# An Object-oriented Matrix Programming Language

Ox™ 6

# An Object-oriented Matrix Programming Language

# Ox™6

## Jurgen A. Doornik

Published by Timberlake Consultants Ltd
www.timberlake.co.uk
www.timberlake-consultancy.com
www.oxmetrics.net

**British Library Cataloguing-in-Publication Data**
A catalogue record of this book is available from the British Library

**Library of Congress Cataloguing-in-Publication Data**
A catalogue record of this book is available from the Library of Congress
Jurgen A. Doornik
p. cm. – (An Object-oriented Matrix Programming Language – Ox™6)

**ISBN 978-0-9552127-5-8**

**Published by**
Timberlake Consultants Ltd
Unit B3, Broomsleigh Business Park
London SE26 5BN, UK
http://www.timberlake.co.uk

842 Greenwich Lane,
Union, NJ 07083-7905, U.S.A.
http://www.timberlake-consultancy.com

---

# Contents

# Figures

# Tables

# Listings

xxix

# Preface

My interest in computer languages was awakened by reading a short book on compiler building written by Niklaus Wirth (see Wirth, 1987). The first opportunity to dabble in this field was the design and implementation of the algebra language in PcGive 7 (also used in later versions). The result was a tiny vector language, not very efficient, but it worked. My ambition was to write a more powerful language, to leverage the growing body of computational code. The next attempt took a few weeks at the end of 1992. It did not lead to a useful program, but the experience helped in the third and serious attempt: Ox. That project was started in April 1994, just after completing version 8 of PcGive. The aim was to use it for the simulations required for my doctoral thesis. Having done most of my programming of recent years in C, I was not pleased with the syntax of the matrix languages I tried. By November I had a preliminary version. It had a database and PcFiml class, and I could use it for my simulations. The Ox library gradually expanded, but my thesis had a higher priority. In the summer of 1995, the number of Ox users tripled: both Neil Shephard and Richard Spady started to use it. Their wishes and comments helped push Ox towards its current form, including Unix versions, support for DLLs, more graphics and many types of random number generators.

The origin of the name Ox is a bit vague. It is the first and last letter of Object-oriented matrix. Initially I was comparing the program to an ox: a solid work animal but quite slow. Since then, however, Ox has become a lot faster, to the point where it is even beating some native C and Fortran programs. Alternatively, the name can be interpreted as a tribute to Oxford and its University.

Of course, there is still much to be added to Ox, and development will continue. OxEdit supplies the integrated environment for development, but a visual debugger remains on the wish-list.

Please keep sending your suggestions for improvements. Questions regarding Ox and Ox packages should primarily be addressed to the ox-users discussion list. You can contact me if you need Ox on a platform which is currently not supported. My work page at www.doornik.com as well as www.oxmetrics.net are regularly updated with pointers to relevant Ox information.

Clearly, I wish to thank Neil Shephard and Richard Spady for adopting Ox early on, and their many comments and suggestions. Also to their students, who were encouraged to use Ox and gave feedback. By now, many more people have downloaded

Ox, and given it a try, among these Francisco Cribari-Neto deserves special thanks. I thank David Hendry for continuing support for this project, and also wish to thank Maureen Baker, Christopher Baum, Charles Bos, Peter Boswijk, Max Bruche, James Davidson, Ola Elerian, Richard Gascoigne, Frank Gerhard, Siem Jan Koopman, Hans-Martin Krolzig, Michal Kurcewicz, Ulrich Küsters, Richard Lewney, Sébastien Laurent, James MacKinnon, Aurora Manrique, Michael Massmann, Sophocles Mavroeidis, Steve Moyle, Bent Nielsen, Marius Ooms, Mike Orszag, Felix Ritchie, Pieter Jelle van der Sluis, Ana Timberlake, Giovanni Urga. And, of course, thanks to all those people who have sent me email messages saying how much they appreciate Ox (I like those!).

As the proverbial last but not least, I wish to thank Kate Doornik: without her support and company I would not have managed.

Oxford, July 2009

I wish you enjoyable and productive use of

# Ox

# Chapter 1

# Prologue

## 1.1 What is Ox?

**Ox** is an object-oriented matrix programming language with a comprehensive mathematical and statistical function library. Matrices can be used directly in expressions, for example to multiply two matrices, or to invert a matrix. The major features of Ox are its speed, extensive library, and well-designed syntax, which leads to programs which are easier to maintain.

## 1.2 Availability

The full Windows version of Ox, called **Ox Professional** is available from Timberlake Consultants. Timberlake can be found on the internet at `www.timberlake.co.uk` and `www.timberlake-consultancy.com`, or contacted via telephone in the UK on: +44 (0)20 8697 3377 , and in the US on: +1 908 686 1251.

The Windows command-line, and Unix versions of Ox can be downloaded from: `www.doornik.com`. These are called **Ox Console**.

Please check the `ox\doc\readme.ox` file before installation (and for Unix installations: `ox/doc/readunix.txt`).

## 1.3 Ox version

This documentation refers to version 6.00. Check the web addresses given in §1.8 for changes which were made after publication of this book.

## 1.4 Learning Ox

The best place to learn Ox is Doornik and Ooms (2006), which gives an introduction to the Ox language, complemented with econometric and statistical examples, as well as

1

many exercises (the tutorial files are installed in `ox\tutorial`). Also see the *Getting started* section in the on-line help system. Chapter 3 gives a shorter introduction.

## 1.5 Ox platforms

Ox is currently available on Windows, Linux for PC, OS X, and Sun/Solaris worksta-
tions. Table 1.1 lists the current set of Ox executables. Console indicates whether the
compiler is launched from the command line, or using an interactive program. The first
yes/no under graphics indicates whether graphs can be created and saved to disk, the
second whether graphs can be displayed on screen by Ox.

**Table 1.1**   Ox executables.

| platform | name | Console | DLL | Debug | graphics |
|---|---|---|---|---|---|
| Windows/Linux/OS X | oxl | yes | yes | no | yes,no |
| Windows | oxli | yes | yes | yes | yes,no |
| Windows/Linux/OS X | OxRun | no | yes | yes | yes,yes |
| Sun (SunOs) | oxl | yes | yes | yes | yes,no |

## 1.6 Ox supported data formats

Ox can read (and write) the following data files directly into a matrix:

- .mat (ASCII matrix file),
- .dat (ASCII data file with load information),
- .in7 (PcGive 7 data file, with data in .bn7 file),
- .xls (Excel spreadsheet and workbook files),
- .wks/.wk1 (Lotus spreadsheet file),
- .dht (Gauss data file, with data in .dat file),
- .fmt (Gauss matrix file),
- .dta (Stata data file, version 4–6).

In addition, there are text and low-level functions for reading and writing binary files.

## 1.7 Extending Ox

Ox can be extended on all platforms. The Ox Appendices documentation provides
examples of what you can do:

- Develop an OxPack compatible interactive package when deriving from the Modelbase class.

- Make extensions to Ox in e.g. C/C++ or Fortran, and put that in a DLL; such functions are then callable from Ox code.
- Use Ox as a mathematics library (e.g. if you are programming in C/C++ but do not want to program in Ox; or to call functions such as Choleski decomposition or a random number generator in your Ox extension DLL).
- Write an interface wrapper around Ox code. Examples using Visual Basic and Visual C++ are given.

Using *OxRun*, Ox can use *OxMetrics* as a front-end, which holds databases, and receives text and graphical output from Ox (and also other modules such as PcGive, STAMP, PcNaive, etc.).

## 1.8 World Wide Web

Check `www.oxmetrics.net` or `www.doornik.com` for information on bugs, bug fixes, new features, benchmarks and other information relevant to Ox.

## 1.9 Online documentation

The Ox help system is implemented as a set of HTML pages which can be read with an internet browser. Open `\ox\docs\index.html` in your browser to start help.

## 1.10 Ox-users discussion list

The ox-users discussion group is an email-based forum to discuss any problems related to Ox programming, and share code and programming solutions. Consult the online help for information on joining the list.

## 1.11 Installation

Installation can be done as follows:

(1) For Windows use the provided setup program, which will do the complete installation (but note that Ox Professional is only available for Windows XP/2000). The settings of §1.12 should have been made automatically.
(2) Under Linux: use the RPM version for automated installation.
(3) Do the zip file installation: copy the zip files to the appropriate Ox directory, and run setup.bat. Then proceed with the next section (Windows). But first, check the supplied `ox\doc\readox.txt` file for the complete set of instructions.

(4) For Unix systems. Installation can proceed along the lines of (3) if you have a compatible unzip program. Otherwise unzip on a PC, and then transfer (binary mode) to the Unix machine. Follow the instructions of §1.12, using the information in §1.15. When in doubt contact your system administrator.

**NO WARRANTY WHATSOEVER IS GIVEN FOR THESE PROGRAMS.
YOU USE THEM AT YOUR OWN RISK!**

All company and product names referred to in this book are either trademarks or registered trademarks of their associated companies.

## 1.12 Completing the basic installation

Under Windows, no further action is required, unless you wish to run the command line version of Ox (that is: `oxl.exe`) from anywhere in your Command prompt (MS-DOS) window. In that case you need to add the `ox\bin` folder to your PATH statement (`ox\bin64` for the 64-bit version) . For example, assuming you, installed on the C drive, add:

```
C:\Program Files\ox\bin
```

to your PATH statement in the autoexec.bat file (Windows ME/9x) or use the system icon in the control panel (Windows XP/2000/NT).

For Unix see §1.15.

## 1.13 Directory structure

```
ox/bin        – executables and DLLs
ox/bin64      – executables and DLLs for 64-bit version
ox/data       – default data directory
ox/dev        – examples on how to extend Ox
ox/doc        – documentation (start index.html)

ox/include    – Ox header files
ox/lib        – useful additional source code files
ox/packages   – Ox extension packages
ox/samples    – Ox samples directory with code for Ch. 2
ox/src        – Ox code for .oxo files in ox/include
ox/tutorial   – Tutorial files accompanying Doornik and Ooms (2006)
```

| | |
|---|---|
| `ox/samples/bench` | – benchmark samples |
| `ox/samples/classes` | – Line and Angle classes from §13.5.6 |
| `ox/samples/database` | – database class examples |
| `ox/samples/graphics` | – graphics examples |
| `ox/samples/inout` | – input/output examples |
| `ox/samples/lib` | – examples for source code files in `ox/lib` |
| `ox/samples/maximize` | – function maximization and differentiation |
| `ox/samples/oxpack` | – application illustrating OxPack dialogs |
| `ox/samples/pcfiml` | – PcFiml examples |
| `ox/samples/ranapp` | – C++ wrapper around Ox code* |
| `ox/samples/simula` | – Simulation class examples |
| `ox/samples/virtual` | – Demonstrates virtual class member functions |

The main executable files are in `ox/bin/`:

| | |
|---|---|
| `oxl.exe` | – standard Ox compiler (Windows) |
| `oxl` | – standard Ox compiler (Unix) |
| `oxli.exe` | – debug/interactive Ox compiler (Windows) |
| `oxrun.exe` | – for using Ox with *OxMetrics* (Windows) |
| `oxpack.exe` | – for interactive use of many packages with *OxMetrics* (Windows) |

## 1.14 OX6PATH

Ox 6.x uses the `OX6PATH` environment variable if this has been set. Under Windows there is no need to set this variables anymore, because the system will use a default (determined from the location of oxwin.dll). If you installed to `c:\ox` it defaults to:

> `c:\ox\include;c:\ox`

Under Unix, the `OX6PATH` variable must always be set, see §1.15.

Ox will read the `OX6PATH` environment variable, so it can still be used. If you do set it, you must include the default. For example, when Ox is run from the network (`X:\apps\ox` for example), and you wish to also use packages installed on the local harddisk at `c:\ox`, you could set:

> `set OX6PATH=X:\apps\ox\include;X:\apps\ox;c:\ox`

Ox 5.x used the `OX5PATH` environment variable, allowing Ox version 5 and 6 installations to exist side by side.

## 1.15 Ox for Unix

The directory structure under Unix should be identical to that under Windows. Setting environment variables, and resolving the dynamic link library works a bit differently. Here are some notes on Unix installation:

(0) Dynamic link libraries have the `.so` extension under Unix, except for HPUX, which uses `.sl`.

(1) Dynamic linking:

For Ox version 5.1, the naming scheme is as follows:

`libox.so.5.10.0`   is the (dynamically linked) Ox library,

`ox1`                 is the executable which links to it.

Normally, step (3) and (4) below would be added to a startup script.

(2) version numbers:

In (e.g.) `ox1.so.5.10.0` the 5 is the major, and 10.0 the minor version number. The executable only looks for a file matching the major version number (`ox1.so.5`). A symbolic link is required to resolve the search:

```
rm libox.so.5
ln -s libox.so.5.00.0 libox.so.5
```

This numbering system is not used for HPUX and AIX. Under HPUX the DLL is called `ox1.sl`, and no symbolic link is required. Under AIX the shared library file is called `libox.o`.

(3) library search paths:

`LD_LIBRARY_PATH` is used to search for the library file when the file is in a nonstandard location. This must be set to the directory where `ox1.so.5` is, unless it has been moved to standard directory which is searched by default. (HPUX uses `SHLIB_PATH`, and AIX uses `LIBPATH`, and OS-X uses `DYLD_LIBRARY_PATH` or `DYLD_FALLBACK_LIBRARY_PATH`.)

(4) `OX6PATH`

set the OX6PATH variable to allow Ox to find include files, e.g. to

```
"$HOME/ox/include:$HOME/ox"
```

Note that setting environment variables is shell specific. For example for bash shells you can use:

- to show contents of `LD_LIBRARY_PATH` environment variable:

```
echo $LD_LIBRARY_PATH
```

- to set to a directory, e.g. to:

```
LD_LIBRARY_PATH="$HOME/ox/bin"; export LD_LIBRARY_PATH
```

- to append a directory (this is one command):

```
LD_LIBRARY_PATH="$LD_LIBRARY_PATH:$HOME/dir";
    export LD_LIBRARY_PATH
```

- to set the OX6PATH variable:

```
OX6PATH="$HOME/ox/include:$HOME/ox"; export OX6PATH
```

Whereas other shells may use setenv/printenv:

- to show contents of LD_LIBRARY_PATH environment variable:
  ```
  printenv $LD_LIBRARY_PATH
  ```
- to set to a directory, e.g. to:
  ```
  setenv LD_LIBRARY_PATH "$HOME/ox/bin"
  ```
- to set the OX6PATH variable:
  ```
  setenv OX6PATH "$HOME/ox/include:$HOME/ox"
  ```

(5) File mode:
On some platforms it might be necessary to set the file mode to executable, for example:

```
chmod +x oxl
```

(6) bin directory
On some systems, when in the bin directory, it is necessary to run Ox as ./oxl instead of just oxl.

(6) developing dynamic link libraries
When developing DLLs for Ox, the ldd command can sometimes help with finding out why a DLL does not link.

(7) The threes example shows how to create and call a dynamic link library. Run make -f threes.mak to compile threes.so (the header file oxexport.h and dependencies must be in the search path). On some platforms there may be unresolved messages from the linker, which may be ignored. Then run oxl threes to see if it works. The dynamic linker must be able to find threes.so, also (7).

(8) When adding a DLL which is to be used from Ox, Ox will try to locate it in the following way:

  1. Try directly
  2. Search along OX6PATH paths
  3. Search along OX6PATH relative to #import statements which have a path component.
  4. Try package/dll_name directory (but only if no path is used in the extern statement).

For example, when the declaration is:

```
extern "arfima,FnFracSigma" fracsigma(....);
```

and arfima.oxo has:

```
#import <modelbase>
#import <lib/testres>
```

and somewhere else is:

```
#import <packages/arfima/arfima>
```

moreover, the `OX6PATH` is set to `$HOME/ox/include:$HOME/ox`
Then Ox will try:

   1.  `./arfima.so`
  2a.  `$HOME/ox/include/arfima.so`
   b.  `$HOME/ox/arfima.so`
  3a.  `$HOME/ox/include/lib/arfima.so`
   b.  `$HOME/ox/lib/arfima.so`
   c.  `$HOME/ox/include/packages/arfima/arfima.so`
   d.  `$HOME/ox/packages/arfima/arfima.so`
  4a.  `$HOME/ox/include/packages/arfima/arfima.so`
   b.  `$HOME/ox/packages/arfima/arfima.so`

So, when Ox is loading a library through the extern statement, the `LD_LIBRARY_PATH` is not used. Also note that under Windows, the operating system automatically searches along the path statement, which does not happen under Unix. (Of course, Unix is also case-sensitive, except for OS X).

DLLs for different platforms can be kept separate by using _64 and platform-specific suffix. For example, Ox will try first one of:

| | |
|---|---|
| `arfima.dll` | Windows 32-bit |
| `arfima_64.dll` | Windows 64-bit |
| `arfima.so` | Linux 32-bit |
| `arfima_64.so` | Linux 64-bit |
| `arfima_osx.so` | OS X 32-bit |
| `arfima_sparc.so` | Solaris on Sparc, 32-bit |
| `arfima_sunx86.so` | Solaris on x86, 32-bit |
| `arfima_sunx86_64.so` | Solaris on x86, 64-bit |

using the search method described above. If that fails, the search is done with just arfima.

# Part I

# Introduction to Ox

# Chapter 2

# Getting started with Ox

## 2.1 Introduction

Ox is an object-oriented matrix language with a comprehensive mathematical and statistical function library. Matrices can be used directly in expressions, for example to multiply two matrices, or to invert a matrix. The basic syntax elements of Ox are similar to the C, C++ and Java languages (however, knowledge if these languages is not a prerequisite for using Ox). This similarity is most clear in syntax items such as loops, functions, arrays and classes. A major difference is that Ox variables have no explicit type, and that special support for matrices is available.

The advantages of object-oriented programming are that it potentially improves the clarity and maintainability of the code, as well as reducing coding effort through inheritance. Several useful classes are provided with Ox.

This chapter will introduce a first Ox program, and discuss the various ways in which the program can be executed. The next chapter will then give a brief overview of the language elements.

## 2.2 A first Ox program

As a first example of an Ox program consider the following Ox code:

.........................................................................*samples/myfirst.ox*

```
#include <oxstd.h>// include the Ox standard library header

main()              // function main is the starting point
{
    decl m1, m2;       // declare two variables, m1 and m2

    m1 = unit(3);   // assign to m1 a 3 x 3 identity matrix
    m1[0][0] = 2;              // set top-left element to 2
    m2 = <0,0,0;1,1,1>;  // m2 is a 2 x 3 matrix, the first
                // row consists of zeros, the second of ones

    print("two matrices", m1, m2);    // print the matrices
}
```
.........................................................................

11

The program is in ox\samples\myfirst.ox; running this program should produce
the following result:

```
two matrices
        2.0000        0.00000        0.00000
        0.00000       1.0000         0.00000
        0.00000       0.00000        1.0000

        0.00000       0.00000        0.00000
        1.0000        1.0000         1.0000
```

An Ox program consists of one or more *source code* files. All source files have the
.ox extension. *Header files* are used to communicate declarations from one source file
to another. Header files have the .h extension.

The next section explains how to run the Ox program on your system. First we
consider the myfirst.ox program in more detail:

- The first line includes the oxstd.h file into the source code (literally: the contents of the file are inserted at that point). This file contains the function declarations of the standard library, so that the function calls can be checked for number
  of arguments. The file name is between < >, indicating that the header file came
  with the Ox program.
- The function main is the starting point, and each program is only allowed one
  such function. Even though main has no arguments, it still requires ().
- Variables may be declared with the decl statement, and have no type until the
  program is actually run.
- unit is a standard library function, which creates an identity matrix; here it is
  called with argument 3. The result is assigned to the variable m1. The type of m1
  has become *matrix*, and until a reassignment is made (or it goes out of scope), m1
  will keep its type and value.
- Note that *indexing starts at zero*, so the top-left element is m1[0][0]: row 0,
  column 0. The first index is the row index: m1[1][2] is row 1, column 2. Ox
  has this convention in common with many other programming languages (but it
  could be changed, see §13.9.5).
- <0,0,0;1,1,1> is a *matrix constant*. Elements are listed by row, whereby rows
  are separated by a semicolon, and elements within a row by a colon. This value
  is stored in m2, which is now also of type matrix.
- print is a library function, which can print any type of variable or constant to the
  standard output screen. It can take any number of arguments. Here it has three: a
  *string constant* and two variables (which both happen to be matrices).

An important advantage of Ox is that we can directly work with matrices, and do not
have to worry about memory allocation and deallocation. Low-level languages may be
faster, although we have encountered several cases in which Ox performed better than
a comparable C program. Ox code has a much closer correspondence to mathematical
expressions used on paper.

# 2.3 Running the first Ox program

### 2.3.1 Ox Professional under Windows

Load the `myfirst.ox` program in OxMetrics and click on Run (the running person icon on the toolbar).

Or right-click on myfirst.ox in the workspace window after it has een loaded into OxMetrics, and select Run Ox.

### 2.3.2 Ox Console under Windows

Load the `myfirst.ox` program in OxEdit and click on Run (the running person icon on the toolbar).

If Ox Console (or Ox Professional) has been installed correctly, the Ox program can also be run from a command window (Command prompt or MS-DOS prompt under Windows) by typing (this assumes Ox is installed in `Program Files\OxMetrics6\ox` on the current drive):

```
cd "\Program Files\OxMetrics6\ox\samples"
```
Followed by
```
oxl myfirst
```
There is no need to add the `.ox` extension. If `oxl` cannot be found, you have to add the path to the executable file, which is in `ox\bin`:

```
..\bin\oxl myfirst
```
Having to add the path to `oxl.exe` everytime is a nuisance, and there are several alternatives which are more convenient:

- Add the `ox\bin` folder to the environment `PATH`. In the default installation this is `C:\Program Files\ox\bin`.
- Use **OxEdit** to run your Ox programs.
- Ox Professional users can run their programs (with graphics) from **OxMetrics**.

In the remainder, we refer to the MS-DOS window as the console window, and to `oxl.exe` as the console version of the Ox compiler.

If you do not get the output listed in the previous section check the installation notes in Chapter 1.11.

### 2.3.3 Ox Professional under Linux and OS X

Load the `myfirst.ox` program in OxMetrics and click on Run (the running person icon on the toolbar).

Or right-click on myfirst.ox in the workspace window after it has een loaded into OxMetrics, and select Run Ox.

### 2.3.4 Ox Console under Linux and OS X

Load the `myfirst.ox` program in OxEdit and click on Run (the running person icon on the toolbar).

If Ox has been installed correctly, the Ox program can also be run from a terminal window by typing (this assumes Ox is installed in /ox on the current drive, which is unlikely to be the correct path):

```
cd /ox/samples
```

Followed by

```
oxl myfirst
```

There is no need to add the `.ox` extension. Currently, there is only the console version under Unix.

If your output is:

```
myfirst.ox (1): 'oxstd.h' include file not found
myfirst.ox (7): 'unit' undeclared identifier
myfirst.ox (12): 'print' undeclared identifier
```

Then the header file was not found, and the `OX6PATH` environment variable is not set, or set wrongly. (Note that the environment variable is specific to the major version of Ox, e.g. `OX5PATH` was used version 5.)


# 2.4 Online help

A large part of this book is part of the online help system. The Ox help system is implemented as a set of HTML pages. To start the help open `\ox\docs\index.html` in your browser.

OxMetrics conveniently lists the Ox Help index in the Help pane in the workspace. When editing an Ox file, press F1 for context-sensitive help for the word under the text caret.


# 2.5 Using file names in Ox

If you specify full path names of files in a string constant, you must either use one forward slash, or two backslashes: `"./data.mat"` or `".\\data.mat"`. Ox will interpret one backslash in a string as an escape sequence (as in `"\n"`, see §13.3.2.2); a single backslash will only work if it does not happen to form an escape sequence. Also note that the Windows and Unix versions of Ox can handle long file names, and that Unix treats file names in a case sensitive manner.

# 2.6 Ox file extensions

Table 2.1 summarizes file types (by extension) used in Ox.

**Table 2.1**   Ox extensions.

| extension | description |
|---|---|
| .dat | ASCII data file with load information, |
| .dht | Gauss data file (with corresponding .dat file) |
| .dll | Dynamic link library (Windows) |
| .eps | Encapsulated PostScript file |
| .fmt | Gauss matrix file |
| .gwg | *OxMetrics* graphics file |
| .h | Ox header file |
| .in7/.bn7 | PcGive 7 data file (with corresponding .bn7 file) |
| .mat | ASCII matrix file |
| .ox | Ox source code file |
| .oxo | compiled Ox code (object file) |
| .ps | PostScript file |
| .so | Dynamic link library (Unix) |
| .xls | Excel worksheet or workbook file |

# 2.7 More on running Ox programs

### 2.7.1 Windows: OxMetrics and OxRun

*OxRun* is a small Windows front end to Ox. It offers the same services as the command-line compilers, but in the form of a dialog. *OxRun* can be started from *OxMetrics*, and text and graphics output from the Ox program will appear in *OxMetrics*. Alternatively, an Ox program can be loaded into OxMetrics, and then run directly by clicking on the Run icon.

   *OxRun* and *OxMetrics* are part of Ox Professional, and cannot be downloaded. More information is in the introduction to Ox, see Doornik and Ooms (2006).

### 2.7.2 Windows: command-line compiler

The Ox command-line compiler under Windows XP/2000 is called `oxl`; starting it without arguments produces a list of options. Dynamic link libraries (DLL) are supported. For debugging and interactive mode, use `oxli.exe` instead of `oxl.exe`.

### 2.7.3 Unix compiler

The Ox compiler under Unix (including Linux) is also called `oxl`. DLLs are supported on all Unix platforms. Under most Unix systems a DLL has the `.so` extension. Debugging and interactive mode are activated as `oxl -d` and `oxl -i` respectively.

### 2.7.4 Running programs with graphics

Many types of graphs are readily produced in Ox, such as graphs over time of several variables, cross-plots, histograms, correlograms, etc. Several examples are in Ch. 10. There is also a GnuPlot package for Ox.

A graph can be saved in various formats: encapsulated PostScript (`.eps`), PostScript (`.ps`), and OxMetrics graphics file (`.gwg`). When using *OxMetrics*, graphs can also be saved in Windows Metafile format (`.wmf`), and copied to the clipboard for pasting into wordprocessors.

Although creating and saving graphs will work on any system supported by Ox, it is only possible to see the result on screen under Windows. This requires Ox Professional, running the Ox program within *OxMetrics*. Then both text and graphical output from the Ox program will appear in *OxMetrics*. There, text and graphs can be edited further, or copied to the clipboard for pasting into other programs.

### 2.7.5 Compilation into `.oxo` file

The `-c` switch compiles the Ox source code into an object file (.oxo file). Such files are binary, and cross-platform compatible. This means that you can create an .oxo file under Windows, then copy it to the Sun (using binary transfer), and use it directly. Thus it provides a way to distribute modules without the source code.

### 2.7.6 The debugger

Ox has debug facilities, which can be useful to locate bugs in your programs. A debug session is started with the `-d` switch (use `oxli.exe` under Windows). More information is in the *Introduction to Ox*, see Doornik and Ooms (2006, Appendix 1).

### 2.7.7 OxEdit

*OxEdit* is a powerful text editor, and a very useful program in its own right. Ox can be installed within OxEdit, and program output captured in an OxEdit window, see `www.doornik.com` and the introduction to Ox: Doornik and Ooms (2006).

### 2.7.8 Windows context menu

Once Ox Professional has been installed there are a couple of convenient shortcuts in the Explorer window:

- (double) clicking on an Ox file will run the file using OxRun,
- right click on an Ox file, and choose:
  - run to run the Ox file with OxRun,
  - open to open the Ox file for editing.

# 2.8 Command line arguments

Arguments before the Ox filename are passed to the compiler, those after to the running program. So in

```
oxl -DMYTEXT1 prog.ox -DMYTEXT2
```

the string "-DMYTEXT2" is not handled by the compiler, but available to the `prog.ox` program when using the `arglist` function. If you just type `oxl` you will get a list of command line options.

### 2.8.1 General switches

**-c** Create an object (`.oxo`) file, there is no linking or running of the file. An `.oxo` file is a binary file which holds compiled Ox code. It can be linked in later (see §3.8).

**-d** Run program in debug mode (with -c: inserts debug information in compiled file).

**-Dtoken** Define tokens, e.g. -DOPTION1+OPTION2 corresponds to the preprocessor statements

```
#define OPTION1
#define OPTION2
```

**-g** The source code is an OxGauss file

**-lfilelist** Link object file, e.g. -lfile1+file2+file3, which links in the named files (the `.oxo` extension is assumed). If the file cannot be found as specified, the linker will search along the include path.

**-i** Run Ox in interactive mode (at start up the file called `ox_init.ox` is run automatically).

**-ipath** Appends path in front of the current include path. Initially, the include path is that specified in the `OX6PATH` environment variable (under Windows when `OX6PATH` is not set, the default is obtained from the location of the binary file); use this switch to prepend directories for searching. Use a semicolon to separate directories. The include path is used to search for files included in search code and link files.

**-w0** Switches off parse warnings. Currently, the parser warns for

- `isolated ; is empty statement`
  This refers to expressions such as `if (i == 10);` where the semicolon terminates the expression. The warning is also issued for `;` after `for` and `while` statements.

- assignment in test expression
  This refers to expressions such as if (i = 10) where an assignment is
  made inside a test expression. The warning is also issued for assignments
  in for, while, and do while statements.

**-x** Clears the current include path. Use this prior to the -i switch if you do not wish to
  search in the directories specified by the OX6PATH environment variables.

### 2.8.2 Optimization switches

**-od** Switch all code optimizations off. By default this is on. Usually, there is no reason
  to switch it off, other than to check for speed differences.
**-on** Switch line numbering off. Use this switch to prevent the emission of line numbers
  into the compiled code. This makes error messages less helpful; moreover, the
  speed improvement is virtually negligable.

### 2.8.3 Run-time switches

**-r-** Do not run code. The code will be compiled and linked. Could be useful to only do
  a syntax check.
**-rc** Sets the matrix cache. By default, the cache stores up to 16 matrices, but only
  matrices which have fewer than 1000 elements (which corresponds to 8 KBytes).
  The first number is the number of matrices, the second the size, separated by a
  colon (no spaces are allowed!), so the default corresponds to -rc16,1000. It
  seems that the marginal benefit of a larger cache, or caching larger matrices is
  small. (Note that the default cache consumes 128 Kbytes in a (highly unlikely)
  worse case.) The cache can be switched off with -rc0,0.
**-rf** Switch FastMath off to save memory. FastMath significantly speeds up: $X'X$,
  correlation, determinant, invertsym, ols2c, variance. In general, the
  overhead is a duplicate of the matrix.
**-rp** Set number of parallel threads (if supported).
  The default is the number of cores or processors;
  use -rp1 to force one thread only (serial code).

**-rr** Prints a cache report, e.g. after running bench1.ox:
  Cache status:  size 16 limit 1000
  hits 189998 misses 6 flushes 0 skipped 0.
**-s** Sets the set symbol table and stack size. The default is -s3000,1000. Setting larger
  sizes is only required when large programs run out of symbol table or stack space.

# 2.9 Extending Ox

Ox is an open system to which you can add functions written in other languages. It is also possible to control Ox from another programming environment such as Visual C++ or Visual Basic.

Extending Ox requires an understanding of the innards of Ox, a decent knowledge of C, as well as the right tools. You also need a version of Ox with developer support. In addition, extending Ox is simpler on some platforms than others. Thus, it is unavoidable that writing Ox extensions is somewhat more complex than writing plain Ox code. However, there could be reasons for extending Ox, e.g. when you need the speed of raw C code (but make sure that the function takes up a significant part of the time it takes to run the program and that it actually will be a lot faster in C than in Ox!), when code is already available in e.g. Fortran, or to add a user-friendly interface.

The documentation on extending Ox is provided as part of the Ox Appendices, which is a separate PDF file. Example code on creating extension dynamic-link libraries are also provided.

# Chapter 3

# Introduction to the Ox language

The previous chapter introduced the first Ox program. We saw that a program always includes header files to define the standard library functions, and that it must have a main function, which is where program control starts. We also saw that the body of the function is enclosed in curly braces. This chapter will give a brief overview of the important elements of the Ox language. A more formal description of the Ox syntax is in Ch. 13. That chapter also has many more examples.

A much more extensive introduction is available, see Doornik and Ooms (2006) and the on-line help system. It is strongly recommended that this is used to learn more about the Ox language. The book contains econometric and statistical examples, and provides tutorial programs as well as many exercises.

## 3.1 Variables, types and scope

Variables are declared using the decl keyword. Unlike C, variables are *implicitly* typed. This means that variables do not have a type when they are declared, but get a type when values are assigned to them. So a variable can change type during its lifetime. The most important implicit types are *int* for an integer value, *double* for a real number, *string* for a text string and *matrix* for a matrix (two-dimensional array) of real numbers. The next Ox program illustrates implicit declaration and scope:

```
#include <oxstd.h>

main()
{
    decl i, d, m, s;

    i = 1;          // assign integer to i --> i is of type int
    d = 1.0;        // assign real number to d --> d is double
    s = "some text";   // assign string to s --> s is string
    m = zeros(3,3);    // assign to m a 3 x 3 matrix of zeros
                            // --> m is of type matrix
    print("i=", i, " d=", d, " s=", s, "\nm=", m);
}
```

This prints (\n is the newline character):

```
i=1 d=1 s=some text
m=
        0.00000         0.00000         0.00000
        0.00000         0.00000         0.00000
        0.00000         0.00000         0.00000
```

The *scope* of a variable refers to the parts of the program which can see the variable. This could be different from its lifetime: a variable can be 'alive' but not 'seen'. If a variable is declared outside any function, its scope is the remainder of the source file. It is possible to export such variables to other source files, as we shall see shortly.

Variables declared inside a function have scope until the closing brace of the level at which it is declared. The following example illustrates:

```
#include <oxstd.h>

decl mX;                                    // external variable
main()
{
    decl i = 0;                             // local variable

    {
        decl i = 1, j = 0;                              // new i
        mX = ones(3,3);
        print("i=", i, " j=", j);           // prints: i=1 j=0
    }                   // brace end: local i and j cease to exist
    print("\ni=", i);           // revert to old i, prints: i=0
}
```

The variable mX (here we use *Hungarian notation*, see §3.10), can be seen everywhere in the main function. To make sure that it can never be seen in other source files, prefix it with the word static. It is good programming practice to use static in such cases, because it is very useful to know that it is not used in any other files (we may than rename it, e.g., without any unexpected side effects). An example will be given in myfunc.ox on page 30.

## 3.2 Indexing matrices

Indexing starts at zero, so m[0][0] is the first element of the matrix m. It is easy to select individual elements or a subset of the matrix. Here are some examples:

```
#include <oxstd.h>

main()
{
    decl m = <0, 1, 2; 3, 4, 5; 6, 7, 8>;

    println("m = ", m);
    println("element 1,0: ", m[1][0]);
```

```
        println("second row: ",  m[1][]);
        println("second column: ", m[][1]);
        println("without 1st row/3rd col: ", m[1:][:1]);
        println("indexed as a vector ", m[2:3]);
    }
```

Which prints as output:

```
m =
        0.00000        1.0000        2.0000
        3.0000         4.0000        5.0000
        6.0000         7.0000        8.0000
element 1,0: 3
second row:
        3.0000         4.0000        5.0000
second column:
        1.0000
        4.0000
        7.0000
without 1st row/3rd col:
        3.0000         4.0000
        6.0000         7.0000
Warning: indexed a matrix as a vector
indexed as a vector
        2.0000
        3.0000
```

These expressions may also be used in assignments, for example:

```
m[1:][:1] = 10;
m[0][1:2] = m[0][0:1];
```

## 3.3 Functions and function arguments

We have already used various functions from the standard library (such as print, ones
and zeros), and written various main functions). Indeed, an Ox program is primarily a
collection of functions. It is important to know that all function arguments are *passed by
value*. This means that the function gets a copy which it can change without changing
the original. For example:

```
#include <oxstd.h>

func(mA)
{
    mA = zeros(1,2);
    print("ma in func()", mA);
}

main()
{
    decl ma;

    ma = ones(1,2);
```

```
            print("ma before func()", ma);
            func(ma);
            print("ma after func()", ma);
    }
```

which prints:

```
ma before func()
         1.0000        1.0000
ma in func()
         0.00000       0.00000
ma after func()
         1.0000        1.0000
```

If the function argument is not changed by the function, it is good programming style to prefix it with the const keyword, as in:

```
func(const mA)
{
    print("ma in func()", mA);
}
```

Then the compiler can generate much more efficient code, especially for matrices and strings.

Of course it is possible to return changed values from the function. If there is only one return value, this is most simply done by using the return statement:

```
#include <oxstd.h>

func(const r, const c)
{
    return rann(r, c);       // return r x c matrix of random
}                            // numbers from standard normal
main()
{
    print("return value from func():", func(1,2) );
}
```

Another way is to pass a *reference* to the variable, rather than the variable itself, as for example in:

```
#include <oxstd.h>

func(const pmA)
{
    pmA[0] = zeros(1,2);
    print("ma in func()", pmA[0]);
}
main()
{
    decl ma;

    ma = ones(1,2);
    print("ma before func()", ma);
    func(&ma);
```

```
        print("ma after func()", ma);
    }
```

which prints:

```
ma before func()
        1.0000          1.0000
ma in func()
        0.00000         0.00000
ma after func()
        0.00000         0.00000
```

Now the change to ma is permanent. The argument to the function was the address of ma, and func received that address as a reference. Now we can modify the contents of the reference by assigning a value to pmA[0]. When func has finished, ma has been changed permanently. Note that we gave the argument a const qualification. This was possible because we did not change pmA itself, but what it referred to.

## 3.4 The for and while loops

Since Ox is a matrix language, there is much less need for loop statements than in C or C++. Indeed, because Ox is compiled and then interpreted, there is a speed penalty for using loop statements when they are not necessary.

The for, while and do while loops have the same syntax as in C. The for loop consists of three parts, an initialization part, a termination check, and an incrementation part. The while loops only have a termination check.

```
#include <oxstd.h>

main()
{
    decl i, d;

    for (i = 0; i < 5; ++i)
    {
        d = i * 0.01;
        println(d);
    }
}
```

which prints (println is like print, but ensures that the next output will be starting on a new line):

```
0
0.01
0.02
0.03
0.04
```

This could also be written, less elegantly, using while as follows:

```
#include <oxstd.h>

main()
{
    decl i, d;

    i = 0;
    while (i < 5)
    {
        d = i * 0.01;
        println(d);
        ++i;
    }
}
```

It is not uncommon to have more than one loop counter in the `for` statement, as the following code snippet illustrates:

```
decl i, j;

for (i = 0, j = 10; i < 5 && j > 0; ++i, --j)
    println(i * j);
```

The `&&` is *logical-and*, whereas `||` is *logical-or*. The `++i` statement is called (prefix) incrementation, and means 'add one to `i`'. Similarly, `--j` subtracts one from `j`. There is a difference between prefix and postfix incrementation (decrementation). For example, the second line in

```
i = 3;
j = ++i;
```

means: add one to `i`, and assign the result to `j`, which will get the value 4. But

```
i = 3;
j = i++;
```

means: leave the value of `i` on the stack for assignment, then afterwards increment `i`. So `j` will get the value 3. In the incrementation part of the `for` loop it does not matter whether you use the prefix or postfix form.

## 3.5 The `if` statement

The `if` statement allows for conditional program flow. In the following example we draw a uniform random number. Such a random number is always between zero and one. The `ranu` returns a matrix, unless we ask it to generate just one number. Then it returns a double, as is the case here.

```
decl d = ranu(1,1);

if (d < 0.5)
    println("less than 0.5");
else if (d < 0.75)
    println("less than 0.75");
```

```
else
    println("greater than 0.75");
```

Again, braces are used to group multiple statements together. They should also be used when nesting if statements, to avoid confusion about which else belongs to which if.

```
decl d1 = ranu(1,1), d2 = ranu(1,1);

if (d1 < 0.5)
{   println("d1 is less than 0.5");
}
else
{   if (d2 < 0.75)
        println("d1 >= 0.5 and d2 < 0.75");
    else
        println("d1 >= 0.5 and d2 <= 0.75");
}
```

The if part is executed if the expression evaluates to a non-zero value (*true*). The else part otherwise, i.e. when the expression evaluates to zero (*false*: either an integer 0, or a double 0.0). Some care is required when using matrices in if statements. A matrix expression is a true statement if all elements are true (non-zero). Even if only one element is zero, the matrix expression is false, so

```
#include <oxstd.h>

main()
{
    if (ones(2,2))  print("yes");
    else            print("no");
    if (unit(2))    print("yes");
    else            print("no");
    if (zeros(2,2)) print("yes");
    else            print("no");
}
```

prints: yesnono.

There are two forms of relational operators. There is < <= > >= == != meaning 'less', 'less than or equal', 'greater', 'greater than or equal', 'is equal' and 'is not equal'. These always produce the integer value 1 (true) or 0 (false). If any of the arguments is a matrix, the result is only true if it is true for each element:

```
#include <oxstd.h>

main()
{
    if (ones(2,2) == 1)  print("yes");   // true for each
    else                 print("no");            // element
    if (unit(2) == 1)    print("yes");//not true for each
    else                 print("no");            // element
    if (zeros(2,2) == 1) print("yes");//not true for each
    else                 print("no");            // element
}
```

prints: yesnono.

The second form are the dot-relational operators .< .<= .> .>= .== .!= meaning 'dot less', 'dot less than or equal', 'dot greater', 'dot greater than or equal', 'is dot equal' and 'is not dot equal'. If any of the arguments is a matrix, the result is a matrix of zeros and ones, with each element indicating the relevant result.

The any library function returns 1 (true) if *any* element of the matrix is non-zero, so that yesyesno will be printed by:

```
#include <oxstd.h>

main()
{
    if (any(ones(2,2)))  print("yes");
    else                 print("no");
    if (any(unit(2)))    print("yes");
    else                 print("no");
    if (any(zeros(2,2))) print("yes");
    else                 print("no");
}
```

To conclude: you can test whether all elements of a matrix m are equal to one (say) by writing: if (m == 1). To test whether any element is equal to one: if (any(m .== 1)). The expression if (m != 1), on the other hand, is only true if none of the elements is equal to one. So, use if (!(m == 1)) to test whether it is true that not all elements are equal to one.

## 3.6 Operations and matrix programming

To a large extent, the same operators are available in Ox as in C or C++. Some of the additional operators are power (^), horizontal concatenation (~), vertical concatenation (|) and the Kronecker product (**). One important distinction is that the operators are also available for matrices, so that, for example, two matrices can be added up directly. For some operators, such as multiplication, there is a distinction between the dot operators (e.g. .* is element by element multiplication and * is matrix multiplication if both arguments are matrices). Not available in Ox are the bitwise operators, instead you need to use the library functions binand and binor.

Because Ox is implicitly typed, the resulting type of the expression will depend on the types of the variables in the expression. When a mixture of types is involved, the result is promoted upwards in the order integer, double, matrix. So in an expression consisting if an integer and a double, the integer will be promoted to a double. An expression of only integers yields an integer. However, there are two important exceptions to this rule:

(1) integer division is done in floating point and yields a double. *This is an important difference with C, where integer division is truncated to an integer.*

(2) power expressions involving integers which yield a result too large to be expressed as an integer give a double result.

To illustrate, we write the Fahrenheit to Celsius example of Kernighan and Ritchie (1988) in Ox:

```
#include <oxstd.h>

const decl LOWER = 0;
const decl UPPER = 100;
const decl STEP  = 20;
main()
{
    decl fahr;

    for (fahr = LOWER; fahr <= UPPER; fahr += STEP)
        print("%3d", fahr, " ",
                "%6.1f", (5.0/9.0) * (fahr-32), "\n");
}
```

which prints:

```
  0   -17.8
 20    -6.7
 40     4.4
 60    15.6
 80    26.7
100    37.8
```

In C we have to write 5.0/9.0, because 5/9 evaluates to zero. In Ox both expressions would be evaluated in floating point arithmetic.

In general we get more more efficient code by vectorizing each program as much as possible:

```
#include <oxstd.h>

const decl LOWER = 0;
const decl UPPER = 100;
const decl STEP  = 20;
main()
{
    decl fahr;

    fahr = range(LOWER, UPPER, STEP)';
    print("%6.1f",  fahr ~ (5.0/9.0) * (fahr-32) );
}
```

- As in the first version of the program, we declare three constants which define the Fahrenheit part of the table.
- The range() function creates a $1 \times n$ matrix with the values LOWER, LOWER+STEP, LOWER + 2STEP, ..., UPPER.
- The transpose operator ' changes this into an $n \times 1$ matrix.

- The conversion to Celsius in the print statement works on the matrix as a whole: multiplication of a matrix by a scalar is equivalent to multiplication by the scalar of each element of the matrix.
- The ˜ operator concatenates the two column vectors into an $n \times 2$ matrix.
- Finally, the print function is different from the printf in C. In Ox each variable to print is simply specified sequentially. It is possible, as done here with "%6.1f", to insert formatting strings for the next variable.

The program prints a table similar to the earlier output:

```
   0.0  -17.8
  20.0   -6.7
  40.0    4.4
  60.0   15.6
  80.0   26.7
 100.0   37.8
```

## 3.7 Arrays

The Ox syntax allows for arrays, so you may use, for example, an array of strings (often useful), an array of matrices, or even an array of an array of matrices (etc.). The following program gives an example.

```
#include <oxstd.h>

const decl MX_R = 2;
const decl MX_C = 2;
main()
{
    decl i, asc, asr, m;

    asr = new array[MX_R];
    asc = new array[MX_C];

    for (i = 0; i < MX_R; ++i)
        asr[i] = sprint("row ", i);
    for (i = 0; i < MX_C; ++i)
        asc[i] = sprint("col ", i);

    m = ranu(MX_R, MX_C);
    print("%r", asr, "%c", asc, m);
}
```

which prints

```
                  col 0        col 1
row 0          0.020192      0.68617
row 1           0.15174      0.74598
```

- The new operator declares a new object. That could be a class object, as discussed in the next chapter, a matrix, a string, or, as used here, an array. The argument in square brackets is the size of the array. (When creating a matrix in this way, note that a matrix is always two-dimensional, and needs two arguments, as in: `m = new matrix[2][2]`.)

- The `sprint` functions return a string, which is stored in the arrays.
- In `print()`, we use `"%r"` followed by an array of strings to specify row labels for the subsequent matrix. Columns labels use `"%c"`.

## 3.8 Multiple files: using #include and #import

The source code of larger projects will often be spread over several source files. Usually the `.ox` file containing the `main` function is only a few tens of lines. We have already seen that information about other source files is passed on through included header files. However, to run the entire program, the code of those files needs to be linked together as well. Ox offers various ways of doing this. As an example, consider a mini-project consisting of two files: a source code file and a header file. The third file will contain the `main` function.

..................................................................... *samples/myfunc.ox*

```
#include <oxstd.h>

static decl s_iCalls = 0;   // counter, initialize to 0

MyFunction(const ma)
{
    ++s_iCalls;                 // increment calls counter
    println("MyFunction has been called ", s_iCalls,
        " times and prints:", ma);
}
```
.......................................................................................

..................................................................... *samples/myfunc.h*

```
    MyFunction(const ma);
```
.......................................................................................

The header file `myfunc.h` *declares* the `MyFunction` function, so that it can be used in other Ox files. Note that the declaration ends in a semicolon. The source code file contains the *definition* of the function, which is the actual code of the function. The header of the definition does not end in a semicolon, but is followed by the opening brace of the body of the function. The `s_iCalls` variable is declared outside any function, making it an *external* variable. Here we also use the `static` *type specifier*, which restricts the scope of the variable to the `myfunc.ox` file: `s_iCalls` is invisible anywhere else (and other files may contain their own `s_iCalls` variable). Variables declared inside a block of curly braces have a more limited lifetime. Their life starts when they are declared, and finishes at the closing brace (matching the brace level of declaration).

It is also possible to share variables between various source files, although there can be only one declaration (physical allocation) of the shared variable. The following modifications would do that for the myfunc.ox program:
(1) delete the static keyword from the declaration,
(2) add to myfunc.h the line (renaming s_iCalls to g_iCalls):

```
extern decl g_iCalls;
```

Any code which includes myfunc.h can now reference or change the g_iCalls variable.

### 3.8.1 Including the code into the main file

The first way of combining the mini project with the main function is to #include the actual code. In that case the myfunc.h header file is not needed:

.......................................................*samples/mymaina.ox*
```
#include <oxstd.h>
#include "myfunc.ox"

main()
{
    MyFunction("one");
}
```
.................................................................................

The result will be just one code file, and mymaina.ox can be run as oxl mymaina.

### 3.8.2 Importing the code into the main file

The drawback of the previous method of including source code using #include, is that it can only be done once. That is not a problem in this short program, but is difficult to ensure if a library is used at many points in a large project. The #import command solves this problem.

..........................................................*samples/mymainc.ox*
```
#include <oxstd.h>
#import "myfunc"

main()
{
    MyFunction("one");
}
```
.................................................................................

Again, mymainc.ox can be run as oxl mymainc.

There is no extension in the argument to `#import`. The effect is as an `#include "myfunc.h"` statement followed by marking `myfunc.ox` for linking.[1] The actual linking only happens when the file is run, and the same `#import` statement may occur multiple times (as well as in compiled files). So even when the same file is imported many times, it will only be linked once.

### 3.8.3 Importing Ox packages

If `myfunc.ox` would require the maximization package, it could have at the top:

```
#include <oxstd.h>
#import <maximize>
```

Partial paths can be used. Searching is relative to the `OX6PATH` environment variable. For example, if the Arfima package is in its default location of `ox/packages/arfima`, we would use:

```
#import <packages/arfima/arfima>
```

The distinction between angular brackets and double quotes in the include and import statements is discussed in §13.9.1. Roughly, the <> form should be used for files which are part of the Ox system, and the double quotes for your own files, which will not be in the Ox tree.

### 3.8.4 Separate compilation

Ox source code files can be compiled into Ox object files. These files have the `.oxo` extension, and are binary. The format is identical across operating systems, but since they are binary, transfer from one platform to another has to be done in binary mode.

To compile `myfunc.ox` into an Ox object file use the `-c` switch:

```
oxl -c myfunc
```

This creates `myfunc.oxo` (the .oxo extension is automatically appended). Remember that `myfunc.oxo` must be recreated every time `myfunc.ox` changes.

Now, when rerunning `mymainc.ox`, it will automatically use the `.oxo` instead of the `.ox` file.

Compiled Ox files can be useful for very large files (although even then compilation will be very fast), or if you do not wish to distribute the source files. They are inconvenient when the code is still under development.

# 3.9 Object-oriented programming

Object-oriented programming involves the grouping together of functions and variables in convenient building blocks. These blocks can then be used directly, or as starting

---

[1] `#import` will actually try to find the `.oxo` file first. If that is not found, it will search for the `.ox` file. If neither is found, the program cannot run. More detail is in §13.9.3.

point for a more specialized implementation. A major advantage of object-oriented programming is that it avoids the use of global variables, thus making the code more re-entrant: several instances will not conflict wiith each other.

The object-oriented features in Ox are not as sophisticated as in some low-level languages. However, this avoids the complexity of a language such as C++, while still providing most of the benefits.

Ox allows you to completely ignore the object-oriented features. However, you will then not be able to use the preprogrammed classes for data management and simulation. It is especially in the latter task that we found a considerable reduction in the required programming effort after writing the base class.

The *class* is the main vehicle for object-oriented programming. A class is nothing more than a group of variables (the data) and functions (the actions) packaged together. This makes it a supercharged `struct` (or `record` in Pascal terminology). Inheritance allows for a new class to add data and functions to the base class, or even redefine functionality of the base class.

In Ox, the default is that all data members of the class are protected (only visible to class members), and all function members are public. Like C++, Ox has the `virtual` keyword to define functions which can be replaced by the derived class. Classes are used by dynamically creating objects of that class. No static objects exist in Ox. When an object is created, the *constructor* function is called, when the object is deleted, the *destructor* function is called. More information on object-oriented programming is given in §13.5.6. Examples based on the preprogrammed classes are in Ch. 12.

## 3.10 Style and Hungarian notation

The readability and maintainability of a program is considerably enhanced when using a consistent style and notation, together with proper indentation and documentation. Style is a personal matter; this section describes the one I have adopted.

In my code, I always indent by one tab (four spaces) at the next level of control (i.e. after each opening brace), jumping back on the closing brace.

I have found Hungarian notation especially useful (see e.g. Petzold, 1992, Ch. 1). Hungarian notation involves the decoration of variable names. There are two elements to Hungarian notation: prefixing of variable names to indicate type (Table 3.1), and using case to indicate scope (Table 3.2, remember that Ox is case sensitive).

As an example consider:

```
#include <oxstd.h>

const decl MX_R = 2;                    /* a constant */
decl g_mX;                       /* exported matrix */
static decl s_iCount;        /* static external variable */
```

**Table 3.1**   Hungarian notation prefixes.

| prefix | type | example |
|--------|------|---------|
| i | integer | iX |
| c | count of | cX |
| b | boolean (f is also used) | bX |
| fl | integer flag | flX |
| d | double | dX |
| m | matrix | mX |
| v | vector ($1 \times n$ or $n \times 1$ matrix) | vX |
| s | string | sX |
| as | array of strings | asX |
| am | array of matrices | amX |
| a | reference in function argument | amX |
| m_ | class member variable | m_mX |
| s_ | static external variable (file scope) | s_mX |
| g_ | external variable with global scope | g_mX |
| fn | function reference | fnX |

**Table 3.2**   Hungarian notation, case sensitivity.

| | |
|---|---|
| function | all lowercase |
| function (exported) | first letter uppercase |
| static external variable | type in lowercase, next letter uppercase (perhaps prefixed with s_) |
| exported external variable | as above, but prefixed with g_ |
| function argument | type in lowercase, next letter uppercase |
| local variables | all lowercase |
| constants | all uppercase |

```
static func1(const pdX)/* argument is pointer to double */
{
}
                                /* exported function */
Func2(const mX, const asX, const cT, const cX)
{
    decl i, m;
}
```

Func2 expects a cT $\times$ cX matrix, and corresponding array of cX variable names. The c prefix is used for the number of elements in a matrix or string. Note however, that it is not necessary in Ox to pass dimensions separately. You can ask mX and asX what dimensions they have:

```
Func2(const mX, const asX)
{
    decl i, m, ct, cx;
    cx = columns(mX);
    ct = rows(mX);
    if (cx != sizeof(asX))
        print("error: dimensions don't match");
}
```

## 3.11 Optimizing for speed

Ox is very fast: current benchmarks suggest that it is faster than most (if not all) other commonly used matrix language interpreters. A program can never be fast enough though, and here are some tips to achieve even higher speed:

- Use matrices as much as you can, avoiding loops and matrix indexing.
- Use the `const` argument qualifier when an argument is not changed in a function: this allows for more efficient function calling.
- Use built-in functions where possible.
- When optimizing a program with loops, it usually only pays to optimize the inner most loop. One option is to move loop invariants to a variable outside the loop.
- Avoid using 'hat' matrices, i.e. avoid using outer products over large dimensions when not necessary.
- Note that matrices are stored by row (the C and C++ default, but transposed from the Fortran default), so it could sometimes be faster to transpose matrices (i.e. have data variables in rows instead of columns).
- If necessary, you can link in C or Fortran code, see the separate Appendices.

## 3.12 OxGauss

Ox has the capability of running a wide range of Gauss (GAUSS is a trademark of Aptech Systems, Inc., Maple Valley, WA, USA) programs. Gauss code can be called from Ox programs, or run on its own. The formal syntax of OxGauss is described in the Ox Appendices, which also lists some of the limitations of OxGauss, and gives a function summary. The remainder of this chapter gives some examples on its use.

### 3.12.1 Running OxGauss programs from the command line

As an example we consider a small project, consisting of a code file that contains a procedure and an external variable, together with a code file that includes the former and calls the function. We shall use `.src` or `.oxgauss` extension for the OxGauss programs.

.................................................. *samples/oxgauss/gaussfunc.src*
```
    declare matrix _g_base = 1;

    proc(0)=gaussfunc(a,b);
        "calling gaussfunc";
        retp(a+_g_base*eye(b));
    endp;
```
..............................................................................

.................................................. *samples/oxgauss/gausscall.src*
```
    #include gaussfunc.src;

    _g_base = 20;
    z = gaussfunc(10,2);
    "result from gaussfunc" z;
```
..............................................................................

To run this program on the command line, enter
```
    oxl -g gausscall.src
```
Which produces the output:
```
Ox version 5.00 (Windows/U) (C) J.A. Doornik, 1994-2007
calling gaussfunc
result from gaussfunc
          30.000000          10.000000
          10.000000          30.000000
```
If there are problems at this stage, we suggest to start by reading the first chapter of the Introduction to Ox.

### 3.12.2 Running OxGauss programs from OxMetrics

Using Ox Professional, the OxGauss program can be loaded into OxMetrics. The syntax highlighting makes understanding the program easier.

Click on Run (the running person) to execute the program. This runs the program using the *OxGauss* application, with the output in a window entitled 'OxGauss Session'. OxMetrics will treat the file as an OxGauss file if it has the .src, .g or .oxgauss extension. If not, the file can still be run by launching *OxGauss* from the OxMetrics workspace window.

### 3.12.3 Calling OxGauss from Ox

The main objective of creating OxGauss was to allow Gauss code to be called from Ox. This helps in the transition to Ox, and increases the amount of code that is available to users of Ox.

The main point to note is that the *OxGauss code lives inside the* gauss *namespace*. In this way, the Ox and OxGauss code can never conflict.

Returning to the earlier example, the first requirement is to make an Ox header file for gaussfunc.src. This must declare the external variables and procedures explicitly in the gauss namespace:

......................................................*samples/oxgauss/gaussfunc.h*

```
namespace gauss
{
    extern decl _g_base;
    gaussfunc(const a, const b);
}
```
....................................................................................

Next, the OxGauss code must be imported into the Ox program. The #import command has been extended to recognize OxGauss imports by prefixing the file name with gauss::, as in the following program:

......................................................*samples/oxgauss/gausscall.ox*

```
#include <oxstd.h>
#import "gauss::gaussfunc"
main()
{
    gauss::_g_base = 20;
    decl z = gauss::gaussfunc(10,2);
    println("result from gaussfunc", z);
}
```
....................................................................................

When the OxGauss functions or variables are accessed, they must also be prefixed with the namespace identifier gauss::. The output is:

```
calling gaussfunc
result from gaussfunc
        30.000      10.000
        10.000      30.000
```

# Chapter 4

# Numerical accuracy

Any computer program that performs numerical calculations is faced with the problem of (loss of) numerical accuracy. It seems a somewhat neglected area in econometric computations, which to some extent could be owing to a perception that the gradual and steady increase in computational power went hand in hand with improvements in accuracy. This, however, is not the case. At the level of software interaction with hardware, the major (and virtually the only) change has been the shift from single precision (4-byte) floating point computation to double precision (8-byte). Not many modern regression packages have problems with the Longley (1967) data set, which severely tests single precision implementations. Of course, there has been a gradual improvement in the understanding of numerical stability of various methods, but this must be offset against the increasing complexity of the calculations involved.

Loss of numerical accuracy is not a problem, provided we know when it occurs and to what extent. Computations are done with finite precision, so it will always be possible to design a problem with analytical solution which fails numerically. Unfortunately, most calculations are too complex to precisely understand to what extent accuracy is lost. So it is important to implement the most accurate methods, and increase understanding of the methods used. The nature of economic data will force us to throw away many correct digits, but only at the end of the computations.

Real numbers are represented as *floating point* numbers, consisting of a sign, a mantissa, and an exponent. A finite number of bytes is used to store a floating point number, so only a finite set can be represented on the computer. The main storage size in Ox is 8 bytes, which gives about 15 to 16 significant digits. Two sources of error result. The first is the *representation error*: most numbers can only be approximated on a computer. The second is *rounding error*. Consider the *machine precision* $\epsilon_m$: this is the smallest number that can be added to one such that the result is different from one:

$$\epsilon_m = \operatorname*{argmin}_{\epsilon} \left(1 + \epsilon \neq 1\right).$$

So an extreme example of rounding error would be $(1 + \epsilon_m/10) - 1$, where the answer would be 0, rather than $\epsilon_m/10$. In Ox: $\epsilon_m \approx 2.2 \times 10^{-16}$.

Due to the accumulation of rounding errors, it is possible that mathematically equivalent formulae can have very different numerical behaviour. For example, computing $V[x]$ as $\frac{1}{T}\sum x_i^2 - \bar{x}^2$ is much less stable than $\frac{1}{T}\sum(x_i - \bar{x})^2$. In the first case, we potentially subtract two quite similar numbers, resulting in cancellation of significant digits (it is even possible to get a negative number). A similar cancellation could occur in the computation of inner products (a very common operation, as it is part of matrix multiplication).

The Windows version of Ox accumulates inner products in extended 10-byte reals, leading to a higher accuracy. In general, one can expect small difference in the results from computations between versions of Ox. Often these are unnoticeable in the accuracy used for printing. The following code example can show the difference between 8 and 10-byte accumulation:

```
#include <oxstd.h>
#include <oxfloat.h>

main()
{
    decl x, y;

    x = <DBL_MAX; DBL_MAX; DBL_MAX-1;
        DBL_MAX; DBL_MAX>;
    y = <10; 10; 1; -10; -10>;

    print("%20.16g", x'y);
}
```

When using extended precision for inner products, it prints the value for DBL_MAX (see Ch. 9) else it prints infinity. When the computations work, it also shows that DBL_MAX $-$ 1 equals DBL_MAX.

An interesting example of harmless numerical inaccuracies is in the case of a grid plot of an autoregressive parameter based on the concentrated likelihood function of an AR($k$) model. Rounding errors make the likelihood function appear non-smooth (not differentiable). This tends to occur in models with many lags of the dependent variable and a high autoregressive order. It also occurs in an AR(1) model of the Longley data set, see Fig. 4.1, which is a grid of 2000 steps between $-1$ and $0$, done in PcGive (ignoring the warning that numerical accuracy is endangered).

It is important to distinguish numerical accuracy from other problems that may occur. Multicollinearity, for example, is first and foremost a statistical problem. A certain parametrization of a model might make the estimates of one or more parameters statistically imprecise (cf. the concept of 'micronumerosity' playfully introduced by Goldberger in Kiefer, 1989). This imprecision could be changed (or moved) by altering the specification of the model. Multicollinearity could induce numerical instability, leading to loss of significant digits in some or all results.

Another example is the determination of the optimum of a non-linear function that is not concave. Here it is possible to end up in a local optimum. This is clearly not

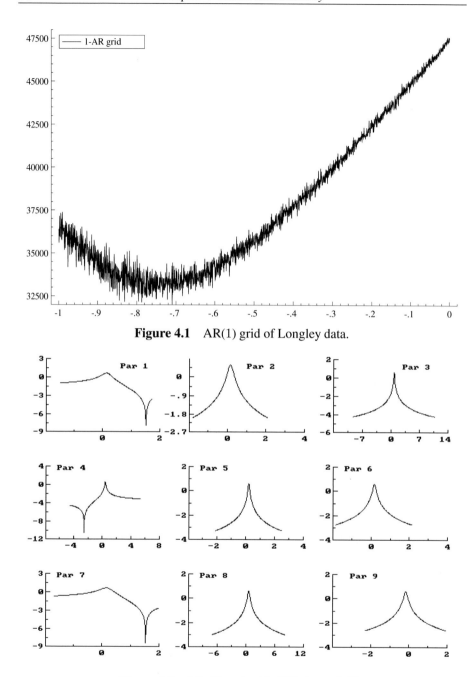

**Figure 4.1**   AR(1) grid of Longley data.

**Figure 4.2**   Likelihood grid of Klein model I.

a problem of numerical stability, but inherent to non-linear optimization techniques. A good example is provided by Klein model I. Figure 4.2 provides a grid plot of the FIML likelihood function for each parameter, centred around the maximum found with the 2SLS estimates as a starting point. These grids are of a different type from the AR grid in Fig. 4.1. In the former, all parameters but one are kept fixed, whereas the AR grid graphs the concentrated likelihood. In the case of one autoregressive parameter, the actual optimum may be read off the graph, as is the case in the AR grid plot above.

A matrix frequently used to show the limitations of numerical techniques is the Hilbert matrix. A Hilbert matrix of dimension $n$, $H_n$, has elements

$$h_{ij} = (i + j + 1)^{-1}, \quad i, j = 0, 1, \ldots, n - 1.$$

For example:

$$H_4 = \begin{pmatrix} 1/1 & 1/2 & 1/3 & 1/4 \\ 1/2 & 1/3 & 1/4 & 1/5 \\ 1/3 & 1/4 & 1/5 & 1/6 \\ 1/4 & 1/5 & 1/6 & 1/7 \end{pmatrix}$$

This matrix is very ill-conditioned, and many computations involving $H_n$ break down even for $n$ as small as 10. The inverse and determinant of $H_n$ are known analytically. Barnett (1990) gives the determinant:

$$\det(H_n) = \prod_{k=0}^{n-1} \frac{(n - k - 1)!(n - k - 1)!k!}{(n + k)!}.$$

We could use the `loggamma` function to compute the (reciprocal of the) determinant: $\log \Gamma(z + 1) = \log(z!)$. Then we can make a stable computation up to $n = 23$. At $n = 24$ the `exp` function overflows. Restricting ourselves to the logarithm of the determinant, we can go quite a bit further. The `determinant` function breaks down much earlier: at $n = 4$ we have about 13 significant digits correct, at $n = 10$ just 5. At $n = 11$, the function reports that the matrix is singular. If we scale the matrix to keep the determinant under control, we get the message that the determinant is unreliable at $n = 11$, which is borne out by only two correct digits. Beyond that, there is no correct answer from the `determinant` function; using the `logdet` function does not help.

To conclude this chapter, we show that using floating point for computations which should result in integers could lead to unexpected results. Most of the time conversion to an integer works, but not always. The following code has been especially written to show that:

```
#include <oxstd.h>

intfuzzy(const d)
{
    return  d > 0 ? int(d * (1 + fuzziness(0)/2))
                  : int(d * (1 - fuzziness(0)/2));
```

```
}
main()
{
    decl i, j;

    for (i = 322, j = 122; i < 327; ++i, ++j)
        println("%20.16f", (i*0.1 - 20) * 10, " ",
                "%5d", int( ((i*0.1) - 20) * 10) - j,
                "%5d", int( ((i*0.1) - 20) * 10),
                "%5d", int(floor( ((i*0.1) - 20) * 10)),
                "%5d", int(ceil( ((i*0.1) - 20) * 10)));

    for (i = 322, j = 122; i < 327; ++i, ++j)
        println("%20.16f", (i*0.1 - 20) * 10, " ",
                "%20.16f", (i*0.1 - 20) * 10 * (1+fuzziness(0)/2),
                "%5d", intfuzzy( ((i*0.1) - 20) * 10) - j);
}
```

which has output on Windows (note that there could be minor differences on other platforms):

```
122.0000000000000300      0   122   122   123
123.0000000000000400      0   123   123   124
123.9999999999999900     -1   123   123   124
125.0000000000000000      0   125   125   125
126.0000000000000100      0   126   126   127


122.0000000000000300  122.0000000000061200      0
123.0000000000000400  123.0000000000061800      0
123.9999999999999900  124.0000000000061800      0
125.0000000000000000  125.0000000000062400      0
126.0000000000000100  126.0000000000063100      0
```

The last two zeros in the floating point print-out are beyond the precision, so can be ignored. We see however, that even then the results are not exact: in general most integers cannot be represented exactly in floating point notation (this is the representation error mentioned earlier). Once we start computing, these inexactitudes propagate. Conversion to an integer involves truncation, hence we find 123 for the third value, and not 124 as expected. This also affects the floor and ceil function. (Another example of this effect is discussed under the range library function.)

There is a potential solution, as shown in the code. Add a little bit to positive numbers (subtract for negative numbers), where the little bit is a fraction determined by the current fuzziness value. This is implemented in the truncf library function. Alternatively, one could round to the nearest integer, using the round function.

Note that, when indexing a matrix by another matrix, a problem like this could occur when the indices are the result from computation, rather than direct storage. Internally, the indices are converted to integers by truncation, so you could decide to round first. When using random indices (e.g. in bootstrapping), such rounding will produce indices out of range, and truncation is precisely what is required.

# Chapter 5

# How to ...

How to compute/get/achieve:

- bootstrap a data set, see under: 'take a random sample ...'.
- censored random variates, for example, a random normal censored at $a$ and $b$ (don't forget any dots; the `setbounds()` function can also be used):

```
x = rann(1000,1);
y = x .< a .? a .: x .> b .? b .: x;
y = setbounds(x, a, b);
```

- check if all elements in a matrix are equal to a value, 1 say:

```
if (x == 1)
```

- check if no element in a matrix is equal to a value, 1 say:

```
if (x != 1)
```

- check if any element in a matrix is not equal to a value, 0 say:

```
if ( !(x == 0) )
if ( max(x .== 0) )
```

- check if any element in a matrix is equal to a value, 1 say:

```
if ( any(x .== 1) )
```

- check if two matrices, x and y, are equal to each other:

```
if (x == y)
```

- check if two matrices, x and y, have any elements in common:

```
if ( any(x .== y) )
```

- concatenation of columns in a loop (inserting columns of zeros):

```
m = <>;
for (i = 0; i < columns(mx); ++i)
{
    m ~= mx[][i];
    m ~= 0;
}
```

Such concatenation can be relatively slow if `columns(m)` is large. An alternative is to pre-allocate the destination matrix:

```
m = zeros(rows(mx), 2 * columns(mx));
for (i = 0; i < columns(mx); i += 2)
{
    m[][i] = mx[][i];
}
```

- concatenation of rows in a loop

```
decl m = <>;
for (i = 0; i < rows(mx); ++i)
    m |= mx[i][];
```

Again, pre-allocation is more efficient.

- correlation matrix out of a variance matrix:

```
decl sdi = 1 ./ sqrt(diagonal(mvar));
corrm = sdi .* mvar .* sdi';
```

- create a tridiagonal matrix, symmetric, $n \times n$:

```
a * unit(n) + b * lag0(unit(n), 1) + b * lag0(unit(n), -1);
```

- delete rows with certain values:

```
deleter(mx, value);
```

  or use:

```
mx[ vecindex( !sumr(mx .== value) )][];
```

- element-by-element maximum (dot-maximum) (or minimum, etc.) of two matrices, or of a matrix and a number:

```
x = y .> 3 .? y .: 3;
x = y .> z .? y .: z;
```

- factorial: see under the `loggamma()` and `gammafact()` library functions, e.g. for $x$!:

```
fact = exp(loggamma(x + 1));
fact = gammafact(x + 1);
```

- gamma function: see under the `loggamma()` and `gammafact()` library functions; for the incomplete gamma function, see under `gammafunc()`.
- index of the maximum value in each column

```
maxindc = maxcindex(x);
```

  Another possibility:

```
maxindc = limits(x)[2][];
```

- maximum of each column:

```
maxc = maxc(x);
```

- median of each data column:

```
quantilec(x);
```

- mode of a data column:

```
max(x[][0]);
```

- $N[\boldsymbol{\mu}, \boldsymbol{\Sigma}]$ random numbers

```
chol_t = choleski(mSigma)';        // use P'
eps = rann(ct, cn) * chol_t + mMu;
```

- $N[\mu, \sigma^2]$ quantiles

```
z = quann(p);
x = z .* sqrt(sigma2) + mu;
```

- Numerical variance
  Following maximum likelihood estimation, compute the second derivative matrix $Q$ using Num2Derivative. Then $-Q^{-1}$ is an estimate of the parameter variance matrix.

- $\pi$ (this requires #include <oxfloat.h>):

```
pi = M_PI;
```

- (homogeneous) Poisson process, simulate first $n$ arrival times:

```
cumulate(ranexp(n, 1, 1.0));
```

- (homogeneous) Poisson process with rate $\mu$, simulate times of events up to time $t$:

```
t * ranuorder(ranpoisson(1, 1, mu * t));
```

- quadratic form:

```
mom = x'x;
mom = outer(x', <>);
```

- select rows with certain values:

```
selectr(mx, value);
```

  or use:

```
mx[ vecindex( sumr(mx .== value) )][];
```

- skewness and kurtosis:

```
mxs = standardize(mx);
n = columns(mx);
skew = sumr(mxs .^ 3) / n;
kurt = sumr(mxs .^ 4) / n;
```

  or use the moments library function.

- sorted column index of a matrix x sorted by the first column (column zero):

```
sortindex = sortcindex(x[][0]);
// or use:
//sortindex =
//    sortbyc(x ~ range(0, rows(x)-1)', 0)[][columns(x)];

// Now sortindex can be used to sort
// another matrix y conformably:
z = y[sortindex][];
```

- sequence from $a$ to $b$ of $n + 1$ equally spaced points (see under the `range` library function for more information):

```
step = (b - a) / n;
seq = range(0, n) *step + a;
```

- substitute certain values only, say change all the 3's to 1 in a matrix x:

```
x = x .== 3 .? 1 .: x;
```

- take a random sample of size n with replacement from the rows of a matrix x:

```
y = x[ ranu(1,n) * rows(x) ][];
```

- take a random sample of size n without replacement from the rows of a matrix x (this requires oxprob.h):

```
y = x[ ransubsample(n, rows(x) - 1) ][];
```

- trim the matrix x by deleting the first top and the last bot rows:

```
trim = x[top:rows(x)-bot-1][];
```

- truncated random variates (i.e. random numbers from truncated distributions, see Devroye, 1986, p.39), with the distribution $F$ truncated on the left at $a$, and on the right at $b$:

$$F^{-1}\left\{F(a) + u \times [F(b) - F(a)]\right\},$$

where $u$ is a uniform random number. In Ox code, for a random normal, truncated at $a$ and $b$:

```
pa = probn(a);        // Pr{value <= a}
    // pa = 0 for no  left truncation
pb = probn(b);        // Pr{value <= b}
    // pb = 1 for no right truncation
y = quann( pa + ranu(1000,1) * (pb - pa) );
```

- two-sided critical values from a $t(k)$ distribution:

```
pvalue = 2 * tailt(fabs(x), k);
```

- unsorting a matrix which is to be sorted by a column i.

```
sorted = sortbyc(x ~ range(0, rows(x)-1)', i)
unsorted = sortbyc(sorted, columns(sorted) - 1);
```

- $y \log y$:

```
y .* log(y .> 0 .? y .: 1);
```

# Chapter 6

# Some matrix algebra

This chapter summarizes the matrix algebra necessary to understand the matrix capabilities of Ox. For a more thorough overview consult Magnus and Neudecker (1988), Dhrymes (1984), Rao (1973, Chapter 1) or Anderson (1984, Appendix A), among many others.

To define the elementary operators on matrices we shall write $(a_{ij})_{m,n}$ for the $m \times n$ matrix $\mathbf{A}$ when this is convenient:

$$\mathbf{A} = (a_{ij})_{m,n} = \begin{pmatrix} a_{11} & \cdots & a_{1n} \\ \vdots & & \vdots \\ a_{m1} & \cdots & a_{mn} \end{pmatrix}.$$

So, for example the $3 \times 2$ matrix of ones is:

$$\begin{pmatrix} 1 & 1 & 1 \\ 1 & 1 & 1 \end{pmatrix}.$$

- *addition,* $\mathbf{A}$ is $m \times n$, $\mathbf{B}$ is $m \times n$:

$$\mathbf{A} + \mathbf{B} = (a_{ij} + b_{ij})_{m,n}.$$

- *multiplication,* $\mathbf{A}$ is $m \times n$, $\mathbf{B}$ is $n \times p$, $c$ is a scalar:

$$\mathbf{AB} = \left( \sum_{k=1}^{n} a_{ik}b_{kj} \right)_{m,p}, \quad c\mathbf{A} = (ca_{ij})_{m,n}.$$

- *dot-multiplication* (hadamard product), $\mathbf{A}$ is $m \times n$, $\mathbf{B}$ is $m \times n$:

$$\mathbf{A} \odot \mathbf{B} = (a_{ij}b_{ij})_{m,n}.$$

For example:

$$\mathbf{\Omega} \odot \mathbf{S} = \begin{pmatrix} \omega_{11}s_{11} & \omega_{12}s_{12} \\ \omega_{21}s_{21} & \omega_{22}s_{22} \end{pmatrix}.$$

- *kronecker product,* $\mathbf{A}$ is $m \times n$, $\mathbf{B}$ is $p \times q$:

$$\mathbf{A} \otimes \mathbf{B} = \left(a_{ij}\mathbf{B}\right)_{mp,nq}.$$

For example, with $\boldsymbol{\Omega} = \left(\omega_{ij}\right)_{2,2}$, $\mathbf{S} = \left(s_{ij}\right)_{2,2}$:

$$\boldsymbol{\Omega} \otimes \mathbf{S} = \begin{pmatrix} \omega_{11}s_{11} & \omega_{11}s_{12} & \omega_{12}s_{11} & \omega_{12}s_{12} \\ \omega_{11}s_{21} & \omega_{11}s_{22} & \omega_{12}s_{21} & \omega_{12}s_{22} \\ \omega_{21}s_{11} & \omega_{21}s_{12} & \omega_{22}s_{11} & \omega_{22}s_{12} \\ \omega_{21}s_{21} & \omega_{21}s_{22} & \omega_{22}s_{21} & \omega_{22}s_{22} \end{pmatrix}.$$

- *transpose,* $\mathbf{A}$ is $m \times n$:

$$\mathbf{A}' = \left(a_{ji}\right)_{n,m}.$$

- *determinant,* $\mathbf{A}$ is $n \times n$:

$$|\mathbf{A}| = \sum (-1)^{c(j_1,\ldots,j_n)} \prod_{i=1}^{n} a_{ij_i}$$

where the summation is over all permutations $(j_1, \ldots, j_n)$ of the set of integers $(1, \ldots, n)$, and $c(j_1, \ldots, j_n)$ is the number of transpositions required to change $(1, \ldots, n)$ into $(j_1, \ldots, j_n)$. In the $2 \times 2$ case the set $(1, 2)$ can be transposed once into $(2, 1)$, so $|\boldsymbol{\Omega}| = (-1)^0 \omega_{11}\omega_{22} + (-1)^1 \omega_{12}\omega_{21}$.

- *trace,* $\mathbf{A}$ is $n \times n$:

$$\mathrm{tr}\mathbf{A} = \sum_{i=1}^{n} a_{ii}.$$

- *rank,* $\mathbf{A}$ is $m \times n$: the rank of $\mathbf{A}$ is the number of linearly independent columns (or rows, row rank always equals column rank) in $\mathbf{A}$, $\mathrm{r}(\mathbf{A}) \leq \min(m, n)$. If $\mathbf{A}$ is $n \times n$ and of full rank then:

$$\mathrm{r}(\mathbf{A}) = n.$$

- *symmetric matrix,* $\mathbf{A}$ is $n \times n$: $\mathbf{A}$ is symmetric if:

$$\mathbf{A}' = \mathbf{A}.$$

- *matrix inverse,* $\mathbf{A}$ is $n \times n$ and of full rank (non-singular, which is equivalent to $|\mathbf{A}| \neq 0$) then $\mathbf{A}^{-1}$ is the unique $n \times n$ matrix such that:

$$\mathbf{A}\mathbf{A}^{-1} = \mathbf{I}.$$

This implies that $\mathbf{A}^{-1}\mathbf{A} = \mathbf{I}$; $\mathbf{I}$ is the $n \times n$ identity matrix:

$$\begin{pmatrix} 1 & 0 & \cdots & 0 \\ 0 & 1 & \cdots & 0 \\ \vdots & \vdots & & \vdots \\ 0 & 0 & \cdots & 1 \end{pmatrix}.$$

- *orthogonal matrix*, $\mathbf{A}$ is $n \times n$: $\mathbf{A}$ is orthogonal if:

$$\mathbf{A}'\mathbf{A} = \mathbf{I}.$$

Then also $\mathbf{A}\mathbf{A}' = \mathbf{I}$; further: $r(\mathbf{A}) = n$, $\mathbf{A}' = \mathbf{A}^{-1}$.
- *orthogonal complement*, $\mathbf{A}$ is $m \times n$, $m > n$ and $r(\mathbf{A}) = n$, define the orthogonal complement $\mathbf{A}_\perp$ as the $m \times (m-n)$ matrix such that: $\mathbf{A}'\mathbf{A}_\perp = \mathbf{0}$ with $r(\mathbf{A}_\perp) = m - n$ and $r(\mathbf{A} : \mathbf{A}_\perp) = m$. $\mathbf{A}_\perp$ spans the *null space* of $\mathbf{A}$; $r(\mathbf{A}_\perp)$ is called the *nullity* of $\mathbf{A}$.
- *idempotent matrix*, $\mathbf{A}$ is $n \times n$: $\mathbf{A}$ is idempotent if:

$$\mathbf{A}\mathbf{A} = \mathbf{A}.$$

An example is the projection matrix $\mathbf{M}_X = \mathbf{I} - \mathbf{X}\left(\mathbf{X}'\mathbf{X}\right)^{-1}\mathbf{X}'$.
- *vectorization*, $\mathbf{A}$ is $m \times n$:

$$\operatorname{vec}\mathbf{A} = \begin{pmatrix} a_{11} \\ \vdots \\ a_{m1} \\ \vdots \\ a_{1n} \\ \vdots \\ a_{mn} \end{pmatrix},$$

which is an $mn \times 1$ vector consisting of the stacked columns of $\mathbf{A}$.

If $\mathbf{A}$ is $n \times n$ and symmetric, we can use the vech operator to vectorize the unique elements, thus ignoring the elements above the diagonal:

$$\operatorname{vech}\mathbf{A} = \begin{pmatrix} a_{11} \\ \vdots \\ a_{n1} \\ a_{22} \\ \vdots \\ a_{n2} \\ \vdots \\ a_{nn} \end{pmatrix},$$

which is a $\frac{1}{2}n(n+1) \times 1$ vector.
- *diagonalization*, $\mathbf{A}$ is $n \times n$:

$$\operatorname{dg}\mathbf{A} = \begin{pmatrix} a_{11} & 0 & \cdots & 0 \\ 0 & a_{22} & \cdots & 0 \\ \vdots & \vdots & & \vdots \\ 0 & 0 & \cdots & a_{nn} \end{pmatrix} = \operatorname{diag}\left(a_{11}, a_{22}, \ldots, a_{nn}\right).$$

- *positive definite,* $\mathbf{A}$ is $n \times n$ and symmetric: $\mathbf{A}$ is positive definite if $\mathbf{x}'\mathbf{A}\mathbf{x} > 0$ for all $n \times 1$ vectors $\mathbf{x} \neq \mathbf{0}$, positive semi-definite if $\mathbf{x}'\mathbf{A}\mathbf{x} \geq 0$ for all $\mathbf{x} \neq \mathbf{0}$, and negative definite if $\mathbf{x}'\mathbf{A}\mathbf{x} < 0$ for all $\mathbf{x} \neq \mathbf{0}$.
- *eigenvalues and eigenvectors,* $\mathbf{A}$ is $n \times n$: the eigenvalues of $\mathbf{A}$ are the roots of the characteristic equation:

$$|\mathbf{A} - \lambda\mathbf{I}| = 0.$$

If $\lambda_i$ is an eigenvalue of $\mathbf{A}$, then $\mathbf{x}_i \neq \mathbf{0}$ is an eigenvector of $\mathbf{A}$ if it satisfies:

$$(\mathbf{A} - \lambda_i\mathbf{I})\,\mathbf{x}_i = \mathbf{0}.$$

- *Choleski decomposition,* $\mathbf{A}$ is $n \times n$ summetric and positive definite, then:

$$\mathbf{A} = \mathbf{PP}',$$

where $\mathbf{P}$ is a unique lower triangular matrix with positive diagonal elements.
- *LU decomposition,* $\mathbf{A}$ is $n \times n$, then:

$$\mathbf{A} = \mathbf{LU}',$$

where $\mathbf{L}$ is a lower triangular matrix with ones on the diagonal and $\mathbf{U}$ is upper diagonal.
- *singular value decomposition,* decomposes an $m \times n$ matrix $\mathbf{A}$, $m \geq n$, into:

$$\mathbf{A} = \mathbf{UWV}',$$

with:

$\mathbf{U}$ is $m \times n$ and $\mathbf{U}'\mathbf{U} = \mathbf{I}_n$,
$\mathbf{W}$ is $n \times n$ and diagonal, with non-negative diagonal elements,
$\mathbf{V}$ is $n \times n$ and $\mathbf{V}'\mathbf{V} = \mathbf{I}_n$.

The diagonal of $\mathbf{W}$ holds the singular values. The number of non-zero singular values is the rank of $\mathbf{A}$, also see §13.8.5.1.

The SVD can be used to find the orthogonal complement of $\mathbf{A}$. Assume $\mathrm{r}(\mathbf{A}) = n$ and compute the singular value decomposition of the $(m \times m)$ matrix $\mathbf{B} = (\mathbf{A} : \mathbf{0})$. The last $m - n$ diagonal elements of $\mathbf{W}$ will be zero. Corresponding to that are the last $m - n$ columns of $\mathbf{U}$ which form $\mathbf{A}_\perp$:

$$\mathbf{B} = (\mathbf{A} : \mathbf{0}) = \mathbf{UWV}' = (\mathbf{U}_1 : \mathbf{U}_2) \begin{pmatrix} \mathbf{W}_1 & \mathbf{0} \\ \mathbf{0} & \mathbf{0} \end{pmatrix} \begin{pmatrix} \mathbf{V}_1' \\ \mathbf{V}_2' \end{pmatrix}.$$

Here $\mathbf{U}$, $\mathbf{V}$ and $\mathbf{W}$ are $(m \times m)$ matrices; $\mathbf{U}_2'\mathbf{U}_1 = \mathbf{0}$ so that $\mathbf{U}_2'\mathbf{A} = \mathbf{U}_2'\mathbf{U}_1\mathbf{W}_1\mathbf{V}_1' = \mathbf{0}$ and $\mathrm{r}(\mathbf{A} : \mathbf{U}_2) = m$ as $\mathbf{U}_2'\mathbf{U}_2 = \mathbf{I}$.

- *differentiation*, define $f\left(\cdot\right):\mathbb{R}^m\mapsto\mathbb{R}$ then:

$$\nabla f=\frac{\partial f\left(\mathbf{a}\right)}{\partial\mathbf{a}}=\begin{pmatrix}\frac{\partial f(\mathbf{a})}{\partial a_1}\\\vdots\\\frac{\partial f(\mathbf{a})}{\partial a_m}\end{pmatrix},\quad\nabla^2 f=\frac{\partial^2 f\left(\mathbf{a}\right)}{\partial\mathbf{a}\partial\mathbf{a}'}=\left(\frac{\partial^2 f\left(\mathbf{a}\right)}{\partial a_i\partial a_j}\right)_{m,m}.$$

If $f\left(\cdot\right)$ is a log-likelihood function we shall write $\mathbf{q}\left(\cdot\right)$ for the first derivative (or score), and $\mathbf{H}\left(\cdot\right)$ for the second derivative (or Hessian) matrix.
For $f\left(\cdot\right):\mathbb{R}^{m\times n}\mapsto\mathbb{R}$ we define:

$$\frac{\partial f\left(\mathbf{A}\right)}{\partial\mathbf{A}}=\left(\frac{\partial f\left(\mathbf{A}\right)}{\partial a_{ij}}\right)_{m,n}.$$

- *Jacobian matrix*, for a vector function $\mathbf{f}\left(\cdot\right):\mathbb{R}^m\mapsto\mathbb{R}^n$ we define the $n\times m$ Jacobian matrix $\mathbf{J}$:

$$\frac{\partial\mathbf{f}\left(\mathbf{a}\right)}{\partial\mathbf{a}'}=\begin{pmatrix}\frac{\partial f_1(\mathbf{a})}{\partial a_1}&\cdots&\frac{\partial f_1(\mathbf{a})}{\partial a_m}\\\vdots&&\vdots\\\frac{\partial f_n(\mathbf{a})}{\partial a_1}&\cdots&\frac{\partial f_n(\mathbf{a})}{\partial a_m}\end{pmatrix}=\begin{pmatrix}\left(\nabla f_1\right)'\\\vdots\\\left(\nabla f_m\right)'\end{pmatrix}=\left(\nabla\mathbf{f}\right)'.$$

The transpose of the Jacobian is called the gradient, and corresponds to the $\mathbf{q}\left(\cdot\right)$ above for $n=1$ (so in that case the Jacobian is $1\times m$ and the score $n\times 1$). The Jacobian is the absolute value of the determinant of $\mathbf{J}$ when $m=n$: $||\mathbf{J}||$.
Normally we wish to compute the Jacobian matrix for a transformation of a coefficient matrix: $\mathbf{\Psi}=\mathbf{F}\left(\mathbf{\Pi}'\right)$ where $\mathbf{F}$ is a matrix function $\mathbf{F}\left(\cdot\right):\mathbb{R}^{m\times n}\mapsto\mathbb{R}^{p\times q}$:

$$\mathbf{J}=\frac{\partial\text{vec}\mathbf{\Psi}}{\partial\left(\text{vec}\mathbf{\Pi}'\right)'},$$

with $\mathbf{\Pi}$ $n\times m$ and $\mathbf{\Psi}$ $p\times q$ so that $\mathbf{J}$ is $pq\times mn$.

# Part II

# Function and Language Reference

# Chapter 7

# Function summary

This chapter lists all library functions by category, and gives a brief description. More detailed descriptions with examples follow in Chapters 8–12.

**date and time functions**

| | |
|---|---|
| date | returns a string with the current date |
| dayofcalendar | translates a date in the day of the calendar |
| dayofeaster | finds the calendar date of Easter |
| dayofmonth | finds the *n*-th weekday in the month |
| dayofweek | translates a date in the day of the week |
| time | returns a string with the current time |
| timeofday | translates the time component of a calendar index |
| timer | returns an integer representing the current time |
| timespan | returns the lapsed time |
| timestr | returns a string from no of seconds since 1 Jan 1970 |
| timing | returns date/time as no of seconds since 1 Jan 1970 |
| today | returns current date/time as no of seconds since 1 Jan 1970 |

**general functions**

| | |
|---|---|
| any | returns TRUE if any element is TRUE |
| arglist | get the argument list specified on the command line |
| binand | binary *and* operation |
| bincomp | binary bit-wise complement operation |
| binor | binary *or* operation |
| columns | get number of columns of argument (0 for int,double) |
| countc | count elements in columns in specified intervals |
| countr | count elements in rows in specified intervals |
| discretize | count elements in columns in regularly-spaced intervals |
| fuzziness | set fuzziness parameter |
| isdotfeq | tests for dot fuzzy equality |
| isdotinf | returns boolean matrix from test for infinity |
| isdotmissing | returns boolean matrix from test for missing values (.NaN,+.Inf,-.Inf) |

| `isdotnan` | returns boolean matrix from test for .NaN |
| `iseq` | tests for equality with fuzziness 0 |
| `isfeq` | tests for fuzzy equality |
| `ismissing` | tests for the presence of a missing value (.NaN,+.Inf,-.Inf) |
| `isnan` | tests for the presence of .NaN |
| `limits` | maximum/maximum values in matrix plus location |
| `max` | maximum value in arguments |
| `maxc` | maximum value of each column |
| `maxcindex` | row index of the maximum value of each column |
| `min` | minimum value in arguments |
| `minc` | minimum value of each column |
| `mincindex` | row index of the minimum value of each column |
| `prodc` | compute column products |
| `prodr` | compute row products |
| `rows` | get number of rows of argument (0 for int,double) |
| `sizec` | get number of columns of argument (1 for int,double) |
| `sizeof` | same as `rows` |
| `sizer` | get number of rows of argument (1 for int,double) |
| `sizerc` | get total number of elements of argument (1 for int,double) |
| `sumc` | compute column sums |
| `sumr` | compute row sums |
| `sumsqrc` | compute column sum of squares |
| `sumsqrr` | compute row sum of squares |
| `va_arglist` | needed to access arguments in a variable argument list |

### graphics functions

| `CloseDrawWindow` | close the drawing window |
| `Draw` | draw a matrix against an $x$-axis |
| `DrawAcf` | draw an ACF (correlogram) and/or PACF |
| `DrawAdjust` | adjust most recent draw object |
| `DrawAxis` | draw an axis |
| `DrawAxisAuto` | draw an automatic axis |
| `DrawBoxPlot` | draw a box plot |
| `DrawCorrelogram` | draw a correlogram |
| `DrawDensity` | draw a histogram and/or density |
| `DrawHistogram` | draw a histogram from vector of heights |
| `DrawLegend` | draw the legend |
| `DrawLine` | draw a line |
| `DrawMatrix` | draw a matrix against an $x$-axis |
| `DrawPLine` | draw a line (pixel coordinates) |
| `DrawPSymbol` | draw a symbol (pixel coordinates) |
| `DrawPText` | draw text (pixel coordinates) |
| `DrawQQ` | draw a QQ plot |
| `DrawSpectrum` | draw a spectral density |

| | |
|---|---|
| DrawSymbol | draw a symbol |
| DrawT | draw a matrix against time |
| DrawText | draw text |
| DrawTitle | set the title text |
| DrawTMatrix | draw a matrix against time |
| DrawX | cross plot of a matrix against a vector |
| DrawXMatrix | cross plot of a matrix against a vector |
| DrawXYZ | draw 3-dimensional graph |
| DrawZ | add error bar/band/fan/Z variable |
| SaveDrawWindow | save the drawing to a file |
| SetDraw | set drawing defaults |
| SetDrawWindow | set the name of the drawing window |
| SetTextWindow | set the name of the text window |
| ShowDrawWindow | show the drawing window |

**input/output**

| | |
|---|---|
| eprint | print to stderr |
| fclose | close a file |
| feof | tests for end of file |
| flush | flushes the file buffer |
| fopen | open a file |
| format | set default print format |
| fprint | print to a file |
| fprintln | as `printf`, ensures the next output will be on a new line |
| fread | read data in binary format from a file |
| fremove | removes a file |
| fscan | read from a file |
| fseek | gets or repositions the file pointer |
| fsize | get the file size in bytes |
| fwrite | write data in binary format from a file |
| loadmat | load a matrix |
| print | print to stdout |
| println | as `print`, ensures the next output will be on a new line |
| savemat | save a matrix |
| scan | read from the console |
| sprint | print to a string |
| sprintbuffer | resize the sprint buffer |
| sscan | read from a string |

**is type functions**

| | |
|---|---|
| classname | returns the class name of a class object |
| isarray | tests if argument is an array |
| isclass | tests if argument is a class object |
| isdouble | tests if argument is a double |

| | |
|---|---|
| isfile | tests if argument is a file |
| isfunction | tests if argument is a function |
| isint | tests if argument is an integer |
| ismatrix | tests if argument is a matrix |
| ismember | tests if a class object has a specified member |
| isstring | tests if argument is a string |

## mathematical functions

| | |
|---|---|
| bessel | bessel functions of order 0 and 1 |
| betafunc | incomplete beta integral |
| binomial | binomial coefficient |
| cabs | complex absolute value |
| cdiv | complex division |
| ceil | ceiling |
| cerf | complex error function |
| cexp | complex exponent |
| clog | complex logarithm |
| cmul | complex multiplication |
| csqrt | complex square root |
| dawson | Dawson integral |
| dfft | discrete Fourier transform |
| erf | error function |
| exp | exponent |
| expint | exponential integral Ei |
| fabs | absolute value |
| factorial | factorial |
| fft | fast Fourier transform, pads to power of two |
| fft1d | fast Fourier transform, any sample size |
| floor | floor |
| fmod | floating point remainder |
| gammafact | gamma function (related to factorial) |
| gammafunc | incomplete gamma function |
| idiv | integer division |
| imod | integer remainder |
| log | natural logarithm |
| log10 | base-10 logarithm |
| loggamma | logarithm of gamma function |
| polygamma | derivatives of loggamma function |
| pow | dot-power (alternative to .^) |
| round | rounds to nearest integer |
| sqr | square |
| sqrt | square root |
| trunc | truncate towards zero |
| truncf | fuzzy truncation towards zero |

**matrix creation**

| | |
|---|---|
| constant | create a matrix and fill with a value |
| diag | create matrix with specified vector on diagonal |
| ones | create a matrix of ones |
| range | create a matrix consisting of a range of numbers (trend) |
| toeplitz | create a symmetric Toeplitz matrix |
| unit | create an identity matrix |
| zeros | create a matrix of zeros |

**matrix decomposition**

| | |
|---|---|
| choleski | Choleski decomposition of symmetric positive definite matrix |
| decldl | square root free Choleski decomposition of sym.pd. matrix |
| decldlband | Choleski decomposition of sym.pd. band matrix |
| declu | LU decomposition |
| decqr | QR decomposition |
| decqrmul | applies $Q$ from the QR decomposition to compute $Q'Y$ |
| decqrupdate | update a QR decomposition via Givens rotations |
| decschur | real Schur decomposition |
| decschurgen | real generalized Schur decomposition |
| decsvd | singular value decomposition |
| eigen | eigenvalues of matrix |
| eigensym | eigenvalues of symmetric matrix |
| eigensymgen | solves generalized symmetric eigen problem |
| polydiv | divides two polynomials |
| polyeval | evaluates a polynomial |
| polymake | gets polynomial coefficients from the (inverse) roots |
| polymul | multiplies two polynomials |
| polyroots | computes the (inverse) roots of a polynomial |
| solveldl | solves AX=B when A is decomposed with decldl |
| solveldlband | solves AX=B when A is decomposed with decldlband |
| solvelu | solves AX=B when A is decomposed with declu |
| solvetoeplitz | solves AX=B when A is symmetric Toeplitz |

**matrix functions**

| | |
|---|---|
| determinant | returns the determinant of a matrix |
| diagcat | concatenates two matrices long the diagonal |
| diagonalize | set off-diagonal elements to zero |
| invert | invert a matrix |
| inverteps | sets inversion/rank epsilon |
| invertgen | (generalized) inversion |
| invertsym | invert a symmetric matrix |
| logdet | returns the log and sign of the determinant |

| | |
|---|---|
| norm | returns the norm of a matrix |
| nullspace | returns the null space of a matrix |
| outer | $XSX'$, or diagonal$(XSX')$ or $\sum x_i x_i'$ |
| rank | returns the rank of a matrix |
| trace | returns the trace of a matrix |

### matrix modification/selection/reordering

| | |
|---|---|
| aggregatec | aggregates the columns of a matrix by taking sums of groups |
| aggregater | aggregates the rows of a matrix by taking sums of groups |
| deletec | deletes columns with specific values (or missing values) |
| deleteifc | deletes columns according to boolean matrix |
| deleteifr | deletes rows according to boolean matrix |
| deleter | deletes rows with specific values (or missing values) |
| diagonal | extract diagonal from a matrix |
| dropc | deletes specified columns |
| dropr | deletes specified rows |
| exclusion | return sorted unique elements which are not in a 2nd matrix |
| insertc | inserts columns of zeros |
| insertr | inserts rows of zeros |
| intersection | return sorted unique intersection of two matrices |
| lower | return the lower diagonal of a matrix |
| reflect | reflect a matrix |
| reshape | reshape a matrix by row |
| reversec | reverse column elements |
| reverser | reverse row elements |
| selectc | selects columns with specific values (or missing values) |
| selectifc | selects columns according to boolean matrix |
| selectifr | selects rows according to boolean matrix |
| selectr | selects rows with specific values (or missing values) |
| selectrc | selects elements from specified rows and columns |
| setbounds | set the lower and upper bounds of a matrix |
| setdiagonal | set the diagonal of a matrix |
| setlower | set the lower diagonal of a matrix |
| setupper | set the upper diagonal of a matrix |
| shape | reshape a matrix by column |
| sortbyc | sort one column, and remaining columns accordingly |
| sortbyr | sort one row, and remaining rows accordingly |
| sortc | sort columns of a matrix, or an array of strings |
| sortcindex | sorted index from applying sortc |
| sortr | sort rows of a matrix |
| submat | extract a submatrix |
| thinc | thin the columns of a matrix |
| thinr | thin the rows of a matrix |

| unique | return the sorted unique elements of a matrix |
| unvech | undoes vech |
| upper | return the upper diagonal of a matrix |
| vec | vectorize the columns of a matrix |
| vech | vectorize the lower diagonal only |
| vecindex | row indices of non-zero elements of the vec of a matrix |
| vecr | vectorize the rows of a matrix |
| vecrindex | row indices of non-zero elements of the vecr of a matrix |

**maximization, differentiation (Maximization package, requires** `maximize.h`**)**

| GetMaxControl | get maximum no of iterations and print control |
| GetMaxControlEps | get convergence tolerances |
| MaxBFGS | maximize a function using BFGS |
| MaxControl | set maximum no of iterations and print control |
| MaxControlEps | set convergence tolerances |
| MaxConvergenceMsg | get convergence message |
| MaxNewton | maximize a function using Newton's method |
| MaxSimplex | maximize a function using the simplex method |
| MaxSQP | maximize a function under nonlinear constraints |
| MaxSQPF | as MaxSQP, using feasible iterates |
| Num1Derivative | numerical computation of 1st derivative |
| Num2Derivative | numerical computation of 2nd derivative |
| NumJacobian | numerical computation of Jacobian matrix |
| SolveNLE | solves systems of nonlinear equations |
| SolveQP | solves quadratic programming problem |

**probability**

| denschi | $\chi^2$ density |
| densf | F density |
| densn | standard normal density |
| denst | Student t density |
| probchi | $\chi^2$ distribution function (also non-central) |
| probf | F-distribution function |
| probn | standard normal distribution function |
| probt | Student t-distribution function |
| quanchi | $\chi^2$ distribution quantiles |
| quanf | F-distribution quantiles |
| quann | standard normal quantiles |
| quant | Student t-distribution quantiles |
| tailchi | $\chi^2$ distribution tail probabilities |
| tailf | F-distribution tail probabilities |
| tailn | standard normal tail probabilities |
| tailt | Student t-distribution tail probabilities |

**probability** (Probability package, requires `oxprob.h`)

| | |
|---|---|
| `densbeta` | $B(a,b)$ density |
| `densbinomial` | Binomial density |
| `denscauchy` | Cauchy density |
| `densexp` | Exponential density |
| `densextremevalue` | Extreme value density |
| `densgamma` | Gamma density |
| `densgeometric` | Geometric density |
| `densgh` | Generalized Hyperbolic density |
| `densgig` | Generalized Inverse Gaussion density |
| `denshypergeometric` | Hypergeometric density |
| `densinvgaussian` | Inverse Gaussian density |
| `denskernel` | kernel densities |
| `denslogarithmic` | logarithmic density |
| `denslogistic` | logistic density |
| `denslogn` | lognormal density |
| `densmises` | von Mises density |
| `densnegbin` | Negative Binomial density |
| `denspareto` | Pareto density |
| `denspoisson` | Poisson density |
| `densweibull` | Weibull density |
| `probbeta` | $B(a,b)$ cumulative distribution function |
| `probbinomial` | Binomial cumulative distribution function |
| `probbvn` | bivariate normal cumulative distribution function |
| `probcauchy` | Cauchy cumulative distribution function |
| `probexp` | exponential cumulative distribution function |
| `probextremevalue` | extreme value cumulative distribution function |
| `probgamma` | Gamma cumulative distribution function |
| `probgeometric` | Geometric cumulative distribution function |
| `probhypergeometric` | Hypergeometric cumulative distribution function |
| `probinvgaussian` | Inverse Gaussian cumulative distribution function |
| `problogarithmic` | logarithmic cumulative distribution function |
| `problogistic` | logistic cumulative distribution function |
| `problogn` | lognormal cumulative distribution function |
| `probmises` | von Mises cumulative distribution function |
| `probmvn` | multivariate normal cdf (up to trivariate) |
| `probnegbin` | Negative Binomial cumulative distribution function |
| `probpareto` | Pareto cumulative distribution function |
| `probpoisson` | cumulative Poisson cumulative distribution function |
| `probweibull` | Weibull cumulative distribution function |
| `quanbeta` | $B(a,b)$ quantiles |
| `quanbinomial` | Binomial quantiles |

| quancauchy | Cauchy quantiles |
|---|---|
| quanexp | exponential quantiles |
| quanextremevalue | extreme value quantiles |
| quangamma | Gamma quantiles |
| quangeometric | Geometric quantiles |
| quanhypergeometric | Hypergeometric quantiles |
| quaninvgaussian | Inverse Gaussian quantiles |
| quanlogarithmic | logarithmic quantiles |
| quanlogistic | logistic quantiles |
| quanlogn | lognormal quantiles |
| quanmises | von Mises quantiles |
| quannegbin | Negative Binomial quantiles |
| quanpareto | Pareto quantiles |
| quanpoisson | Poisson quantiles |
| quanweibull | Weibull quantiles |

**random numbers**

| rann | standard normal distributed random numbers |
|---|---|
| ranseed | set and get seed; choose unform random number generator |
| ranu | uniform $[0, 1]$ distributed random numbers |

**random numbers** (Probability package, requires oxprob.h)

| ranbeta | $B(a, b)$ distributed random numbers |
|---|---|
| ranbinomial | binomially distributed random numbers |
| ranbrownianmotion | realizations from a Brownian motion |
| rancauchy | Cauchy random numbers |
| ranchi | $\chi^2$ distributed random numbers |
| randirichlet | Dirichlet$(\alpha_1, \ldots, \alpha_{c+1})$ random numbers |
| ranexp | $\exp(\lambda)$ distributed random numbers |
| ranextremevalue | extreme value random numbers |
| ranf | F-distributed random numbers |
| rangamma | gamma-distributed random numbers |
| rangeometric | Geometric random numbers |
| rangh | Generalized Hyperbolic random numbers |
| rangig | Generalized Inverse Gaussion random numbers |
| ranhypergeometric | Hypergeometric random numbers |
| raninvgaussian | inverse Gaussian-distributed random numbers |
| ranlogarithmic | logarithmic distributed random numbers |
| ranlogistic | logistic distributed random numbers |
| ranlogn | log normal distributed random numbers |
| ranmises | von Mises distributed random numbers |
| ranmultinomial | multinomial distributed random numbers |
| rannegbin | negative binomial distributed random numbers |

| | |
|---|---|
| ranpareto | Pareto random numbers |
| ranpoisson | poisson distributed random numbers |
| ranpoissonprocess | realizations from a poisson process |
| ranshuffle | samples from a vector without replacement |
| ranstable | stable-distributed random numbers |
| ransubsample | samples from a set of integers without replacement |
| rant | Student t-distributed random numbers |
| ranuorder | uniform order statistics |
| ranweibull | Weibull random numbers |
| ranwishart | Wishart$(1, \mathbf{I}_r)$ distributed random drawing |

**statistics**

| | |
|---|---|
| correlation | correlation matrix of matrix (data in columns) |
| meanc | compute column means |
| meanr | compute row means |
| moments | compute column moment ratios (skewness,kurtosis, etc.) |
| ols2c | OLS based on normal equations (data in columns) |
| ols2r | OLS based on normal equations (data in rows) |
| olsc | OLS based on orthogonal decomposition (data in columns) |
| olsr | OLS based on orthogonal decomposition (data in rows) |
| quantilec | quantiles of a matrix (data in columns) |
| quantiler | quantiles of a matrix (data in rows) |
| spline | natural cubic spline smoother (data in columns) |
| standardize | standardize a matrix (data in columns) |
| varc | compute column variances |
| variance | variance matrix of matrix (data in columns) |
| varr | compute row variances |

**string functions**

| | |
|---|---|
| strfind | finds a string/character in an array of strings/string |
| strfindr | finds last occurrence |
| strifind | case insensitive version of strfind |
| strifindr | case insensitive version of strfindr |
| strlwr | convert a string to lower case |
| strtrim | removes leading and trailing white space |
| strupr | convert a string to upper case |

**system functions**

| | |
|---|---|
| chdir | change directory |
| exit | exits Ox |
| getcwd | get current working directory |
| getenv | get the value of an environment variable |
| getfiles | get list of files matching the specified mask |
| oxfilename | returns the name of the Ox file it is called from |

| | |
|---|---|
| oxprintlevel | global control of printing |
| oxrunerror | raises a run-time error |
| oxversion | returns the Ox version |
| oxwarning | controls run-time warnings |
| systemcall | make an operating system call |

**time series (data in columns)**

| | |
|---|---|
| acf | autocorrelation function of matrix |
| cumprod | cumulate autoregressive product |
| cumsum | cumulate autoregressive sum |
| cumulate | cumulate (vector) autoregressive process |
| diff0 | $i$th difference, $(1 - L^i)y$ |
| findsample | determines the selected sample |
| lag0 | $i$th lag |
| periodogram | periodogram, smoothed periodogram (spectral density) |

**time series** (Arma package, requires `arma.h`)

| | |
|---|---|
| arma0 | residuals of an ARMA$(p, q)$ filter |
| armaforc | forecasts from an ARMA$(p, q)$ process |
| armagen | fitted values of an ARMA$(p, q)$ process |
| armavar | autocovariances of an ARMA$(p, q)$ process |
| diffpow | $d$th fractional difference, $(1 - L)^d y$ |
| modelforc | forecasts of a dynamic model |
| pacf | partial autocorrelation function of matrix or applies Choleski factor of a Toeplitz matrix |

**trigonometric functions**

| | |
|---|---|
| acos | arccosine |
| asin | arcsine |
| atan | arctangent |
| atan2 | arctangent of $y/x$ |
| cos | cosine |
| cosh | cosine hyperbolicus |
| sin | sine |
| sinh | sine hyperbolicus |
| tan | tangent |
| tanh | tangent hyperbolicus |

**standard classes**

| | |
|---|---|
| Database | Data loading, saving; model selection |
| Modelbase | Model formulation and estimation, interactive facilities |
| PcFiml | OLS, VAR, cointegration, simultaneous equations |
| PcFimlDgp | General reduced form dynamic model DGP |
| PcNaiveDgp | DGP with up to two lags, may be equilibrium correction |

| RanMC | Error generation for Monte Carlo experiments |
|-------|-----------------------------------------------|
| Sample | Basic sample: year (period) |
| Simula | Monte Carlo experimentation |

`ox/lib/` **code snippets** (examples in `ox/samples/lib/`)

| acffft.ox | compute the ACF using the FFT |
|-----------|-------------------------------|
| coigamma.ox | asymptotic distribution of I(1) and I(2) tests |
| densest.ox | density estimation |
| hacest.ox | heteroscedasticity and autocorrelation consistent covariance |
| hpfilter.ox | compute the Hodrick-Prescott filter |
| longrun.ox | dynamic analysis of dynamic systems |
| normtest.ox | Normality test |
| quantile.ox | compute quantiles given a density and cdf |
| spline3w.ox | computes a cubic spline weight matrix |
| probimhof.ox | Imhof procedure for cdf of the ratio of quadratic form |
| ranktest.ox | tests the rank of a matrix |
| testres.ox | residual-based tests (ARCH, Normality, Portmanteau) |

# Chapter 8

# Function reference

Ox has implicit typing, so function declarations contain no type information. However, at run time, type information is known and checked for validity. The following argument types are distinguished in the function summary (the conversion rules are described in §13.8.2.3):

| argument type | legal actual argument | conversion inside function to |
|---|---|---|
| int | int, double, $1 \times 1$ matrix | int |
| double | int, double, $1 \times 1$ matrix | double |
| matrix | int, double, matrix | matrix |
| arithmetic type | int, double, matrix | int $\rightarrow$ double |
| any type | any type | none |
| string | string | none |
| array | array | none |
| address | address | none |

All functions documented in this chapter require the `oxstd.h` header file, which must be included by writing

```
#include <oxstd.h>
```

at the top of your source code. A few functions need an additional header file, which is indicated explicitly.

Some functions have a variable argument list. An example is the `fread` function. This function is documented as:

```
fread(const file, const am, ...);
fread(const file, const am, const type, const r, const c);
```

which means that the following calls are allowed:

```
fread(file, am);
fread(file, am, type);
fread(file, am, type, r);
fread(file, am, type, r, c);
```

The function documentation will indicate what the default values are when arguments are omitted.

# acf

```
acf(const ma, const ilag);
```
>    ma            in:  $T \times n$ matrix
>    ilag          in:  int, the highest lag

*Return value*
> Returns a $(\text{ilag} +1) \times n$ matrix with the autocorrelation function of the columns of ma up to lag ilag. Returns 0 if $\text{ilag} \le 0$. If any variance is $\le 10^{-20}$, then the corresponding autocorrelations are set to 0.

*Description*
> Computes the autocorrelation functions of the columns of a $T \times n$ matrix $A = (a_0, a_1, \ldots, a_{n-1})$. The autocorrelation function of a $T$-vector $x = (x_0 \cdots x_{T-1})'$ up to lag $k$ is defined as $\text{r} = (\hat{r}_0 \cdots \hat{r}_k)'$:

$$\hat{r}_j = \frac{\sum_{t=j}^{T-1} (x_t - \bar{x})(x_{t-j} - \bar{x})}{\sum_{t=0}^{T-1} (x_t - \bar{x})^2}, \tag{8.1}$$

> with the mean defined in the standard way as:

$$\bar{x} = \frac{1}{T} \sum_{t=0}^{T-1} x_t.$$

> Note that $\hat{r}_0 = 1$. The approximate standard error for $\hat{r}_j$ is $1/\sqrt{T}$.

*See also*
> DrawCorrelogram, pacf, lib/AcfFft.ox

*Example*
> The example computes a correlogram twice, once using the library function, and once 'manually' (in the matrix macf).

```
#include <oxstd.h>
main()
{
    decl i, m1 = rann(200,2), m1m, macf, ilag = 5;

    macf = new matrix[ilag + 1][2];
    m1m = m1 - meanc(m1);            // in deviation from mean

    for (i = 0; i <= ilag; ++i)
        macf[i][] = diagonal(m1m'lag0(m1m, i));
    macf = macf ./ macf[0][];        // scale by variance

    print( acf(m1, ilag) ~ macf);
}
```

> produces

```
     1.0000          1.0000          1.0000          1.0000
    -0.0021973      -0.046870       -0.0021973      -0.046870
    -0.041011       -0.051470       -0.041011       -0.051470
    -0.050879       -0.039346       -0.050879       -0.039346
     0.056525       -0.093980        0.056525       -0.093980
     0.021034        0.12671         0.021034        0.12671
```

# acos

```
acos(const ma);
```
    ma            in:   arithmetic type

*Return value*
    Returns the arccosine of ma, of double or matrix type.

*See also*
    asin, atan, cos, cosh, sin, sinh, tan, tanh

*Example*
```
#include <oxstd.h>
main()
{
    print( acos(<0,1>) );
    print( asin(<0,1>) );
    print( atan(<0,1>) );
    print( cos(<0,1>) );
    print( cosh(<0,1>) );
    print( sin(<0,1>) );
    print( sinh(<0,1>) );
    print( tan(<0,1>) );
    print( tanh(<0,1>) );
}
```

produces

```
     1.5708          0.00000
     0.00000         1.5708
     0.00000         0.78540
     1.0000          0.54030
     1.0000          1.5431
     0.00000         0.84147
     0.00000         1.1752
     0.00000         1.5574
     0.00000         0.76159
```

# aggregatec, aggregater

```
aggregatec(const ma, const istep);
aggregater(const ma, const istep);
    ma          in:  m × n matrix A
    istep       in:  int, size of groups, s
```

*Return value*

The aggregatec function returns a ceil$(m/s)$ × n matrix where each group of s observations in every column is replaced by the sum.

The aggregater function returns a m × ceil$(n/s)$ matrix where each group of s observations in every row is replaced by the sum.

*See also*

thinc, thinr

*Example*

```
#include <oxstd.h>
main()
{
    decl x = ones(20,1) ~ range(1,20)';

    println(aggregatec(x, 5));
    println(aggregatec(x, 6));
    println(aggregater(x', 5));
    println(aggregater(x', 6));
}
```

produces

```
        5.0000        15.000
        5.0000        40.000
        5.0000        65.000
        5.0000        90.000

        6.0000        21.000
        6.0000        57.000
        6.0000        93.000
        2.0000        39.000

        5.0000        5.0000        5.0000        5.0000
        15.000        40.000        65.000        90.000

        6.0000        6.0000        6.0000        2.0000
        21.000        57.000        93.000        39.000
```

# any

```
any(const ma);
     ma           in:  arithmetic type
```

*Return value*

Returns TRUE if any element of ma is TRUE, of integer type.

*Description*

If any element is non-zero, the return value is 1. This is in contrast with the `if` statement, which evaluates to TRUE if *all* elements are TRUE.

*See also*

§13.8.9

*Example*

```
#include <oxstd.h>
main()
{
    decl m1 = unit(2), m2 = zeros(2,2);

    if (m1 == 0)        print ("TRUE ");
    else                print ("FALSE ");
    if (any(m1 .== 0))  print ("TRUE ");
    else                print ("FALSE ");
    if (!(m1 == 0))     print ("TRUE ");
    else                print ("FALSE ");
    if (any(m1 .!= 0))  print ("TRUE ");
    else                print ("FALSE ");

    if (m2 == 0)        print ("TRUE ");
    else                print ("FALSE ");
    if (any(m2 .== 0))  print ("TRUE ");
    else                print ("FALSE ");
    if (m2 != 0)        print ("TRUE ");
    else                print ("FALSE ");
    if (any(m2 .!= 0))  print ("TRUE ");
    else                print ("FALSE ");
}
```

produces: FALSE TRUE TRUE TRUE TRUE TRUE FALSE FALSE

# arglist

```
arglist();
```

*Return value*

Returns an array of strings holding the command line arguments passed to the Ox program. The first entry is the name of the program that was specified on the command line.

*Example*

Running the following program `arglist.ox`:

```
#include <oxstd.h>
main()
{
    decl args = arglist(), s, i, j;

    for (i = 0; i < sizeof(args); ++i)
    {
        sscan(args[i], "%d", &j);
        println("argument ", i, ": ", args[i],
                " integer value:", j);
    }
}
```

as `oxl arglist.ox a 12 c` (the arguments before `arglist.ox` are passed to `oxl`, those after to `arglist.ox`), produces:

```
argument 0: arglist.ox integer value:0
argument 1: a integer value:0
argument 2: 12 integer value:12
argument 3: c integer value:0
```

# array

`array(const ma);`

    `ma`           in:   any type

*Return value*

Casts the argument to an array, unless it already is an array.

*Example*

The array cast can be useful when an array indexing must remain an array. For example, a single index on an array of strings returns a string, whereas a multiple index returns an array of strings.

```
#include <oxstd.h>
main()
{
    decl as = {"ax", "bx", "cx"};

    print("single index is string: ", as[0],
        "\nmultiple index is array of strings:", as[0:1],
        "keep single index as array:", array(as[0]) );
}
```

which produces:

```
single index is string: ax
multiple index is array of strings:
[0] = ax
[1] = bx
keep single index as array:
[0] = ax
```

# asin

```
asin(const ma);
```
     ma         in:   arithmetic type

*Return value*

    Returns the arcsine of ma, of double or matrix type.

*See also*

    acos (for examples), atan, cos, cosh, sin, sinh, tan, tanh

# atan, atan2

```
atan(const ma);
atan2(const my, const mx);
```
    ma         in:   arithmetic type
    my         in:   arithmetic type
    mx         in:   arithmetic type

*Return value*

    The atan function returns the arctangent of ma, of double or matrix type, between $-\pi/2$ and $\pi/2$.

    The atan2 function returns the arctangent of my ./ mx, between $-\pi$ and $\pi$. The return type is double if both my and mx are int or double. If my or mx is a matrix, the return type is a matrix of the same size.

*See also*

    acos (for examples), asin, cos, cosh, sin, sinh, tan, tanh

# bessel

```
bessel(const mx, const type, const n01);
bessel(const mx, const type, const nu);
```
    mx         in:   $x$, arithmetic type, points at which to evaluate
    type      in:   character, type of Bessel function: 'J', 'Y', 'I', 'K'
                   or string: "IE", "KE", for scaled Bessel functions
    n01       in:   0 or 1: order of Bessel function
    nu         in:   double, fractional order of Bessel function

*Return value*

    Returns a $m \times n$ matrix with the requested Bessel function, or a double when x is scalar. The following are available: $J_0(x)$, $Y_0(x)$, $J_1(x)$, $Y_1(x)$, and the modified Bessel functions $I_0(x)$, $K_0(x)$, $I_1(x)$, $K_1(x)$. Similarly, the fractional Bessel functions $J_\nu(x)$, $Y_\nu(x)$, $I_\nu(x)$, $K_\nu(x)$. The modified Bessel functions are also available in scaled form: $e^{-x}I_\nu(x)$ and $e^x K_\nu(x)$.

    The result is accurate to about 15 digits.

*Description*

The implementation is based on the code by W. Fullerton (Los Alamos scientific lab), as available in the FN library of netlib. The fractional Bessel functions are based on the Fortran code in Netlib by W.J. Cody.

# betafunc

```
betafunc(const mx, const ma, const mb);
        mx          in:   x, arithmetic type
        ma          in:   a, arithmetic type
        mb          in:   b, arithmetic type
```

*Return value*

Returns the incomplete beta integral $B_x(a, b)$. Returns 0 if $a \leq 0$, $b \leq 0$ or $x \leq 0$. The accuracy is to about 10 digits.

The return type is derived as follows:

| returns | mx | ma,mb |
|---|---|---|
| $m \times n$ matrix | $m \times n$ matrix | scalar |
| $m \times n$ matrix | scalar | $m \times n$ matrix |
| $m \times n$ matrix | $m \times n$ matrix | $m \times n$ matrix |
| double | scalar | scalar |

*Description*

The incomplete beta integral is defined as:

$$B_x(a, b) = \int_0^x t^{a-1} (1-t)^{b-1} \, \mathrm{d}t, \quad a > 0, b > 0.$$

Note that the complete beta integral is:

$$B(a, b) = B_1(a, b) = \frac{\Gamma(a)\Gamma(b)}{\Gamma(a+b)}.$$

Using the `loggamma` function, $B(a, b)$ can be computed as:

```
exp(loggamma(a) + loggamma(b) - loggamma(a+b))
```

which avoids overflow in the gamma function.

Also note that `betafunc` computes the incomplete beta integral, and *not* $I_x(a, b) = B_x(a, b)/B(a, b)$. $I_x(a, b)$ corresponds to the beta distribution, and can be computed with `probbeta`.

The approximation is based on the continued fraction representation given in Press, Flannery, Teukolsky and Vetterling (1988, §6.3).

*See also*

`gammafunc`, `probbeta`, `probf`, `tailf`

# binand, bincomp, binor

```
binand(const ia, const ib, ...);
bincomp(const ia);
binor(const ia, const ib, ...);
    ia          in:   int
    ib          in:   int
    ...         in:   optional additional integers
```

*Return value*

binand returns the result from *and*-ing all arguments (the & operator in C/C++).
binor returns the result from *or*-ing all arguments (the | operator in C/C++).
bincomp returns the binary (bit-wise) complement of the argument (the ˜ operator in C/C++).

*Example*

```
#include <oxstd.h>
main()
{
    print( binand(1,2,4), " ", binor(1,2,4) );
}
```

produces: 0  7

# binomial

```
binomial(const n, const k);
    n           in:   arithmetic type
    k           in:   arithmetic type
```

*Return value*

Returns the binomial function at the rounded value of each element, of double or matrix type.
For negative integers, the function returns .NaN.

*Description*

Computes the binomial coefficient:

$$\binom{n}{k} = \frac{n!}{(n-k)!k!}.$$

When $\max(n-k, k) \geq 50$ the computation uses the loggamma function:

$$\binom{n}{k} = \exp\left(\log \Gamma(n+1) - \log \Gamma(n-k+1) - \log \Gamma(k+1)\right).$$

which has about 13 significant digits.

*See also*

factorial, gammafunc, loggamma

# cabs, cdiv, cerf, cexp, clog, cmul, csqrt

```
cabs(const ma);
cdiv(const ma, const mb);
cerf(const ma);
cexp(const ma);
clog(const ma);
cmul(const ma, const mb);
csqrt(const ma);
```
> ma, mb        in:  $2 \times n$ matrix (first row is real part, second row imaginary
>                 part), or $1 \times n$ matrix (real part only)

*Return value*

cabs returns a $1 \times n$ matrix with the absolute value of the vector of complex numbers.

cdiv returns a $2 \times n$ matrix with the result of the division of the two vectors of complex numbers. If both ma and mb have no imaginary part, the return value will be $1 \times n$.

cerf returns a $2 \times n$ matrix with the result of the complex error function of the vector of (complex) numbers.

cexp returns a $2 \times n$ matrix with the result of the complex exponential of the vector of (complex) numbers.

clog returns a $2 \times n$ matrix with the result of the complex logarithm of the vector of (complex) numbers.

cmul returns a $2 \times n$ matrix with the result of the multiplication of the two vectors of complex numbers. If both ma and mb have no imaginary part, the return value will be $1 \times n$.

csqrt returns a $2 \times n$ matrix with the square root of the vector of complex numbers.

*Description*

Using subscript $r$ for the real part of $a, b$ and subscript $i$ for the imaginary part:
cabs: modulus of complex number: $|a| = (a_r^2 + a_i^2)^{1/2}$.
cmul: complex multiplication: $ab = (a_r + ia_i)(b_r + ib_i)$.
cdiv: complex division: $a/b = (a_r + ia_i)/(b_r + ib_i)$.
csqrt: square root of complex number: $a^{1/2} = (a_r + ia_i)^{1/2}$.
cexp: complex exponential: $\exp(a) = \exp(a_r)(\cos(a_i) + i\sin(a_i))$.
clog: complex logarithm: $\log(a) = \log(|a|) + i\arctan(a_i/a_r)$.
complex conjugate: $(a_r - ia_i)$.

*Example*

```
#include <oxstd.h>
main()
{
    decl v = <1, -1, -2>, rv = csqrt(v);
    rv[0][1] = 1;/* change to a more interesting value */
```

```
    print(v, rv, cabs(rv), cdiv(rv, rv), cmul(rv, rv),
        cmul(rv, cdiv(ones(1,3), rv)) );
    print(cexp(clog(rv)) );
}
```

produces

```
    1.0000        -1.0000        -2.0000

    1.0000         1.0000         0.00000
    0.00000        1.0000         1.4142

    1.0000         1.4142         1.4142

    1.0000         1.0000         1.0000
    0.00000        0.00000        0.00000

    1.0000         0.00000       -2.0000
    0.00000        2.0000         0.00000

    1.0000         1.0000         1.0000
    0.00000        0.00000        0.00000

    1.0000         1.0000    8.6593e-017
    0.00000        1.0000         1.4142
```

In the second example the complex functions are used to check if the computed
roots of a polynomial indeed correspond to zeros of the polynomial:

```
#include <oxstd.h>
main()
{
    decl v1, roots, cr;

    v1 = <-1, 1.2274, -0.017197, -0.28369, -0.01028>;

    polyroots(v1, &roots);

    cr = columns(roots);
    print("roots", roots,
        "inverse roots", cdiv(ones(1,cr), roots) );

    decl x1, x2, x3, x4, check;
    x1 = roots;
    x2 = cmul(x1, x1);                      /* roots ^ 2 */
    x3 = cmul(x2, x1);                      /* roots ^ 3 */
    x4 = cmul(x2, x2);                      /* roots ^ 4 */
    check = v1[0][4] * (ones(1,cr) | zeros(1,cr)) +
            v1[0][3] * x1 + v1[0][2] * x2 +
            v1[0][1] * x3 + v1[0][0] * x4;

    print("check (near-zeros could be different "
        "with other Ox versions):", check);
}
```

which produces:

```
roots
        0.82865         0.82865        -0.39337      -0.036535
        0.16923        -0.16923        0.00000        0.00000
inverse roots
        1.1585          1.1585         -2.5422        -27.371
       -0.23659         0.23659         0.00000        0.00000
check (near-zeros could be different with other Ox versions):
        0.00000         0.00000  -1.7000e-016  -8.4441e-018
     -2.2204e-016   2.2204e-016        0.00000        0.00000
```

# ceil

```
ceil(const ma);
     ma              in:   arithmetic type
```

*Return value*

Returns the ceiling of each element of ma, of double or matrix type. The ceiling is the smallest integer larger than or equal to the argument

*See also*

floor, round, trunc

*Example*

```
#include <oxstd.h>
main()
{
    print( ceil(<-1.8, -1.2, 1.2, 1.8>) );
    print( floor(<-1.8, -1.2, 1.2, 1.8>) );
    print( round(<-1.8, -1.2, 1.2, 1.8>) );
    print( trunc(<-1.8, -1.2, 1.2, 1.8>) );

    print( int(-1.8), " ", int(-1.2), " ",
        int(1.2), " ", int(1.8) );
}
```

produces

```
        -1.0000         -1.0000         2.0000         2.0000
        -2.0000         -2.0000         1.0000         1.0000
        -2.0000         -1.0000         1.0000         2.0000
        -1.0000         -1.0000         1.0000         1.0000
   -1 -1 1 1
```

# chdir

```
chdir(const s);
```
      s            in:   new directory

*Return value*

    Returns 1 if successful, 0 otherwise.

*Description*

    Changes the current directory.

    *Windows specific*: if the string starts with a drive letter followed by a semicolon, the current drive is also changed. For example, use `chdir("c:")` to change to the C drive.

*See also*

    `getcwd`, `systemcall`

# choleski

```
choleski(const ma);
```
      ma         in:   symmetric, positive definite $m \times m$ matrix $A$

*Return value*

    Returns the Choleski decomposition $P$ of a symmetric positive definite matrix $A$: $A = PP'$; $P$ is lower triangular (has zeros above the diagonal).

    Returns 0 if the decomposition failed.

*Error and warning messages*

    choleski(): decomposition failed (this implies a negative definite or numerically singular matrix $A$).

*See also*

    `decldl`, `invertsym`, `solvelu`, `RanMC::Choleski`

*Example*

    The example also shows how `solvelu` may be used to obtain $P^{-1}$.

```
#include <oxstd.h>
main()
{
    decl mp;

    mp = choleski(<4,1;1,3>);
    print(mp, mp*mp');

    print(1/mp ~ solvelu(mp, 0, 0, unit(2)) );
}
```

    produces

```
        2.0000        0.00000
     0.500000          1.6583

        4.0000          1.0000
        1.0000          3.0000

      0.50000        0.00000        0.50000        0.00000
     -0.15076        0.60302       -0.15076        0.60302
```

# classname

```
classname(const obj);
     obj            in:  object of a class
```

*Return value*

    Returns a string with the class name of the object (or 0 if the argument is not an object).

*See also*

    `isclass`

# columns

```
columns(const ma);
     ma             in:  any type
```

*Return value*

    Returns an integer value with the number of columns in the argument `ma`:

| type | returns |
|------|---------|
| $m \times n$ matrix | $n$ |
| string | number of characters in the string |
| array | number of elements in the array |
| file | number of columns in the file |
|  | (only if opened with f format, see `fopen`) |
| other | 0 |

*See also*

    `rows, sizec, sizeof, sizer, sizerc`

*Example*

```
#include <oxstd.h>
main()
{
    println(columns(<0,1;1,2;3,4>), " ", columns("taylor"));
    println(   rows(<0,1;1,2;3,4>), " ",    rows("taylor"));
    println( sizerc(<0,1;1,2;3,4>), " ", sizeof("taylor"));
}
```

produces

```
2 6
3 6
6 6
```

# constant

```
constant(const dval, const r, const c);
constant(const dval, const ma);
```
|       |     |        |
|-------|-----|--------|
| dval  | in: | double |
| r     | in: | int    |
| c     | in: | int    |
| ma    | in: | matrix |

*Return value*

constant(dval,r,c) returns an r by c matrix filled with dval.

constant(dval,ma) returns a matrix of the same dimension as ma, filled with dval.

*See also*

ones, unit, zeros

*Example*

```
#include <oxstd.h>
main()
{
    print( constant(1.5, 2, 2) );
}
```

produces

```
        1.5000        1.5000
        1.5000        1.5000
```

# correlation

```
correlation(const ma);
```
|      |                             |
|------|-----------------------------|
| ma   | in:  $T \times n$ matrix $A$ |

*Return value*

Returns a $n \times n$ matrix holding the correlation matrix of ma. If any variance is $\leq 10^{-20}$, then the corresponding row and column of the correlation matrix are set to 0.

*Description*

Computes the correlation matrix $R = (r_{ij})$ of a $T \times n$ matrix $A = (a_{tj})$:

$$\bar{a}_j = \frac{1}{T} \sum_{t=0}^{T-1} a_{tj}$$

$$\hat{\sigma}_j^2 = \frac{1}{T} \sum_{t=0}^{T-1} (a_{tj} - \bar{a}_j)^2$$

$$r_{ij} = \frac{1}{T \hat{\sigma}_i \hat{\sigma}_j} \sum_{t=0}^{T-1} (a_{ti} - \bar{a}_i)(a_{tj} - \bar{a}_j)$$

Note that $r_{ii} = 1$.

*See also*

acf, meanc, meanr, standardize, varc, varr, variance

*Example*

```
#include <oxstd.h>
main()
{
    decl m1 = rann(100,2), m2;

    m2 = standardize(m1);
    print( correlation(m1), m2'm2/rows(m2) );
}
```

produces

```
    1.0000    -0.039218
   -0.039218    1.0000

    1.0000    -0.039218
   -0.039218    1.0000
```

# cos, cosh

```
cos(const ma);
cosh(const ma);
```
     ma　　　　　　in:  arithmetic type

*Return value*

cos returns the cosine of ma, of double or matrix type.
cosh returns the cosine hyperbolicus of ma, of double or matrix type.

*See also*

acos (for examples), asin, atan, cosh, sin, sinh, tan, tanh

# countc

```
countc(const ma, const va);
    ma          in:  $m \times n$ matrix
    va          in:  $1 \times q$ or $q \times 1$ matrix
```

*Return value*

Returns a matrix r which counts of the number of elements in each column of ma which is between the corresponding values in va:

r[0][0] = # elements in column 0 of ma $\leq$ va[0]
r[1][0] = # elements in column 0 of ma $>$ va[0] and $\leq$ va[1]
r[2][0] = # elements in column 0 of ma $>$ va[1] and $\leq$ va[2]
r[q][0] = # elements in column 0 of ma $>$ va[q-1]
...

r[0][1] = # elements in column 1 of ma $\leq$ va[0]
r[1][1] = # elements in column 1 of ma $>$ va[0] and $\leq$ va[1]
r[2][1] = # elements in column 1 of ma $>$ va[1] and $\leq$ va[2]
r[q][1] = # elements in column 1 of ma $>$ va[q-1]
...

If ma is $m \times n$, and va is $1 \times q$ (or $q \times 1$) the returned matrix is $(q+1) \times n$ (any remaining columns of va are ignored). If the values in va are not ordered, the return value is filled with missing values.

*Description*

Counts the number of elements in each column which is in a supplied interval.

*See also*

countr

*Example*

```
#include <oxstd.h>
main()
{
    print( countc(<0:3;1:4;2:5>, <2,4>) );
    print( countr(<0:3;1:4;2:5>, <2>) );
}
```

produces

| | | | |
|---|---|---|---|
| 3.0000 | 2.0000 | 1.0000 | 0.00000 |
| 0.00000 | 1.0000 | 2.0000 | 2.0000 |
| 0.00000 | 0.00000 | 0.00000 | 1.0000 |

| | |
|---|---|
| 3.0000 | 1.0000 |
| 2.0000 | 2.0000 |
| 1.0000 | 3.0000 |

# countr

```
countr(const ma, const va);
    ma          in:  m × n matrix
    va          in:  1 × q or q × 1 matrix
```

*Return value*

Returns a matrix r which counts of the number of elements in each row of ma which is between the corresponding values in va:

r[0][0] = # elements in row 0 of ma $\leq$ va[0]
r[0][1] = # elements in row 0 of ma $>$ va[0] and $\leq$ va[1]
r[0][2] = # elements in row 0 of ma $>$ va[1] and $\leq$ va[2]
r[0][q] = # elements in row 0 of ma $>$ va[q-1]

...

r[1][0] = # elements in row 1 of ma $\leq$ va[0]
r[1][1] = # elements in row 1 of ma $>$ va[0] and $\leq$ va[1]
r[1][2] = # elements in row 1 of ma $>$ va[1] and $\leq$ va[2]
r[1][q] = # elements in row 1 of ma $>$ va[q-1]

...

If ma is $m \times n$, and va is $1 \times q$ (or $q \times 1$) the returned matrix is $m \times (q + 1)$ (any remaining columns of va are ignored). If the values in va are not ordered, the return value is filled with missing values.

*Description*

Counts the number of elements in each row which is in a supplied interval.

*See also*

countc (for an example)

# cumprod

```
cumprod(const mfac);
cumprod(const mfac, const cp);
cumprod(const mfac, const cp, const mz);
    mfac        in:  T × n or 1 × n matrix of multiplication factors S
    cp          in:  int: autoregressive order p (optional argument; default is 1)
    mz          in:  (optional argument) T × n or 1 × n matrix of known compo-
                     nents Z (optional argument; default is 0)
```

*Return value*

Returns a $T \times n$ matrix with the cumulated autoregressive product. The first $p$ rows of the return value will be identical to the sum of those in mz and mfac; the recursion will be applied from the $p$th term onward. If either mz or mfac is $1 \times n$, the same values are used for every $t$.

*Description*

For a column $(z_0, \ldots, z_{T-1})'$ of known values $X$, and multiplication factors $(s_0, \ldots s_{T-1})'$ the cumprod function computes:

$$
\begin{aligned}
a_t &= z_t + s_t, & t &= 0, \ldots, p-1, \\
a_t &= z_t + s_t(a_{t-1} \times \ldots \times a_{t-p}) & t &= p, \ldots, T-1.
\end{aligned}
$$

*See also*

cumsum (for an example), cumulate

## cumsum

```
cumsum(const mx, const vp);
cumsum(const mx, const vp, const mstart);
```

| | | |
|---|---|---|
| mx | in: | $T \times n$ matrix of known component $X$ |
| vp | in: | $1 \times p$ or $n \times p$ or $T \times p$ matrix with autoregressive coefficients $\phi_1, \phi_2, \ldots, \phi_p$ |
| mstart | in: | (optional argument) $s \times n$ matrix of starting values $S$, $s \geq p$; default is mx |

*Return value*

Returns a $T \times n$ matrix with the cumulated autoregressive sum. The first $p$ rows of the return value will be identical to those of mstart; the recursion will be applied from the $p$th term onward.

If vp is $1 \times p$, the same coefficients are applied to each column.

If vp is $n \times p$, each row will have coefficients specific to each column of the recursive series.

Finally, if vp is $T \times p$, the same coefficients are applied to each column, but the coefficients are specific to each row (time-varying coefficients).

*Description*

For a column $(x_0, \ldots, x_{T-1})'$ of known values $X$, and starting values $(s_0, \ldots s_{p-1})'$ the cumsum function computes:

$$
\begin{aligned}
a_t &= s_t, & t &= 0, \ldots, p-1, \\
a_t &= x_t + \phi_1 a_{t-1} + \ldots + \phi_p a_{t-p}, & t &= p, \ldots, T-1.
\end{aligned}
$$

When $\phi$ is $n \times p$, the AR coefficients are different for each data column, for $j = 0, \ldots, n-1$:

$$
\begin{aligned}
a_{t,j} &= s_{t,j}, & t &= 0, \ldots, p-1, \\
a_{t,j} &= x_{t,j} + \phi_{j,1} a_{t-1} + \ldots + \phi_{t,p} a_{j-p}, & t &= p, \ldots, T-1.
\end{aligned}
$$

When $\phi$ is $T \times p$ (and $T \neq n$), the AR coefficients are time-varying:

$$
\begin{aligned}
a_t &= s_t, & t &= 0, \ldots, p-1, \\
a_t &= x_t + \phi_{t,1} a_{t-1} + \ldots + \phi_{t,p} a_{t-p}, & t &= p, \ldots, T-1.
\end{aligned}
$$

*See also*
```
cumprod, cumulate
```

*Example*
```
#include <oxstd.h>
main()
{
    decl mx = ones(5,1);
    print( mx ~ cumsum(mx, <0.5>)
              ~ cumsum(mx, <1, 0.5>, <1;2>)
              ~ cumprod(mx * 2)
              ~ cumprod(mx * 2, 2) );

    print(cumsum(mx, <0.5;0.5;0.5;1;1>)' );
}
```

produces

```
        1.0000      1.0000      1.0000      2.0000      2.0000
        1.0000      1.5000      2.0000      4.0000      2.0000
        1.0000      1.7500      3.5000      8.0000      8.0000
        1.0000      1.8750      5.5000      16.000      32.000
        1.0000      1.9375      8.2500      32.000      512.00

        1.0000      1.5000      1.7500      2.7500      3.7500
```

# cumulate

```
cumulate(const ma);
cumulate(const ma, const m1, ...);
cumulate(const ma, const am);
```
|        |     |                                                              |
|--------|-----|--------------------------------------------------------------|
| ma     | in: | $T \times n$ matrix $A$                                      |
| m1     | in: | $n \times n$ matrix, coefficients of first lags (optional argument) |
| ...    | in: | $n \times n$ matrix, coefficients of lags 2, ...            |
| am     | in: | array of length $k$ with $n \times n$ matrices of coefficients |

*Return value*
Returns a $T \times n$ matrix.

The simplest version returns a matrix which holds the cumulated (integrated) columns of ma.

The second form cumulates (integrates) the (vector) autoregressive process with current values ma using the specified coefficient matrices. The function has a variable number of arguments, and the number of arguments determines the autoregressive order (minimum 2 arguments, which is an AR(1) process). Note that `cumulate(m)` corresponds to `cumulate(m,unit(columns(m)))`.

*Description*
The version with one arguments cumulates the columns of its argument.

For the form with additional arguments, assume that ma and $k$ coefficient matrices have been supplied ($k \geq 1$: at least two arguments) and write $A_0^{T-1} = A = $ ma, $M_1 = $ m1, ... $M_k$. Also define $A_{-i}^{T-1-i}$ as the $i$th lag, whereby each column is lagged: each column of $A$ is shifted down, and missing values are replaced by zeros, so that e.g. $A_{-1}^{T-2} = $ lag0(ma, 1).
The cumulate function returns:

$$A_0^{T-1} + A_{-1}^{T-2}M_1 + A_{-2}^{T-3}M_2 + \cdots A_{-k}^{T-1-k}M_k,$$

which has the same dimensions as ma.
The univariate case is easier to explain. For example, with three arguments, $(a_0, \ldots, a_{T-1})'$, $\beta_0$ and $\beta_1$, this function computes $y_t$:

$$
\begin{aligned}
y_0 &= a_0, \\
y_1 &= a_1 + \beta_0 y_0, \\
y_2 &= a_t + \beta_0 y_1 + \beta_1 y_2, \\
y_t &= a_t + \beta_0 y_{t-1} + \beta_1 y_{t-2}, \quad t = 2, \ldots, T-1.
\end{aligned}
$$

*See also*
    cumsum, lag0

*Example*

```
#include <oxstd.h>
main()
{
    print( ones(5,1)
            ~ cumulate(ones(5,1))
            ~ cumulate(ones(5,1), <0.5>)
            ~ cumulate(ones(5,1), <1>, <0.5>)
            ~ cumulate(ones(5,1), {<1>, <0.5>}) );
}
```

produces

```
    1.0000      1.0000      1.0000      1.0000      1.0000
    1.0000      2.0000      1.5000      2.0000      2.0000
    1.0000      3.0000      1.7500      3.5000      3.5000
    1.0000      4.0000      1.8750      5.5000      5.5000
    1.0000      5.0000      1.9375      8.2500      8.2500
```

# date

date();

*Return value*
    A string holding the current date.

*See also*
    time

*Example*
```
#include <oxstd.h>
main()
{
    println("\ntime=", time(), " date=", date());
}
```

prints the current time and date.

# dawson

```
dawson(const ma);
```
      ma          in:   arithmetic type

*Return value*
    Returns the Dawson integral

$$F(x) = e^{-x^2} \int_0^x e^{t^2} dt$$

of each element of ma, of double or matrix type.

*Description*
    The function is based on the Fortran code in Netlib by W.J. Cody.

*See also*
    erf

# dayofcalendar, dayofeaster, dayofmonth, dayofweek

```
dayofcalendar(const index);
dayofcalendar(const year, const month, const day);
dayofeaster(const year);
dayofmonth(const year, const month, const dayofweek, const nth);
dayofweek(const index);
dayofweek(const year, const month, const day);
```
| | | |
|---|---|---|
| index | in: | in: arithmetic type, calendar index of a certain date, as returned by dayofcalendar(year, month, day) |
| year | in: | arithmetic type |
| month | in: | arithmetic type, January=1, etc. |
| day | in: | arithmetic type |
| dayofweek | in: | arithmetic type, day of the week (Sunday = 1, Monday = 2, ...) |
| nth | in: | arithmetic type, $> 0$: n-th from start of month, $< 0$: n-th from end of month |

*Return value*

The dayofcalendar function with three arguments returns the calendar index of the specified date (this is the Julian day number, see below). If all arguments are an integer, the return value will be an integer.

The dayofcalendar function with one argument takes a calendar index (or vector of indices), as returned by dayofcalendar(year, month, day) as argument, returning a $n \times 3$ matrix with the triplet year, month, day in each row ($n$ is the number of elements in the input).

The dayofeaster function returns the calendar index of Easter.

The dayofmonth function returns the calendar index of the $n$-th day of the week in the specified month ($n$-th from last for a negative value). For example dayofmonth(2005, 5, 2, -1) returns the index of the last Monday in May 2005.

The dayofweek function with three arguments returns the day of the week (Sunday = 1, Monday = 2, ...). If all arguments are an integer, the return value will be an integer.

The dayofweek function with one argument takes a calendar index (r vector of) as argument, returning the day of the week (Sunday = 1, Monday = 2, ...).

*Description*

The calendar[1] index is the Julian day number, and the dayof... functions convert from or to the index. For example, Julian day 2453402 corresponds to 2005-01-31. An optional fractional part specifies the fraction of the day: 2453402.75 corresponds to 2005-01-01T18:00. If the day number is zero, it is interpreted as a time only, so 0.75 is just 18:00 (6 PM).[2]

Use dayofcalendar(year, month, day) - dayofcalendar(year, 1, 1) + 1 to compute the day in the year. Similarly, the function can be used to compute the number of days between two dates.

The "%C" print format is available to print a calendar index.

*See also*

print, timeofday, timing

*Example*

```
#include <oxstd.h>
main()
{
    println("1-Jan-2000 was weekday ",
        dayofweek(2000, 1, 1), " (7 is Saturday)");
    println("1-Jan-2000 was yearday ",
        dayofcalendar(2000, 1, 1));
    println("2000 had ", dayofcalendar(2001, 1, 1)
```

---

[1]The calendar is Gregorian from 15 October 1582 onwards, and Julian before (so there is no year 0: year $-1$ precedes year 1; day 0 is on Julian date 1 January -4713).

[2]This is similar to how Excel stores date and time. The main difference is that Excel uses 1=1900-01-01 (wrongly treating 1900 as a leap year).

```
                 - dayofcalendar(2000, 1, 1), " days");
         println("2001 had ", dayofcalendar(2002, 1, 1)
             - dayofcalendar(2001, 1, 1), " days");

         println("%c", {"Easter Sunday", "Last Wed in May"},
             "%17C", dayofeaster(range(2005, 2010)')
                   ~ dayofmonth(range(2005, 2010)', 5, 2, -1));

}
```

produces

```
1-Jan-2000 was weekday 7 (7 is Saturday)
1-Jan-2000 was yearday 2451545
2000 had 366 days
2001 had 365 days

    Easter Sunday  Last Wed in May
       2005-03-27       2005-05-30
       2006-04-16       2006-05-29
       2007-04-08       2007-05-28
       2008-03-23       2008-05-26
       2009-04-12       2009-05-25
       2010-04-04       2010-05-31
```

# decldl

```
decldl(const ma, const aml, const amd);
```
| | |
|---|---|
| ma | in:  symmetric, positive definite $m \times m$ matrix $A$ |
| aml | in:  address of variable |
| | out: $m \times m$ lower diagonal matrix $L$, $LDL' = A$ |
| amd | in:  address of variable |
| | out: $1 \times m$ matrix with reciprocals of $D$ |

*Return value*

Returns the result of the Choleski decomposition:

　1　no error;

　0　the Choleski decomposition failed: the matrix is negative definite or the matrix is (numerically) singular.

*Description*

Computes the square root free Choleski decomposition of a symmetric positive definite matrix $A$ stored in argument ma: $A = LDL'$. $L$ has zeros above the diagonal and ones on the diagonal.

Note that the *reciprocals* of $D$ are stored in amd.

*Error and warning messages*

decldl(): decomposition failed (the matrix is numerically singular or negative definite)

*See also*

choleski, decldlband, solveldl

*Example*

```
#include <oxstd.h>
main()
{
    decl ma = <4,1;1,3>, md, ml, mi;

    print("result = ", decldl(ma, &ml, &md));
    print(" L =", ml, "D =", md);
    print(ml*diag(1 ./ md)*ml');

    mi = solveldl(ml, md, unit(2));
    print(mi*ma);
}
```

Note that diag(1 ./ md) and diag(1./md) are not the same. The program produces (the final matrix could have values of around 1e-16 instead of 0):

```
result = 1 L =
         1.0000        0.00000
         0.25000       1.0000
D =
         0.25000       0.36364

         4.0000        1.0000
         1.0000        3.0000

         1.0000        0.00000
         0.00000       1.0000
```

# decldlband

decldlband(const ma, const aml, const amd);

| | | |
|---|---|---|
| ma | in: | $p \times m$ vector specifying the $A^b$ matrix |
| aml | in: | address of variable |
| | out: | holds $p \times m$ lower diagonal matrix $L$ |
| amd | in: | address of variable |
| | out: | $1 \times m$ matrix with reciprocals of $D$ |

*Return value*

Returns the result of the Choleski decomposition:

1 no error;

0 the Choleski decomposition failed: the matrix is negative definite or the matrix is (numerically) singular.

*Description*

Computes the square root free Choleski decomposition of a symmetric positive definite band matrix $A$ stored in argument ma: $A = LDL'$. $L$ has zeros above the diagonal and ones on the diagonal. Note that the reciprocals of $D$ are stored. If $A = (a_{ij}), i, j = 0, \ldots m - 1$ is the underlying $m \times m$ symmetric positive definite band matrix, with bandwidth $p$, so that $a_{ij} = 0$ for $|i - j| > p$, then the input matrix ma $= A^b$ is formed as:

$$
\begin{pmatrix}
0 & \cdots & \cdots & 0 & a_{0,p-1} & \cdots & a_{m-p,m-1} \\
\vdots & & & & & & \vdots \\
0 & a_{0,1} & a_{1,2} & \cdots & \cdots & \cdots & a_{m-2,m-1} \\
a_{0,0} & \cdots & \cdots & \cdots & \cdots & \cdots & a_{m-1,m-1}
\end{pmatrix}
$$

The example below also shows how to create $A^b$ out of $A$ and vice versa.

*Error and warning messages*

decldlband(): decomposition failed (the matrix is numerically singular or negative definite)

*See also*

diagonal, solveldlband, solvetoeplitz

*Example*

```
#include <oxstd.h>
main()
{
    decl i, j, k, m, mab, ma, ml, md, ct = 5, cb = 2;

    ma = toeplitz(<5,4,3>, ct);    // create test matrix ma
    for (i = 0; i < ct; ++i)
        ma[i][i] += i;

    mab = diagonal(ma, cb);  // create band matrix version
    print("original matrix", ma, "band version", mab);

    if (decldlband(mab, &ml, &md))  // decompose and solve
        print("solved:", solveldlband(ml, md, <1;2;3;4;5>)' );

    // undo banded storage:store L in lower diagonal of ma
    for (i = 0, m = -cb; i < ct; ++i, m++)
        for (j = max(0,m), k = j - m; j < i; ++j, ++k)
            ma[i][j] =  ml[k][i];

    print("band L=", ml, "L:U=", ma);
}
```

produces

```
original matrix
      5.0000        4.0000        3.0000       0.00000       0.00000
      4.0000        6.0000        4.0000        3.0000       0.00000
      3.0000        4.0000        7.0000        4.0000        3.0000
     0.00000        3.0000        4.0000        8.0000        4.0000
```

|          |          |          |          |          |
|----------|----------|----------|----------|----------|
| 0.00000  | 0.00000  | 3.0000   | 4.0000   | 9.0000   |

band version

|          |          |          |          |          |
|----------|----------|----------|----------|----------|
| 0.00000  | 0.00000  | 3.0000   | 3.0000   | 3.0000   |
| 0.00000  | 4.0000   | 4.0000   | 4.0000   | 4.0000   |
| 5.0000   | 6.0000   | 7.0000   | 8.0000   | 9.0000   |

solved:

|          |          |           |          |          |
|----------|----------|-----------|----------|----------|
| 0.012378 | 0.26172  | -0.036251 | 0.17507  | 0.48983  |

band L=

|          |          |          |          |          |
|----------|----------|----------|----------|----------|
| 0.00000  | 0.00000  | 0.60000  | 1.0714   | 0.70000  |
| 0.00000  | 0.80000  | 0.57143  | 0.53333  | 0.67290  |
| 1.0000   | 1.0000   | 1.0000   | 1.0000   | 1.0000   |

L:U=

|          |          |          |          |          |
|----------|----------|----------|----------|----------|
| 5.0000   | 4.0000   | 3.0000   | 0.00000  | 0.00000  |
| 0.80000  | 6.0000   | 4.0000   | 3.0000   | 0.00000  |
| 0.60000  | 0.57143  | 7.0000   | 4.0000   | 3.0000   |
| 0.00000  | 1.0714   | 0.53333  | 8.0000   | 4.0000   |
| 0.00000  | 0.00000  | 0.70000  | 0.67290  | 9.0000   |

# declu

`declu(const ma, const aml, const amu, const amp);`

| ma  | in:  | square $m \times m$ matrix $A$ |
|-----|------|--------------------------------|
| aml | in:  | address of variable |
|     | out: | $m \times m$ matrix lower diagonal matrix $L$, has ones on the diagonal |
| amu | in:  | address of variable |
|     | out: | $m \times m$ matrix upper diagonal matrix $U$, $LU = PA$ |
| amp | in:  | address of variable |
|     | out: | $2 \times m$ matrix, the first row holds the permutation matrix $P'$, $A = (LU)[P'][]$, the second row holds the interchange permutations |

*Return value*

Returns the result of the LU decomposition:

1 no error;

2 the decomposition could be unreliable;

0 the LU decomposition failed: the matrix is (numerically) singular.

*Description*

Computes the LU decomposition of a matrix $A$ as: $PA = LU$ by Gaussian elimination (using accumulation of inner-products) with partial pivoting, as described, e.g. in Wilkinson (1965, §4.39) (also see Golub and Van Loan, 1989 §3.4 for an analysis). *Note that $L$ has ones on the diagonal.*

The permutation matrix $P'$ is stored as a vector of row indices so that $A = (LU)[P'][]$ (see the example below). The actual permutation matrix $P' = P^{-1}$ can be created as pt = (unit(rows(ma)))[vp] [] where ma is the original matrix, and vp holds the row indices as returned by declu (in the first row of amp,

the last argument). $P$ can be computed as vp[][vp]. The second row of amp
holds the interchange permutations $p$, such that rows $p[0][i]$ and $i$ are swapped.

*Error and warning messages*

    declu(): decomposition failed (the matrix is numerically singular)

*See also*

    determinant, invert, solvelu

*Example*

```
#include <oxstd.h>
main()
{
    decl ma, ml, mu, vp, mx;

    ma = <3,17,10;2,4,-2;6,18,-12>;
    declu(ma, &ml, &mu, &vp);
    print( (ml*mu)[ vp[0][] ][], (unit(rows(ma)))[ vp[0][] ][] );

    mx = solvelu(ml, mu, vp, ma);
    print(mx);
}
```

produces (note that the last matrix is the identity matrix: whether it has zeros, or
nearly zeros, could dependent on which Ox version was used):

```
       3.0000            17.000           10.000
       2.0000            4.0000          -2.0000
       6.0000            18.000          -12.000

      0.00000            1.0000          0.00000
      0.00000           0.00000           1.0000
       1.0000           0.00000          0.00000

       1.0000    -3.7007e-017           0.00000
 -3.7007e-017            1.0000          0.00000
 1.8504e-017     -1.8504e-017            1.0000
```

# decqr

```
decqr(const ma, const amq, const amr, const amp);
```

| | | |
|---|---|---|
| ma | in: | $m \times n$ matrix $A$ |
| amq | in: | address of variable |
| | out: | $n \times m$ matrix upper diagonal matrix $H'$, has ones on the diagonal |
| amr | in: | address of variable |
| | out: | $n \times n$ matrix upper diagonal matrix $R_1$ |
| amp | in: | address of variable |
| | | (use 0 as argument to avoid pivoting; note that pivoting is recommended) |
| | out: | $2 \times n$ matrix, the first row holds the permutation matrix $P'$, the second row holds the interchange permutations |

*Return value*

Returns the result of the QR decomposition:

0:      out of memory,

1:      success,

2:      ratio of diagonal elements of $A'A$ is large, rescaling is advised, (ratio of smallest to largest $\leq \epsilon_{inv}$)

$-1$:   $(A'A)$ is (numerically) singular
$$(|R_{ii}| \leq \epsilon_{inv} \left[\max_j(A'A)_{jj}\right]^{1/2}),$$

$-2$:   combines 2 and $-1$.

The inversion epsilon, $\epsilon_{inv}$, is set by the `inverteps` function.

*Description*

Computes the QR decomposition of a matrix $A$ as: $AP = QR$ based on House-holder transformations with column pivoting, as described, e.g. in Golub and Van Loan (1989, §5.4). $A$ is $m \times n$, $Q$ is an $m \times m$ orthogonal matrix, and $R$ is an $m \times n$ upper diagonal matrix. Note that this function does *not* return $Q$ and $R$. Instead it returns $R_1$, which is the $\min(n,m) \times n$ upper block of $R$ (the rest of $R$ is zero). $Q'$ is returned as an $\min(n,m) \times m$ matrix $H'$ which stores the Householder vectors. $H$ is lower diagonal with ones on the diagonal. $H$ will have columns of zeros if $A$ is reduced rank (in that case pivoting is essential). The `decqrmul` function uses $H'$ to compute $Q'Y$.

The permutation matrix $P'$ is stored in the same way as for `declu`.

*See also*

`decqrmul` (for another example), `decqrupdate`, `inverteps`, `olsc`, `solvelu`

*Example*

```
#include <oxstd.h>
main()
{
    decl ma, mht, mr, mp, vp;
    ma = <2,1,4;5,1,7;8,1,9;11,1,12>;

    decqr(ma, &mht, &mr, &mp);
    vp = mp[0][];
    print("A=", ma, "A\'A", ma'ma,
        "R\'R (ignoring pivoting)", mr'mr,
        "R\'R (after undoing pivoting)", (mr'mr)[vp][vp]);
    println("Note that mp[0][] contains P':", vp);
    println("The pivots on A (where AP=QR) are:",
        sortcindex(vp') ');
}
```

```
A=
        2.0000      1.0000      4.0000
        5.0000      1.0000      7.0000
        8.0000      1.0000      9.0000
        11.000      1.0000      12.000
A'A
```

```
           214.00          26.000          247.00
           26.000          4.0000          32.000
           247.00          32.000          290.00
R'R (ignoring pivoting)
           290.00          247.00          32.000
           247.00          214.00          26.000
           32.000          26.000          4.0000
R'R (after undoing pivoting)
           214.00          26.000          247.00
           26.000          4.0000          32.000
           247.00          32.000          290.00
Note that mp[0][] contains P':
           1.0000          2.0000         0.00000
The pivots on A (where AP=QR) are:
           2.0000         0.00000          1.0000
```

# decqrmul

```
decqrmul(const mht, const my);
decqrmul(const mht);
```
|            |     |                                   |
| ---------- | --- | --------------------------------- |
| mht        | in: | $n \times m$ matrix $H'$ from decqr |
| my         | in: | $m \times p$ matrix $Y$            |

*Return value*

Returns $Q'Y$, where $Q$ is the orthogonal matrix derived from the QR decomposition. The version with one argument returns the $m \times m$ matrix $Q'$.

*Description*

The decqr composition returns $Q$ in the form of householder vectors $H'$. This function may be used to obtain $Q'Y$ or $Q'$ (the latter can be costly as it requires an $m \times m$ identity matrix). To compute $QY$, reverse the elements in each column of $H'$: decqrmul(reversec(mht), my).

*See also*

decqr, olsc, solvelu

*Example*

The example shows how to obtain $Q'$, reconstructs the original matrix, and implements regression using the QR decomposition (note that olsc is also QR based). Because the input matrix is singular, the solution is not unique. Different versions of Ox may find different solutions depending on differences in accumulation of rounding errors.

```
#include <oxstd.h>
main()
{
    decl iret, ma, maa, mht, mr, mp, mq, mb, vy;

    ma = <1,2,3;1,5,6;1,8,9;1,11,12>;
```

```
    iret = decqr(ma, &mht, &mr, &mp);
    if (iret < 0)
        println("Input matrix is singular");
    print("H\'=", mht', "R1=", mr, "pivots", mp);

    mq = decqrmul(mht);
    maa = mq' * (mr | <0,0,0>);
    print("Q\'=", mq', "ma (pivoted)=", maa,
        "ma=", maa[][mp[0][]]);

    vy = <2;1;2;4>;
    olsc(vy, ma, &mb);
    print("regression coefficients (transposed)", mb');

    decl rank = sumr(fabs(diagonal(mr)) .> 1e-14);
    println("rank=", rank);
    mr[rank:][] = 0;

    mb = solvelu(0, mr, 0, decqrmul(mht, vy)[:2][]);
    print("from QR", mb', "in correct order", mb[mp[0][]][]');
}
```

```
Input matrix is singular
H'=
        1.0000       0.00000       0.00000
        0.30877       1.0000       0.00000
        0.46316      -0.32710       1.0000
        0.61755      -0.78925       0.95191
R1=
      -16.432       -14.606       -1.8257
        0.00000       0.81650      -0.81650
        0.00000       0.00000   -6.9793e-016
pivots
        2.0000       1.0000       0.00000
        2.0000       1.0000       2.0000
Q'=
       -0.18257      -0.81650       0.39332       0.38118
       -0.36515      -0.40825      -0.80854      -0.21508
       -0.54772   -3.0378e-016       0.43712      -0.71339
       -0.73030       0.40825      -0.021902       0.54728
ma (pivoted)=
        3.0000       2.0000       1.0000
        6.0000       5.0000       1.0000
        9.0000       8.0000       1.0000
       12.000       11.000       1.0000
ma=
        1.0000       2.0000       3.0000
        1.0000       5.0000       6.0000
        1.0000       8.0000       9.0000
        1.0000       11.000       12.000
regression coefficients (transposed)
        0.00000      -0.50000       0.73333
```

```
rank=
        2.0000
from QR
        0.73333        -0.50000        0.00000
in correct order
        0.00000        -0.50000        0.73333
```

# decqrupdate

```
decqrupdate(const amq, const amr, const i1, const i2);
decqrupdate(const amq, const amr, const i1);
```
    amq        in:  address of $m \times m$ matrix $Q$
               out: updated matrix $Q$
    amr        in:  address of $m \times n$ matrix $R$
               out: updated matrix $R$

*No return value.*

*Description*

Updates the QR decomposition using Givens rotations.

The version with only the i1 argument zeroes the subdiagonal elements from subdiagonal i1 to the diagonal (i.e. subdiagonal 0). It is assumed that subdiagonals below i1 are already zero.

The version with both the i1 and i2 arguments zeroes the subdiagonal from column i1 to column i2. It is assumed that columns before i1 are already zero below the diagonal.

Both decqrupdate(&q, &a, 0, columns(r)); and decqrupdate(&q, &a, rows(r)); compute a complete QR decomposition (like decqr, although decqr does not compute $Q$ explicitly). However, the decqrupdate function is primarily intended to update a QR factorization.

*See also*

decqr, decqrmul

*Example*

The example shows first how the QR decomposition of an upper Hessenberg matrix (a matrix with zeros below the subdiagonal) can be computed, and then updates after appending a column to a lower triangular matrix.

```
#include <oxstd.h>
main()
{
    decl ma, maa, mht, mr, mp, mq, mb, vy;

    ma = <1,2,3,4,5;1,5,6,7,8;0,1,8,9,10;0,0,1,11,12>;

    println("Upper Hessenberg matrix A", ma);
    mr = ma;
    mq = unit(sizer(ma));
```

```
        decqrupdate(&mq, &mr, 1);
        println("triangular R:", mr);
        println("original:", mq*mr);

        mr[1:][0] = 1;
        mq = unit(sizer(ma));
        println("Column 0 changed:", mr);
        decqrupdate(&mq, &mr, 0, sizer(mr));
        println("Made triangular:", mr);
        println("original:", mq*mr);
}
```

```
Upper Hessenberg matrix A
        1.0000      2.0000      3.0000      4.0000      5.0000
        1.0000      5.0000      6.0000      7.0000      8.0000
        0.00000     1.0000      8.0000      9.0000     10.000
        0.00000     0.00000     1.0000     11.000      12.000
triangular R:
        1.4142      4.9497      6.3640      7.7782      9.1924
        0.00000     2.3452      5.3300      5.7564      6.1828
        0.00000     0.00000     6.4102      8.8637      9.9131
        0.00000     0.00000     0.00000     9.7365     10.583
original:
        1.0000      2.0000      3.0000      4.0000      5.0000
        1.0000      5.0000      6.0000      7.0000      8.0000
        0.00000     1.0000      8.0000      9.0000     10.000
        0.00000     0.00000     1.0000     11.000      12.000
Column 0 changed:
        1.4142      4.9497      6.3640      7.7782      9.1924
        1.0000      2.3452      5.3300      5.7564      6.1828
        1.0000      0.00000     6.4102      8.8637      9.9131
        1.0000      0.00000     0.00000     9.7365     10.583
Made triangular:
        2.2361      4.1793      9.2753     15.812      17.745
        0.00000     3.5403      1.4789     -3.9779     -4.0002
        0.00000     0.00000     4.6671     -0.80946    -0.78739
        0.00000     0.00000     0.00000    -0.70954    -1.2216
original:
        1.4142      4.9497      6.3640      7.7782      9.1924
        1.0000      2.3452      5.3300      5.7564      6.1828
        1.0000   3.8760e-016    6.4102      8.8637      9.9131
        1.0000   3.8760e-016 8.6736e-018    9.7365     10.583
```

# decschur, decschurgen

```
decschur(const ma, const amval, const ams, ...);
decschur(const ma, const amval, const ams, const amv,
    const dselmin, const dselmax);
decschurgen(const ma, const mb, const amalpha, const ambeta,
    const ams, const amt, ...);
decschurgen(const ma, const mb, const amalpha, const ambeta,
    const ams, const amt, const amvl, const amvr, const dselmin,
    const dselmax);
```

| | | |
|---|---|---|
| ma | in: | $m \times m$ matrix $A$ |
| amval | in: | address of variable |
| | out: | complex eigenvalues: $2 \times m$ matrix with eigenvalues of $A$ first row is real part, second row imaginary part |
| | | only real eigenvalues: $1 \times m$ matrix |
| | | The eigenvalues are not ordered unless dselmin and dselmax are specified. |
| ams | in: | address of variable |
| | out: | upper quasi-triangular Schur form $S$, such that $A = VSV'$ |
| amv | in: | (optional) address of variable |
| | out: | orthogonal matrix $V$ with Schur vectors, such that $A = VSV'$ |
| dselmin | in: | (optional) double, minimum absolute eigenvalue to move forward |
| dselmax | in: | (optional) double, maximum absolute eigenvalue to move forward |
| ma | in: | $m \times m$ matrix $A$ |
| mb | in: | $m \times m$ matrix $B$ for generalized Schur decomposition |
| amalpha | in: | address of variable |
| | out: | complex values: $2 \times m$ matrix with $\alpha$ first row is real part, second row imaginary part |
| | | only real $\alpha$s: $1 \times m$ matrix |
| | | The generalized eigenvalues are $(\alpha_r[j] + i\alpha_i[j])/\beta[j]$, $j = 0, \ldots, m - 1$. |
| | | The generalized eigenvalues are not ordered unless dselmin and dselmax are specified. |
| ambeta | in: | address of variable |
| | out: | $1 \times m$ matrix with $\beta$ |
| ams | in: | address of variable |
| | out: | upper quasi-triangular Schur form $S$, such that $A = V_l S V_r'$ |
| amt | in: | address of variable |
| | out: | upper-triangular Schur form $T$, such that $B = V_l T V_r'$ |

| | | |
|---|---|---|
| `amvl` | in: | (optional) address of variable |
| | out: | orthogonal matrix $V_l$ with left Schur vectors |
| `amvr` | in: | (optional) address of variable |
| | out: | orthogonal matrix $V_r$ with right Schur vectors |
| `dselmin` | in: | (optional) double, minimum absolute generalized eigenvalue to include move forward |
| `dselmax` | in: | (optional) double, maximum absolute generalized eigenvalue to include move forward |

*Return value*

Returns the result of the Schur decomposition:

0  no error;
1  maximum no of iterations reached;
-1  ill conditioning prevented ordering;
-2  rounding errors in ordering affected complex eigenvalues.

*Description*

The `decschur` function computes the Schur decomposition of a real matrix $A$:

$$A = VSV',$$

where $V$ is orthogonal, and $S$ upper quasi-triangular, with $2 \times 2$ blocks on the diagonal corresponding to complex eigenvalues.

The `decschurgen` function computes the generalized Schur decomposition of two real matrices $A, B$:

$$A = V_l S V_r', \quad B = V_l T V_r',$$

where $V$ is orthogonal, and $S$ upper quasi-triangular, with $2 \times 2$ blocks on the diagonal corresponding to complex eigenvalues. $T$ is an upper-triangular matrix. The generalized eigenvalues are $\alpha[i]/\beta[i]$, where $\alpha$ may be complex and $\beta$ is real. The Schur decomposition can be ordered if the `dselmin` and `dselmax` arguments are specified. Any (generalized) eigenvalues that are $\geq$ `dselmin` and $\leq$ `dselmax` in absolute value, are selected for reordering, and moved top left. Note the reordering may affect complex eigenvalue when the matrices are ill-conditioned. Sources: these routines are based on LAPACK 3.0 (see LAPACK, 1999).

*Error and warning messages*

decschur(): maximum no. of iterations reached
decschurgen(): maximum no. of iterations reached

*Example*

```
#include <oxstd.h>

main()
{
    decl a, b, ev, t, s, v, i, alpha, beta, vl, vr;
```

```
a = rann(4,4);   b = rann(4,4);
print("a", a);

i = decschur(a, &ev, &s);

print("eigenvalues", ev);
print("S", s);

i = decschur(a, &ev, &s, &v);

print("v*s*v'", v*s*v');

i = decschur(a, &ev, &s, &v, 0, 1);

print("cabs(eigenvalues) between 0 and 1 first, S=", s);

i = decschurgen(a, b, &alpha, &beta, &s, &t, &vl, &vr);

print("b", b);
println("decschurgen i=", i);
print("alpha", alpha);
print("beta", beta);
print("s", s, "vl*s*vr'", vl*s*vr');
print("t", t, "vl*t*vr'", vl*t*vr');

i = decschurgen(a, unit(rows(a)), &alpha, &beta, &s, &t,
    &vl, &vr, 0, 1);

println("selecting gen. eigen values between 0 and 1 first");
print("generalized eigen values", alpha ./ beta);
}
```

produces

```
a
        0.22489         1.7400       -0.20426       -0.91760
       -0.67417        -0.34353       0.22335       -0.14139
       -0.18338         0.68035       0.090558      -0.83328
        0.81350         1.1174        0.31499       -0.50031
eigenvalues
       -0.25959        -0.25959      -0.0046060     -0.0046060
        1.3775          -1.3775       0.32694       -0.32694
S
       -0.25959        -2.1654       -1.2665        -0.37296
        0.87631         -0.25959     -0.51481        0.18777
        0.00000          0.00000     -0.0046060      0.16910
        0.00000          0.00000     -0.63214       -0.0046060
v*s*v'
        0.22489         1.7400       -0.20426       -0.91760
       -0.67417        -0.34353       0.22335       -0.14139
       -0.18338         0.68035       0.090558      -0.83328
        0.81350         1.1174        0.31499       -0.50031
cabs(eigenvalues) between 0 and 1 first, S=
```

```
       -0.0046060      -0.20780       0.49340       0.64443
        0.51441       -0.0046060      0.66321       0.24688
        0.00000        0.00000       -0.25959       0.78487
        0.00000        0.00000       -2.4177       -0.25959
b
       -1.6268         0.61943       -1.4574       -1.8035
        2.0016         0.57912       -0.70797       0.59336
       -0.58939        1.4674        -0.020230      0.73706
        1.4795        -0.26881        1.2282        1.5784
decschurgen i=0
alpha
        1.9293         0.70758       -0.68938      -0.22323
beta
        0.089639       3.2454         2.0066        1.7759
s
        1.9293         1.4371        -0.80659       0.35450
        0.00000        0.70758        0.12850      -0.28463
        0.00000        0.00000       -0.68938       0.61345
        0.00000        0.00000        0.00000      -0.22323
vl*s*vr'
        0.22489        1.7400        -0.20426      -0.91760
       -0.67417       -0.34353        0.22335      -0.14139
       -0.18338        0.68035        0.090558     -0.83328
        0.81350        1.1174         0.31499      -0.50031
t
        0.089639       0.68167       -0.46602      -0.52514
        0.00000        3.2454         1.6897       -0.89339
        0.00000        0.00000        2.0066       -0.75847
        0.00000        0.00000        0.00000       1.7759
vl*t*vr'
       -1.6268         0.61943       -1.4574       -1.8035
        2.0016         0.57912       -0.70797       0.59336
       -0.58939        1.4674        -0.020230      0.73706
        1.4795        -0.26881        1.2282        1.5784
selecting gen. eigen values between 0 and 1 first
generalized eigen values
       -0.0046060     -0.0046060     -0.25959      -0.25959
        0.32694       -0.32694        1.3775       -1.3775
```

# decsvd

```
decsvd(const ma);
decsvd(const ma, const amu, const amw);
decsvd(const ma, const amu, const amw, const amv);
```

| | | |
|---|---|---|
| ma | in: | $m \times n$ matrix $A$ |
| amu | in: | address of variable |
| | out: | $m \times n$ matrix $U$, $U'U = I_n$ |
| amw | in: | address of variable |
| | out: | $1 \times n$ matrix with diagonal of $W$ |
| amv | in: | (optional argument) address of variable |
| | out: | if not 0 on input: $n \times n$ matrix $V$, $UWV' = A$, $V'V = I_n$ |

*Return value*

Returns the result of the singular value decomposition:

- one argument: returns a $1 \times \min(m, n)$ matrix with the singular values, or 0 if the decomposition failed.
- two or more arguments: returns an integer indicating the result from the decomposition:

  0  no error;

  k  if the $k$-th singular value (with index $k - 1$) has not been determined after 50 iterations.

Note that the singular values are in *decreasing order*, with the columns of $U, V$ sorted accordingly.

*Description*

Decomposes a $m \times n$ matrix $A$, rank$(A) = r > 0$, into $A = UWV'$:

$U$ is $m \times n$ and $U'U = I_n$,

$W$ is $n \times n$ and diagonal, with positive diagonal elements,

$V$ is $n \times n$ and $V'V = I_n$.

The rank of $A$ is the number of non-zero diagonal elements of $W$.

*Error and warning messages*

decsvd(): decomposition failed

*See also*

§13.8.5.1, §13.8.5

*Example*

```
#include <oxstd.h>
main()
{
    decl x=<1,2;3,4;5,6>, mu, mv, mw;

    print("singular values: ", decsvd(x));
    print("result = ", decsvd(x, &mu, &mw, &mv));
    print(" A =", mu * diag(mw) * mv');
```

```
        decsvd(x', &mu, &mw, &mv);
        print(" A =", mu * diag(mw) * mv');
}
```

produces

```
singular values:
        9.5255        0.51430
result = 0 A =
        1.0000        2.0000
        3.0000        4.0000
        5.0000        6.0000
  A =
        1.0000        3.0000        5.0000
        2.0000        4.0000        6.0000
```

# deletec, deleter
# deleteifc, deleteifr

```
deletec(const ma);
deletec(const ma, const mval);
deleter(const ma);
deleter(const ma, const mval);
deleteifc(const ma, const mifc);
deleteifr(const ma, const mifr);
```

| | | |
|---|---|---|
| ma | in: | $m \times n$ matrix to delete from |
| mval | in: | $p \times q$ matrix with values to use for deletion |
| mifc | in: | $p \times n$ boolean matrix specifying columns to delete |
| mifr | in: | $m \times q$ boolean matrix specifying rows to delete |

*Return value*

The `deletec` function with one argument returns an $m \times s$ matrix, deleting columns from `ma` which have a missing value (NaN: not a number).

The `deleter` function with one argument returns an $s \times n$ matrix, deleting rows from `ma` which have a missing value (NaN: not a number).

The remaining forms have no special treatment of missing values.

The `deleter` function with two arguments returns an $s \times n$ matrix, deleting the rows from `ma` which have at least one element equal to an element in the matrix `mval`.

The `deletec` function with two arguments returns an $m \times s$ matrix, deleting the columns from `ma` which have at least one element equal to an element in the matrix `mval`.

The deleteif functions can be used to delete rows or columns based on a logical expression: all rows (columns) wich have a zero in the corresponding row (column) are kept, the remainder is dropped.

The `deleteifc` function returns an $m \times s$ matrix, deleting only those columns from ma which have at least one non-zero element in the corresponding column of `mifc`.

The `deleteifr` function returns an $s \times n$ matrix, deleting only those rows from ma which have at least one non-zero element in the corresponding row of `mifr`.

All functions return an empty matrix (<>) if the result is empty.

*See also*

dropc, dropr, selectc, selectr, selectrc, selectifc, selectifr, hasnandot, vecindex

*Example*

```
#include <oxstd.h>
main()
{
    decl m = <.,1,2,3;4:7;8,9,.,11;12:15>, m1,
        del = <1,9,14>;
    print(m, "NaN deleted", m1 = deleter(m));
    print("delete", deleter(m1, del));
    print("deleteif", deleteifr(m1, m1 .< 0 || m1 .> 14));
}
```

produces:

```
            .NaN       1.0000       2.0000       3.0000
          4.0000       5.0000       6.0000       7.0000
          8.0000       9.0000        .NaN       11.000
          12.000       13.000       14.000       15.000
NaN deleted
          4.0000       5.0000       6.0000       7.0000
          12.000       13.000       14.000       15.000
delete
          4.0000       5.0000       6.0000       7.0000
deleteif
          4.0000       5.0000       6.0000       7.0000
```

# denschi, densf, densn, denst

```
denschi(const ma, const df);
densf(const ma, const df1, const df2);
densn(const ma);
denst(const ma, const df);
```

|        |     |                                                          |
|--------|-----|----------------------------------------------------------|
| ma     | in: | arithmetic type                                          |
| df     | in: | arithmetic type, degrees of freedom                      |
| df1    | in: | arithmetic type, degrees of freedom in the numerator     |
| df2    | in: | arithmetic type, degrees of freedom in the denominator   |

*Return value*

Returns the requested density at `ma` (the returned densities are positive):

| | |
|---|---|
| denschi | $\chi^2(df)$ density |
| densf   | $F(df1, df2)$ density |
| densn   | standard normal density |
| denst   | student-t$(df)$ density |

The return type is derived as follows:

| returns | ma | degrees of freedom arguments |
|---------|-----|------------------------------|
| $m \times n$ matrix | $m \times n$ matrix | scalar |
| $m \times n$ matrix | scalar | $m \times n$ matrix |
| $m \times n$ matrix | $m \times n$ matrix | $m \times n$ matrix |
| double | scalar | scalar |

*See also*

`prob...`, `quan...`, `tail...`, Probability package (§11.3)

# determinant

```
determinant(const ma);
```

|      |     |                      |
|------|-----|----------------------|
| ma   | in: | $m \times m$ matrix  |

*Return value*

Returns the determinant of `ma`. Return type is double.

*Description*

Computes the determinant of a matrix. The determinant is obtained from the LU decomposition of the matrix (see `declu`). Use `invert` if both the inverse and determinant are required. Note that for ill-conditioned or large matrices, the determinant could be a very large or very small number.

*Error and warning messages*

determinant(): overflow (determinant set to DBL_MAX_E_EXP)
determinant(): underflow (determinant set to 0)
determinant(): matrix is singular (determinant set to 0)

determinant(): unreliable (warns that the result may be unreliable)

*See also*
```
declu, invert, logdet
```
*Example*
```
#include <oxstd.h>
main()
{
    print( determinant(<2,1;1,4>) );
}
```

produces: 7

# dfft

```
dfft(const ma);
dfft(const ma, const inverse);
    ma          in:  2 × n matrix (first row is real part, second row imaginary
                     part), or 1 × n matrix (real part only, imaginary part is zero)
    inverse     in   (optional argument), int:
                     1: do inverse discrete FT
                     2: do inverse discrete real FT
```

*Return value*
If only one argument is used, the return value is a $2 \times n$ matrix which holds the
Fourier transform.
If inverse equals 1, the return value is a $2 \times n$ matrix which holds the inverse
Fourier transform.
If inverse equals 2, the return value is a $1 \times n$ matrix which holds the inverse
real Fourier transform.

*Description*
Performs an (inverse) discrete Fourier transform. Computing the discrete Fourier
transform is of order $n^2$, whereas the FFT is of order $n \log_2(n)$, so much faster
for large sample sizes.
If the input has no complex part, in the absence of the inverse argument, a real
FT is performed.

*See also*
```
fft1d
```
*Example*
```
#include <oxstd.h>
main()
{
    print( "dfft", dfft(<1,0,1>), "fft1d", fft1d(<1,0,1>),
        "inverse dfft(dfft))", dfft(dfft(<1,0,1>), 2) );
}
```

produces

```
dfft
        2.0000        0.50000        0.50000
        0.00000       0.86603       -0.86603
fft1d
        2.0000        0.50000        0.50000
        0.00000       0.86603       -0.86603
inverse dfft(dfft))
        1.0000 -1.4599e-016        1.0000
```

# diag

```
diag(const ma);
```
    ma         in:   double, or $m \times 1$ or $1 \times m$ matrix

*Return value*

    Returns a $m \times m$ matrix with `ma` on the diagonal.

*See also*

    `diagonal`, `diagonalize`, `toeplitz`

*Example*

```
#include <oxstd.h>
main()
{
    print( diag(<1,1>), diag(<1;1>) );
}
```

produces

```
        1.0000        0.00000
        0.00000       1.0000

        1.0000        0.00000
        0.00000       1.0000
```

# diagcat

```
diagcat(const ma, const mb);
```
    ma        in:   $m \times n$ matrix
    mb        in:   $p \times q$ matrix

*Return value*

    Returns a $(m+p) \times (n+q)$ matrix with `mb` concatenated to `mb` along the diagonal; the off-diagonal blocks are set to zero.

*Example*

```
#include <oxstd.h>
main()
{
    print( diagcat(<2,2>, unit(2)) );
}
```

produces

```
     2.0000        2.0000      0.00000      0.00000
    0.00000       0.00000       1.0000      0.00000
    0.00000       0.00000      0.00000       1.0000
```

# diagonal

```
diagonal(const ma);
diagonal(const ma, const upr);
diagonal(const ma, const upr, const lwr);
```
        ma          in:   arithmetic type
        upr         in:   (optional argument), int: upper bandwidth ($\geq 0$, default 0)
        lwr         in:   (optional argument), int: lower bandwidth ($\leq 0$, default 0)

*Return value*

The version with one argument returns a matrix with the diagonal from the specified matrix in the first row. *Note that the diagonal is returned as a row vector, not a column.* If ma is $m \times n$, the returned matrix is $1 \times \min(m, n)$ (exception: $0 \times 0$ when $m = 0$); if ma is scalar, the returned matrix is $1 \times 1$.

The version with more than one argument extracts the matrix in band format. If $A = (a_{ij})$ is $m \times n$ input matrix, then the output matrix ma $= A^b$ is formed as:

$$
\begin{pmatrix}
 & \vdots & & & \\
0 & 0 & a_{2,3} & \cdots & \\
0 & a_{0,1} & a_{1,2} & \cdots & \\
a_{0,0} & a_{1,1} & a_{2,2} & \cdots & \\
a_{1,0} & a_{2,1} & a_{3,2} & \cdots & \\
 & \vdots & & & 0
\end{pmatrix}
$$

The diagonal is returned with diagonal(., 0, 0).

*See also*

decldlband (for another example), diag, diagonalize, setdiagonal

*Example*

```
#include <oxstd.h>
main()
{
    decl x = <1:5;11:15;21:25>;
    print( "%6.0f", diagonal(x) );
    print( "%6.0f", diagonal(x, 1, -1) );
}
```

produces

```
    1    12    23

    0     2    13    24
    1    12    23     0
   11    22     0     0
```

# diagonalize

```
diagonalize(const ma);
     ma          in:   arithmetic type
```

*Return value*

Returns a matrix with the diagonal of ma on its diagonal, and zeros in off-diagonal elements. If ma is $m \times n$, the returned matrix is $m \times n$; if ma is scalar, the returned matrix is $1 \times 1$.

*See also*

diag, diagonal, setdiagonal

*Example*

```
#include <oxstd.h>
main()
{
    print( diagonalize( constant(2, 3, 4) ) );
}
```

produces

```
     2.0000      0.00000      0.00000      0.00000
     0.00000      2.0000      0.00000      0.00000
     0.00000      0.00000      2.0000      0.00000
```

# diff0

```
diff0(const ma, const ilag);
diff0(const ma, const ilag, const dmisval);
     ma         in:  $T \times n$ matrix $A$
     ilag       in:  int, lag length of difference (1 for first difference)
     dmisval    in:  (optional argument) double, value to set missing observa-
                     tions to (default is 0)
```

*Return value*

Returns a $T \times n$ matrix with the ilagth difference of the specified matrix, whereby missing values are replaced by zero. E.g. the result matrix r using second differences (ilag = 2) is:

```
r[0][0] = 0                    r[0][1] = 0                    ...
r[1][0] = 0                    r[1][1] = 0                    ...
r[2][0] = ma[2][0]-ma[0][0]   r[2][1] = ma[2][1]-ma[0][1]   ...
r[3][0] = ma[3][0]-ma[1][0]   r[3][1] = ma[3][1]-ma[1][1]   ...
r[4][0] = ma[4][0]-ma[2][0]   r[4][1] = ma[4][1]-ma[2][1]   ...
...
```

The result has the same dimensions as ma.

*Description*

Differences the specified matrix, missing values are replaced by zero (unless a missing value is specified as the third argument). Using the lag operator $L$, for a column $a = (a_0, \ldots, a_{T-1})'$ of $A$, this function computes $(1 - L^d)a$. For $d = 1$, this is: $(0, a_1 - a_0, \ldots, a_{T-1} - a_{T-2})'$. The value of $d$ must be integer, but may be negative (a forward difference). Note that $(1 - L^0)a = 0$.

*See also*

lag0

*Example*

```
#include <oxstd.h>
main()
{
    print( diff0(<1:5>',2) );
}
```

produces

```
     0.00000
     0.00000
     2.0000
     2.0000
     2.0000
```

# discretize

```
discretize(const vx, const dmin, const dmax,
    const icount, const ioption);
    mx         in:  1 × T data vector
    dmin       in:  double, first point a
    dmax       in:  double, last point b
    icount     in:  int, number of points M
    ioption    in:  int, 0: raw discretization; 1: weighted discretization
```

*Return value*

Returns a $1 \times M$ matrix with the discretized data.

*Description*

Define a horizontal axis $a, a + \delta, a + 2\delta, \ldots, b$, where $\delta = (b-a)/(M-1)$. The return value is the observation count, where each data value is assigned to the nearest point on the horizontal axis (this is raw discretization). Points outside the interval $[a - \delta/2, b + \delta/2)$ are ignored. The sum of the return value corresponds to the number of data points actually used.

In weighted discretization, an observation wich falls between two points is distributed to both points, with weight proportional to the distance.

*See also*

countc, lib/DensEst.ox (for an application)

*Example*

In this example, the three intervals are $[-3, -1)$, $[-1, 1)$ and $[1, 3)$. So the last observation of x will be ignored. The raw discretization simply counts the numbers in each interval, giving the first line of output. The weighted version looks at the distance to the points $-2, 0, 2$ (also printed as the last output line): $-3$ is to the left of the minimum, so fully assigned to the first interval. Apart from $-1$, all observations are exactly on a point, so fully assigned; $-1$ falls halfway between $-2$ and $0$, so half is assigned to the first interval, and half to the second (if the value would have been $-1.5$, $0.75$ would go to the first interval, $0.25$ to the second.

```
#include <oxstd.h>
main()
{
    decl a = -2, b = 2, m = 3, t;
    decl x = <-3,-2,-1,0,2,3>;

    t = a + (b - a) * range(0, m - 1) / (m - 1);
    print( discretize(x, a, b, m, 0)
        | discretize(x, a, b, m, 1) | t);
}
```

produces

```
    2.0000          2.0000          1.0000
    2.5000          1.5000          1.0000
   -2.0000          0.00000         2.0000
```

# double

```
double(const ma);
     ma          in:   arithmetic type
```

*Return value*

Casts the argument to a double:

| input | returns |
|---|---|
| integer | converted to a double |
| double | unchanged |
| matrix | element 0,0 |
| string | see §13.8.2.3 (also see the example under fread) |
| other types | error |

*See also*

    int, matrix, string, §13.8.2.3

# dropc, dropr

```
dropc(const ma, const midxc);
dropr(const ma, const midxr);
dropr(const aa, const midxr);
```
|       |     |                                                            |
|-------|-----|------------------------------------------------------------|
| ma    | in: | $m \times n$ matrix to delete from                         |
| aa    | in: | $m$ array to delete from                                   |
| midxc | in: | scalar or $p \times q$ matrix specifying the index of columns to delete |
| midxr | in: | scalar or $p \times q$ matrix specifying the index of rows to delete |

*Return value*

The dropc function returns a copy of the input matrix with the specified columns deleted.

The dropr function returns a copy of the input matrix with the specified rows deleted; dropr also works for arrays.

All functions return an empty matrix (<>) if all rows or columns are deleted (or empty array for arrays).

*Example*

```
#include <oxstd.h>
main()
{
    decl x = <1,2,3;4,5,6>;
    print( dropc(x, 1) );
    print( dropr(x, 1) );
    print( insertc(x, 0, 1) );
    print( insertr(x, 0, 1) );

    decl a = {{"A","B"},{1,2},{<1>,<2>}};
    println("a=", a, "dropr(a,<1,2>)", dropr(a,<1,2>));
    println("a[0]=", a[0], "dropr(a[0],<1>)", dropr(a[0],<1>));
    println("insertr(a[0],0,2)", insertr(a[0],0,2));
}
```

produces

```
    1.0000        3.0000
    4.0000        6.0000

    1.0000        2.0000        3.0000

    0.00000       1.0000        2.0000        3.0000
    0.00000       4.0000        5.0000        6.0000

    0.00000       0.00000       0.00000
```

```
        1.0000        2.0000        3.0000
        4.0000        5.0000        6.0000
a=
[0][0] = A
[0][1] = B
[1][0] = 1
[1][1] = 2
[2][0] =
        1.0000
[2][1] =
        2.0000
dropr(a,<1,2>)
[0][0] = A
[0][1] = B
a[0]=
[0] = A
[1] = B
dropr(a[0],<1>)
[0] = A
insertr(a[0],0,2)
[0] = .Null
[1] = .Null
[2] = A
[3] = B
```

*See also*
    deleteifc, deleteifr, insertc, insertr, vecindex


# eigen, eigensym


```
eigen(const ma, const amval);
eigen(const ma, const amval, const amvec);
eigensym(const ms, const amsval);
eigensym(const ms, const amsval, const amsvec);
```

| ma | in: | $m \times m$ matrix $A$ |
|---|---|---|
| amval | in: | address of variable |
| | out: | complex eigenvalues: $2 \times m$ matrix with eigenvalues of $A$ |
| | | first row is real part, second row imaginary part |
| | | only real eigenvalues: $1 \times m$ |
| | | *The eigenvalues are not sorted.* |

| | | |
|---|---|---|
| `amvec` | in: | address of variable |
| | out: | complex eigenvectors: $2m \times m$ matrix with eigenvectors of $A$ in columns top $m \times m$ block is real part, bottom $m \times m$ block is imaginary part |
| | | only real eigenvalues: $m \times m$ matrix with eigenvectors in columns |
| | | (the vectors are scaled by the largest absolute element in the vector) |
| `ms` | in: | symmetric $m \times m$ matrix $A^s$ |
| `amsval` | in: | address of variable |
| | out: | $1 \times m$ matrix with eigenvalues of $A^s$, sorted in decreasing order |
| `amsvec` | in: | address of variable |
| | out: | $m \times m$ matrix with eigenvectors of $A^s$ in columns |

*Return value*

Returns the result of the eigenvalue decomposition:

0  no error;
1  maximum no of iterations (50) reached.

*Description*

Computes the eigenvalues of a real matrix and a symmetric real matrix. The `eigensym` function delivers the eigenvalues sorted, with the *largest first*. If eigenvectors are requested, these are in corresponding order.

The `eigen` function uses the balanced form of the matrix. (`eigensym`: if the matrix has elements of widely varying order of magnitude, the smaller elements should be in the bottom right hand corner.)

Sources: these routines are based on algorithms by J.H. Wilkinson and colleagues in Numerische Mathematik (Martin, Reinsch and Wilkinson, 1968, Martin and Wilkinson, 1968b, Martin and Wilkinson, 1968a, Parlett and Reinsch, 1969, Peters and Wilkinson, 1970, Dubrulle, 1970). From Ox version 3.2 onwards, the non-symmetric eigenvalue code is based on LAPACK 3.0 (see LAPACK, 1999).

*Error and warning messages*

eigen(): maximum no. of iterations reached
eigensym(): maximum no. of iterations reached

*Example*

```
#include <oxstd.h>
main()
{
    decl meval, mevec;

    print("result=", eigensym(<2,1;1,3>, &meval, &mevec));
    print(" eigenvalues:", meval, "eigenvectors:", mevec);

    print("result=", eigen(<2,1;-3,1>, &meval));
```

```
    print(" eigenvalues:", "%r",
        {"real", "imaginary"}, meval);
}
```

produces

```
result=0 eigenvalues:
      3.6180        1.3820
eigenvectors:
   -0.52573       0.85065
   -0.85065      -0.52573
result=0 eigenvalues:
real                1.5000        1.5000
imaginary           1.6583       -1.6583
```

# eigensymgen

eigensymgen(const ma, const mb, const amval,const amvec);

| | | |
|---|---|---|
| ma | in: | symmetric $m \times m$ matrix $A$ |
| mb | in: | symmetric positive definite $m \times m$ matrix $B$ |
| amval | in: | address of variable |
| | out: | $1 \times m$ matrix with sorted (generalized) eigenvalues of $A$ |
| amvec | in: | address of variable |
| | out: | $n \times m$ matrix (generalized) eigenvectors of $A$ in columns |

*Return value*

Solves the general eigenproblem $Ax = \lambda Bx$. returning the result of the eigenvalue decomposition:

   0  no error;
   1  maximum no of iterations (50) reached.
  −1  Choleski decomposition failed.

*Description*

Solves the general eigenproblem $Ax = \lambda Bx$, where $A$ and $B$ are symmetric, $B$ is also positive definite. The problem is transformed in standard eigenproblem by decomposing $B = CC' = LDL'$ and solving $Py = \lambda y$, where $y = C'x$, $P = C^{-1}AC'^{-1}$

*Error and warning messages*

eigensymgen(): matrices not conformant
eigensymgen(): maximum no. of iterations reached
eigensymgen(): decomposition failed (Choleski decomposition)

*See also*

decldl, eigensym

*Example*

```
#include <oxstd.h>
main()
{
    decl meval, mevec;

    print("result = ",
        eigensymgen(<2,1;1,3>,<1,0;0,1>, &meval, &mevec));
    print(" generalized eigenvectors:", mevec);
}
```

produces

```
result = 0 generalized eigenvectors:
      -0.52573        0.85065
      -0.85065       -0.52573
```

# eprint

```
eprint(const a, ...);
    a           in:  any type
    ...         in:  any type
```

*Return value*

Returns the number of arguments supplied to the function.

*Description*

Prints to stderr. See `print` for a further description.

*See also*

`fprint`, `print`, `sprint`

*Example*

```
#include <oxstd.h>
main()
{
    eprint( "\nerror message\n" );
}
```

prints `error message` to the console (even when the output is redirected to a file).

# erf

```
erf(const ma);
    ma          in:  arithmetic type
```

*Return value*

Returns the error function of each element of ma, of double or matrix type.

*Description*

The error function is related to the normal CDF as follows:

$$\text{erf} = 2\Phi(x\sqrt{2}) - 1.$$

*See also*

cerf, probn

# exclusion

```
exclusion(const ma, const mb);
exclusion(const ma, const mb, const amidx);
```
| | | |
|---|---|---|
| ma | in: | matrix |
| mb | in: | matrix |
| amidx | in: | address of matrix |
| | out: | $2 \times c$ matrix, first row is index of exclusion in ma, second row is index in mb. |

*Return value*

Returns the sorted unique elements of ma which are not in mb as a row vector. Returns an empty matrix if the result is empty. Missing values are skipped.

*See also*

intersection, unique

*Example*

```
#include <oxstd.h>
main()
{
    decl x = <-1,1,.,-2,-2,.,4>, y = <3,3,.,-2,1>;
    format("%5.1g");
    print("exclusion", exclusion(x, y) );
    print("intersection", intersection(x, y) );
    print("union", unique(x ~ y) );
}
```

produces

```
exclusion
   -1    4
intersection
   -2    1
union
   -2   -1    1    3    4
```

# exit

```
exit(const iexit);
```
      iexit      in:  integer, exit code

*No return value.*

*Description*
    Exits the Ox run-time environment. The specified exit code is ignored.

# exp

```
exp(const ma);
```
      ma      in:  arithmetic type

*Return value*
    Returns the exponent of each element of ma, of double or matrix type.

*See also*
    log

*Example*
```
#include <oxstd.h>
main()
{
    print( exp(<0,1>) );
}
```

    produces

      1.0000        2.7183

# expint

```
expint(const ma);
```
      ma      in:  arithmetic type

*Return value*
    Returns the exponential integral $\text{Ei}(x)$ of each element of ma, of double or matrix type.

*Description*
    Note that $E_1(x) = -\text{Ei}(-x)$. The function is based on the Fortran code in Netlib by W.J. Cody.

# fabs

```
fabs(const ma);
```
        ma              in:   int, double, matrix

*Return value*
    Returns the absolute value of each element of ma, of the same type as ma.

*Example*
```
#include <oxstd.h>
main()
{
    print( fabs(<-1.1,1.1>) );
}
```

    produces

        1.1000          1.1000

# factorial

```
factorial(const ma);
```
        ma              in:   arithmetic type

*Return value*
    Returns the factorial function at the rounded value of each element of ma, of double or matrix type.
    For negative integers, the function returns .NaN.

*Description*
    Computes the factorial:

$$n! = n \times (n-1) \times (n-2)\ldots 2 \times 1.$$

    The gamma function is related to the factorial for integer arguments: if $n$ is integer then $\Gamma(n+1) = n!$.
    Often a ratio of factorials functions is needed. Note that the factorial can overflow rapidly. However, often there is an offsetting factor in the denominator/numerator, and it is advised to use the loggamma or binomial function instead in that case.
    Computation is based on the gammafunc function.

*See also*
    binomial, gammafunc

# fclose

```
fclose(const file);
```
      `file`        in:   an open file which is to be closed

*Return value*
    Returns 0.

*Description*
    Closes the specified file, which was previously opened by a call to `fopen`. All
    open files are automatically closed when the program exits. On some operating
    systems, there is a limit on the number of open files.
    Use `fclose("l")` to close the log file.

*See also*
    `fopen`, `fprint` (for an example)

# feof, fflush

```
feof(const file);
fflush(const file);
```
      `file`      in:   an open file

*Return value*
    The `feof` function checks for end of file; returns 0 if not at end of file, a non-zero
    value otherwise. `fflush` flushes the file buffer.

# fft, fft1d

```
fft(const ma);
fft(const ma, const inverse);
fft1d(const ma);
fft1d(const ma, const inverse);
```
      `ma`         in:   $2 \times n$ matrix (first row is real part, second row imaginary
                        part), or $1 \times n$ matrix (real part only, imaginary part is zero)
      `inverse`   in   (optional argument), int:
                        1: do inverse FFT
                        2: do inverse real FFT

*Return value*
    If only one argument is used, the return value is a $2 \times s$ matrix which holds the
    Fourier transform.
    If `inverse` equals 1, the return value is a $2 \times s$ matrix which holds the inverse
    Fourier transform.

If `inverse` equals 2, the return value is a $1 \times s$ matrix which holds the inverse real Fourier transform.

For `fft1d`, $s = n$, so it returns the same number of columns as the input.

But `fft` pads with zeros until a power of two is reached: $s$ is the smallest power of 2 which is $\geq n$.

*Description*

Performs an (inverse) fast Fourier transform. The code is based on FFTE 2.0 by Daisuke Takahashi, see `www.ffte.jp`. FFTE provides Discrete Fourier Transforms of sequences of length $2^p 3^q 5^r$, which has been extended to work for all sample size.

If the input has no complex part, in the absence of the `inverse` argument, a real FFT is performed.

*See also*

for some applications: `lib/AcfFft.ox`, `lib/DensEst.ox`

*Example*

```
#include <oxstd.h>
main()
{
    print( fft(<1,0,1>), fft(fft(<1,0,1>), 2) );
}
```

produces

```
        2.0000      0.00000      2.0000      0.00000
      0.00000      0.00000      0.00000      0.00000

        1.0000      0.00000      1.0000      0.00000
```

# findsample

```
findsample(const mdata, const vvarsel, const vlagsel,
    const it1, const it2, const imode, const ait1, const ait2);
```

| | | |
|---|---|---|
| mdata | in: | $T \times n$ data matrix |
| vvarsel | in: | $p$-dimensional selection vector with indices in `mdata` |
| | | or empty matrix to use whole `mdata` as selection |
| vlagsel | in: | $p$-dimensional vector with lag lengths for selection |
| | | or empty matrix to use no lags |
| it1 | in: | int, first observation index to consider ($\geq 0$) |
| it2 | in: | int, last observation index to consider (can use $-1$ for $T-1$) |

| mode | in: | int, sample selection mode |
| | | SAM_ALLVALID: all observations must be valid |
| | | SAM_ENDSVALID: only the first and last observation must be wholly valid (there may be missing observations in between) |
| | | SAM_ANYVALID: the first and last observation must have some valid data |
| ait1 | in: | address of variable |
| | out: | the first observation index |
| ait2 | in: | address of variable |
| | out: | the last observation index |

*Return value*

The number of observation in the selected sample.

*Example*

```
#include <oxstd.h>
main()
{
    decl x = range(0,5)' ~ range(10,15)', t1, t2;

    x[2][1] = x[5][1] = .NaN;
    x[4][] = .NaN;

    println(x);
    findsample(x, <>, <>, 0, -1, SAM_ALLVALID, &t1, &t2);
    println("SAM_ALLVALID:  t1=", t1, " t2=", t2);
    findsample(x, <>, <>, 0, -1, SAM_ENDSVALID, &t1, &t2);
    println("SAM_ENDSVALID: t1=", t1, " t2=", t2);
    findsample(x, <>, <>, 0, -1, SAM_ANYVALID, &t1, &t2);
    println("SAM_ANYVALID:  t1=", t1, " t2=", t2);

    findsample(x, <0,0>, <0,1>, 0, -1, SAM_ALLVALID, &t1, &t2);
    println("SAM_ALLVALID:  t1=", t1, " t2=", t2,
        " column 0, lags 0-1");
}
```

produces

```
      0.00000        10.000
      1.0000         11.000
      2.0000          .NaN
      3.0000         13.000
       .NaN           .NaN
      5.0000          .NaN
SAM_ALLVALID:  t1=0 t2=1
SAM_ENDSVALID: t1=0 t2=3
SAM_ANYVALID:  t1=0 t2=5
SAM_ALLVALID:  t1=1 t2=3 column 0, lags 0-1
```

# floor

```
floor(const ma);
```
    ma          in:   arithmetic type

*Return value*

Returns the floor of each element of ma, of double or matrix type. The floor is the largest integer less than or equal to the argument.

*See also*

ceil (for an example), round, trunc

# fmod

```
fmod(const ma, const mb);
```
    ma          in:   arithmetic type
    mb          in:   arithmetic type

*Return value*

Returns the floating point remainder of ma / mb. The sign of the result is that of ma. The return type is double if both ma and mb are int or double. If ma is a matrix, the return type is a matrix of the same size, holding the floating point remainders ma$[i][j]$/mb$[i][j]$, etc. The return type is derived as follows:

| returns | ma | mb |
|---|---|---|
| $m \times n$ matrix | $m \times n$ matrix | scalar |
| $m \times n$ matrix | scalar | $m \times n$ matrix |
| $m \times n$ matrix | $m \times n$ matrix | $m \times n$ matrix |
| double: | scalar | scalar |

*See also*

imod

*Example*

```
#include <oxstd.h>
main()
{
    print( fmod(3,2), " ", fmod(-3,2), " ",
            fmod(3,-2), " ", fmod(-3,-2) );
}
```

produces: 1 -1 1 -1

# fopen

```
fopen(const filename);
fopen(const filename, const smode);
     filename            in:   name of file to open
     smode               in:   text with open mode
```

*Return value*

Returns the opened file if successful, otherwise the value 0.

*Description*

Opens a file. The first form, without the smode argument opens a file for *reading* (equivalent to using "r"). The smode argument can be:

"w"     open for writing;

"a"     open for appending;

"r"     open for reading;

"r+"    open for reading and writing (update);

"l"     open a log file for writing (use "la" to append).

The binary mode makes a difference under MS-DOS and Windows, but only for the treatment of end-of-line characters. Binary leaves a \n as \n, whereas non-binary translates \n to \r\n on output (and vice versa on input). When using "r+", it is necessary to use fseek or fflush when switching from reading to writing.

In addition, the following letters can be used in the smode argument:

b Opens the file in binary mode. This makes a difference under MS-DOS and Windows, but only for the treatment of end-of-line characters. Binary leaves a \n as \n, whereas non-binary translates \n to \r\n on output (and vice versa on input). On Windows/MS-DOS systems, it is customary to open text files without the b, and binary files (when using fread and fwrite) with the b.

f When the file has a .fmt extension, and the letter f is appended to the format (as e.g. "rbf"), the matrix file is opened in formatted mode. In that case, reading and writing can occur by blocks of rows. When writing, the file must be explicitly closed through a call to fclose. Note that .fmt files written by Gauss on Unix platforms cannot be opened this way (unless the v96 format is used).

This can also be used for a v96 .dat file, which stores variable names as well as binary data. When writing, the first fwrite should be an array of strings, which also determines the number of variables. When reading, used fread(file, &as, 's') to read the variable names; this resets the file pointer to the first row.

F Same as 'f', except using the v96 format instead of extended v89.

e Forces the file reading and writing (using fread and fwrite) to be in little-endian mode. This allows Ox on Unix (not Linux on Intel) to handle files which use the MS-DOS byte ordering (which is little-endian).

E  Forces the file reading and writing (using fread and fwrite) to be in big-endian mode. This allows Ox on Windows/MS-DOS to handle files which use the Unix (not Linux on Intel) byte ordering (which is big-endian).

To send the output from all `print` and `println` statements to a file (in addition to the screen), use `fopen`(*filename*`,"l"`).

*See also*
    `fclose`, `fflush`, `fprint` (for an example), `fread`, `fscan`, `fseek`, `fwrite`

# format

```
format(const sfmt);
```
    sfmt       in:   string: new default format for double or int
                       int: new line length for matrix printing

*No return value.*

*Description*
Use this function to specify the default format for double and int types. The function automatically recognizes whether the format string is for int or double (otherwise it is ignored). The specified double format will also be used for printing matrices. See under the `print` function for a complete description of the formatting strings.

Use an integer argument to set the line length for matrix printing (default is 80, the maximum is 1024).

The default format strings are:
    int       `"%d"`
    double   `"%5g"`
    matrix   each element `"%#13.5g"`, 6 elements on a
              line (depending on the line length).

Notes:

- The `print` function allows setting of format for the next argument only.
- Be careful with the `%f` format. For example, when printing 1e-300, the output field will need 302 characters.
- By default, integers and doubles are printed without a leading space. To use a space as separator: `format(" %d");`. Specifying a wider field can also insert extra spaces: `format("%6d");`. For a double, you could set the field to `"%#13.5g"`. Because at most 7 characters are needed on top of the 5 for significant digits, this format will always have at least one space.
- When a matrix is printed, no extra space is inserted between elements. So, make sure that the field width is at least one character larger than the maximum number of printed characters (as is the case for `"%#13.5g"` and `"%13.5g"`).

*See also*
    `fprint`, `print`, `sprint`

# fprint, fprintln

```
fprint(const file, const a, ...);
fprintln(const file, const a, ...);
     file       in:  file which is open for writing
     a          in:  any type
     ...        in:  any type
```

*Return value*

> Returns the number of arguments supplied to the function.

*Description*

> Prints to the specified file. See print for a further description. fprintln is as fprint but ensures the next output will be on a new line.

*See also*

> fclose, fopen, print

*Example*

```
#include <oxstd.h>
main()
{
    decl file = fopen("test.tmp", "w");

    fprintln(file, "some text" );

    fclose(file);
}
```

> produces a file test.tmp with the specified text.

# fread

```
fread(const file, const am, ...);
fread(const file, const am, const type, const r, const c);
     file       in:  file which is open for writing
     am         in:  address, address for storing read item
     type       in:  (optional argument), type of object to read, see below
     r          in:  (optional argument), number of rows to read; default is 1 if
                     argument is omitted
     c          in:  (optional argument), number of columns to read; default is 1
                     if argument is omitted, unless file is opened with f, in which
                     case the number of columns is read from the file
```

*Return value*

> Returns an integer:

> $-1$ nothing read, because end-of-file was reached;

0  nothing read, unknown error;

> 0  object read, return value is size which was actually read:

| type | data type read | return value |
|------|---------------|--------------|
| 'i', 'd' | integer | 1 |
| 'e', 'f' | double | 1 ($r$ and $c$ omitted, or both equal to 1) |
| 'e', 'f' | matrix | $r \times c$ |
| 'e', 'f' | matrix | $r$ (number of complete rows read; file opened with f in format) |
| 'c' | integer | 1 (if $r = 1$: just one byte read) |
| 'c' | string | $r$ (if $r > 1$: $r$ bytes read) |
| 's' | string | string length |
| '4' | float | 1 ($r$ and $c$ omitted, or both equal to 1) |
| '4' | float matrix | $r \times c$ |

When reading a matrix, for example as fread(file,&x,'f',r,c), the size of x will always be r by c. If less than rc elements could be read, the matrix is padded with zeros. If no elements could be read at all, because the end of the file was reached, the return value is –1.

The '4' format reads 4-byte real values ('float'), these are not written by Ox, but may be needed to read externally created files.

The 's' type reads a string up to (and including) the first null character or the end of file.

*Description*

Reads binary data from the specified file. The byte ordering is the platform specific ordering, unless the f format was used (also see fopen and fwrite).

*See also*

fclose, fopen, fscan, fseek, fwrite (for example using f format)

*Example*

A number of input/output examples is in the samples/inout directory. Below is samples/inout/inout7.ox. The programs inout10 and inout11 show how data can be read and written in blocks when the file is not a .fmt file.

This example writes a matrix as a .fmt file using savemat. Then the matrix is written using fread, in such a way that the same format is used.

Note that under Windows and MS-DOS these files are identical, but that on some platforms (such as the Sun) the files differ: iotest7.ox is little endian, but reading here assumes the platform ordering (which is big endian on a Sun).

```
#include <oxstd.h>
main()
{
    decl file, x;
    decl s, r, c, rc8;

    x = rann(2,3);
```

```
        x[0][] = double("tinker");
        savemat("iotest7.fmt", x);
                    // open mode: read, binary, little-endian
        file = fopen("iotest7.fmt", "rbe");
        fread(file, &s, 'c', 4);

        if (s == "\xDD\xEE\x86")
            println("signature OK");
        else
        {   println("signature NOT OK!");
            exit(1);
        }

        fread(file, &r, 'i');
        fread(file, &c, 'i');
        println("rows=", r, " columns=", c);

        fread(file, &rc8, 'i');
        fread(file, &x, 'f', r, c);
        println("-1 indicates eof: ", fread(file, &s, 'c', 1));
        if (feof(file))
            println("Was indeed end of file.");

        fclose(file);

        println(string(x[0][0]), x[1:][]);
    }
```

produces:

```
signature OK
rows=2 columns=3
-1 indicates eof: -1
Was indeed end of file.
tinker
        -0.91760      -0.67417       -0.34353
```

# fremove

```
fremove(const filename);
```
        filename                in:   name of file to remove

*Return value*

        Returns 1 if the file was removed successfully, 0 otherwise.

# fscan

```
fscan(const file, const a, ...);
    file      in:  file which is open for writing
    a         in:  any type
    ...       in:  any type
```

*Return value*

Returns the number of arguments successfully scanned and assigned, or -1 when the end of the file was encountered and nothing was read.

*Description*

Reads text from a file. The arguments are a list of scanning strings and the addresses of variables.

A scanning string consists of text, optionally with a format specifier which starts with a % symbol. The string is truncated after the format. Any text which precedes the format, is skipped in the file. A space character will skip any white space in the file.

If the scanning string holds a format (and assignment is not suppressed in the format), the string must be followed by the address of a variable.

The format specification is similar to that for the scanf function of the C language:

$$\%[* \text{ or } \#][width]type$$

The *width* argument specifies the width of the input field. A * suppresses assignment. A # can only be used with m and M.

Notes:

- The "%m" and "%M" formats can be used to read a matrix from a file. They first read the number of rows and columns, and then the matrix row by row; this corresponds to the format used by loadmat.
  No dimensions are read by "%#m" and "%#M", in that case the scanning string has to be followed by two integers indicating the number of rows and columns to be read. For fscan the two integers can be $-1$. In that case all numbers are read and returned as a column vector.
- The "%z" format reads a whole line up to \n, the \n (and \r) are removed from the return value. The line can be up to 2048 characters long (or whatever buffer size is set with sprintbuffer). If the line in the file is too long, the remainder is skipped.
- When scanning a string, the maximum string length which can be read is 2048. The sprintbuffer function can be used to enlarge the buffer size.
- The "%t" and "%T" formats can be used to read a token, using a simplified syntax that is similar to Ox code. Five types of tokens are distinguished:
  SCAN_EOF     End of the file or text.
  SCAN_IDENTIFIER   An identifier.
  SCAN_LITERAL   A literal integer, double or string.

**Table 8.1**   Formatting types for scanning.

| double *type*: | |
|---|---|
| e,f,g | field is scanned as a double value |
| le,lf,lg | field is scanned as a double value |
| C | field is scanned as a calendar double value |

| integer *type*: | |
|---|---|
| d | signed decimal notation, |
| i | signed decimal notation, |
| o | unsigned octal notation, |
| x | unsigned hexadecimal notation, |
| u | unsigned decimal notation, |
| c | (no width) scan a single character (i.e. one byte), |

| string *type*: | |
|---|---|
| s | scan a string up to the next white space, |
| z | scan a whole line, |
| c | (width > 1) scan a number of characters, |

| matrix *type*: | |
|---|---|
| m,M | scan a matrix row by row, |

| token *type*: | |
|---|---|
| t | scan a token, returning the value, |
| T | scan a token, returning a triplet. |

| *any type*: | |
|---|---|
| v | scan an Ox constant. |

SCAN_SYMBOL    A symbol.
SCAN_SPACE    White space.

The "%t" version returns the value that was read, while "%T" returns an array with three elements: the value, the actual text that was read and the token type (SCAN_...).

Note that a negative number is read as two tokens: a minus symbol and the value. Space is returned as a token. To skip leading spaces use " %t" and " %T".

The token format can be useful when a simple parser is required, or to read strings that are not delimited by white space. An example is given under sscan.

- The "%C" format is used to scan a date/time field written in ISO format: *yyyy-mm-dd*, *hh:mm::ss.hh*, or *yyyy-mm-ddThh:mm::ss.hh*. Examples are 1999-03-31, 13:10 (a 24-hour clock is used, seconds and hundreds are optional) and 1999-3-31T13:10.

Years with week number are also recognised, e.g. 1976-W3 returns the calendar index for the Monday of week 3 in 1976. (Week 1 is the first week that contains the first Thursday; or equivalently, the week that contains 4 January.)

- The "%v" format reads a variable that has been written in the format of an Ox constant. It is especially useful to read a variable that consist of a derived types, such as an array or a class object, but also for a matrix. When scanning a class object, the variable must already have the type of that class (using new), because the scan functions cannot create the object themselves. An example is given in ox/samples/inout/percent_v.ox and under the print function.

*See also*

fprint, fread, print, scan, sscan (for another example)

*Example*

The example (samples/inout/iotest2.ox) writes a file, and reads it twice. The first time, the string read is tinker123, but then reading gets stuck, because the word tailor can not be read is an integer, double or matrix. Failure to read the matrix dimension generates an error message.

The second time, the file is read properly.

```
#include <oxstd.h>
main()
{
    decl file;

    file = fopen("iotest2.txt", "w");
    fprint(file, "tinker123\ntailor456.78\n 2 2 1 0 0 1\n");
    fclose(file);

    decl c = -2, s, i = 0, d = 0, m = 0;

    file = fopen("iotest2.txt");
    println("Next statement will print message: "
        "\"load matrix: no matrix elements\"");

    c = fscan(file, "%s", &s,        // stops after &s
        "%d", &i, "%f", &d, "%m", &m);
    fclose(file);

    print("\nitems read=", c, " s=", s, " int=", i,
        " dbl=", d, " mat=", m);

    file = fopen("iotest2.txt");
    c = fscan(file, "tinker%d", &i, " tailor%f", &d, "%m", &m);
    fclose(file);

    print("\nitems read=", c, " int=", i, " dbl=", d,
        " mat=", m);

    // token example:
    decl str = "GMM(\"a\", 1.5, -3);";
```

```
    decl func, arg0, arg1, arg2, arg3;

    println("\ntoken string: ", str);
    sscan(str, "%t", &func, "( %t", &arg0, ", ", %f", &arg1,
        ", %d", &arg2);
    println("scanned using \"%t\": ", func, " ", arg0,
        " ", arg1, " ", arg2);

    sscan(str, "%T", &func, "(%T", &arg0, ", %T", &arg1,
        ", %T", &arg2, "%T", &arg3);
    println("scanned using \"%T\":", func, arg0, arg1, arg2, arg3);
}
```

produces

```
Next statement will print message: "load matrix: no matrix elements"
load matrix: no matrix elements

items read=1 s=tinker123 int=0 dbl=0 mat=0
items read=3 int=123 dbl=456.78 mat=
        1.0000          0.00000
        0.00000         1.0000

token string: GMM("a", 1.5, -3);
scanned using "%t": GMM a 1.5 -3
scanned using "%T":
[0] = GMM
[1] = GMM
[2] = 0

[0] = a
[1] = "a"
[2] = 1

[0] = 1.5
[1] = 1.5
[2] = 1

[0] = -
[1] = -
[2] = 2

[0] = 3
[1] = 3
[2] = 1
```

# fseek

```
fseek(const file);
fseek(const file, const type);
fseek(const file, const type, const r);
```
    `file`      in:  file which is open for writing

    `type`     in:  (optional argument), type of object use in seeking, see below

    `r`        in:  (optional argument), number of rows to move; default is 1 if argument is omitted

*Return value*

The first form, with only the `file` argument, tells the current position in the file as an offset from that start of the file (as the standard C function `ftell`).

The second and third form return 0 if the seek was successful, else a non-zero number,

*Description*

Repositions the file pointer to a new position specified from the start of a file. The `type` argument is interpreted as follows:

| type | seek data type | byte equivalent |
|------|----------------|-----------------|
| 'i', 'd' | integer | $4r$ |
| 'e', 'f' | double | $8r$ |
| 'e', 'f' | matrix rows | $16 + 8rc$ (file opened with f in format) |
| 'c' | character | $r$ |

So when a file is opened as `"rbf"`, `fseek(file,'f',r)` moves the file pointer to row $r$ in the `.fmt` file.

To position the file pointer at the end specify $-1$ for the third argument. This can be used to determine the length of a file, as the following example shows:

```
fseek(file, 'c', -1);        // move to end
length = fseek(file);        // get byte position at end
::fseek(file, 'c', 0);       // move to beginning
fread(file, &s, 'c', length); // read the whole file into s
```

*See also*

    `fclose`, `fopen`

*Example*

This example (`samples/inout/iotest9.ox`) reads and writes to a matrix opened with the f format. In that case, the number of columns applies to the whole file, and seeking is by row. Once the file file holds data, each subsequent write must match the number of columns already in the file.

```
#include <oxstd.h>
main()
{
    decl file, x, i;

    file = fopen("iotest9.fmt", "wbf");  // write
```

```
        fwrite(file, ones(1, 4));
        fwrite(file, 1 + ones(1, 4));
        fwrite(file, zeros(27, 4));

        fclose(file);

        file = fopen("iotest9.fmt", "abf");   // append
        println("file is ", rows(file), " by ", columns(file));

        fwrite(file, 2 + ones(1, 4));
        fclose(file);

        file = fopen("iotest9.fmt", "rbf");      // read
        println("file is ", rows(file), " by ", columns(file));

        fseek(file, 'f', 1);                 // second row
        fread(file, &x, 'f', 1);              // read it
        print("row of twos:", x);

        fseek(file, 'f', rows(file)-1);  // second row
        fread(file, &x, 'f', 1);   // read it
        print("row of threes:", x);
    }
```

produces:

```
file is 29 by 4
file is 30 by 4
row of twos:
        2.0000       2.0000       2.0000       2.0000
row of threes:
        3.0000       3.0000       3.0000       3.0000
```

# fsize

```
fsize(const file);
    file      in:  an open file
```

*Return value*

Returns the size of the file in bytes (an integer).

# fwrite

```
fwrite(const file, const a);
    file      in:  file which is open for writing
    a         in:  int, double, matrix or string
```

*Return value*

Returns 0 if failed to write, or the number of items written to the file:

| input | return value (integer) |
|---|---|
| integer | 1, |
| double | 1, |
| $m \times n$ matrix | number of elements written (normally $m \times n$), |
| $m \times n$ matrix | opened with f format: no of rows written (normally $m$), |
| string | number of characters written. |

*Description*

Writes binary data to the specified file. The byte ordering is the platform specific ordering, unless the f format was used (also see fopen), in which case writing is to a .fmt file in little-endian mode (also see savemat). When data is written to a .fmt file, the number of columns must match that already in the file (use columns(file) to ask for the number of columns in the file).

*See also*

fclose, fopen, fread, fseek (for example using f format)

*Example*

A number of input/output examples is in the samples/inout directory. Below is samples/inout/inout6.ox, which saves a matrix as a .ftm file using savemat. Then the matrix is written using fwrite, in such a way that the same format is used. See under fread for a read example.

Note that under Windows and MS-DOS these files are identical, but that on some platforms (such as the Sun) the files differ: iotest6a.fmt is little endian, but iotest6b.fmt big endian. So on a Sun, using loadmat on iotest6b.fmt fails to read the matrix correctly.

The example also shows how a short string can be stores in matrix, and retrieved from it.

```
#include <oxstd.h>
main()
{
    decl file, x = rann(2,3);
    x[0][] = double("tinker");
    savemat("iotest6a.fmt", x);
                                    // force little-endian mode
    file = fopen("iotest6b.fmt", "wbe");
//  two ways if writing signature, first:
//  decl s = new string[4];      // need four bytes
//  s[0:2] = "\xDD\xEE\x86";     // signature is DDEE8600
//  fwrite(file, s);
//
//  and second way:
    fprint(file, "%c", 0xdd, "%c", 0xee, "%c", 0x86, "%c", 0x00);

    fwrite(file, rows(x));
    fwrite(file, columns(x));
    fwrite(file, rows(x) * columns(x) * 8);
    fwrite(file, x);
```

```
        fclose(file);

        decl y = loadmat("iotest6b.fmt");

        println(string(x[0][0]), string(y[0][0]), x[1][1]-y[1][1]);
    }
```

produces: `tinkertinker0`

# fuzziness

```
fuzziness(const deps);
        deps        in:   double, 0 or new fuzziness value
```

*Return value*

Sets and returns the new fuzziness parameter if `deps` $> 0$. If `deps` $\leq 0$, no new fuzziness value is set, but the current one is returned. The default fuzziness is $10^{-13}$.

*See also*

`isfeq`

# gammafact

```
gammafact(const ma);
        ma          in:   arithmetic type
```

*Return value*

Returns the complete gamma function at the value of each element of `ma`, of double or matrix type.

For argument zero, or a negative integer, the function returns .NaN.

*Description*

Computes the gamma function at the argument:

$$\Gamma(a) = \int_0^\infty x^{a-1} e^{-x} \mathrm{d}x.$$

Note that:

$$a\Gamma(a) = \Gamma(a+1).$$

The gamma function is related to the factorial for integer arguments: if $a = i$ is integer then $\Gamma(i+1) = i!$.

Often a ratio of gamma functions is needed. Since the Gamma function can overflow quite rapidly, it is advised to use the `loggamma` function instead.

The function is accurate to about 14 to 15 significant digits (a table is used to look up integer values up to 13). The approximation uses a series expansion of the reciprocal for arguments $\leq 13$ (see Abramowitz and Stegun, 1984, §6.1.34). Otherwise the exponential of the loggamma is used. For negative arguments the following relation is used:

$$\Gamma(a) = -\frac{\pi}{\sin(\pi a)a\Gamma(-a)}.$$

*See also*
>    factorial, gammafunc, loggamma, polygamma

# gammafunc

```
gammafunc(const dx, const dr);
```
|   |   |   |
|---|---|---|
| mx | in: | $x$, arithmetic type |
| mr | in: | $r$, arithmetic type |

*Return value*
>    Returns the incomplete gamma function $G_x(r)$. Returns 0 if $r \leq 0$ or $x \leq 0$. The accuracy is to about 10 digits.
>    The return type is derived as follows:

| returns | mx | mr |
|---|---|---|
| $m \times n$ matrix | $m \times n$ matrix | scalar |
| $m \times n$ matrix | scalar | $m \times n$ matrix |
| $m \times n$ matrix | $m \times n$ matrix | $m \times n$ matrix |
| double | scalar | scalar |

*Description*
>    The incomplete gamma function is defined as:

$$G_x(r) = \int_0^t \frac{1}{\Gamma(r)} x^{r-1} e^{-t} \mathrm{d}t, \quad t > 0, r > 0.$$

>    Source: gammafunc uses Applied Statistics algorithm AS 239 (Shea, 1988).

*See also*
>    betafunc, loggamma, probgamma

*Example*
```
#include <oxstd.h>
#include <oxprob.h>        // required for probgamma
main()
{
    print(probgamma(5.99, 1, 0.5), " ",
            gammafunc(5.99 * 0.5, 1), "\n");
    print(probgamma(5.99, 0.5, 1), " ",
            gammafunc(5.99, 0.5) );
}
```
produces
```
0.949963 0.949963
0.999462 0.999462
```

# getcwd

```
getcwd();
```

*Return value*

Returns the current directory.
*Windows specific*: returns the current directory on the current drive. Use chdir
to change the current drive.

*See also*

chdir, getfiles (for example), systemcall

# getenv

```
getenv(const senv);
    senv        in:   string
```

*Return value*

Returns a string with the value of the environment variable, or an empty string if
the environment variable is undefined.

# getfiles

```
getfiles(const sfilemask);
    sfilemask  in:   string, mask for files, may have a path or wild cards
```

*Return value*

Returns an array of strings with filenames matching the specified mask.

*See also*

chdir, getcwd

*Example*

```
#include <oxstd.h>

main()
{
    println("Current folder = ", getcwd());
    chdir("D:\\OxMetrics6\\ox\\include");
    //default:chdir("C:\\Program Files\\OxMetrics6\\ox\\include");
    println("Current folder = ", getcwd());
    println("Files in folder: ", getfiles("*.ox"));
}
```

produces

```
Current folder = D:\Waste
Current folder = D:\OxMetrics6\ox\include
Files in folder:
[0] = g2ox.ox
[1] = oxgauss.ox
[2] = ox_init.ox
```

# idiv, imod

```
idiv(const ia, const ib);
imod(const ia, const ib);
    ia          in:  arithmetic type
    ib          in:  arithmetic type
```

*Return value*

The imod function returns the integer remainder of int(ia) / int(ib). The sign of the result is that of ia.

The idiv function returns the result of the integer division int(ia) / int(ib). The return type is a matrix of integer values if either arguments is a matrix, else it is a scalar int.

*See also*

fmod

*Example*

```
#include <oxstd.h>
main()
{
    print( idiv(3,2), " ", idiv(-4,2), " ",
           idiv(3,-2), " ", idiv(-4,-2), " ");
    print( imod(3,2), " ", imod(-3,2), " ",
           imod(3,-2), " ", imod(-3,-2) );
}
```

produces: 1 -2 -1 2 1 -1 1 -1

# insertc, insertr

```
insertc(const ma, const c, const cadd);
insertr(const ma, const r, const radd);
insertr(const aa, const r, const radd);
    ma          in:  $m \times n$ matrix to insert into
    aa          in:  $m$ array to delete from
    c           in:  scalar, column index of insertion
    cadd        in:  scalar, number of columns of zeros to add
    r           in:  scalar, row index of insertion
    radd        in:  scalar, number of rows of zeros to add
```

*Return value*

The insertc function returns a copy of the input matrix with the specified columns of zeros inserted.

The insertr function returns a copy of the input matrix with the specified rows of zeros inserted; insertr also works for arrays.

*See also*

dropc (for an example), dropr

# int

```
int(const ma);
```
        ma              in:   arithmetic type

*Return value*

Casts the argument to an integer:

| input | returns |
|-------|---------|
| integer | unchanged |
| double | rounded towards zero |
| matrix | element 0,0 rounded towards zero |
| string | element 0 |
| other types | error |

*See also*

ceil (for an example), double , matrix , trunc, §13.8.2.3

# intersection

```
intersection(const ma, const mb);
intersection(const ma, const mb, const amidx);
```
        ma              in:   matrix
        mb              in:   matrix
        amidx           in:   address of matrix
                        out:  $2 \times c$ matrix, the first row is the index of the common
                              elements in vecr(ma), the second row is the index in
                              vecr(mb). The order of the indices correspond to the order
                              of the return value.

*Return value*

Returns the sorted unique elements of ma which are also in mb as a $1 \times c$ vector,
where $c$ is the number of elements ma and mb have in common. Returns an empty
matrix if the result is empty. Missing values are skipped.

*See also*

exclusion (for an example), unique

# invert

```
invert(const ma);
invert(const ma, const alogdet, const asign);
```

| | | |
|---|---|---|
| ma | in: | $m \times m$ real matrix $A$ |
| alogdet | in: | (optional argument) address of variable |
| | out: | double, the *logarithm* of the absolute value of the determinant of $A$ |
| asign | in: | (optional argument) address of variable |
| | out: | int, the sign of the determinant of $A$; 0: singular; $-1, -2$: negative determinant; $+1, +2$: positive determinant; $-2, +2$: result is unreliable |

*Return value*

Returns the inverse of $A$, or the value 0 if the decomposition failed.

*Description*

Inverts the matrix $A$ using the LU decomposition (see under declu). The exponent of the log-absolute-determinant can only be computed for values $\leq$ DBL_MAX_E_EXP and $\geq$ DBL_MIN_E_EXP (see Ch. 9).

Note that 1 / ma also returns the inverse (more precisely: if ma is square, invert is tried, if that fails, or the matrix is not square, the generalized inverse is used), see §13.8.5 and invertgen.

*Error and warning messages*

invert(): decomposition failed (the matrix is numerically singular)

*See also*

declu, invertgen, invertsym, logdet

*Example*

```
#include <oxstd.h>
main()
{
    decl mp;

    mp = <4,1;1,3>;
    print(invert(mp)*mp, invertsym(mp)*mp);
}
```

produces (note that the both matrices are the identity matrix: whether it has zeros, or nearly zeros, could dependent on which Ox version was used):

```
     1.0000 -2.7756e-017
    0.00000       1.0000

     1.0000 -2.7756e-017
    0.00000       1.0000
```

# inverteps

```
inverteps(const dEps);
```
    dEps        in:  sets the inversion epsilon $\epsilon_{inv}$ to dEps if dEps $> 0$, to the default if dEps $< 0$; leaves the value unchanged if dEps $==$ 0

*Return value*

    Returns the inversion epsilon (the new value if dEps != 0).

*Description*

    The following functions return singular status if the pivoting element is less than or equal to $\epsilon_{inv}$: decldl, declu, decldlband, invert, invertsym, orthmgs. Less than $10\epsilon_{inv}$ is used by olsc and olsr.

    A singular value is considered zero when less than $||A||_\infty 10\epsilon_{inv}$ in rank, nullspace, and when using the generalized inverse.

    The default value for $\epsilon_{inv}$ is $1000 \times$ DBL_EPSILON.

# invertgen

```
invertgen(const ma);
invertgen(const ma, const mode);
```
    ma          in:  $m \times n$ matrix $A$

    mode       in:  int, mode of inversion (optional argument, default is 0)

*Return value*

    Returns the (generalized) inverse of $A$, or the value 0 if the decomposition failed.

*Description*

| mode | description | $A$ |
|------|-------------|-----|
| 0 | generalized inverse using SVD | |
| 1 | gen. symmetric p.s.d. inverse using SVD | $m = n$, symmetric p.s.d. |
| 2,20 | first try invert then mode 0 | $m = n$ |
| 3,30 | first try invertsym then mode 1 | $m = n$, symmetric p.s.d. |
| 4,40 | use olsc (QR dec.) for inverse of $A'A$ | $m \geq n$ |
| $\geq 10$ | print warning if matrix is singular | |

  0.  When mode equals 0, or the mode argument is omitted, invertgen defaults to the generalized inverse (see §13.8.5.1) when only one argument is used.

  1.  When mode equals 1, the matrix must be symmetric positive semi-definite. The generalized inverse can use the fact that $\mathbf{U} = \mathbf{V}$ in the singular value decomposition. *Do not use this mode for negative definite matrices.*

2. Mode 2 first tries the normal inversion routine (`invert`), and then, if the matrix is singular, uses the generalized inverse. This mode is the same as using `1 / x`.
3. Mode 3 first tries the normal inversion routine (`invertsym`), and then, if the matrix is singular, uses the generalized inverse (as mode 1). *Do not use this mode for negative definite matrices.*
4. Mode 4 uses the QR decomposition, and the inverse is the same as obtained from using `olsc`. This is a different type of generalized inverse, so that, when the matrix is singular a different value is obtained then from the other modes.

If the matrix is full rank, the generalized inverse equals the normal inverse (for modes 1,3 this also requires symmetry and positive definiteness).

When the mode argument is multiplied by ten, a warning is printed if the matrix is singular (or negative definite for mode 30), but the return value is not affected.

*Error and warning messages*
 invertgen: invert failed, proceeding with generalized inverse (mode 20
 invertgen: invertsym failed, proceeding with generalized p.s.d. inverse (mode 30)
 invertgen: matrix has reduced rank (mode 40)
 invertgen: decomposition failed (some other problem)

*See also*
 `invert, invertsym`

*Example*
```
#include <oxstd.h>
main()
{
    decl x, xx;
    x = rann(20,2);
    x = x ~ x[][0];
    xx = x'x;

    println("\nAA^A=A:");
    print(xx * invertgen(xx, 30) * xx - xx);
    print(xx * invertgen(x, 40) * xx - xx);

    println("These generalized inverses are different:");
    print("Choleski failed, so use SVD", invertgen(xx, 3));
    print("Using QR", invertgen(x, 4));
}
```

produces (note that the exact value of the zeros can depend on the computer platform and the version of Ox):

```
AA^A=A:
Warning: invertgen: singular matrix
```

```
invertgen.ox (10): main

   3.5527e-015 -1.3323e-015  3.5527e-015
  -1.3323e-015  3.5527e-015 -1.3323e-015
   3.5527e-015 -1.3323e-015  3.5527e-015
Warning: invertgen: singular matrix
invertgen.ox (11): main

   3.5527e-015  4.4409e-016  3.5527e-015
   4.4409e-016 -3.5527e-015  4.4409e-016
   3.5527e-015  4.4409e-016  3.5527e-015
These generalized inverses are different:
Choleski failed, so use SVD
      0.014260    -0.0023020       0.014260
     -0.0023020    0.049276      -0.0023020
      0.014260    -0.0023020       0.014260
Using QR
      0.057041    -0.0046039       0.00000
     -0.0046039     0.049276       0.00000
      0.00000       0.00000        0.00000
```

# invertsym

```
invertsym(const ma);
invertsym(const ma, const alogdet);
```

|           |      |                                                          |
|-----------|------|----------------------------------------------------------|
| ma        | in:  | symmetric, positive definite $m \times m$ matrix $A$     |
| alogdet   | in:  | (optional argument) address of variable                  |
|           | out: | double, the *logarithm* of the determinant of $A$        |

*Return value*

Returns the inverse of $A$, or the value 0 if the decomposition failed.

*Description*

Inverts the symmetric positive definite matrix $A$ using the Choleski decomposition (see under decldl). The exponent of the log-determinant can only be computed for values $\leq$ DBL_MAX_E_EXP and $\geq$ DBL_MIN_E_EXP (see Ch. 9).

*Error and warning messages*

invertsym(): decomposition failed (the matrix is numerically singular or negative definite)

*See also*

decldl, invert (for an example), invertgen

# isarray, isclass, isdouble, isfile, isfunction, isint, ismatrix, ismember, isstring

```
isarray(const a);
isclass(const a);
isclass(const a, const sclass);
isdouble(const a);
isfile(const a);
isfunction(const a);
isint(const a);
ismatrix(const a);
ismember(const a, const smember);
isstring(const a);
```
|        |     |                        |
|--------|-----|------------------------|
| a      | in: | any type               |
| sclass | in: | string, class name     |
| smember| in: | string, member name    |

*Return value*

Returns TRUE (i.e. the value 1) if the argument is of the correct type, FALSE (0) otherwise.

`isclass(a, "class")` returns TRUE if a is an object of type `"class"`, or derived from `"class"`.

`ismember` returns 1 if a is an object of a class and has a function member `"smember"`; 2 if `"smember"` is a data member and 0 otherwise.

*See also*

classname

# isdotfeq, isfeq

```
isdotfeq(const ma, const mb);
isfeq(const ma, const mb);
```
|    |     |                 |
|----|-----|-----------------|
| ma | in: | arithmetic type |
| mb | in: | arithmetic type |

*Return value*

`isfeq` always returns an integer: it returns 1 if the argument ma is fuzzy equal to mb, 0 otherwise. When strings are compared, the comparison is case insensitive.

`iseq` is as `isfeq`, but using fuzziness of zero. When strings are compared, the comparison is case sensitive.

`isdotfeq` returns a matrix if either argument is a matrix; the matrix consists of 0's and 1's: 1 if the comparison holds, 0 otherwise. If both arguments are scalar, `isdotfeq` is equal to `isfeq`.

In both cases the current fuzziness value is used.

*See also*

> fuzziness

*Example*

```
#include <oxstd.h>
main()
{
    decl m1 = <1+1e-17,1-1e-17;1+1e-17,1-1e-17 >;
    decl m2 = <1+1e-17,1-1e-10;1+1e-17,1-1e-17 >;

    print( "m1 is ", isfeq(m1,1) ? "" : "*** not *** ",
        "fuzzy equal to 1\n");
    print( "m2 is ", isfeq(m2,1) ? "" : "*** not *** ",
        "fuzzy equal to 1\n");
    print(isdotfeq(m1,1));
}
```

produces

```
m1 is fuzzy equal to 1
m2 is *** not *** fuzzy equal to 1
        1.0000          1.0000
        1.0000          1.0000
```

# isdotinf

```
isdotinf(const ma);
    ma              in:   arithmetic type
```

*Return value*

> Returns a matrix of the same dimensions if the input is a matrix; the returned matrix consists of 0's and 1's: 1 if the element is +/- infinity, 0 otherwise. If the arguments is a double, isdotinf returns 1 if the double is +/- infinity.

*See also*

> isdotmissing, isdotnan

# isdotmissing, isdotnan, ismissing, isnan

```
isdotmissing(const ma);
isdotnan(const ma);
ismissing(const ma);
isnan(const ma);
    ma              in:   arithmetic type
```

*Return value*

> isnan always returns an integer: it returns 1 if *any* element in ma is .NaN (not a number), 0 otherwise. .NaN can be used to indicate a missing value.

isdotnan returns a matrix of the same dimensions if the input is a matrix; the returned matrix consists of 0's and 1's: 1 if the element is NaN, 0 otherwise. If the arguments is a double, isdotnan returns 1 if the double is NaN.

ismissing and isdotmissing are similar to isnan and isdotnan respectively. However, in addition to NaN, they also treat $+/-$ infinity as a missing value.

*See also*

deletec, deleter, selectc, selectr

*Example*

```
#include <oxstd.h>
main()
{
    decl m1 = <1,2,3;4,5,6;7,8,9 >;
    decl m2 = <1,.,3;4,5,.;7,8,9 >;

    print( "m1 has ", isnan(m1) ? "" : "*** no *** ",
        "missing values\n");
    print( "m2 has ", isnan(m2) ? "" : "*** no *** ",
        "missing values\n");

    print(isdotnan(m2));
    print("m2", m2, "rows with NaN deleted",
        deleter(m2), deleteifr(m2, isdotnan(m2)));
}
```

produces

```
m1 has *** no *** missing values
m2 has missing values

        0.00000        1.0000        0.00000
        0.00000        0.00000        1.0000
        0.00000        0.00000        0.00000
m2
        1.0000          .NaN        3.0000
        4.0000        5.0000          .NaN
        7.0000        8.0000        9.0000
rows with NaN deleted
        7.0000        8.0000        9.0000

        7.0000        8.0000        9.0000
```

# lag0

```
lag0(const ma, const ilag);
lag0(const ma, const ilag, double dmisval);
```
|  |  |  |
|--|--|--|
| ma | in: | $T \times n$ matrix |
| ilag | in: | int, lag length, or matrix with lag lengths |
| dmisval | in: | (optional argument) double, value to set missing observations to (default is 0) |

*Return value*

Returns a $T \times n$ matrix with the lags of the specified matrix, whereby missing values are replaced by zero. E.g. the result matrix r using two lags is:

```
r[0][0] = 0           r[0][1] = 0         ...
r[1][0] = 0           r[1][1] = 0         ...
r[2][0] = m[0][0]     r[2][1] = m[0][1]   ...
r[3][0] = m[1][0]     r[3][1] = m[1][1]   ...
...
```

The result has the same dimensions as ma.

If ilag is a matrix the return value corresponds to lag0(.,ilag[0]) ~ lag0(.,ilag[1]) ~...

*Description*

Lags the specified matrix, missing values are replaced by zero (unless a missing value is specified as the third argument). Using the lag operator (also called backshift operator) $L$: this computes:

$$L^k a_t = a_{t-k} \quad \text{for} \quad t - k \geq 0,$$

and 0 for $t - k < 0$.

Note that a negative value for ilag will create leads.

*See also*

diff0

*Example*

```
#include <oxstd.h>
#include <oxfloat.h>              // reguired for M_NAN
main()
{
    print( lag0(<1:5>',2) ~ lag0(<1:5>',2, M_NAN) );
}
```

produces

```
    0.00000        .NaN
    0.00000        .NaN
    1.0000        1.0000
    2.0000        2.0000
    3.0000        3.0000
```

# limits

```
limits(const ma);
       ma              in:  m × n matrix
```

*Return value*

Returns a $4 \times n$ matrix:

| | |
|---|---|
| 1st row: | minimum of each column of ma |
| 2nd row: | maximum of each column of ma |
| 3rd row: | row index of minimum (lowest index if more than one exists) |
| 4th row: | row index of maximum (lowest index if more than one exists) |

*See also*

max, maxc, maxcindex, min, mincindex

*Example*

```
#include <oxstd.h>
main()
{
    decl m = rann(7,2);
    print( range(0, rows(m)-1)' ~ m,
        "%r", {"column min","column max",
        "row index of min","row index of max"}, limits(m) );
}
```

produces

```
       0.00000       0.22489        1.7400
       1.0000       -0.20426       -0.91760
       2.0000       -0.67417       -0.34353
       3.0000        0.22335       -0.14139
       4.0000       -0.18338        0.68035
       5.0000        0.090558      -0.83328
       6.0000        0.81350        1.1174

column min            -0.67417       -0.91760
column max             0.81350        1.7400
row index of min       2.0000         1.0000
row index of max       6.0000         0.00000
```

# loadmat

```
loadmat(const sname);
loadmat(const sname, const iFormat);
loadmat(const sname, const aasVarNames);
```
|  |  |  |
|---|---|---|
| sname | in: | string containing an existing file name |
| iFormat | in: | (optional argument, .mat matrix file only) |
|  |  | 1: file has no matrix dimensions; then the matrix is returned as a column vector, and shape could be used to create a differently shaped matrix. |
|  | in: | (optional argument, .xls Excel file only) |
|  |  | 1: strings are loaded as values and dates translated to Ox dates, as in OxMetrics or the database class. |
|  |  | 0 (the default): strings are treated as empty cells, unless a dot or starting with #N/A), and dates are read using the Excel numbering instead of Ox. For a date after 1-Mar-1900: oxdate = exceldate + 2415019. |
| aasVarNames | in: | (optional argument, not for .mat matrix files) address of variable |
|  | out: | array of strings, names of data columns. |

*Return value*

Returns the matrix which was read, or 0 if the operation failed.

*Description*

The type of file read depends on the extension of the file name:

|  |  |
|---|---|
| .mat | matrix file (text file), described below, |
| .dat | data file (text file) with load information, |
| .in7 | PcGive 7 data file (with corresponding .bn7 file), |
| .xls | Excel worksheet or workbook file (binary file), |
| .csv | comma-separated spread sheet file (text file), |
| .dta | Stata data file (version 4–6), |
| .dht | Gauss data file (v89, with corresponding .dat file), |
| .fmt | Gauss matrix file (v89 and v96), |
| any other | as .mat file. |

This function does not retrieve information on data frequency and sample periods. To retrieve such information, use the Database class.

A matrix file holds a matrix, preceded by two integers which specify the number of rows and columns of the matrix. It will normally have the .mat extension. White space and a comma between numbers is skipped. If a symbol is found which is not a number, then the rest of the line will be skipped (so, e.g. everything following ; or // is treated as comments). The exception to this is an isolated dot, the letter m or M or the word .NaN: these are interpreted as a missing element with value NaN (Not a Number); .Inf is interpreted as infinity. An example of a matrix file is:

```
2 3          //<-- dimensions, a 2 by 3 matrix
//comment    //<-- a line of comment
1 0 0        //<-- first row of the matrix
0 1 .5       //<-- second row of the matrix
```

If the iFormat argument equals 1, the file is assumed not to contain matrix dimension (if it does, they will be the first two elements in the matrix).

The other file formats are described in more detail in the the Database class, under the Load functions, and in the *OxMetrics* book. Note that all file formats work identically on whatever platform Ox runs on. So an .xls file could be written with Ox on a Sun, then transferred (in binary mode) to a Windows machine, and read into Ox for Windows. Ox takes care of differences in byte ordering when writing and reading binary files (always using little-endian format). This also means that a v89 .fmt written by Ox on the Sun can be read by Ox under Windows. Gauss under Unix writes v89 .fmt files in a different format. The only exception are v96 .fmt files, which write the data in the format that is native to the platform on which Ox is running. The file stores information on the byte ordering, and such a file can be read on any platform.

*Warning: Excel may write csv files with only single precision (9 significant digits, rather than the 17 that are needed for loss-less saving).*

*Error and warning messages*
 loadmat(): file not found
 loadmat(): no matrix elements
 loadmat(): not enough matrix elements

*See also*
 Database class, savemat, shape

*Example*
```
#include <oxstd.h>
main()
{
    decl m = unit(2), as;

    savemat("t.mat", m);
    print(m, loadmat("t.mat"));

    savemat("t.in7", m, {"AA", "BB"});
    loadmat("t.in7", &as);
    println("names", as);
}
```
produces

```
              1.0000        0.00000
              0.00000       1.0000

              1.0000        0.00000
              0.00000       1.0000
names
[0] = AA
[1] = BB
```

and a file called t.mat:

```
2 2
     1.0000000000000000e+000    0.0000000000000000e+000
     0.0000000000000000e+000    1.0000000000000000e+000
```

# log, log10

```
log(const ma);
log10(const ma);
     ma              in:   arithmetic type
```

*Return value*

The log function returns the natural logarithm of each element of ma, of double or matrix type.

The log10 function returns the logarithm (base 10) of each element of ma, of double or matrix type.

*See also*

exp

*Example*

```
#include <oxstd.h>
main()
{
    print( log(<1,10>) );
    print( log10(<1,10>) );

    // the following shows how to prevent log(0)
    // in the computation of y*log(y) using the
    // dot-conditional operator:
    decl y = range(0,4);
    print(y .* log(y .> 0 .? y .: 1));
}
```

produces

```
          0.00000    2.3026
          0.00000    1.0000
          0.00000    0.00000    1.3863    3.2958    5.5452
```

# logdet

```
logdet(const ma, const asign);
```
    ma        in:  $m \times m$ real matrix $A$

    asign     in:  address of variable

                out: int, the sign of the determinant of $A$;  0:  singular; $-1, -2$: negative determinant; $+1, +2$: positive determinant; $-2, +2$: result is unreliable

*Return value*

    Returns a double: the *logarithm* of the absolute value of the determinant of $A$ (1.0 if the matrix is singular).

*Description*

    Computes the determinant (the log of the absolute value and the sign) of a matrix using the LU decomposition of the matrix (see declu). The exponent of log-absolute-determinant can only be computed for values $\leq$ DBL_MAX_E_EXP and $\geq$ DBL_MIN_E_EXP (see Ch. 9).

*See also*

    determinant, invert

# loggamma

```
loggamma(const ma);
```
    ma        in:  arithmetic type

*Return value*

    Returns the logarithm of the complete gamma function at the value of each element of ma, of double or matrix type.

    Returns .Inf for argument zero, and .NaN for any argument less than zero.

*Description*

    Computes the logarithm of the gamma function at the argument:

$$\log \Gamma(a) = \log \int_0^\infty x^{a-1} e^{-x} \mathrm{d}x \quad \text{for } a > 0.$$

If $a = i$ is integer then $\Gamma(i+1) = i!$.

Often the ratio of two gamma functions needs te be computed. This can be done as $\Gamma(a)/\Gamma(b) = \exp(\log \Gamma(a) - \log \Gamma(b))$, thus reducing the risk of overflow for large arguments.

The function is accurate to about 14 to 15 significant digits (a table is used to look up integer values up to 50). The approximation uses the recurrence relation to obtain an argument greater than $8.5$; then an asymptotic formula with eight terms is applied (see Abramowitz and Stegun, 1984, §6.1.40).

*See also*
    gammafact, gammafunc, polygamma

*Example*
```
#include <oxstd.h>
main()
{
    print( loggamma(<0.5,1,10>) );
}
```

produces

        0.57236        0.00000        12.802


# lower

```
lower(const ma);
```
    ma              in:  $m \times n$ matrix

*Return value*
    Returns the lower diagonal (including the diagonal), i.e. returns a copy of the
    input matrix with strict upper-diagonal elements set to zero.

*See also*
    setdiagonal, setupper, setlower, upper

*Example*
```
#include <oxstd.h>
main()
{
    print( lower(ones(3,3)) );
    print( upper(ones(3,3)) );
}
```

produces

        1.0000        0.00000        0.00000
        1.0000        1.0000         0.00000
        1.0000        1.0000         1.0000

        1.0000        1.0000         1.0000
        0.00000       1.0000         1.0000
        0.00000       0.00000        1.0000


# matrix

```
matrix(const ma);
```
    ma              in:  arithmetic type

*Return value*

Casts the argument to a matrix:

| input | returns |
|---|---|
| integer | a $1 \times 1$ matrix |
| double | a $1 \times 1$ matrix |
| matrix | unchanged |
| string | a $1 \times 1$ matrix |
| other types | error |

*See also*

int, double, §13.8.2.3

# max

```
max(const a, ...);
    a           in:  arithmetic type
    ...         in:  arithmetic type
```

*Return value*

Returns the maximum value in all the arguments. The return type is int if all arguments are of type int; otherwise the return type is double.

*Description*

Finds the maximum value in the arguments, ignoring missing values. Use the dot-relational operator to find the element-by-element maximum or mimimum, see Ch. 5.

*See also*

limits, maxc, min

*Example*

```
#include <oxstd.h>
main()
{
    print( min(<1.5,12.5>, 1, 6), " ", max(<1.5,12.5>, 1, 6) );
}
```

produces: 1 12.5

# maxc, maxcindex

```
maxc(const ma);
maxcindex(const ma);
    ma          in:  T × n matrix A
```

*Return value*

The maxc function returns a $1 \times n$ matrix holding the maximum of each column of ma.

The maxcindex function returns a $1 \times n$ matrix holding the row index of the maximum of each column of ma.

*Description*

Finds the maximum value in each column, ignoring missing values. If no maximum is found (a column has all missing values), then the maximum is .NaN, and the index $-1$.

*See also*

limits, max, minc, mincindex

*Example*

```
#include <oxstd.h>
main()
{
    decl x = <11,12;10,15>;
    print("x = ", x);
    println("maxc and maxcindex", maxc(x) ~ maxcindex(x));
    println("minc and mincindex", minc(x) ~ mincindex(x));
}
```

produces

```
x =
        11.000        12.000
        10.000        15.000
maxc and maxcindex
        11.000        15.000       0.00000        1.0000
minc and mincindex
        10.000        12.000        1.0000       0.00000
```

# meanc, meanr

```
meanc(const ma);
meanr(const ma);
```
    ma              in:  $T \times n$ matrix $A$

*Return value*

The meanc function returns a $1 \times n$ matrix holding the means of the columns of ma.

The meanr function returns a $T \times 1$ matrix holding the means of the rows of ma.

*See also*

sumc, sumr, varc, variance (for an example), varr

# min

```
min(const a, ...);
    a           in:  arithmetic type
    ...         in:  arithmetic type
```

*Return value*

Returns the minimum value in all the arguments, ignoring missing values. The return type is int if all arguments are of type int; otherwise the return type is double.

*Description*

Finds the minimum value in the arguments. Use the dot-relational operator to find the element-by-element maximum, see Ch. 5.

*See also*

limits, max (for an example), minc

# minc, mincindex

```
minc(const ma);
mincindex(const ma);
    ma          in:  $T \times n$ matrix $A$
```

*Return value*

The minc function returns a $1 \times n$ matrix holding the minimum of each column of ma.

The mincindex function returns a $1 \times n$ matrix holding the row index of the minimum of each column of ma.

*Description*

Finds the minimum value in each column, ignoring missing values. If no minimum is found (a column has all missing values), then the minimum is .NaN, and the index $-1$.

*See also*

limits, maxc, maxcindex, min

# moments

```
moments(const ma);
moments(const ma, const k);
moments(const ma, const k, const fratio);
    ma          in:  $T \times n$ matrix $A$
    k           in:  (optional argument) no of moments $k$ (default is $k = 4$)
    fratio      in:  (optional argument) 0: no ratios (default is moment ratios)
```

*Return value*

Returns an $(k + 1) \times n$ matrix holding in each column for the corresponding column of ma:

| row | holds | description |
|---|---|---|
| 0 | $T^*$ | effective sample size |
| 1 | $m_1$ | sample mean |
| 2 | $m_2^{1/2}$ | sample standard deviation |
| 3 | $\sqrt{b_1} = m_3/(m_2^{3/2})$ | sample skewness |
| 4 | $b_2 = m_4/(m_2^2)$ | sample kurtosis |
| ... | | |
| k | $m_k/(m_2^{k/2})$ | sample $k$th central moment ratio (i.e. in deviation from mean) |

If fratio equals 0, the moments are not divided:

| row | holds | description |
|---|---|---|
| 0 | $T^*$ | effective sample size |
| 1 | $m_1$ | sample mean |
| 2 | $m_2$ | sample variance |
| ... | | |
| k | $m_k$ | sample $k$th central moment (i.e. in deviation from mean) |

*Description*

Computes the central moment ratios or central moments. Skips missing values.

*See also*

meanc, meanr, standardize, varc, varr

*Example*

The normal distribution $N[\mu, \sigma^2]$ has central moments:

$$\mu_r = \mathsf{E}\left[X - \mathsf{E}X\right]^r = \begin{cases} 0 & \text{if } r \text{ is odd,} \\ \frac{r!}{(r/2)!} \frac{\sigma^r}{2^{r/2}} & \text{if } r \text{ is even.} \end{cases}$$

So the standard normal distribution has skewness

$$\sqrt{\beta_1} = \mu_3/\mu_2^{3/2} = 0,$$

and kurtosis

$$\beta_2 = \mu_4/\mu_2^2 = 3.$$

The exponential distribution $\exp(\lambda)$ has moments about zero:

$$\mu_r' = \mathsf{E}X^r = \frac{r!}{\lambda^r}.$$

Therefore, when $\lambda = 2$, the mean is $1/2$, the variance $1/2 - 1/4 = 1/4$, etc.

```
#include <oxstd.h>
#include <oxprob.h>
main()
{
    decl m1 = rann(10000,1) ~ ranexp(10000,1, 2);

    print("moment ratios",
          "%r", {"T","mean","std.dev.","skewness","kurtosis"},
          "%c", {"normal", "exp(2)"}, moments(m1));
    print("first 6 central moments",
          "%r", {"mean", "variance", "m3", "m4", "m5", "m6"},
          moments(m1, 6, 0)[1:][]);
}
```

produces

```
moment ratios
                      normal        exp(2)
T                     10000.        10000.
mean               -0.011605       0.49592
std.dev.              1.0033        0.50088
skewness           0.010556         1.9876
kurtosis              3.0314        8.4267
first 6 central moments
mean               -0.011605       0.49592
variance              1.0066        0.25088
m3                 0.010660        0.24976
m4                    3.0713        0.53039
m5                  0.13868         1.1581
m6                    15.774        2.9434
```

# norm

```
norm(const ma);
norm(const ma, const itype);
```

    ma          in:   arithmetic type
    itype       in:   int, type of norm

*Return value*

Returns the norm of a matrix.

*Description*

Computes the norm of a matrix $A$. The type of norm depends on the `itype` argument. When $A$ is a matrix:

| itype | norm |
|-------|------|
| 0 | $\|A\|_\infty = \max_{0 \le i < m} \sum_{j=0}^{n-1} \|a_{ij}\|,$ |
| 1 | $\|A\|_1 = \max_{0 \le j < n-1} \sum_{i=0}^{m-1} \|a_{ji}\|,$ |
| 2 | $\|A\|_2 = $ largest singular value, |
| 'F' | $\|A\|_2 = \left( \sum_i \sum_j \|a_{ij}\|^2 \right)^{1/2},$ |
| $-1$ | $\|A\|_{-\infty} = \min_{0 \le i < m} \sum_{j=0}^{n-1} \|a_{ij}\|.$ |

The last one is the Frobenius norm. `norm(x)` corresponds to `norm(x,0)`. When $A$ is a vector:

| itype | norm |
|-------|------|
| 0 | $\|a\|_\infty = \max_i \|a_i\|,$ |
| 1 | $\|a\|_1 = \sum_i \|a_i\|,$ |
| 2 | $\|a\|_2 = \left( \sum_i (a_i)^2 \right)^{1/2},$ |
| $p$ | $\|a\|_p = \left( \sum_i \|a_i\|^p \right)^{1/p},$ |
| $-1$ | $\|a\|_{-\infty} = \min_i \|a_i\|.$ |

Again note that `norm(x)` corresponds to `norm(x,0)`.

*See also*

    `decsvd, rank`

*Example*

```
#include <oxstd.h>
main()
{
    decl x = <1,2;3,4;5,6>;

    print( norm(x), " " );
    print( norm(x, 1), " " );
    print( norm(x, 2), " " );
    print( norm(x, 'F') );
}
```

produces: `11 12 9.52552 9.53939`

# nullspace

`nullspace(const ma);`

    `ma`           in:   $m \times n$ matrix $A$

*Return value*

Returns the null space of `ma`, or 0 (`ma` is square and full rank) (or if the SVD fails).

*Description*

Uses the SVD to compute the null space $A_\perp$ of an $m \times n$ matrix $A$, as explained in

Appendix 6. If rank$(A) = r$ and $m \geq n$, the rank of the null space is $p = m - r$, and $A_\perp$ is an $m \times p$ matrix such that $A'_\perp A_\perp = I$ and $A'A_\perp = 0$. The rank of $A$ is the number of non-zero singular values, which is determined as explained under `inverteps`.

*Error and warning messages*
    nullspace(): decomposition failed

*See also*
    `decsvd, inverteps`

*Example*
```
#include <oxstd.h>
main()
{
    decl ma = zeros(4,2);
    ma[0][0] = ma[0][1] = 1;

    print(ma, nullspace(ma));
}
```
produces
```
        1.0000          1.0000
        0.00000         0.00000
        0.00000         0.00000
        0.00000         0.00000

        0.00000         0.00000   3.4152e-017
        0.00000         0.00000      -1.0000
        0.00000         1.0000    0.00000
        1.0000          0.00000   0.00000
```

# ols2c, ols2r, olsc, olsr

```
olsc(const my, const mx, const amb);
olsc(const my, const mx, const amb, const amxtxinv);
olsc(const my, const mx, const amb, const amxtxinv, const amxtx);
ols2c(const my, const mx, const amb);
ols2c(const my, const mx, const amb, const amxtxinv);
ols2c(const my, const mx, const amb, const amxtxinv, const amxtx);
```
| | | |
|---|---|---|
| my | in: | $T \times n$ matrix $Y$ |
| mx | in: | $T \times k$ matrix $X$ |
| amb | in: | address of variable |
| | out: | $k \times n$ matrix of OLS coefficients, $B$ |
| amxtxinv | in: | (optional argument) address of variable |
| | out: | $k \times k$ matrix $(X'X)^{-1}$, |
| amxtx | in: | (optional argument) address of variable |
| | out: | $k \times k$ matrix $(X'X)$, |

```
olsr(const my, const mx, const amb);
olsr(const my, const mx, const amb, const amxtxinv);
olsr(const my, const mx, const amb, const amxtxinv, const amxtx);
ols2r(const my, const mx, const amb);
ols2r(const my, const mx, const amb, const amxtxinv);
ols2r(const my, const mx, const amb, const amxtxinv, const amxtx);
```

| | | |
|---|---|---|
| my | in: | $n \times T$ matrix $Y'$ |
| mx | in: | $k \times T$ matrix $X'$, $T \geq k$ |
| amb | in: | address of variable |
| | out: | $n \times k$ OLS coefficient matrix, $B'$ |
| amxtxinv | in: | (optional argument) address of variable |
| | out: | $k \times k$ matrix $(X'X)^{-1}$, |
| amxtx | in: | (optional argument) address of variable |
| | out: | $k \times k$ matrix $(X'X)$, |

*Return value*

| | |
|---|---|
| 0: | out of memory, |
| 1: | success, |
| 2: | ratio of diagonal elements of $X'X$ is large, rescaling is advised, (ratio of smallest to largest $\leq \epsilon_{inv}$) |
| $-1$: | $(X'X)$ is (numerically) singular, (decision made in decqr and decldl respectively). |
| $-2$: | combines 2 and $-1$. |

The inversion epsilon, $\epsilon_{inv}$, is set by the inverteps function.

*Description*

olsc and olsr do ordinary least squares using the Householder QR decomposition with pivoting (see, e.g., Golub and Van Loan, 1989, Ch. 5).

ols2c and ols2r form $(X'X)$ and solve the normal equations using the Choleski decomposition (see decldl).

The QR based method for computing OLS is more accurate, but about half as fast (unless $T \approx k$), and more memory intensive than the normal equations approach (the QR method uses a copy of the data to work on).

If $(X'X)$ is singular, the QR based method computes $B$ and $(X'X)^{-1}$ with zeros at the positions corresponding to the singular variables; $X'X$ remains based on the full $X$. So $(X'X)^{-1}$ is not the normal generalized inverse when $X$ does not have full column rank. The normal equation approach does not produce a meaningful result in case of singularity.

*See also*

decldl, decqr, inverteps

*Example*

```
#include <oxstd.h>
main()
```

```
{
    decl mx, my, cy = 2, ct = 50, ck = 3, mb, mxtx, mxtxi;
    mx = ranu(ct,ck);
    my = rann(ct,cy) / 10 + mx * ones(ck,1);

    olsc(my, mx, &mb);
    print(mb);
    olsr(my', mx', &mb, &mxtxi, &mxtx);
    print(mb, mxtx ~ mxtxi);

    print((1/mx)*my, mx'mx ~ invert(mx'mx));
}
```

produces:

```
    1.0992    0.98022
    1.1068    0.95734
   0.78966     1.0401

    1.0992     1.1068    0.78966
   0.98022    0.95734     1.0401

    16.842     13.139     12.740    0.23380  -0.11726  -0.10967
    13.139     15.095     11.872   -0.11726   0.24566 -0.098336
    12.740     11.872     14.467   -0.10967 -0.098336   0.24639

    1.0992    0.98022
    1.1068    0.95734
   0.78966     1.0401

    16.842     13.139     12.740    0.23380  -0.11726  -0.10967
    13.139     15.095     11.872   -0.11726   0.24566 -0.098336
    12.740     11.872     14.467   -0.10967 -0.098336   0.24639
```

# ones

```
ones(const r, const c);
ones(const ma);
    r          in:  int
    c          in:  int
    ma         in:  matrix
```

*Return value*

ones(r,c) returns an r by c matrix filled with ones.

ones(ma) returns a matrix of the same dimension as ma, filled with ones.

*See also*

constant, unit, zeros

*Example*

```
#include <oxstd.h>
main()
{
    print( ones(2, 2) );
}
```

produces

```
1.0000        1.0000
1.0000        1.0000
```

# outer

```
outer(const mx, const ms);
outer(const mx, const ms, const mode);
```
|        |     |                                                    |
|--------|-----|----------------------------------------------------|
| mx     | in: | $m \times n$ matrix $X$                            |
| ms     | in: | $n \times n$ symmetric matrix $S$ or empty matrix  |
| mode   | in: | int, operation mode: 'd' or 'o' (optional argument) |

*Return value*

outer(mx,ms) returns $XSX'$ which is $m \times m$.

outer(mx,ms,'d') returns diagonal$(XSX')$ which is $1 \times m$. For large matrices this is much faster than using the diagonal function.

outer(mx,<>,'o') returns $\sum_{i=1}^{m} x_i x_i'$ which is $n \times n$, writing $X' = (x_1, \ldots, x_m)$.

*See also*

diagonal

*Example*

```
#include <oxstd.h>
main()
{
    decl x = rann(2,3), y = ranu(3,3), s = y'y;
    print( outer(x, s, 'd') | diagonal(outer(x, s))
        | diagonal(x * s * x') );
}
```

produces

```
3.7646        4.2561
3.7646        4.2561
3.7646        4.2561
```

# oxfilename

```
oxfilename(const itype);
```
  itype  in: int, determines output format

*Return value*
  Returns a string with the name of the Ox source file from which it is called:

| itype | returns | example 1 | example 2 |
|-------|---------|-----------|-----------|
|       |         | oxl D:\waste\func | oxl func |
| 0 | full file name | D:\waste\func.ox | func.ox |
| 1 | path of file name | D:\waste\ | |
| 2 | base name | func | func |
| 3 | file extension | .ox | .ox |

In the first two cases the return value depends on how the program was started (the path may not have been specified).

# oxprintlevel

```
oxprintlevel(const ilevel);
```
  ilevel  in: int, print level, see below

*No return value.*

*Description*
  Controls printing:
   oxprintlevel(1);  default: prints as normal,
   oxprintlevel(0);  switches printing off (`print` and `println` have no output),
   oxprintlevel(2);  disallows further calls to `oxprintlevel`,
   oxprintlevel(-1);  switches printing off, including warnings.
  This function can be useful in simulations (e.g.), where the code being simulated has no other mechanism for switching printing on and off (Modelbase derived code normally uses `SetPrint`).

*See also*
  oxwarning

*Example*
```
#include <oxstd.h>
test()
{
    oxprintlevel(0);        // output off
    // do some simulations which otherwise have output
    for (decl i = 0; i < 1000; ++i)
        println("i=", i);
    oxprintlevel(1);        // output on

    // do some simulations which has output and warning
```

```
    oxprintlevel(-1);         // output and warnings off
    for (decl i = 0; i < 1000; ++i)
        println("i=", i, " invert(0):", invert(0));
    oxprintlevel(1);          // output on


    // do some simulations which have warnings
    decl oldwarnings = oxwarning(0);    // all warnings off
    for (decl i = 0; i < 1000; ++i)
        invert(0);
    oxwarning(oldwarnings);                // reset warning levels
}
main()
{
    // comment the next line in to overrule oxprintlevel calls
    //oxprintlevel(2);
    test();
}
```

Prints nothing unless the `oxprintlevel(2)` statement is commented in.

## oxrunerror

```
oxrunerror(const smsg);
oxrunerror(const smsg, const i01);
```
     smsg       in:   string, error message text
     i01        in:   int, 0 (the default) or 1

*No return value.*

*Description*
    Prints the specified run-time error message and location, and exits the program.
    If `i01`=0, the standard Ox call trace is printed; if `i01`=1, the top level function
    call is skipped (in case the error is raised in an error handler function). Use 2 to
    omit the trace.

## oxversion

```
oxversion();
```

*Return value*
    Returns an integer with the version of Ox multiplied by 100. So for version 4.10
    the return value is 410.

# oxwarning

```
oxwarning(const smsg);
oxwarning(const flset);
```
      smsg      in:  string, user-determined warning message
      flset     in:  int, new warnings settings

*Return value*
      Returns the previous warnings settings.

*Description*
      When given a string as argument, the function will print a user-determined warn-
ing message.

      Otherwise, `oxwarning` controls the reporting of run-time warning messages. The
following types of messages are controlled by this function:

| flag | context |
| --- | --- |
| WFL_DECFAILED | decomposition failed, |
| WFL_ITMAX | maximum no. of iterations reached, |
| WFL_CONCAT | concatenation dimensions don't match, |
| WFL_VECIDXMAT | indexed a matrix as a vector, |
| WFL_DETERMINANT | determinant-related warning, |
| WFL_USER | user-determined warning message. |

      The first occurs when an inversion or decomposition fails, the second could hap-
pen in an eigenvalue based function. The concatenation message is printed when
the dimensions don't match, and the results has been padded with zeros. The
message related to `WFL_VECIDXMAT` is given when a matrix which is not a row or
column vector is indexed with just one index. However, the message is not given
when using an empty single index

      , which has the same effect as the `vecr` function.
      You can add the flags together to specify warning settings. Use `oxwarning(0)`
to switch all messages off, and `oxwarning(-1)` to switch them all on.

*See also*
      `oxprintlevel`(for an example)

# periodogram

```
periodogram(const ma);
periodogram(const ma, const itrunc, const cpoints,
    const imode);
```
|          |     |                                                               |
|----------|-----|---------------------------------------------------------------|
| ma       | in: | arithmetic type, $T \times n$ matrix                          |
| itrunc   | in: | int, truncation parameter $m$, if $\leq 0, \geq T$ then $T-1$ is used |
| cpoints  | in: | int, no of points $N$ at which to evaluate periodogram        |
| imode    | in: | 0: (truncated) periodogram (multiplied by $T$),               |
|          |     | 1: smoothed periodogram (multiplied by $T$) using Parzen window, |
|          |     | 2: estimated spectral density using Parzen window (as option 1, but divided by $c_0$). |

*Return value*

- `periodogram(ma);`
  Returns $T$ times the periodogram, evaluated at the Fourier frequencies $0, 2\pi/T, 4\pi/T, \ldots, (\mathrm{int}(T/2)2\pi)/T$. The dimensions of the returned matrix are $\mathrm{int}(T/2) + 1 \times n$.
- `periodogram(ma, itrunc, N, 0);`
  Returns a $N \times n$ matrix with ($T$ times) the periodogram of the columns of ma using autocovariances up to lag `itrunc`, computed at frequencies $0, \pi/(N-1), 2\pi/(N-1), \ldots, \pi$.
- `periodogram(ma, itrunc, N, 1);`
  Returns a $N \times n$ matrix with ($T$ times) the smoothed periodogram of the columns of ma using autocovariances up to lag `itrunc`, computed at frequencies $0, \pi/(N-1), 2\pi/(N-1), \ldots, \pi$.
- `periodogram(ma, itrunc, N, 2);`
  Returns a $N \times n$ matrix with the spectral density of the columns of ma using autocorrelations up to lag `itrunc`, computed at frequencies $0, \pi/(N-1), 2\pi/(N-1), \ldots, \pi$.

*Description*

Computes the periodogram or spectral density of the columns of a $T \times n$ matrix $A = (a_0, a_1, \ldots, a_{n-1})$.

Define the autocovariance function of a $T$-vector $x = (x_0 \cdots x_{T-1})'$ up to lag $k$ as $c = (\hat{c}_0 \cdots \hat{c}_k)'$:

$$\hat{c}_j = \frac{1}{T} \sum_{t=j}^{T-1} (x_t - \bar{x})(x_{t-j} - \bar{x}), \tag{8.2}$$

with the mean defined in the standard way as:

$$\bar{x} = \frac{1}{T} \sum_{t=0}^{T-1} x_t$$

Note that $\hat{r}_j = \hat{c}_j/\hat{c}_0$, see equation (8.1) on page 68.
The sample periodogram is then defined as:

$$\hat{p}(\omega) = \frac{1}{2\pi} \sum_{j=-T+1}^{T-1} \hat{c}_{|j|} \cos(j\omega) = \frac{\hat{c}_0}{2\pi} \sum_{j=-T+1}^{T-1} \hat{r}_{|j|} \cos(j\omega), \quad 0 \le \omega \le \pi,$$

(8.3)

and the sample spectral density as:

$$\hat{s}(\omega) = \frac{1}{2\pi} \sum_{j=-m}^{m} K(j) \hat{r}_{|j|} \cos(j\omega), \quad 0 \le \omega \le \pi.$$

The $K(\cdot)$ function is called the *lag window*, $m$ is called the *lag truncation parameter*.
The value of the imode parameter affects the computations as follows:

0: Computes $T\hat{p}(\omega)$.
1: Computes the smoothed periodogram $T\hat{c}_0\hat{s}(\omega)$. The smoothing is achieved using the Parzen window:

$$
\begin{aligned}
K(j) &= 1 - 6\left(\frac{j}{m}\right)^2 + 6\left|\frac{j}{m}\right|^3, & \left|\frac{j}{m}\right| &\le 0.5, \\
&= 2\left(1 - \left|\frac{j}{m}\right|\right)^3, & 0.5 \le \left|\frac{j}{m}\right| &\le 1.0, \\
&= 0, & \left|\frac{j}{m}\right| &> 1.
\end{aligned}
$$

2: Computes the estimated spectral density $\hat{s}(\omega)$ using the Parzen window.

We have that $K(-j) = K(j)$, so that the sign of $j$ does not matter. The $c_j$s are based on fewer observations as $j$ increases. The window function attaches decreasing weights to the autococorrelations, with zero weight for $j > m$. The larger $m$, the less smooth the spectrum becomes, but the lower the bias. For more information see Priestley (1981, Ch.6), Granger and Newbold (1986, §2.6) and Brockwell and Davis (1991, §10.1).
In each case, when $N = \text{cpoints} > 0$, the periodogram is evaluated at $N$ frequencies between 0 and $\pi$:

$$0, \frac{\pi}{N-1}, \frac{2\pi}{N-1}, \dots, \frac{(N-1)\pi}{N-1} = \pi,$$

so that the horizontal axis could be computed as:
    M_PI * range(0, cpoints-1) / (cpoints-1)
When cpoints is 0 on input, or when the version with one argument is used, $N = \text{int}(T/2)$, and the periodogram is evaluated at:

$$0, \frac{2\pi}{T}, \frac{4\pi}{T}, \dots, \frac{2N\pi}{T},$$

so that the horizontal axis could be computed as:

```
M_2PI * range(0, int(ct/2)) / ct
```

*See also*

fft1d, DrawSpectrum (for another example).

*Example*

```
#include <oxstd.h>
#include <oxfloat.h>          // required for M_2PI

main()
{
    decl ct = 2^3 + 7, x, y, yzt, p1, p2;

    y = cumulate(rann(ct,1), 0.9);
    p1 = periodogram(y) / ct;
    x = M_2PI * range(0, int(ct/2))' / ct;

    yzt = (y - meanc(y))';// FFT expects data in row
    p2 = sqr(cabs(fft1d(yzt))') / (ct * M_2PI );
    print("%c", {"periodogram", "frequencies", "FFT"},
        p1 ~ x ~ p2);
}
```

produces (the zeros at the end of the periodogram and frequencies are added in the concatenation with fft):

```
periodogram  frequencies         FFT
    0.00000      0.00000   1.1253e-033
    0.49542      0.41888       0.49542
    0.060270     0.83776      0.060270
    0.024741     1.2566       0.024741
    0.16432      1.6755        0.16432
    0.036133     2.0944       0.036133
    0.019385     2.5133       0.019385
    0.023846     2.9322       0.023846
    0.00000      0.00000      0.023846
    0.00000      0.00000      0.019385
    0.00000      0.00000      0.036133
    0.00000      0.00000       0.16432
    0.00000      0.00000      0.024741
    0.00000      0.00000      0.060270
    0.00000      0.00000       0.49542
```

# polydiv

```
polydiv(const ma, const mb, const cp);
```

| | | |
|---|---|---|
| ma | in: | $1 \times m$ matrix $A = (a_0 \ldots a_{m-1})$ specifying the $A$ polynomial (see below) |
| mb | in: | $1 \times n$ matrix $B = (b_0 \ldots b_{n-1})$ specifying the $B$ polynomial (see below) |
| cp | in: | int, required length, $p$, of polynomial resulting from division |

*Return value*

Returns a $1 \times p$ matrix with the coefficients of polynomial resulting from dividing the $A$ polynomial by the $B$ polynomial. The integer 0 is returned when $b_0$ is 0, or $p = 0$.

*Description*

Defining the two polynomials

$$A(x) = a_0 + a_1 x + a_2 x^2 + \ldots a_{m-1} x^{m-1},$$
$$B(x) - b_0 + b_1 x + b_2 x^2 + \ldots b_{n-1} x^{n-1},$$

polydiv returns ($p$ is specified in the function call):

$$D(x) = A(x)/B(x) = d_0 + d_1 x + d_2 x^2 + \ldots d_{p-1} x^{p-1}.$$

*See also*

polyeval, polymake, polymul (for an example), polyroots

# polyeval

polyeval(const ma, const mx);

| | | |
|---|---|---|
| ma | in: | $1 \times m$ matrix $A = (a_0 \ldots a_{m-1})$ specifying the $A$ polynomial (see below) |
| mx | in: | arithmetic type |

*Return value*

Returns the polynomial evaluated at mx.

*Description*

Defining the polynomial

$$A(x) = a_0 + a_1 x + a_2 x^2 + \ldots a_{m-1} x^{m-1},$$

polyeval returns $A(x)$.

*See also*

polydiv, polymake, polymul, polyroots

*Example*

```
#include <oxstd.h>
main()
{
    decl a = <1,-0.8,-0.1>;

    println("a(x)=a[0]+a[1]*x+a[2]*x^2; a(3)=", polyeval(a, 3));
}
```

produces

```
a(x)=a[0]+a[1]*x+a[2]*x^2; a(3)=-2.3
```

# polygamma

```
polygamma(const ma, const mn);
        ma              in:  arithmetic type
        mn              in:  arithmetic type, order of derivative: 0 = first derivative, 1 =
                             second derivative, etc.
```

*Return value*

Returns the derivative of the logarithm of the complete gamma function at the value of each element of ma, of double or matrix type. The second argument specifies the order of the derivative.

Returns zero for any argument less than or equal to zero, or derivative order less than 0.

The return type is derived as follows:

| returns | ma | order arguments |
|---|---|---|
| $m \times n$ matrix | $m \times n$ matrix | scalar (int) |
| $m \times n$ matrix | scalar | $m \times n$ matrix |
| $m \times n$ matrix | $m \times n$ matrix | $m \times n$ matrix |
| double | scalar | scalar (int) |

*Description*

Computes the derivatives of the loggamma function at the argument $a$:

$$\psi^{(n)}(a) = \frac{d^{n+1}}{da^{n+1}} \log \Gamma(a) \quad \text{for } a > 0.$$

Most commonly used are:

$n = 0$     digamma (psi) function
$n = 1$     trigamma function
$n = 2$     tetragamma function
$n = \ldots$     etc.

The function is accurate to about 15 significant digits. The approximation uses the recurrence relation

$$\psi^{(n)}(a+1) = \psi^{(n)}(a) + (-1)^n n! z^{-n-1}.$$

to obtain an $a$ value greater than 8.5; then an asymptotic formula with eight terms is applied (see Abramowitz and Stegun, 1984, §6.4.11).

*See also*

loggamma

*Example*

```
#include <oxstd.h>
#include <oxfloat.h>          // required for M_EULER

main()
```

```
{
    print(polygamma(<0.5,1>, 0), -M_EULER - 2*log(2) ~ -M_EULER);
    print("%12.7g", polygamma(0.5, <0,1,2,3>));
}
```

produces

```
        -1.9635      -0.57722
        -1.9635      -0.57722
        -1.96351      4.934802       -16.8288        97.40909
```

# polymake

```
polymake(const roots);
```
    roots       in:  $2 \times m$ matrix with (inverse) roots of the polynomial, first row
                     is real part, second row imaginary part (or $1 \times m$ matrix if all
                     roots are real).

*Return value*

Returns the coefficients of the polynomial ($a_0 = 1$) as a $2 \times (m + 1)$ matrix if
the roots had a complex part, else $1 \times (m + 1)$.

*Description*

Computes the polynomial coefficients from the inverse roots. The constant term
($a_0$) is set to one, so returned is the $a_i$ from:

$$1 + a_1 x + a_2 x^2 + \dots a_m x^m.$$

*See also*

polyroots (for an example)

# polymul

```
polymul(const ma, const mb);
```
    ma          in:  $1 \times m$ matrix $A = (a_0 \dots a_{m-1})$ specifying the $A$ polyno-
                     mial (see below)
    mb          in:  $1 \times n$ matrix $B = (b_0 \dots b_{n-1})$ specifying the $B$ polynomial
                     (see below)

*Return value*

Returns a $1 \times m + n - 1$ matrix with the coefficients of the product of the polynomials.

*Description*

Defining the two polynomials

$$A(x) = a_0 + a_1 x + a_2 x^2 + \dots a_{m-1} x^{m-1},$$
$$B(x) = b_0 + b_1 x + b_2 x^2 + \dots b_{n-1} x^{n-1},$$

the `polymul` function returns:

$$C(x) = A(x)B(x) = c_0 + c_1 x + c_2 x^2 + \dots c_{p-1} x^{p-1}, \quad p = m + n - 2.$$

The coefficients $c_i$ correspond to the convolution of the coeficients $a_i$ and $b_i$:

$$c_i = \sum_{j=\max(0,i-n+1)}^{\min(i,m-1)} a_j b_{i-j}, \quad i = 0, \dots, p - 2.$$

The `polymul` function computes the sum directly. For large polynomials, faster computation can be based on the fast Fourier transform, as the example shows.

*See also*

     `fft1d, polydiv, polyeval, polymake, polyroots`

*Example*

```
#include <oxstd.h>
main()
{
    decl a, b, c, ff;
    format("%10.4f");

    a = <1,-0.9>;   b = <1,-0.8,-0.1>;

    print(polymul(a, b));
    c = polymul(b, a);
    print(polydiv(c, a, 5));

        // multiply the two FFTs, padded with zeros
    ff = cmul( fft(a~zeros(b)), fft(b~zeros(a)) );
    ff = fft(ff, 2);     // apply inverse real FFT
    print( ff[][:columns(a)+columns(b)-2] );

        // divide the two FFTs, padded with zeros
    ff = cdiv( fft(c~zeros(a)), fft(a~zeros(c)) );
    ff = fft(ff, 2);     // apply inverse real FFT
    print( ff[][:4] );
}
```

produces

```
    1.0000    -1.7000     0.6200     0.0900
    1.0000    -0.8000    -0.1000    -0.0000    -0.0000
    1.0000    -1.7000     0.6200     0.0900
    1.0000    -0.8000    -0.1000     0.0000     0.0000
```

# polyroots

```
polyroots(const ma, const amroots);
```
    ma        in:  $1 \times (m+1)$ matrix $A = (a_0 \dots a_m)$ specifying the polynomial of order $m$ (see below)

    amroots  in:  address of variable

              out: $2 \times m$ matrix with roots of the polynomial, first row is real part, second row imaginary part (all zeros if the roots are real). The roots are *not* sorted.

*Return value*

    Returns the result of the eigenvalue decomposition:

      0  no error;

      1  maximum no of iterations (50) reached.

*Description*

    Computes the inverse roots of a polynomial

$$a_0 + a_1 x + a_2 x^2 + \dots a_m x^m.$$

    The inverse roots are found as the eigenvalues of the companion matrix (which is already in upper Hessenberg form), e.g. when $m = 4$ and $a_0 = 1$:

$$
\begin{matrix}
-a_1 & -a_2 & -a_3 & -a_4 \\
1 & 0 & 0 & 0 \\
0 & 1 & 0 & 0 \\
0 & 0 & 1 & 0
\end{matrix}
$$

    Note that the implementation assumes that $a_0 \neq 0$. Also note that the inverse roots of $1 + a_1 x + a_2 x^2 + \dots a_m x^m$, correspond to the roots of $x^m + a_1 x^{m-1} + a_2 x^{m-2} + \dots a_1$.

*Error and warning messages*

    polyroots(): maximum no. of iterations reached

*See also*

    cabs (for another example), eigen, polydiv, polyeval, polymake, polymul

*Example*

```
#include <oxstd.h>
main()
{
    decl v1, roots, cr;
    v1 = <-1, 1.2274, -0.017197, -0.28369, -0.01028>;

    polyroots(v1, &roots);
```

```
    cr = columns(roots);
    print(v1, "roots", roots,
        "inverse roots", cdiv(ones(1,cr), roots),
        "polynomial", polymake(roots) );
}
```

produces

```
    -1.0000        1.2274    -0.017197    -0.28369    -0.010280
roots
    0.82865        0.82865    -0.39337    -0.036535
    0.16923       -0.16923     0.00000     0.00000
inverse roots
     1.1585         1.1585     -2.5422     -27.371
    -0.23659        0.23659     0.00000     0.00000
polynomial
     1.0000        -1.2274    0.017197     0.28369     0.010280
     0.00000        0.00000    0.00000     0.00000     0.00000
```

# pow

```
pow(const ma, const p);
    ma          in:  arithmetic type
    p           in:  arithmetic type, power
```

*Return value*

Returns ma .^ p. This is identical to using the dot-power operator, with the exception that if both ma and p are an integer, the return type is a double.

*See also*

sqr (for an example), ^ .^ (§13.8.3)

# print, println

```
print(const a, ...);
println(const a, ...);
    a           in:  any type
    ...         in:  any type
```

*Return value*

Returns the number of arguments supplied to the function.

*Description*

Each argument is printed to stdout using default formatting. A formatting string can be input in the input stream: a formatting string starts with a % symbol, and is followed by one or more characters. If a formatting string is encountered, it is not printed, but applied to the next argument.

There is an additional option to add column and row labels for a matrix, specify a different format for each matrix column, or only print the lower diagonal:

%r      the next argument contains row labels (array of strings)
%c      the next argument contains column labels (array of strings)
%cf     the next argument contains column formats (array of strings)
%lwr    only print the lower diagonal of the matrix

The default format strings are:

| no value | "null" |
| int | "%d" |
| double | "%g" |
| matrix | "\n", then each element "%#13.5g", 6 elements on a line (5 if row is labelled), no labels. |
| string | "%s" |
| array | "&0x%p" |
| function | "&%d" |
| class | "&0x%p" |
| library function | "&0x%p" |

The format function may be used to set a different default format; it also lists the format options.

The format specification is similar to that for the printf function of the C language:

$$\%[\mathit{flag}][\mathit{width}][.\mathit{precision}]\mathit{type}$$

**Table 8.2**    Formatting flags for doubles and integers.

| *flag* | |
| --- | --- |
| – | left adjust in output field, |
| + | always print a sign, |
| *space* | prefix space if first character is not a sign |
| 0 | pad with leading zeros, |
| # | alternate output form: |
| | type is o: first digit will be 0, |
| | type is xX: prefix with 0x or 0X (unless value is 0), |
| | type is eEfgG: always print decimal point, |
| | type is gG: keep trailing zeros. |
| | type is mM: omit dimensions. |

The *width* argument specifies the width of the output field. The *precision* argument specifies the number of significant digits (type is gG) number of digits after the decimal point (type is eEf); the default is 6 if *precision* is absent.

Table 8.3 explains the format strings; some notes:

• The format function allows setting a default format.

**Table 8.3**   Formatting types for printing.

| double *type*: | (also used for matrices) |
| --- | --- |
| g,G | %e or %E if the exponent is $< -4$ |
| | or $>=$ *precision*; else use %f, |
| e,e | scientific notation: with exponent, |
| f | print without exponent, |
| C | print as a calendar date |
| **specials for matrices:** | |
| r | followed by row labels (array of strings), |
| c | followed by column labels (array of strings), |
| cf | followed by column formats (array of strings), e.g. |
| | `print("%c",{"a","b"},"%cf",{"%8.4g","%6.2g"},m);` |
| integer *type*: | |
| d,i | signed decimal notation, |
| o | unsigned octal notation, |
| x,X | unsigned hexadecimal notation, |
| u | unsigned decimal notation, |
| c | print as a single character (i.e. one byte), |
| string *type*: | |
| s | string format, |
| matrix *type*: | |
| m | print matrix row by row using %25.26e, |
| M | print matrix row by row using default format, |
| *any type*: | |
| v | any variable in Ox constant format. |

- Be careful with the %f format, for example, when printing 1e-300, the output field will need 302 characters.
- By default, integers are printed without leading spaces, to use a space as separator: " %d" alternatively specify a wider field: "%6d".
- Matrices always use one space between elements.
- The "%m" and "%M" formats must be followed by a matrix. First the number of rows and columns is written, which is followed by the matrix, row by row; this corresponds to the format used by savemat. The dimensions are omitted by "%#m" and "%#M".
  This format is most useful when the matrix has to be read from a file at a later stage.
- The "%C" format prints date and/or time. If there is no fraction the calendar date is printed as yyyy-mm-dd; if there is only a fraction the time is printed as hh:mm or hh:mm:ss or hh:mm:ss.hh. If both are present yyyy-mm-ddThh:mm[:ss[.hh]] is printed (so using the ISO standard for date/time

formatting). Also see day of calendar.

- The "%v" format prints a variable in the format of an Ox constant, and can be used for any variable. It can be especially useful to read and write variables that consist of derived types, such as an array or a class object, but also for a matrix. An example is given below and in ox/samples/inout/percent_v.ox.

The println function is as print but ensures the next output will be on a new line.

To print text starting with a percentage symbol that is also a format specifier, use either %s as the format, or a double percentage, as in println("%s", "%GDP", " or:  ", "%%GDP").

*See also*

eprint, format, fprint, fscan, fwrite, sprint

*Example*

```
main()
{
    print( "%r", {"row 1", "row 2"},
            "%c", {"col 1", "col 2"}, "%6.1g", unit(2) );

    decl xp = 9*rann(2,1)~ranu(2,1);
    print( "%c", {"x ", "p "},
            "%cf",{"%8.4g", " [%4.2f]"}, xp);

    decl x = rann(10,2);
    print("\nLower diagonal:", "%lwr", x'x);
}
```

produces

```
        col 1 col 2
row 1     1     0
row 2     0     1

        x       p
    2.024 [0.42]
    15.66 [0.16]

Lower diagonal:
        10.585
        3.1110        7.1178
```

In the second example we show the output from the "%v" format.

```
#include <oxstd.h>

class VClass
{
    decl m_mMatrix;
    decl m_aArray;
```

```
        VClass();
    }
    VClass::VClass()
    {
        m_mMatrix = range(1,3);
        m_aArray = {"a", "b", "c"};
    }
    main()
    {
        print( "%r", {"row 1", "row 2"},
               "%c", {"col 1", "col 2"}, "%6.1g", unit(2) );

        decl xp = 9*rann(2,1)~ranu(2,1);
        print( "%c", {"x ", "p "},
               "%cf",{"%8.4g", " [%4.2f]"}, xp);

        decl x = rann(10,2);
        print("\nLower diagonal:", "%lwr", x'x);

        decl vc = new VClass();
        print("\nobject using %v:\n", "%v", vc);
    }
```

produces

```
object using %v:
::VClass
{
.m_mMatrix = <1,2,3>;
.m_aArray = {"a","b","c"};
}
```

# probchi, probf, probn, probt

```
probchi(const ma, const df);
probchi(const ma, const df, const nc);
probf(const ma, const df1, const df2);
probf(const ma, const df1, const df2, const nc);
probn(const ma);
probt(const ma, const df);
probt(const ma, const df, const nc);
```

|        |     |                                                        |
|--------|-----|--------------------------------------------------------|
| ma     | in: | arithmetic type                                        |
| df     | in: | arithmetic type, degrees of freedom                    |
| df1    | in: | arithmetic type, degrees of freedom in the numerator   |
| df2    | in: | arithmetic type, degrees of freedom in the denominator |
| nc     | in: | arithmetic type, non-centrality parameter              |

*Return value*

Returns the requested probabilities at ma (between zero and one):

probchi  probabilities from $\chi^2(df)$ distribution,
probchi  probabilities from non-central $\chi^2(df)$ distribution,
probf    probabilities from $F(df1, df2)$ distribution,
probf    probabilities from non-central $F(df1, df2)$ distribution,
probn    one-sided probabilities from the standard normal $N(0, 1)$,
probt    one-sided probabilities from student-t$(df)$ distribution,
probt    one-sided probabilities from non-central student-t$(df)$ distribution.

The normal probabilities are accurate to 14-15 significant digits for probabilities $> 10^{-20}$. The other probabilities are accurate to at least 10 digits.
The return type is derived as follows:

| returns | ma | degrees of freedom arguments |
|---|---|---|
| $m \times n$ matrix | $m \times n$ matrix | scalar |
| $m \times n$ matrix | scalar | $m \times n$ matrix |
| $m \times n$ matrix | $m \times n$ matrix | $m \times n$ matrix |
| double | scalar | scalar |

*Description*

Sources: probchi uses gammafunc and Applied Statistics algorithm AS 275 (Mardia and Zemroch, 1975, and a modified version of Ding, 1992) for the non-central distribution; probf uses betafunc, probn and tailn use Ooura (1998) and AS 66 (Hill, 1973), probt uses AS 3 (Cooper, 1968) for two arguments and integer degrees of freedom, and a modification of AS 243 (Lenth, 1989 otherwise. The non-central F is based on a modified version of AS 266 (Lenth, 1987).

*See also*

dens..., quan..., tail..., Probability package (§11.3) for probbvn, probmvn

*Example*

```
#include <oxstd.h>
main()
{
    decl m = <0,4.61,5.99>;

    print("%r", {"chi:    "}, probchi(m, 2));
    print("%r", {"normal:"}, probn(<-1.96, 0, 1.96>) );
    print("%r", {"t:      "}, probt(<-1.96, 0, 1.96>, 4) );
                      /* additional argument types: */
    print("%r", {"chi:    "}, probchi(5.99, <2,3,4>),
          "%r", {"chi:    "}, probchi(<6,7,8>, <2,3,4>) );
    print("%r", {"nc chi:"}, probchi(m, 2, 5));
    print("%r", {"nc t:  "}, probt(<-1.96, 0, 1.96>, 4, 5));
}
```

produces

```
chi:              0.00000      0.90024       0.94996
normal:           0.024998     0.50000       0.97500
t:                0.060777     0.50000       0.93922
chi:              0.94996      0.88790       0.80010
chi:              0.95021      0.92810       0.90842
nc chi:           0.00000      0.37210       0.49621
nc t:           7.3581e-010  2.8665e-007   0.0052148
```

# prodc, prodr

```
prodc(const ma);
prodr(const ma);
```
      ma          in:   $T \times n$ matrix $A$

*Return value*

The prodc function returns a $1 \times n$ matrix which holds the product of all column elements of ma.

The prodr function returns a $T \times 1$ matrix which holds the product of all row elements of ma.

*See also*

    sumc, sumr

*Example*

```
#include <oxstd.h>
main()
{
    print( prodc(<0:3;1:4;2:5>) );
    print( prodr(<0:3;1:4;2:5>) );
}
```

produces

```
    0.00000       6.0000       24.000       60.000

    0.00000
    24.000
    120.00
```

# quanchi, quanf, quann, quant

```
quanchi(const ma, const df);
quanf(const ma, const df1, const df2);
quann(const ma);
quant(const ma, const df);
```
| | | |
|---|---|---|
| ma | in: | arithmetic type, probabilities: all values must be between 0 and 1 |
| df | in: | arithmetic type, degrees of freedom |
| df1 | in: | arithmetic type, degrees of freedom in the numerator |
| df2 | in: | arithmetic type, degrees of freedom in the denominator |

*Return value*

Returns the requested quantiles (inverse probability function; percentage points) at ma:

| | |
|---|---|
| quanchi | quantiles from $\chi^2(df)$ distribution |
| quanf | quantiles from $F(df1, df2)$ distribution |
| quann | standard normal quantiles |
| quant | quantiles from student-t$(df)$ with integer degrees of freedom |

The quantiles are accurate to about 10 digits.

The return type is derived as follows:

| returns | ma | degrees of freedom arguments |
|---|---|---|
| $m \times n$ matrix | $m \times n$ matrix | scalar |
| $m \times n$ matrix | scalar | $m \times n$ matrix |
| $m \times n$ matrix | $m \times n$ matrix | $m \times n$ matrix |
| double | scalar | scalar) |

*Description*

Sources: quanchi uses a modified version of Applied Statistics algorithm AS 91 (Best and Roberts, 1975) and AS R85 (Shea, 1991), quanf uses AS 109 (Cran, Martin and Thomas, 1977) and AS 64 (Majunder and Bhattacharjee, 1973) to obtain starting values for a Newton Raphson refinement (it does not use the iterative procedure from AS 109 because this was found to be not accurate enough; AS R83 (Berry, Mielke Jr and Cran, 1977) does not seem to solve this), quann uses AS 241 (Wichura, 1988), quant is based on Hill (1981), using Newton Raphson for refinement.

*See also*

dens..., prob..., tail..., lib/Quantile.ox (to compute quantiles of other distributions), Probability package (§11.3)

*Example*

```
#include <oxstd.h>
main()
{
    decl t = range(1,10), tt = (t - 5) / 5;

    print("%14.10g",
        probf(t,10,10)' ~ quanf(probf(t,10,10),10,10)'
      ~ probt(tt,2)' ~ quant(probt(tt,2),2)' );
}
```

produces

```
        0.5           1    0.253817018       -0.8
  0.855154194         2    0.3047166335      -0.6
  0.9510726929        3    0.3639172365      -0.4
  0.98041856          4    0.4299859958      -0.2
  0.9910499384        5         0.5           0
  0.9954702686        6    0.5700140042       0.2
  0.9975177199        7    0.6360827635       0.4
```

| | | | |
|---|---|---|---|
| 0.9985507194 | 8 | 0.6952833665 | 0.6 |
| 0.99910908 | 9 | 0.746182982 | 0.8 |
| 0.9994284475 | 10 | 0.7886751346 | 1 |

# quantilec, quantiler

```
quantilec(const ma);
quantiler(const ma);
quantilec(const ma, const mq);
quantiler(const ma, const mq);
```

     ma        in:  $T \times n$ matrix $A$

     mq        in:  (optional argument) $1 \times q$ matrix of quantiles

*Return value*

The quantilec function returns a $q \times n$ matrix holding the requested quantiles of the columns of ma. If no second argument is used the return value is a $1 \times n$ matrix holding the medians.

The quantiler function returns a $T \times q$ matrix holding the requested quantiles of the rows of ma. If no second argument is used the return value is a $T \times 1$ matrix holding the medians.

*Description*

The $q$-th quantile $\xi_q$, $0 \leq q \leq 1$, of a random variable $X$ is defined as the smallest $\xi$ which satisfies $P(X \leq \xi) = q$. So $\xi_{0.5}$, the median, divides the distribution in half.

For a sample of size $T$, $x = (x_0 \cdots x_{T-1})'$, the $q$-th quantile is found by interpolating the nearest two values. Write $(y_0 \cdots y_{T-1})$ for the ordered $x$-values, $y_0 \leq y_1 \leq \cdots \leq y_{T-1}$, the quantiles are computed as:

$$\xi_q = [k + 1 - q\,(T - 1)]\,y_k + [q\,(T - 1) - k]\,y_{k+1}, \qquad (8.4)$$

where

$$k = \text{int}[q\,(T - 1)].$$

when $q(T - 1)$ is integer, the expression simplifies to $\xi_q = y_k$.

For example, for the quartiles ($\xi_{0.25}$, $\xi_{0.5}$ and $\xi_{0.75}$) when $T = 4$: $q(T - 1) = 0.75, 1.5, 2.25$ and $k = 0, 1, 2$ respectively. In this case, the median is the average of the middle two observations: $\xi_{.5} = 0.5y_1 + 0.5y_2$, and the lower quartile: $\xi_{.25} = 0.25y_0 + 0.75y_1$.

The example below shows how to obtain quantiles without using interpolation.

*See also*

    meanc, meanr, varc, varr

*Example*

```
#include <oxstd.h>
main()
{
    print( quantilec(<3;2;1;4>, <1/4,2/4,3/4>) );
    print( quantilec(<3;2;1;4>) );

    decl m = rann(2,10000);          /* generate m */

    print( quantiler(m, <0.8,0.9,0.95,0.975>) );
    print( quantilec(m', <0.8,0.9,0.95,0.975>) );

    m = sortr(m);                    /* sort m */
    print( m[][columns(m) * <0.8,0.9,0.95,0.975> ] );
}
```

produces:

```
       1.7500
       2.5000
       3.2500

       2.5000

       0.83516      1.2728      1.6457      1.9635
       0.84842      1.2740      1.6248      1.9570

       0.83516      0.84842
       1.2728       1.2740
       1.6457       1.6248
       1.9635       1.9570

       0.83536      1.2734      1.6459      1.9638
       0.84871      1.2744      1.6255      1.9585
```

# range

```
range(const min, const max);
range(const min, const max, const step);
        min       in:  int or double, first value m
        max       in:  int or double, last value n
        step      in:  int or double, (optional argument) increment
```

*Return value*

Returns a $1 \times (n - m + 1)$ matrix with the values with values $m, m + 1, \ldots, n$. If $n < m$, range returns a $1 \times (m - n + 1)$ matrix with the values with values $m, m - 1, \ldots, n$.

The version which uses the step argument uses that as the incrementor (rather than the default $+1$ or $-1$), the returned matrix is a row vector of the required length.

*Description*

When all arguments are integers, the incrementation arithmetic is done using integers, else using doubles. Integer arithmetic could be a bit more precise when using longer ranges. The following example illustrates the difference:

```
range(-1.1, 1.1, 0.11);
range(-110, 110, 11) / 100;
```

The first line has the loop using floating point arithmetic, and will not have exactly zero, but something like -1.9e-16 as its 11th element. In the second line, the loop is incremented in integer arithmetic before conversion to floating point numbers. Here the 11th number will be exactly zero. Because if these rounding errors, it is best to use the integer version, and scale afterwards.

*See also*

constant

*Example*

```
#include <oxstd.h>
main()
{
    print( range(1,4), range(4,1), range(1,6,2));
    print( range(1.2,4), range(1,6,2.1));
}
```

produces

| 1.0000 | 2.0000 | 3.0000 | 4.0000 |
|--------|--------|--------|--------|
| 4.0000 | 3.0000 | 2.0000 | 1.0000 |
| 1.0000 | 3.0000 | 5.0000 |        |
| 1.2000 | 2.2000 | 3.2000 |        |
| 1.0000 | 3.1000 | 5.2000 |        |

# rank

```
rank(const ma);
rank(const ma, const eps);
```

      ma         in:  arithmetic type
      eps       in:  arithmetic type, optional tolerance

*Return value*

Returns the rank of a matrix, of type int. The rank of a scalar is 1, except for the rank of zero, which is zero.

*Description*

Computes the rank of a matrix $A$. The rank is the number of singular values $> 10\epsilon_{inv}\|A\|_\infty$, with $\epsilon_{inv}$ is set by the inverteps function (the default is the machine precision for doubles times $1000 \approx 2 \times 10^{-13}$) and

$$\|A\|_\infty = \max_{0 \le i < m} \sum_{j=0}^{n-1} |a_{ij}|.$$

Note that, by default, the rank is relative to the norm, so that, for example, the rank of `<1e-200>` is 1.

When the two argument version is used, the rank is computed as the number of singular values > eps.

*See also*

> `decsvd, inverteps, norm`

*Example*

```
#include <oxstd.h>
main()
{
    print( rank(<1,0;1,0>), " " );
    print( rank(<1e-200>), " " );
    print( rank(0), " " );
    print( rank(<1e-200>, inverteps(0)) );
}
```

produces: 1  1  0  0

# rann

`rann(const r, const c);`
>       r            in:   int, number of rows
>       c            in:   int, number of columns

*Return value*

> Returns a $r \times c$ matrix of random numbers from the standard normal distribution. The matrix is filled by row. Note that, if both $r$ and $c$ are 1, the return value is a scalar of type double.

*Description*

> The `rann` function generates pseudo-random draws from the standard normal distribution. This uses uniform random numbers as described under `ranu`.
>
> Using `ranseed("MWC_52")` (the default uniform generator) or `ranseed ("MWC_32")` will generate standard normal samples using the ziggurat method (Doornik, 2005), while the others use the polar-Marsaglia method. In the polar method, the draws are generated in pairs. As a consequence, the seed may be one state further advanced than expected.

*See also*

> `ranseed, ranu`, Probability package ($\S 11.3$),

*Example*

```
#include <oxstd.h>
main()
{
    print( sumc( rann(1000,1) ) / 1000 );
```

```
        ranseed(-1);
        print(rann(1,5));
        ranseed(-1);
        print(rann(1,3) ~ rann(1,2));
}
```

produces

```
    -0.035817

    0.22489      1.7400    -0.20426    -0.91760    -0.67417
    0.22489      1.7400    -0.20426    -0.91760    -0.67417
```

# ranseed

```
ranseed(const iseed);
        iseed       in:  int (1 seed), or array of ints (multiple seeds), or
                    in:  string, name of random number generator to use.
```

*Return value*

Returns the current seed(s) of the random number generator. If the generator only uses one seed, the return type is int. Otherwise it is an array holding all the seeds (all array elements are integers).

A call to ranseed(0) only returns the current seed, without changing it; ranseed(-1) resets to the initial seed and returns the initial seed.

A call with a string argument to set the RNG returns the name of the new RNG. Use ranseed("") to get the name of the current RNG without changing it.

*Description*

Sets and gets the seed(s); ranseed can also change the random number generator (see under ranu for more information). Some examples are:

| | |
|---|---|
| ranseed(0) | just returns the seed(s) |
| ranseed(-1) | resets the initial seed(s) |
| ranseed(111) | sets seed to 111 |
| ranseed(111, 1111) | sets two seeds (e.g. for two seed rng, "GE") |
| ranseed("MWC_52") | MWC822_52 generator (the default generator) |
| ranseed("PM") | Park & Miller generator (the Ox 3 default) |
| ranseed("GM") | George Marsaglia's generator |
| ranseed("LE") | Pierre L'Ecuyer's generator |

*The seed is not set according to the date and time.* Ox always uses a fixed seed, so that statistical results can be replicated on the next run. Thus, in many cases it is not necessary to set the seed explicitly. To set the seed according to the current time use ranseed(today()).

Note that each generator has its own set of seeds. When using L'Ecuyer, the four seeds must be ($> 1, > 7, > 15, > 127$), otherwise the call is ignored.

Note that the ranseed("MWC_32") and ranseed("MWC_52") generators have 256 seeds and a state and carry, so ranseed(0) returns a vector with 258

elements.   It is possible to set the seed with one element, for example
ranseed(111). In that case 111 is used as a starting point for a procedure
that generates 256 seeds, and the default state and carry are used.  For other
RNGs which use more than one seed, if only one seed is set then all seeds are set
to this value.

*See also*

    ran..., ranu

*Example*

```
#include <oxstd.h>
main()
{
    decl seed = ranseed(0);
    print("RNG=", ranseed(""), " initial seeds: ",
        seed[0], " ... ", seed[sizeof(seed) - 1]);
    print( meanc(rann(10000,2)) | meanc(rann(10000,2)) );
    seed = ranseed(0);
    print("current seed: ",
        seed[0], " ... ", seed[sizeof(seed) - 1]);
    ranseed(-1);
    print( meanc(rann(10000,2)) );

    ranseed("GM");
    print("RNG=", ranseed(""), " initial seed: ", ranseed(0) );
    print( meanc(rann(10000,2)) | meanc(rann(10000,2)) );
    ranseed(-1);
    print( meanc(rann(10000,2)) );
}
```

produces

```
RNG=MWC_52 initial seeds: 1013904223 ... 43164928
     0.0011722    -0.0070313
    -0.0024659    -0.0065795
current seed: 866497328 ... -969946603
     0.0011722    -0.0070313
RNG=GM initial seed:
[0] = 362436069
[1] = 521288629

    -0.0046842     0.015912
     0.0037562     0.017064

    -0.0046842     0.015912
```

# ranu

```
ranu(const r, const c);
    r          in:  int
    c          in:  int
```

*Return value*

Returns a $r \times c$ matrix of uniform random numbers. The matrix is filled by row. When both r and c are 1, the return value is a scalar of type double.

*Description*

Generates random numbers uniformly distributed in the range 0 to 1. Each call to ranu will produce a different set of numbers, unless the seed is reset (this is achieved through the ranseed function). There is a choice between five random number generators (made using ranseed). The following two tables list the origin and properties of the (pseudo) random number generators (see Doornik, 2006 for a more detailed discussion):

| code | name | reference |
|------|------|-----------|
| "PM" | LCG31 | modified version of Park and Miller (1988) (this was the Ox 1–3 default) |
| "GM" | MWC60 | Marsaglia (1997) |
| "LE" | LFSR113 | L'Ecuyer (1999) |
| "MWC_32" | MWC8222 | Marsaglia (2003) |
| "MWC_52" | MWC8222_52 | Marsaglia (2003) and Doornik (2007) |
| "default" | | Set the default generator, same as "MWC_52". |

| code | period | seeds | speed |
|------|--------|-------|-------|
| "PM" | $2^{31} - 1 \approx 2 \times 10^9$ | 1 | 0.8 |
| "GM" | $\approx 0.6 \times 2^{60} \approx 7 \times 10^{17}$ | 2 | 0.9 |
| "LE" | $\approx 2^{113} \approx 4 \times 10^{34}$ | 4 | 1.1 |
| "MWC_32" | $\approx 2^{8222} \approx 10^{2475}$ | 256 | 0.8 |
| "MWC_52" | $\approx 2^{8221} \approx 10^{2475}$ | 256 | 1 |

"MWC_52" generates a random number that makes full use of the available floating point precision (this carries over to all other random number functions). The others only use 32 bits, instead of 52. This is now the default uniform RNG (in Ox 3.4 and earlier, "PM" was the default).

Note that "MWC_32" and "MWC_52" have 256 seeds, so ranseed(0) returns a vector with 256 elements. It is possible to set the seed with one element, for example ranseed(111). In that case 111 is used as a starting point for a procedure that generates 256 seeds.

The relative speed ratio is only a rough indicator (and will be platform specific). All random number generators for the non-uniform distributions use the active uniform generator as input. A C-code listing of the generators is given in the Ox Appendices.

*See also*

    ran..., ranseed

*Example*

```
#include <oxstd.h>
main()
{
    print( ranu(2,3) );
}
```

produces

| | | |
|---|---|---|
| 0.56444 | 0.76994 | 0.41641 |
| 0.15881 | 0.098209 | 0.37477 |

# reflect

```
reflect(const ma);
```
    ma             in:   square $m \times m$ matrix

*Return value*

Returns the reflected version of ma.

*Description*

Reflects a matrix around its secondary diagonal (from element $m-1, 0$ to element $0, m-1$). A matrix which is unchanged under reflection is called *persymmetric*.

*See also*

    transpose operator '

*Example*

```
#include <oxstd.h>
main()
{
    print( reflect(<2,1;1,4>) );
}
```

produces

| | |
|---|---|
| 4.0000 | 1.0000 |
| 1.0000 | 2.0000 |

# reshape

```
reshape(const ma, const r, const c);
```
    ma             in:   arithmetic type
    r              in:   int
    c              in:   int

*Return value*

Returns an r × c matrix, filled by row from vecr(ma). If there are less than rc elements in ma, the input matrix is repeated.

*Description*

Reshapes a matrix. It runs through the rows of ma from top to bottom. When all the elements of ma are used, the function starts again at the begining of ma.

*See also*

shape, vecr

*Example*

```
#include <oxstd.h>
main()
{
    print( reshape(<1:3>, 4, 3)' );
}
```

produces

```
        1.0000      1.0000      1.0000      1.0000
        2.0000      2.0000      2.0000      2.0000
        3.0000      3.0000      3.0000      3.0000
```

# reversec, reverser

```
reversec(const ma);
reverser(const ma);
    ma              in:  m × n matrix A
```

*Return value*

The reversec function returns an $m \times n$ matrix which is ma, except that the elements within each column are in reverse order.

The reverser function returns an $m \times n$ matrix which is ma, except that the elements within each row are in reverse order.

*See also*

sortc, sortr

*Example*

```
#include <oxstd.h>
main()
{
    decl m = <0:3;4:7;8:11;12:15>;
    print( m, reversec(m), reverser(m) );
}
```

produces:

```
0.00000        1.0000        2.0000        3.0000
4.0000        5.0000        6.0000        7.0000
8.0000        9.0000        10.000        11.000
12.000        13.000        14.000        15.000


12.000        13.000        14.000        15.000
8.0000        9.0000        10.000        11.000
4.0000        5.0000        6.0000        7.0000
0.00000        1.0000        2.0000        3.0000

3.0000        2.0000        1.0000        0.00000
7.0000        6.0000        5.0000        4.0000
11.000        10.000        9.0000        8.0000
15.000        14.000        13.000        12.000
```

# round

```
round(const ma);
```
    ma          in:   arithmetic type

*Return value*

    Returns the rounded elements of ma, of double or matrix type. Rounds to the nearest integer.

*See also*

    ceil (for an example), floor, trunc

# rows

```
rows(const ma);
```
    ma          in:   any type

*Return value*

    Returns an integer value which is the number of rows in the argument:

| type | returns |
|------|---------|
| $m \times n$ matrix | $m$ |
| string | number of characters in the string |
| array | number of elements in the array |
| file | number of rows in the file |
| | (only if opened with f format, see fopen) |
| other | 0 |

*Description*

    Computes the number of rows in the argument.

*See also*

    columns (for an example), sizec (for an example), sizeof, sizer, sizerc

# savemat

```
savemat(const sname, const ma);
savemat(const sname, const ma, const iFormat);
savemat(const sname, const ma, const asVarNames);
```
| | | |
|---|---|---|
| sname | in: | string containing a destination file name (with extension) |
| ma | in: | matrix |
| iFormat | in: | (optional argument) |
| | | 1: omit the matrix dimensions (.mat file only) |
| | | 1: save in universal v96 format (.fmt file only) |
| asVarNames | in: | (optional argument) |
| | | array of strings with names for data columns |

*Return value*

Returns 0 if the operation failed, 1 otherwise.

*Description*

The type of file saved depends on the extension of the file name:

| | |
|---|---|
| .mat | matrix file (text file), |
| .dat | data file (text file) with load information, |
| .in7 | PcGive 7 data file (with corresponding .bn7 file), |
| .xls | Excel version 2.1 spreadsheet file, |
| .csv | comma-separated spread sheet file (text file), |
| .fmt | Gauss matrix file: extended v89 (default) or universal v96 |
| .dht | Gauss data file: extended v89, with corresponding .dat file), |
| any other | as .mat file. |

The .mat and .dat formats save the data in human readable (ascii) format, the rest in binary format. For general matrices, use .mat for flexibility and easy of use, and .fmt format for speed (it can be an order of magnitude faster than .mat for large files). The other formats are more appropriate for database style data, where the number of rows (observations) is larger than the number of columns (variables). In that case .in7 is the fastest. Spreadsheet files (.xls, .wks, .wk1) cannot save matrices larger than $65\,536 \times 256$, although Ox allows up to $65\,536$ columns. For more information on spreadsheet files see Database::LoadXls(); for an example of a .mat file see loaddata().

Where required, the sample start is set to 1 (1), the frequency to 1, and the variable names to Var1, Var2, .... The Database class allows proper treatment of sample periods and variable names.

When writing a matrix file (see loadmat for an example), the values are written to full precision (16 significant digits). A NaN (Not a Number) is written as a dot.

All written files (including .fmt) are identical on each platform, so that a file can be written under Windows, transferred to a Sun in binary mode, and then read

again using `loadmat`. So, the files are written in Windows byte ordering (little endian; also see `fwrite`). Gauss under Unix writes .fmt files in a different format. The only exception are v96 .fmt files, which write the data in the format that is native to the platform on which Ox is running. The file stores information on the byte ordering, and such a file can again be read on any platform.
The `loadmat` function has a further discussion of the formats.

*Error and warning messages*
> savemat(): cannot open file
> Can only save ... variables

*See also*
> `Database` class, `loadmat` (for an example)

# scan

```
scan(const a, ...);
    a           in:  any type
    ...         in:  any type
```

*Return value*
> Returns the number of arguments successfully scanned and assigned.

*Description*
> This function works as `fscan`, but reading from the console, not a file. Any text in the scanning string which does not have an input format is *echoed to the console* (this is different from the standard C `scanf` function).

*See also*
> `fscan`, `fwrite`, `sscan`

*Example*
> The following example reads one input line at a time (leading spaces in each line are skipped, because of the starting space in " %z", and reads from that string using `scan`. The * in "%*d" suppresses assignment, so the integer is skipped in the file.

```
#include <oxstd.h>
main()
{
    decl c, i, d, m;

    c = scan("Enter an integer: %d", &i,
            "Enter a double:   %f", &d);
    print("items read=", c, " int=", i, " dbl=", d, "\n");

    c = scan("Enter a 2 x 2 matrix: %#m", 2, 2, &m);
```

```
        print("items read=", c, " mat=", m);

        c = scan("Enter a matrix with dimensions: %m", &m);
        print("items read=", c, " mat=", m);
}
```

This program produces (keyboard input is written in italics):
Enter an integer: *24*
Enter a double:    *25*
items read=2 int=24 dbl=25
Enter a 2 x 2 matrix: *1 0 0 1*

items read=1 mat=
        1.0000       0.00000
        0.00000      1.0000

Enter a matrix with dimensions: *2 2 1 0 0 1*

items read=1 mat=
        1.0000       0.00000
        0.00000      1.0000

# selectc, selectr
# selectifc, selectifr
# selectrc

```
selectc(const ma);
selectc(const ma, const mval);
selectr(const ma);
selectr(const ma, const mval);
selectifc(const ma, const mifc);
selectifr(const ma, const mifr);
selectrc(const ma, const mr, const mc);
```

| ma | in: | $m \times n$ matrix to select from |
|---|---|---|
| mval | in: | $p \times q$ matrix with values to use for selection |
| mifc | in: | $p \times n$ boolean matrix specifying columns to select |
| mifr | in: | $m \times q$ boolean matrix specifying rows to select |
| mc | in: | $p \times n$ matrix with indices of columns to select |
| mr | in: | $m \times q$ matrix with indices of rows to select |

*Return value*

The selectc function with one argument returns an $m \times s$ matrix, selecting columns from ma which have a missing value (.NaN: not a number).
The selectr function with one argument returns an $s \times n$ matrix, selecting rows from ma which have a missing value (.NaN: not a number).

The remaining forms do not have special treatment of missing values.

The `selectc` function with two arguments returns an $m \times s$ matrix, selecting the columns from `ma` which have at least one element equal to an element in `mval`.
The `selectr` function with two arguments returns an $s \times n$ matrix, selecting the rows from `ma` which have at least one element equal to an element in `mval`.
The selectif functions can be used to select rows or columns based on a logical expression: all rows (columns) wich have a zero in the corresponding row (column) are dropped.
The `selectifc` function returns an $m \times s$ matrix, selecting columns from `ma` which have at least one non-zero element in the corresponding column of `mifc`.
The `selectifr` function returns an $s \times n$ matrix, selecting only those rows from `ma` which have at least one non-zero element in the corresponding row of `mifr`.
The `selectrc` function returns a $1 \times \max(pn, mq)$ matrix, which holds the selected elements. If an index is outside the matrix bounds of `ma` the corresponding element in the return value is NaN.

All functions return an empty matrix (`<>`) if the selection is empty.

*See also*

deletec (for an example involving NaNs), deleter, deleteifc, deleteifr, hasnandot, vecindex

*Example*

```
#include <oxstd.h>
main()
{
    decl m = <0:3;4:7;8:11;12:15>, sel = <1,9,10,14>;
    print(m, "select", selectc(m, sel), selectr(m, sel));
    print("selectif", selectifr(m, m .< 0 || m .> 14));
    print("selectrc", selectrc(m, <2,3,4>, <2,3,4>));
}
```

produces:

| | | | |
|---|---|---|---|
| 0.00000 | 1.0000 | 2.0000 | 3.0000 |
| 4.0000 | 5.0000 | 6.0000 | 7.0000 |
| 8.0000 | 9.0000 | 10.000 | 11.000 |
| 12.000 | 13.000 | 14.000 | 15.000 |

select

| | |
|---|---|
| 1.0000 | 2.0000 |
| 5.0000 | 6.0000 |
| 9.0000 | 10.000 |
| 13.000 | 14.000 |

| | | | |
|---|---|---|---|
| 0.00000 | 1.0000 | 2.0000 | 3.0000 |
| 8.0000 | 9.0000 | 10.000 | 11.000 |
| 12.000 | 13.000 | 14.000 | 15.000 |

selectif

| | | | |
|---|---|---|---|
| 12.000 | 13.000 | 14.000 | 15.000 |

selectrc

| | | |
|---|---|---|
| 10.000 | 15.000 | .NaN |

# setbounds

```
setbounds(const ma, const dlo, const dhi);
```
    ma        in:  $m \times n$ matrix

    dlo      in:  scalar, lower bound (may be `-.Inf`)

    dhi      in:  scalar, upper bound (may be `+.Inf`)

*Return value*

Returns the specified matrix, replacing values smaller than dlo by dlo and values greater that dhi by dhi. Missing values remain missing.

*See also*

Ch. 5 (censored random variates)

*Example*

```
#include <oxstd.h>
main()
{
    decl x = <1,2,3;4,5,6>;
    print( setbounds(x, 3, 4) );
    print( setbounds(x, -.Inf, 4) );
    print( setbounds(x, 2, .Inf) );
}
```

produces

```
        3.0000        3.0000        3.0000
        4.0000        4.0000        4.0000

        1.0000        2.0000        3.0000
        4.0000        4.0000        4.0000

        2.0000        2.0000        3.0000
        4.0000        5.0000        6.0000
```

# setdiagonal, setlower, setupper

```
setdiagonal(const ma, const mdiag);
setlower(const ma, const ml);
setupper(const ma, const mu);
setlower(const ma, const ml, const mdiag);
setupper(const ma, const mu, const mdiag);
```
    ma       in:  $m \times n$ matrix

    mdiag    in:  $1 \times \min(m, n)$ or $\min(m, n) \times 1$ or matrix $m \times n$ matrix or scalar

    ml       in:  scalar or $m \times n$ matrix with new strict lower diagonal

    mu       in:  scalar or $m \times n$ matrix with new strict upper diagonal

*Return value*

setdiagonal returns a matrix with the diagonal replaced by mdiag, which is either a vector with the new diagonal elements, or a matrix from which the diagonal is copied. If mdiag is scalar, all diagonal elements of the returned matrix have that value.

setlower returns ma with the strict lower diagonal replaced by that of ml.

setupper returns ma with the strict upper diagonal replaced by that of ml.

The following are equivalent:

```
setlower(ma,ml,mdiag)   setdiagonal(setlower(ma,ml),mdiag)
setupper(ma,ml,mdiag)   setdiagonal(setupper(ma,ml),mdiag)
```

*See also*

diag, diagonal, diagonalize, lower, upper

*Example*

```
#include <oxstd.h>
main()
{
    decl ma = ones(2,2);
    print(setdiagonal(ma, zeros(2,1)),
          setdiagonal(ma, 0),
          setdiagonal(ma, zeros(2,2)) );

    ma = ones(3,3);
    decl mb = rann(3,3);

    print(setlower(ma, mb, mb), setupper(ma, 0),
          setupper(ma, 0, 2) );
}
```

produces

```
      0.00000        1.0000
       1.0000        0.00000

      0.00000        1.0000
       1.0000        0.00000

      0.00000        1.0000
       1.0000        0.00000

      0.22489        1.0000        1.0000
     -0.91760       -0.67417       1.0000
      0.22335       -0.14139      -0.18338

       1.0000        0.00000       0.00000
       1.0000        1.0000        0.00000
       1.0000        1.0000        1.0000

       2.0000        0.00000       0.00000
       1.0000        2.0000        0.00000
       1.0000        1.0000        2.0000
```

# shape

```
shape(const ma, const r, const c);
    ma          in:  arithmetic type
    r           in:  int
    c           in:  int
```

*Return value*

Returns an r × c matrix, filled by column from vec(ma). If there are fewer than rc elements in ma, the value 0 is used for padding.

*Description*

Shapes a matrix. It runs through the columns of ma from left to right, and can be used e.g. to undo a vec operation. So shape puts the first r elements of ma in the first column of the return matrix, etc. To do the opposite, namely put the first c elements in the first row of the return matrx, use shape(ma, c, r)'.
Shape is closely related to vec:

```
        v = shape(x, rows(x)*columns(x), 1)
```

is the same as v = vec(x).

```
        shape(v, rows(x), columns(x))
```

undoes the vectorization.

*See also*

reshape, vec

*Example*

```
#include <oxstd.h>
main()
{
    print( shape(<0:5>, 2, 4) );
    print( shape(<0:5>, 4, 2)' );
}
```

produces

```
    0.00000      2.0000      4.0000      0.00000
    1.0000       3.0000      5.0000      0.00000

    0.00000      1.0000      2.0000      3.0000
    4.0000       5.0000      0.00000     0.00000
```

# sin, sinh

```
sin(const ma);
sinh(const ma);
    ma              in:  arithmetic type
```

*Return value*

 sin returns the sine of ma, of double or matrix type.

 sinh returns the sine hyperbolicus of ma, of double or matrix type.

*See also*

 acos (for examples), asin, atan, cos, cosh, sinh, tan, tanh

## sizec, sizeof, sizer, sizerc

```
sizec(const ma);
sizeof(const ma);
sizer(const ma);
sizerc(const ma);
```

*Return value*

 Returns an integer value which is the number of elements in the argument:

| type | rows<br>sizeof | columns | sizer | sizec | sizerc |
|---|---|---|---|---|---|
| int, double | 0 | 0 | 1 | 1 | 1 |
| $m \times n$ matrix | $m$ | $n$ | $m$ | $n$ | $m \times n$ |
| string, length $c$ | $c$ | $c$ | 1 | $c$ | $c$ |
| array, length $c$ | $c$ | $c$ | 1 | $c$ | $c$ |
| file $(r \times c)$ | $r$ | $c$ | $c$ | $c$ | $r \times c$ |
| other | 0 | 0 | 0 | 0 | 0 |

A file type variable only has dimensions if it was opened using the 'f' format.

*See also*

 columns, rows

*Example*

```
#include <oxstd.h>
main()
{
    decl i, d, m, s, a, res;
    i = 0; d = 0.0;
    m = unit(3,2);
    s = "aap", a = {"a", "b"};
    res = columns(i)~rows(i)~sizec(i)~sizer(i)~sizerc(i)
        | columns(d)~rows(d)~sizec(d)~sizer(d)~sizerc(d)
        | columns(m)~rows(m)~sizec(m)~sizer(m)~sizerc(m)
        | columns(s)~rows(s)~sizec(s)~sizer(s)~sizerc(s)
        | columns(a)~rows(a)~sizec(a)~sizer(a)~sizerc(a);

    print("%r",
        {"int","double","matrix[3][2]","string[3]","array[2]"},
        "%c",
        {"columns","rows","sizec","sizer","sizerc"},
        "%8.1g", res);
}
```

produces:

```
              columns   rows   sizec   sizer   sizerc
int               0       0      1       1        1
double            0       0      1       1        1
matrix[3][2]      2       3      2       3        6
string[3]         3       3      3       1        3
array[2]          2       2      2       1        2
```

# solveldl

```
solveldl(const ml, const md, const mb);
```

| | | |
|---|---|---|
| ml | in: | $m \times m$ lower diagonal matrix $L$, $LDL' = A$ |
| md | in: | $1 \times m$ matrix with reciprocals of $D$ |
| mb | in: | $m \times n$ matrix $B$, the right-hand side |

*Return value*

Returns the $m \times n$ matrix $X$ from solving $AX = B$.

*Description*

Solves $AX = B$ for $X$ following a square root free Choleski decomposition of $A$ using decldl ($A$ is symmetric and positive definite).

*See also*

decldl (for an example), invertsym

# solveldlband

```
solveldlband(const ml, const md, const mb);
```

| | | |
|---|---|---|
| ml | in: | $p \times m$ vector specifying the $L^b$ matrix |
| md | in: | $1 \times m$ matrix with reciprocals of $D$ |
| mb | in: | $m \times n$ matrix $B$, the right-hand side |

*Return value*

Returns the $m \times n$ matrix $X$ from solving $AX = B$.

If md is the empty matrix, the return value is $m \times n$ matrix $X = L^{-1}B$.

*Description*

Solves $AX = B$ for $X$ when A is a symmetric positive definite band matrix. $A^b$, the band form of $A$, must have been decomposed using decldlband first. See under decldlband for the storage format of $A^b$ and examples to move between $A^b$ and $A$.

*See also*

decldlband (for an example), solvetoeplitz

# solvelu

```
solvelu(const ml, const mu, const mp, const mb);
```
| | | |
|---|---|---|
| ml | in: | $m \times m$ lower diagonal matrix $L$ (use 0 to indicate absence of $L$) |
| mu | in: | $m \times m$ upper diagonal matrix $U$ (use 0 to indicate absence of $U$) |
| mp | in: | $2 \times m$ matrix with interchange permutations in the second row (use 0 to indicate absence of permutations) |
| mb | in: | $m \times n$ matrix $B$, the right-hand side |

*Return value*

Returns the $m \times n$ matrix $X$ from solving $AX = B$, where $A$ is supplied in decomposed form.

*Description*

Solves $AX = B$ for $X$ following a LU decomposition of $A$ using `declu`: $PA = LU$, where $L$ is lower diagonal and $U$ upper diagonal. First $LW = PB$ is solved for $W$ by forward substitution, then $W = UX$ is solved for x by backward substitution. When a diagonal element of $L$ or $U$ is zero, the corresponding element of $X$ will be set to zero.

This function may be used to only do the forward or backward substitution part:
      `solvelu(L,0,0,B)` solves $LX = B$,
      `solvelu(0,U,0,B)` solves $UX = B$.
So can be used to invert a triangular matrix.

*See also*

`declu` (for an example), `invert`

# solvetoeplitz

```
solvetoeplitz(const mr, const cm, const mb);
solvetoeplitz(const mr, const cm, const mb, alogdet);
```
| | | |
|---|---|---|
| mr | in: | double, or $r \times 1$ or $1 \times r$ matrix, specifying the symmetric positive definite (band) Toeplitz matrix |
| cm | in: | dimension of complete Toeplitz matrix: $m \times m, m \geq r$ |
| mb | in: | $m \times n$ matrix $B$, the right-hand side |
| alogdet | in: | (optional argument) address of variable |
| | out: | double, the *logarithm* of (the absolute value of) the determinant of $A$ |

*Return value*

Returns the $m \times n$ matrix $X$ from solving $AX = B$, or 0 if the Toeplitz matrix is singular.

*Description*

Solves $AX = B$ for $X$ when A is symmetric Toeplitz. A Toeplitz matrix has the same values along each diagonal (see under `toeplitz`). The algorithm is based on the Levinson algorithm in Golub and Van Loan (1989, algorithm 4.7.2, page 187).

The algorithm also accepts a non-positive (non-singular) Toeplitz matrix, but note that it computes $\log[\text{abs}(|A|)]$ for the optional third argument. The exponent of that can only be computed for values $\leq$ DBL_MAX_E_EXP and $\geq$ DBL_MIN_E_EXP (see Ch. 9).

*See also*

pacf, toeplitz

*Example*

```
#include <oxstd.h>
main()
{
    decl ct = 10, mb, mt, mx;

    mb = <2;3;4;5;6>;
    mx = solvetoeplitz(<3,.5,.2,.1>, 5, mb);
    print(mx');
    mx = invertsym( toeplitz(<3,.5,.2,.1>,5) ) * mb;
    print(mx');
}
```

produces

| | | | | |
|---|---|---|---|---|
| 0.46189 | 0.63974 | 0.88536 | 1.1737 | 1.7240 |
| 0.46189 | 0.63974 | 0.88536 | 1.1737 | 1.7240 |

# sortbyc, sortbyr

```
sortbyc(const ma, const icol);
sortbyr(const ma, const irow);
```

| | | |
|---|---|---|
| ma | in: | matrix |
| icol | in: | scalar: index of column to sort, or |
| | | matrix: specifying the columns to sort by. |
| irow | in: | index of row to sort |

*Return value*

The reordered (sorted in ascending order) matrix.

*Description*

The `sortbyc` function sorts the rows of a matrix according to the specified column; `sortbyr` sorts the columns of a matrix according to the specified row. Sorting is in ascending order using combsort (Lacey and Box, 1991).

If you want the sorting to be in descending order, you can use `reversec` after `sortbyc`, and `reverser` after `sortbyr`.

The sortbyc function can also sort on multiple columns. In that case specify a vector of columns on which to sort. The sorting is on the first specified column, within that on the second, etc. The elements in the icol argument when it is a matrix are processed by row, so corresponding to vecr(icol).

*See also*

reversec, reverser, sortc, sortr

*Example*

```
#include <oxstd.h>
main()
{
    decl m = <1,0,3;0,4,4;4,3,0>;
    print( sortbyc(m,0), sortbyr(m,0) );

    m = <1,3;1,2;3,4;3,5;2,3;2,2>;

    print("%4.1g", m ~ sortbyc(m, 0) ~ sortbyc(m, 0~1));
}
```

produces

```
    0.00000        4.0000        4.0000
    1.0000         0.00000       3.0000
    4.0000         3.0000        0.00000

    0.00000        1.0000        3.0000
    4.0000         0.00000       4.0000
    3.0000         4.0000        0.00000

   1    3    1    3    1    2
   1    2    1    2    1    3
   3    4    2    2    2    2
   3    5    2    3    2    3
   2    3    3    5    3    4
   2    2    3    4    3    5
```

# sortc, sortcindex, sortr

```
sortc(const ma);
sortr(const ma);
sortcindex(const mb);
```

|      |     |                                    |
|------|-----|------------------------------------|
| ma   | in: | matrix, array or string            |
| mb   | in: | row vector, column vector, array or string |

*Return value*

If ma is a matrix, the return value is ma with each column (sortc) or row (sortr) sorted in ascending order. If ma is scalar the return type and value are that of ma. If ma is an array of strings, the strings are sorted in increasing order (all non-string entries are pushed to the end, and will be in reverse order). If ma is a string, the string is returned unchanged.

The sorting method used is combsort.

The `sortcindex` returns a column vector with the sorted index which results from applying `sortc(mb)` (so `v[sortcindex(v)]` equals `sortc(v)`). A matrix argument to `sortcindex` must be a column vector or a row vector (the transpose is used in the latter case, so `sortcindex(v)` and `sortcindex(v')` are the same).

Applying `sortcindex` twice, as in `sortcindex(sortcindex(v))`, returns the ranking.

*See also*

> `sortbyc, sortbyr`

*Example*

```
#include <oxstd.h>
main()
{
    decl m = <1,0,3;0,4,4;4,3,0>;
    print( sortc(m), sortr(m) );
    print( sortcindex(m[0][]) );
    print( sortc( {"x", "", 2, "aa", 1} ) );
}
```

produces

```
        0.00000        0.00000        0.00000
        1.0000         3.0000         3.0000
        4.0000         4.0000         4.0000

        0.00000        1.0000         3.0000
        0.00000        4.0000         4.0000
        0.00000        3.0000         4.0000

        1.0000
        0.00000
        2.0000

[0] =
[1] = aa
[2] = x
[3] = 1
[4] = 2
```

# spline

```
spline(const my, const mx, const alpha);
spline(const my, const mx, const alpha, agcv);
```

| | | |
|---|---|---|
| my | in: | $T \times n$ matrix with variables (observations in columns) to smooth |
| mx | in: | 0 for evenly spaced $Y$, else $T \times m$ matrix with $X$ (where $m = 1$: same $X$ used for all $Y$s, or $m = n$: corresponding $X$ is used with $Y$) |
| alpha | in: | double, bandwidth $\alpha$ (also see below), 0: automatic bandwidth selection using GCV, $< 0$: absolute value is bandwidth, $> 0$: specifies equivalent number of parameters. |
| agcv | in: | (optional) address, returns GCV (generalized cross validation score) and $k_e$ (equivalent number of parameters) |

*Return value*

Returns a $T \times n$ matrix with the smooth from applying the natural cubic spline. The optional agcv argument is a $2 \times n$ matrix, with the generalized cross validation (GCV) score in the first row, and the equivalent number of parameters in the second.

*Description*

The spline smoothes the cross plot of $Y$ against time (mx argument is 0), or against an $x$ variable. Consider a plot of $y_t$, against $x_t$, and sort the data according to $x$: $a < x_{[1]} < \ldots < x_{[T]} < b$. In a spline model, the sum of squared deviations from a function $g$ is minimized, subject to a roughness penalty:

$$\min \sum_{t=1}^{T} \left[ y_t - g\left(x_{[t]}\right)\right]^2 + \alpha \int_a^b \left[g''(x)\right]^2 \, \mathrm{d}x.$$

Ox uses a *natural cubic spline*, which is cubic because the function $g$ is chosen as a third degree polynomial, and natural because the smooth is a straight line between $a$ and $x_{[1]}$ and between $x_{[1]}$ and $b$. Two good references on splines and nonparametric regression are Green and Silverman (1994) and Hastie and Tibshirani (1994).

The $\alpha$ parameter is the bandwidth: the smaller $\alpha$, the lower the roughness penalty, and hence the closer the smooth will track the actual data.

There are three ways of specifying the bandwidth $\alpha$ :

0 use automatic bandwidth selection based on GCV;
   The GCV criterion is computed as:

$$GCV(\alpha) = T \left( \frac{RSS}{T - 1.25k_e + 0.5} \right).$$

A bracketing search algorithm is used to minimize GCV.

$< 0$  the absolute value is used for the bandwidth;
         No iteration is required.
$> 0$  specifies the equivalent number of parameters $k_e$ to be used.
         A bracketing search algorithm is used to locate the specified $k_e$ ($k_e$ is approximately comparable to the number of regressors used in a linear regression)

The spline is evaluated at the data points, where missing $y_t$ values (both in and outside sample) are estimated by the fit from the smooth. Observations where both $y_t$ and $x_t$ are missing are omitted in the calculations. The missing values used are .NaN.

The spline procedure handles ties in the $x$ variable. The algorithm used to compute the spline is of order $T$, and consists of the Reinsch algorithm combined with the Hutchinson-de Hooch algorithm for computing the GCV score (see Green and Silverman, 1994, Chs. 2 & 3).

For evenly spaced data (e.g. cross plot against time), a natural cubic spline is very close to the Hodrick–Prescott filter which is popular in macro-economics. By default, the Hodrick–Prescott filter uses a bandwidth of 1600, in which case the smoothers from both methods are virtually identical. Also see the OxMetrics book.

*See also*
   lib/Spline3w.ox, lib/HPfilter.ox,

*Example*
   The following example first smoothes the four variables in the variable my using time as the $X$ variable, and automatic bandwidth selection. The second observation of the first variable is set to a missing value.
   The second spline smoothes the cross plot of the last three variables against the first, choosing the bandwidth as 12 equivalent parameters.

```
#include <oxstd.h>
#include <oxfloat.h>

main()
{   decl my, ms, gcv;

    my = loadmat("data/data.in7");
    my[1][0] = M_NAN;
    ms = spline(my, 0, 0);
    print( "%c", {"CONS", "smooth"}, my[:4][0] ~ ms[:4][0]);

    ms = spline(my[][1:], my[][0], 12, &gcv);
    print( "%r", {"GCV", "k_e"}, gcv);
}
```

produces

```
        CONS        smooth
      890.45        890.01
```

```
        .NaN        888.19
      886.33        886.58
      884.88        885.38
      885.25        884.66

GCV                 13.932      1.4645      24.309
k_e                 12.000      11.999      11.999
```

# sprint

```
sprint(const a, ...);
    a           in:  any type
    ...         in:  any type
```

*Return value*

Returns a string containing the written text, or 0 if the sprint buffer was too small (see sprintbuffer).

*Description*

Each argument is printed to a string. See print for a description of formatting. The maximum text length is 2048 characters by default. The sprintbuffer function can be used to enlarge the buffer size.

*Error and warning messages*

sprint(): no string buffer

sprint(): string buffer length exceeded

*See also*

eprint, print, sprintbuffer

*Example*

```
#include <oxstd.h>
main()
{
    decl s = sprint("a", "_", "%0X", 10);
    print( s );
}
```

produces: a_A

# sprintbuffer

```
sprintbuffer(const len);
    len         in:  int
```

*Return value*

Returns 0 of type int.

*Description*

    Sets the size of the internal sprint buffer. The default is 2048 characters, and this function is only needed if texts of more than 2048 characters will be written using `sprint`.

*See also*

    `sprint`

## sqr, sqrt

```
sqr(const ma);
sqrt(const ma);
        ma          in:   arithmetic type
```

*Return value*

    `sqrt` returns the square root of the elements of ma, of double or matrix type.

    `sqr` returns the square of the elements of ma. If the input to `sqr` is a double or matrix, the return type is a double or matrix. If the input is an integer, the return type is integer unless the result would overflow in integer computation. In that case the return type is double in order to represent the result.

*Example*

```
#include <oxstd.h>
main()
{
    print( sqrt(<2,3>), <2,3> .^ 0.5 );
    print( sqr(<2,3>), <2,3> .^ 2 );

    println( sqr(2^14), isint(sqr(2^14)) ? " int" : " double");
    println( sqr(2^15), isint(sqr(2^15)) ? " int" : " double");
    println( pow(2,15), isint(pow(2,15)) ? " int" : " double");
}
```

    produces

```
         1.4142        1.7321
         1.4142        1.7321
         4.0000        9.0000
         4.0000        9.0000
268435456 int
1.07374e+009 double
32768 double
```

*See also*

    `pow, ^ .^` (§13.8.3)

# sscan

```
sscan(const string, const a, ...);
sscan(const astring, const a, ...);
```
|            |     |                                                                                |
|------------|-----|--------------------------------------------------------------------------------|
| string     | in: | string to scan from                                                            |
| astring    | in: | address of string to scan from, on return the scanned text has been removed from the string |
| a          | in: | any type                                                                       |
| ...        | in: | any type                                                                       |

*Return value*

Returns the number of arguments successfully scanned and assigned. If s is a string, then sscan(s,...will leave the string unchanged, whereas sscan(&s,...will remove the read characters from the string. Returns −1 when at the end of the string.

*Description*

This function works as fscan, but reading from a string, not a file. See fscan for a description of formatting; the "%#m" and "%#M" formats may not be used in sscan.

*See also*

fscan, fwrite, scan

*Example*

The following example (samples/inout/inout5.ox) reads one input line at a time (leading spaces in each line are skipped, because of the starting space in " %z"), and reads from that string using sscan. The * in "%*d" suppresses assignment, so the integer is skipped in the file.

```
#include <oxstd.h>
main()
{
    decl file, s, c;
    decl svar, address;

    file = fopen("data/data.in7");
    if (!isfile(file))
    {
        print("failed to open file\n");
        exit(1);
    }
    do
    {   c = fscan(file, " %z", &s);
        if (c > 0 && s[0] == '>')
        {
            sscan(&s, ">%s", &svar, "%*d", "%*d", "%*d",
                "%*d", "%*d", "%d", &address, " ");
            println("variable : ", svar, " address:", address);
            println("remainder: ", s);
```

```
        }
    } while (c > 0);

    fclose(file);
}
```

If the .in7 file can be found, this program produces:

```
variable : CONS address:32
remainder: data 10-04-1992 13:20:38.33
variable : INC address:1336
remainder: data 10-04-1992 13:20:38.33
variable : INFLAT address:2640
remainder: data 10-04-1992 13:20:38.33
variable : OUTPUT address:3944
remainder: data 10-04-1992 13:20:38.33
```

# standardize

```
standardize(const ma);
    ma           in:  T × n matrix A
```

*Return value*

Returns a $T \times n$ matrix holding the standardized columns of ma. If any variance is $\leq 10^{-20}$, then the corresponding column is set to 0.

*Description*

Standardization implies subtracting the mean, and then dividing by the standard deviation. A standardized vector has mean zero and variance one.

*See also*

correlation (for an example), meanc, meanr, varc, varr, variance

# string

```
string(const ma);
    ma          in:  arithmetic type
```

*Return value*

Casts the argument to a string, see §13.8.2.3.

*See also*

double, sprint (for printing to a string)

# strfind, strfindr, strifind, strifindr

```
strfind(const where, const what);
strfindr(const where, const what);
strifind(const where, const what);
strifindr(const where, const what);
```

*Return value*

| where | what | return type |
|---|---|---|
| array of strings | array of $c$ string | $1 \times c$ matrix with indices of occurrence ($-1$ if not found) |
| array of strings | string | int: index of occurrence of string what, or $-1$ if not found |
| string | string | int: index of occurrence of substring what, or $-1$ if not found |
| string | $r \times c$ matrix with character values | $1 \times rc$ matrix with indices of occurrence ($-1$ if not found) |
| string | character | int: index of occurrence of character what, or $-1$ if not found |

*Example*

```
#include <oxstd.h>
main()
{
    decl as1 = {"aa", "bb", "cc", "cc"};
    decl as2 = {"cc", "dd", "aa"};

    print("index = ", strfind(as1, "cc"), "\n",
            "index = ", strfindr(as1, "cc"), "\n",
            "index = ", strfind(as1, "ee"), "\n",
            "index = ", strfind(as1,   as2),
            "packed: ", deletec(strfind(as1, as2), -1) );
    println("first ox is at position ", strfind("ooxox", "ox"),
            " in \"ooxox\"");
    println("last  ox is at position ", strifindr("oOXoX", "ox"),
            " in \"oOXoX\" (no case)");
    println("x is at position ", strfind("ox", 'x'), " in \"ox\"");
    println("x is at position ", strfind("OX", 'x'), " in \"OX\"");
    println("x is at position ", strifind("OX", 'x'),
            " in \"OX\" (no case)");
    println("index of x,o in \"OX\" (no case):",
            strifind("OX", 'x'~'o'));
}
```

produces (remember that the first entry has index 0):

```
index = 2
index = 3
index = -1
```

```
index =
        2.0000       -1.0000        0.00000
packed:
        2.0000        0.00000
first ox is at position 1 in "ooxox"
last  ox is at position 3 in "oOXoX" (no case)
x is at position 1 in "ox"
x is at position -1 in "OX"
x is at position 1 in "OX" (no case)
index of x,o in "OX" (no case):
        1.0000        0.00000
```

## strlwr, strtrim, strupr

```
strlwr(const s);
strtrim(const s);
strupr(const s);
```
     s          in:   the strings to convert

*Return value*

Returns a copy of the string, which is converted to lower case (`strlwr`) or upper-case (`strupr`). `strtrim` returns the string with leading and trailing white space removed.

*Example*

```
#include <oxstd.h>
main()
{
    decl s = "A StrinG\n";
    print( strlwr(s), strupr(s), s);
    s = "  aa  bb \t\n";
    print( "{", strtrim(s), "}");
}
```

produces

```
a string
A STRING
A StrinG
{aa bb}
```

## submat

```
submat(const ma, const r1, const r2, const c1, const c2);
```
    ma       in:  matrix
    r1,r2   in:  int
    c1,c2   in:  int

*Return value*

Returns the submatrix of ma from row indices r1 to r2 and column indices c1 to c2. This is equivalent to ma[r1:r2][c1:c2], apart from that indices below the lower bound are set to the lower bound, and indices above the upper bound set to the upper bound.

*See also*

selectrc, [] (§13.8.2.4)

## sumc, sumr

```
sumc(const ma);
sumr(const ma);
```
      ma           in:  $T \times n$ matrix $A$

*Return value*

The sumc function returns a $1 \times n$ matrix r which holds the sum of the column elements of ma.

The sumr function returns a $T \times 1$ matrix which holds the sum of the row elements of ma.

*See also*

meanc, meanr, prodc, prodr, sumsqrc, sumsqrr, varc, varr

*Example*

```
#include <oxstd.h>
main()
{
    print( sumc(<0:3;1:4;2:5>) | sumsqrc(<0:3;1:4;2:5>));
    print( sumr(<0:3;1:4;2:5>) ~ sumsqrr(<0:3;1:4;2:5>));
}
```

produces

```
        3.0000      6.0000      9.0000      12.000
        5.0000      14.000      29.000      50.000

        6.0000      14.000
        10.000      30.000
        14.000      54.000
```

## sumsqrc, sumsqrr

```
sumsqrc(const ma);
sumsqrr(const ma);
```
      ma           in:  $T \times n$ matrix $A$

*Return value*

The sumsqrc function returns a $1 \times n$ matrix r which holds the sum of the squares of the column elements of ma.

The sumsqrr function returns a $T \times 1$ matrix which holds the sum of the squares of the row elements of ma.

*See also*

sumc (for an example), sumr, varc, varr

# systemcall

```
systemcall(const s);
    s              in:   system command
```

*Return value*

Returns the exit code from the system call.

*Description*

Performs a operating system call, and waits for the call to finish.

*See also*

chdir, getcwd

# tailchi, tailf, tailn, tailt

```
tailchi(const ma, const df);
tailf(const ma, const df1, const df2);
tailn(const ma);
tailt(const ma, const df);
       ma           in:   arithmetic type
       df           in:   arithmetic type, degrees of freedom
       df1          in:   arithmetic type, degrees of freedom in the numerator
       df2          in:   arithmetic type, degrees of freedom in the denominator
```

*Return value*

Returns the requested tail probabilities at ma (the returned tail probabilities are between zero and one):

    tailchi    tail probabilities from $\chi^2(df)$ distribution

    tailf      tail probabilities from $F(df1, df2)$ distribution

    tailn     one-sided standard normal tail probability

    tailt     one-sided tail probabilities from student-$t(df)$ distribution

The tail probabilities are accurate to about 10 digits.

The return type is derived as follows:

| returns | ma | degrees of freedom arguments |
|---|---|---|
| $m \times n$ matrix | $m \times n$ matrix | scalar (int for `tailt`) |
| $m \times n$ matrix | scalar | $m \times n$ matrix |
| $m \times n$ matrix | $m \times n$ matrix | $m \times n$ matrix |
| double | scalar | scalar (int for `tailt`) |

*See also*
>    dens..., prob..., quan...

*Example*
```
#include <oxstd.h>
main()
{
    print("%r", {"chi(2):"}, tailchi(<0,4.61,5.99>, 2));
    print("%r", {"normal:"}, tailn(<-1.96, 0, 1.96>) );
    print("%r", {"t(4):  "}, tailt(<-1.96, 0, 1.96>, 4) );
    print("%r", {"t(50): "}, tailt(<-1.96, 0, 1.96>, 50) );
}
```

produces

```
chi(2):         1.0000      0.099759     0.050037
normal:         0.97500     0.50000      0.024998
t(4):           0.93922     0.50000      0.060777
t(50):          0.97221     0.50000      0.027790
```

# tan, tanh

```
tan(const ma);
tanh(const ma);
```
>    ma             in:   arithmetic type

*Return value*
>    `tan` returns the tangent of `ma`, of double or matrix type.
>    `tanh` returns the tangent hyperbolicus of `ma`, of double or matrix type.

*See also*
>    acos (for examples), asin, atan, cos, cosh, sin, sinh, tanh

# thinc, thinr

```
thinc(const ma, const c);
thinr(const ma, const r);
```
>    ma             in:   $m \times n$ matrix $A$
>    c              in:   int, desired number of columns to extract
>    r              in:   int, desired number of rows to extract

*Return value*

The thinc function returns an $m \times$ c matrix consisting of a selection of columns of the original matrix.

The thinr function returns an r $\times n$ matrix consisting of a selection of rows of the original matrix.

*Description*

The thinc function selects columns as follows:

$$0, \ g, \ 2g, \ 3g, \ldots, \ (c-1)g,$$

$$\text{where} \quad g = 1 + \text{int}\left(\frac{n-c}{c-1}\right) \text{ if } c > 1.$$

The thinr function selects rows similarly.

The example below also indicates how to draw a random sample.

*See also*

aggregatec, aggregater

*Example*

Note in the example that, strictly speaking, it is not necessary to truncate the random indices in idx, as this is done automatically when using a matrix to index another matrix.

```
#include <oxstd.h>
main()
{
    decl m = rann(1000, 2), idx;
    print( thinr(m, 3) ~ m[<0,499,998>][] );
    print( thinc(m', 3)' ~ m[<0,499,998>][] );
                /* get three random indices in idx */
    idx = trunc(ranu(1,3) * rows(m));
    print(idx, m[idx][] ~ m[sortr(idx)][] );
}
```

produces

```
     0.22489        1.7400       0.22489        1.7400
    -0.21417       -1.0037      -0.21417       -1.0037
    0.084549       0.83591      0.084549       0.83591

     0.22489        1.7400       0.22489        1.7400
    -0.21417       -1.0037      -0.21417       -1.0037
    0.084549       0.83591      0.084549       0.83591

      408.00        852.00        877.00

      1.9639      0.073371        1.9639      0.073371
     0.25375       -1.2006       0.25375       -1.2006
     -1.1932      -0.52929       -1.1932      -0.52929
```

# time

```
time();
```

*Return value*
> A string holding the current time.

*See also*
> date (for an example)


# timeofday

```
timeofday(const index);
timeofday(const hours, const minutes);
timeofday(const hours, const minutes, const seconds);
timeofday(const hours, const minutes, const seconds, const h100s);
```

|         |     |                                                                                   |
|---------|-----|-----------------------------------------------------------------------------------|
| index   | in: | in: arithmetic type, calendar index of a certain date with fractional time        |
| hours   | in: | arithmetic type, hours on 24-hour clock                                            |
| minutes | in: | arithmetic type, minutes                                                           |
| seconds | in: | arithmetic type, seconds                                                           |
| h100s   | in: | arithmetic type, hundreds                                                          |

*Return value*
> The timeofday function with two or more arguments returns the fraction of the calendar index of the specified time (see below). If all arguments are an integer, the return value will be an integer.
>
> The timeofday function with one argument takes a calendar index (or vector of indices), as argument, returning a $n \times 4$ matrix with the quadruplet hours, minutes, seconds, hundreds in each row ($n$ is the number of elements in the input).

*Description*
> The calendar index is the Julian day number, with an optional fractional part to specifies the fraction of the day: 2453402.75 corresponds to 2005-01-01T18:00. If the day number is zero, it is interpreted as a time only, so 0.75 is just 18:00 (6 PM).
>
> The "%C" print format is available to print or scan a calendar index.

*See also*
> dayofcalendar, print, timing

*Example*
```
#include <oxstd.h>
main()
{
    decl timeidx = range(0,4)' / 6 + range(0,4)' / 360;
```

```
        println("%5.0f", timeofday(timeidx),
            "%20C", timeidx + dayofcalendar(2005,1,1) );
}
```

produces

```
    0     0     0     0
    4     4     0     0
    8     8     0     0
   12    12     0     0
   16    16     0     0

           2005-01-01
   2005-01-01T04:04
   2005-01-01T08:08
   2005-01-01T12:12
   2005-01-01T16:16
```

# timer, timespan

```
timer();
timespan(const time);
timespan(const time, const time0);
    time        in:  double, value from previous call to timer
    time0       in:  double, (optional argument) start time
```

*Return value*

The `timer` function returns a double representing the current elapsed processor time in one 100th of a second. (Under Windows this is the elapsed time since the process started; under Linux/Unix, it is the CPU time used so far, ignoring time taken by other processes.)

The `timespan(time)` function with returns a string holding the processor time lapsed since the `time` argument.

The `timespan(time, time0)` function with returns a string holding the time lapsed between `time` and `time0`. Both arguments must be measured in one 100th of a second.

*See also*

today

*Example*

```
#include <oxstd.h>
main()
{
    decl i, time, m = rann(100,10), m2;

    time = timer();

    for (i = 0; i < 1000; ++i)
        m2 = m'm;
```

```
        print("time lapsed: ", timespan(time), "\n");
        print("or in seconds: ", (timer() - time) / 100, "\n");
        print("time lapsed: ", timespan(time, timer()), "\n");
}
```

prints the time it took to do the for loop.

## timestr, timing, today

```
timestr(const time);
timing(const mdates);
timing(const mtimes, const mode);
today();
```

| | | |
|---|---|---|
| time | in: | double, date expressed as number of seconds since 1 January 1970 at 00:00:00 (e.g. a value from `timing`) |
| mdates | in: | $T \times k$ matrix with date and time, in order: year, month, day, hour, minute, second (see below). |
| mtimes | in: | $m \times n$ matrix with dates expressed in seconds. |
| mode | in: | int, 0 (or absent): convert date/time to seconds; 1: convert seconds to date/time; 2: convert seconds to calendar index as used in `dayofcalendar` and `timeofday`. |

*Return value*

The `timing` function with `mode` 0 (or no mode specified) converts a $T \times k$ matrix of year, month, ..., seconds (see below) to a $T \times 1$ vector with the date/time expressed as the number of seconds since 1 January 1970 at 00:00:00.

The `timing` function with `mode` 1 converts an $m \times n$ matrix of seconds, returning an $mn \times 6$ matrix with respectively year, month, day, hour, min, sec in the columns.

The `timing` function with `mode` 2 converts an $m \times n$ matrix (or a single double) of seconds to calendar indices, returning an $m \times n$ matrix (or a double).

The `timestr` function returns the date/time expressed as a text string: `"year-month-day hour:min:sec"`. The time is omitted if it is 00:00:00.

The `today` function returns a double with the current date/time expressed in seconds.

*Description*

These functions work with time in seconds: the number of seconds since 1 January 1970 at 00:00:00. This is more restrictive and less convenient than the calendar index (with fraction for time) that is used in `dayofcalendar` and `timeofday`.

The input matrix for `timing` with `mode` 0 (or no mode specified) has a specified data and time in each row, with the columns organized as:

| column | item  | values                                        |
|--------|-------|-----------------------------------------------|
| 0      | year  | full year (e.g. 1970)                         |
| 1      | month | month in year, $1 \ldots 12$ (e.g. 2 for February) |
| 2      | day   | day in month, $1 \ldots 31$                   |
| 3      | hour  | hour in day, $0 \ldots 23$                     |
| 4      | min   | minutes, $0 \ldots 59$                         |
| 5      | sec   | seconds, $0 \ldots 59$                         |

The actual input matrix may have fewer columns, in which case the remainder is assumed to be zero (one for month and day).

*See also*

dayofcalendar, timeofday, timer

*Example*

```
#include <oxstd.h>
main()
{
    decl time1, time2;

    time1 = timing(<1990, 12, 1; 1991, 1, 1>);
    time2 = timing(<1990, 12, 1, 12, 0, 1>);

    println("time1[0]: ", timestr(time1[0]));
    println("time1[1]: ", timestr(time1[1]));
    println("time2:    ", timestr(time2));
    println("today:    ", timestr(today()));
    println("today:    ", "%6.0f", timing(today(), 1));
    println("today:    ", "%C", timing(today(), 2));
}
```

which produces as output:

```
time1[0]: 1990-12-01
time1[1]: 1991-01-01
time2:    1990-12-01 12:00:01
today:    2007-07-19 10:34:24
today:
   2007     7     19     10     34     24
today:    2007-07-19T10:34:24
```

# toeplitz

```
toeplitz(const ma);
toeplitz(const ma, const cm);
```
|         |     |                                                      |
|---------|-----|------------------------------------------------------|
| ma      | in: | double, or $r \times 1$ or $1 \times r$ matrix       |
| cm      | in: | (optional argument) $m$: dimension of matrix to be created, $m \geq r$; if the argument is missing, $m = r$ is used. |

*Return value*

Returns a symmetric Toeplitz matrix.

*Description*

Creates a symmetric Toeplitz matrix using the supplied argument. A Toeplitz matrix has the same values along each diagonal. Here we allow for a banded Toeplitz matrix, e.g. when $r = 3$ and $m = 5$:

$$\begin{pmatrix} a_0 & a_1 & a_2 & 0 & 0 \\ a_1 & a_0 & a_1 & a_2 & 0 \\ a_2 & a_1 & a_0 & a_1 & a_2 \\ 0 & a_2 & a_1 & a_0 & a_1 \\ 0 & 0 & a_2 & a_1 & a_0 \end{pmatrix}$$

When the bandwith equals the dimension (i.e. there are no zeros: $m = r$), we write $\mathcal{T}(a_0, a_1, \ldots, a_{m-1})$ for the Toeplitz matrix.

*See also*

diag, pacf, solvetoeplitz (for an example)

# trace

```
trace(const ma);
    ma          in:  arithmetic type
```

*Return value*

Returns the trace of ma (the sum of its diagonal elements). Return type is double.

*See also*

determinant

*Example*

```
#include <oxstd.h>
main()
{
    print( trace(<2,1;1,4>) );
}
```

produces: 6

# trunc, truncf

```
trunc(const ma);
truncf(const ma);
    ma              in:  arithmetic type
```

*Return value*

trunc returns the truncated elements of ma, of double or matrix type.
truncf is fuzzy truncation.

*Description*

Truncation is rounding towards zero, however, the result remains a double value. Note that conversion to an integer also results in truncation, but that in that case the result is undefined if the real number is too big to be represented as an integer. truncf multiplies positive numbers by one plus the current fuzziness (one minus fuzziness for negative numbers) before truncation.

*See also*

ceil, floor, fuzziness, round,

*Example*

```
#include <oxstd.h>
main()
{
    print( trunc(<-2.0-1e-15, -2.0+1e-15, 2.0-1e-15, 2.0+1e-15>));
    print(truncf(<-2.0-1e-15, -2.0+1e-15, 2.0-1e-15, 2.0+1e-15>));
}
```

produces

```
    -2.0000      -1.0000      1.0000      2.0000
    -1.0000      -1.0000      2.0000      2.0000
```

# unique

unique(const ma);
    ma        in:   matrix

*Return value*

Returns the sorted unique elements of ma as a row vector. Returns an empty matrix if the result is empty. Missing values are skipped.

*See also*

exclusion (for an example), intersection

# unit

unit(const rc);
unit(const r, const c);
    rc        in:   int
    r         in:   int
    c         in:   int

*Return value*

Returns an rc by rc identity matrix (one argument), or a r by c matrix with ones on the diagonal (rest zero).

*See also*

    constant, unit, zeros

*Example*

```
#include <oxstd.h>
main()
{
    print( unit(2) );
}
```

produces

       1.0000      0.00000
       0.00000      1.0000

# unvech

```
unvech(const va);
```
        va          in:  arithmetic type, (column or row) vector to make into sym-
                         metric matrix

*Return value*

    Returns a symmetric matrix, given the vectorized lower diagonal of a symmetric
    matrix.

*Description*

    Undoes the vech operation.

*See also*

    vech (for an example)

# upper

```
upper(const ma);
```
        ma           in:  $m \times n$ matrix

*Return value*

    Returns the upper diagonal (including the diagonal), i.e. returns a copy of the
    input matrix with strict lower-diagonal elements set to zero.

*See also*

    lower (for an example), setdiagonal, setlower, setupper

# va_arglist

```
va_arglist();
```

*Return value*

Returns an array holding the arguments starting with the first variable in the
variable argument list.

*Description*

See §13.5.5.2.

*Example*

```
#include <oxstd.h>
test(const a, ...)
{
    decl i, args = va_arglist();

    println("number of extra arguments: ", sizeof(args));
    for (i = 0; i < sizeof(args); i++)
        println("vararg [", i, "] = ", args[i]);
}
main()
{
    test("tinker", "tailor", "soldier");
}
```

which prints

```
number of extra arguments: 2
vararg [0] = tailor
vararg [1] = soldier
```

# varc, varr

```
varc(const ma);
varr(const ma);
```
    ma              in:   $T \times n$ matrix $A$

*Return value*

The varc function returns a $1 \times n$ matrix holding the variances of the columns
of ma.
The varr function returns a $T \times 1$ matrix holding the variances of the rows of
ma.

*Description*

The variance of $x_t, t = 1, \ldots T$ is computed as:

$$\frac{1}{T} \sum_{t=1}^{T} (x_t - \bar{x})^2, \quad \text{where } \bar{x} = \frac{1}{T} \sum_{t=1}^{T} x_t.$$

*See also*

    meanc, meanr, sumc, sumr, variance

*Example*

```
#include <oxstd.h>
main()
{
    decl m1 = rann(100,2), m2;
    print( variance(m1), varc(m1), varr(m1') );
}
```

produces

```
      1.0356     -0.037133
  -0.037133       0.86569

      1.0356       0.86569

      1.0356
      0.86569
```

# variance

```
variance(const ma);
```
    ma          in:  $T \times n$ matrix $A$

*Return value*

Returns an $n \times n$ matrix holding variance-covariance matrix of ma.

*Description*

Computes the variance-covariance matrix of a $T \times n$ matrix $A = (a_0, a_1, \ldots, a_{n-1})$:

$$T^{-1}\breve{A}'\breve{A}, \quad \text{where } \breve{A} = (a_0 - \bar{a}_0, a_1 - \bar{a}_1, \ldots a_{n-1} - \bar{a}_{n-1}),$$

and

$$\bar{a}_i = \frac{1}{T} \sum_{t=0}^{T-1} a_{it}.$$

*See also*

    acf, correlation, meanc, meanr, standardize, varc, varr

*Example*

```
#include <oxstd.h>
main()
{
    decl m1 = rann(100,2), m2;

    m2 = m1 - meanc(m1);
    print( variance(m1), m2'm2/rows(m2) );
}
```

produces

```
      1.0356      -0.037133
  -0.037133        0.86569

      1.0356      -0.037133
  -0.037133        0.86569
```

# vec

```
vec(const ma);
    ma              in:  arithmetic type
```

*Return value*

If ma is an $m \times n$ matrix, the return value is an $mn \times 1$ matrix consisting of the stacked columns of ma. If ma is scalar, the return value is an $1 \times 1$ matrix consisting of the value ma.

*Description*

Vectorizes a matrix by stacking columns. The shape function can be used to undo the vectorization.

*See also*

shape, vech, vecr

*Example*

```
#include <oxstd.h>
main()
{
    print( vec(<0,1;2,3>) );
}
```

produces

```
    0.00000
    2.0000
    1.0000
    3.0000
```

# vech

```
vech(const ma);
    ma              in:  arithmetic type
```

*Return value*

If ma is an $m \times n$ matrix, the return value is an $(m(m + 1)/2 - j(j + 1)/2) \times 1$ matrix, where $j = \max(m - n, 0)$, consisting of the stacked columns of the lower diagonal of ma. If ma is scalar, the return value is a $1 \times 1$ matrix consisting of the value ma.

*Description*

Vectorizes the lower diagonal of a matrix by stacking columns. use unvech to undo this vectorization.

*See also*

unvech, vec, vecr

*Example*

```
#include <oxstd.h>
main()
{
    decl m = <0,1;2,3>;
    print( vech(m), unvech(vech(m)) );
}
```

produces

```
        0.00000
        2.0000
        3.0000

        0.00000        2.0000
        2.0000         3.0000
```

# vecindex

```
vecindex(const ma);
vecindex(const ma, const mfind);
    ma          in:   matrix
    mfind       in:   matrix (optional argument)
```

*Return value*

vecindex with one argument returns a $p \times 1$ matrix holding the row index of the non-zero elements of vec(ma), where $p$ is the number of non-zero elements in ma. If there is no non-zero element, the function returns the empty matrix (<>).

vecindex with two arguments returns a $p \times 1$ matrix holding the row indices of the elements of vec(ma) which appear in mfind. If none are found, the function returns the empty matrix (<>).

*See also*

shape, vec

*Example*

```
#include <oxstd.h>
main()
{
    decl x = <0,1,2;0,2,0>;
    print(vec(x), vecindex(x)', vecindex(x, 0)' );
}
```
produces

```
          0.00000
          0.00000
          1.0000
          2.0000
          2.0000
          0.00000

          2.0000        3.0000        4.0000

          0.00000       1.0000        5.0000
```

# vecr

```
vecr(const ma);
     ma               in:   arithmetic type
```

*Return value*

If ma is an $m \times n$ matrix, the return value is an $mn \times 1$ matrix consisting of the stacked transposed rows of ma. If ma is scalar, the return value is a $1 \times 1$ matrix consisting of the value ma.

*Description*

Vectorizes a matrix by stacking rows into a column vector. This is compatible with using one empty index on a matrix (see the example).

*See also*

reshape, vec, vech, vecrindex

*Example*

```
#include <oxstd.h>
main()
{
    decl x = <0,1;2,3>;
    print( vecr(x) ~ x[] );
}
```

produces

```
          0.00000       0.00000
          1.0000        1.0000
          2.0000        2.0000
          3.0000        3.0000
```

# vecrindex

```
vecrindex(const ma);
vecrindex(const ma, const mfind);
vecrindex(const ma, const mfind, const bunique);
    ma          in:  matrix
    mfind       in:  matrix (optional argument)
    bunique     in:  1 (optional argument when mfind is present)
```

*Return value*

vecrindex with one argument returns a $p \times 1$ matrix holding the row index of the non-zero elements of vecr(ma), where $p$ is the number of non-zero elements in ma. If there is no non-zero element, the function returns the empty matrix (<>). vecrindex with two argument returns a $p \times 1$ matrix holding the row indices of the elements of vecr(ma) which appear in mfind. In this case, the optional third argument may be used to only report the first occurrence in ma. If none are found, the function returns the empty matrix (<>).

*See also*

vecindex, vecr

*Description*

vecrindex is compatible with using one index on a matrix. When ma is a vector, vecrindex and vecindex will give identical results.

*Example*

```
#include <oxstd.h>
main()
{
    decl x = <0,1,2;0,2,0>;

    print(vecr(x),
        "1 argument:",   vecrindex(x)',
        "2 arguments:",  vecrindex(x, 0)',
        "3 arguments:",  vecrindex(x, <0,2>, 1)');
    print("non-zeros:", vecr(x)[vecrindex(x)]',
        "zeros:", vecr(x)[vecrindex(x, 0)]' );
}
```

produces

```
        0.00000
        1.0000
        2.0000
        0.00000
        2.0000
        0.00000
1 argument:
        1.0000        2.0000        4.0000
2 arguments:
        0.00000       3.0000        5.0000
```

```
3 arguments:
      0.00000        2.0000
non-zeros:
      1.0000         2.0000         2.0000
zeros:
      0.00000        0.00000        0.00000
```

## zeros

```
zeros(const r, const c);
zeros(const ma);
     r              in:   int
     c              in:   int
     ma             in:   matrix
```

*Return value*

zeros(r,c) returns an r by c matrix filled with zeros.

zeros(ma) returns a matrix of the same dimension as ma, filled with zeros.

*See also*

ones, unit, new

*Example*

```
#include <oxstd.h>
main()
{
    print( zeros(2, 2) );
}
```

produces

```
     0.00000        0.00000
     0.00000        0.00000
```

# Chapter 9

# Predefined Constants

**oxstd.h** defines (requires #include <oxstd.h>):

| | |
|---|---|
| FALSE | 0 |
| TRUE | 1 |

**oxfloat.h** defines (requires #include <oxfloat.h>):

| | |
|---|---|
| M_PI | $\pi$ |
| M_2PI | $2\pi$ |
| M_PI_2 | $\pi/2$ |
| M_1_PI | $1/\pi$ |
| M_SQRT2PI | $\sqrt{(2\pi)}$ |
| M_E | $e = \exp(1)$ |
| M_EULER | Euler's constant, $\gamma$ |
| M_NAN | .NaN (Not a Number), also see isnan and isdotnan |
| M_INF | .Inf (Infinity) |
| M_INF_POS | +.Inf (Infinity) |
| M_INF_NEG | -.Inf (minus Infinity) |
| DBL_DIG | number of decimal digits of precision |
| DBL_EPSILON | machine precision $\epsilon_m$, smallest number such that $1.0 + \epsilon_m \,! = 1.0$ |
| DBL_MANT_DIG | number of bits in mantissa |
| DBL_MAX | maximum double value |
| DBL_MIN | minimum positive double value |
| DBL_MIN_EXP | minimum 2 exponent |
| DBL_MAX_EXP | maximum 2 exponent |
| DBL_MIN_E_EXP | minimum $e$ exponent |
| DBL_MAX_E_EXP | maximum $e$ exponent |
| DBL_MIN_10_EXP | minimum 10 exponent |
| DBL_MAX_10_EXP | maximum 10 exponent |
| INT_MAX | maximum integer value |
| INT_MIN | minimum integer value |

The following constants are predefined by the Ox compiler:

| | |
|---|---|
| OX_64_BIT | when running 64-bit Ox |
| OX_AIX | when running on IBM/AIX |
| OX_BIG_ENDIAN | only on a big-endian machine (Unix workstations) |
| OX_DecUNIX | when running on Dec/UNIX |
| OX_HPUX | when running on HP-UX |
| OX_Irix | when running on SGI/Irix |
| OX_Linux | when running on Linux/PC |
| OX_OS_X | when running on Sun |
| OX_Sun | when running on Mac/OS X |
| OX_Windows | when running under Windows |

# 9.1 Missing values (NaN)

The hardware-defined missing value is called *Not a Number*, or .NaN for short. Any computation involving a .NaN results in a .NaN. The format used when printing output is .NaN.

In a matrix constant, either .NaN, M_NAN or a dot may be used to represent a missing value (M_NAN requires oxfloat.h). If the dot is the first or last element, an extra space is required to avoid confusion with dot-greater/less than.

In a double constant, either .NaN or M_NAN may be used to represent a missing value (M_NAN requires oxfloat.h).

A number of procedures are available to deal with missing values, most importantly:

- deletec(): deletes all columns which have a .NaN,
- deleter(): deletes all rows which have a .NaN,
- isdotnan(): returns matrix of 0's and 1's: 1 if the element is a .NaN, 0 otherwise,
- isnan(): returns 1 if *any* element is a .NaN, 0 otherwise.
- selectc(): selects all columns which have a .NaN,
- selectr(): selects all rows which have a .NaN,

# 9.2 Infinity

Infinity also exists as a special value supported by the hardware. Infinity can be positive or negative (printed as +.Inf and -.Inf), and can be used in comparisons as any normal number. You can use .Inf, +.Inf and -.Inf in your code. Alternatively, the predefined constants M_INF, M_INF_POS, and M_INF_NEG are defined in oxfloat.h. The isdotinf() function tests for infinity.

# Chapter 10

# Graphics function reference

## 10.1 Introduction

Graphs in Ox are drawn on a graphics worksheet, consisting of 15 000 by 10 000 pixels, with (0,0) in the bottom left corner:

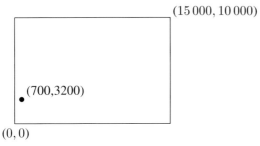

Positions can be specified in pixel coordinates, as for example $(p_x, p_y) = (70, 3200)$. More often it is convenient to use real world coordinates. This is done by specifying an area on the graphics worksheet, and attaching real world coordinates to it. These areas are allowed to overlap, but need not:

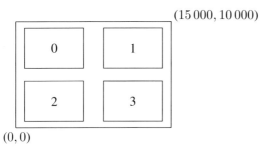

Suppose we have set up all areas as being from $(x, y) = (0.0, 0.0)$ to $(x, y) = (1.0, 1.0)$ (again within each area the origin is the lower left corner). Then we can draw a line through area 2 in two ways:

(1) in real coordinates within an area

step 1: select area 2;
step 2: move to (0.0, 0.0);
step 3: draw a line to (1.0,1.0).

(2)  using pixel coordinates on the worksheet

step 1: move to pixel coordinates (600,600);
step 2: draw a line to pixel coordinates (3600, 3600),

where we assume that (600,600) to (3600,3600) are the pixel coordinates chosen for area 2. Drawing in real world coordinates has the advantage that it corresponds more closely to our data.

In general we use high level drawing functions. These select an area, and a type of graph, and give the data to plot. Note that the supplied matrix must have the data in *rows* (unlike, for example,. the Database, where it is in columns). Several functions documented below expect an $m \times T$ matrix for $T$ observations on $m$ variables. The header file to be included for graphics is oxdraw.h.

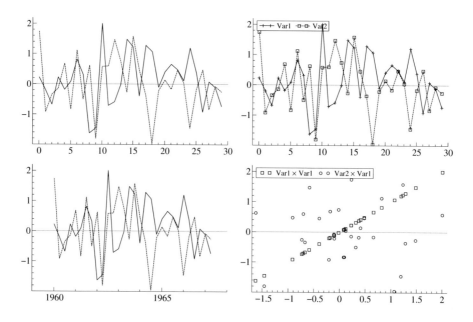

**Figure 10.1**   draw1.eps.

*Example*

................................................*samples/graphics/draw1.ox*

```
#include <oxstd.h>
#include <oxdraw.h>

main()
{
    decl m = rann(30,2);

    Draw(0, m', 0, 1);
    DrawMatrix(1, m', {"Var1", "Var2"}, 0, 1, 2);
    DrawT(2, m', 1960, 1, 4);
    DrawXMatrix(3, m', {"Var1", "Var2"}, m', "Var1", 1, 3);

    SetDrawWindow("draw1");
    ShowDrawWindow();
    SaveDrawWindow("draw1.ps");
}
```

.................................................................................

The file `draw1.eps` produces Fig. 10.1. The `SetDrawWindow` function is only relevant when you use *OxRun* to run the program. Then it may be used to specify the name of the graphics window in *OxMetrics*.

*Example*

................................................*samples/graphics/draw2.ox*

```
#include <oxstd.h>
#include <oxdraw.h>

main()
{
    decl m = rann(100,2);

    DrawAcf(0, m[][0]', "var", 9);
    DrawDensity(1, m[][0]', "var", TRUE, TRUE, TRUE);
    DrawQQ(2, m[][0]', "var", QQ_N, 0, 0);
    DrawQQ(3, m[][0]', "var", QQ_U, 0, 0);

    ShowDrawWindow();
    SaveDrawWindow("draw2.eps");
}
```

.................................................................................

The file `draw2.eps` produces Fig. 10.2.

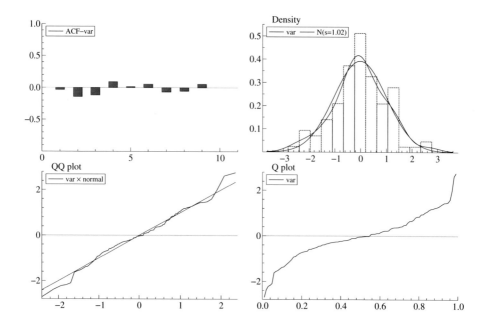

**Figure 10.2**   `draw2.eps`.

## 10.2 Symbol and line types

**Table 10.1**   Symbol types in graphics.

| | | | |
|---|---|---|---|
| `PL_FILLBOX` | filled box | `PL_FILLCIRCLE` | filled circle |
| `PL_BOX` | open box | `PL_TRIANGLE` | triangle |
| `PL_PLUS` | plus | `PL_FILLTRIANGLE` | filled triangle |
| `PL_DASH` | dash | `PL_DIAMOND` | diamond |
| `PL_CIRCLE` | circle | `PL_FILLDIAMOND` | filled diamond |
| `PL_LINE` | line | `PL_CROSS` | cross |

**Table 10.2**  Line types in graphics.

| | |
|---|---|
| TP_SOLID | solid line |
| TP_DOTTED | dotted line |
| TP_DASHED | dashed line |
| TP_LDASHED | long-dashed line |
| TP_USER | user-defined line |

**Table 10.3**  Plotting styles in graphics.

| | |
|---|---|
| ST_LINE | line (points connected) |
| ST_SYMBOLS | symbols |
| ST_LINESYMBOLS | line and symbols |
| ST_INDEX | index line |
| ST_INDEXSYMBOLS | index line with symbols |
| ST_BARS | bars |
| ST_SHADING | shading |

**Table 10.4**  Default line attributes in graphics.

| index | color | line type | width | symbol | size |
|---|---|---|---|---|---|
| 0 | white | solid | 10 | plus | 90 |
| 1 | black | solid | 6 | plus | 90 |
| 2 | red | solid | 10 | plus | 90 |
| 3 | blue | solid | 10 | box | 90 |
| 4 | blue/green | solid | 10 | circle | 90 |
| 5 | purple | dotted | 10 | plus | 90 |
| 6 | green | dotted | 10 | plus | 90 |
| 7 | brown/yellow | long dash | 10 | plus | 90 |
| 8 | dark purple | long dash | 10 | plus | 90 |
| 9 | pastel yellow | dotted | 10 | plus | 90 |
| 10 | pastel green | dotted | 10 | plus | 90 |
| 11 | pastel blue | solid | 10 | plus | 90 |
| 12 | | solid | 10 | plus | 90 |
| 13 | light grey | solid | 10 | plus | 90 |
| 14 | grey | solid | 10 | plus | 90 |
| 15 | light grey | solid | 10 | plus | 90 |

**Table 10.5**  Default palette and error fan attributes in graphics.

| index | color | index | color | index | color |
|---|---|---|---|---|---|
| -1 | wireframe | 2 | red | 5 | purple |
| 0 | white | 3 | blue | 6 | green |
| 1 | black | 4 | blue/green | 7 | brown/yellow |

## 10.3 Function reference

## CloseDrawWindow

```
CloseDrawWindow();
```
*No return value.*

*Description*
    Starts a new draw window for subsequent graphs. Note that the *OxMetrics* graphics window will remain active there. A call to ShowDrawDrawing also clears the graphics buffer, so does not need to be followed by a call to CloseDrawWindow.

## Draw

```
Draw(const iArea, const mYt);
Draw(const iArea, const mYt, const dXfirst, const dXstep);
```

| | | |
|---|---|---|
| iArea | in: | int, area index |
| mYt | in: | matrix, $m \times T$ matrix with $m$ rows of data |
| dXfirst | in: | (optional) double, $X$-value of first observation, $x$, default is 1 |
| dXstep | in: | (optional) double, gap between $X$-values, $d_x$, default is 1 |

*No return value.*

*Description*
    This function draws $m$ variables against an $X$ variable, where the $X$ variable consists of evenly spaced observations $x, x + d_x, x + 2d_x, x + 3d_x, \ldots$. Each variable is drawn by linking up the points. The first line index is 2.

## DrawAcf

```
DrawAcf(const iArea, const vY, const sY, const cLag, ...);
DrawAcf(const iArea, const vY, const sY, const cLag, const fAcf,
    const fPacf, const fErrorBand, int iIndex, const fBar);
```

| | | |
|---|---|---|
| iArea | in: | int, area index |
| mY | in: | $k \times T$ matrix, each *row* is a new plot |
| sY | in: | string, variable name, or array of strings ($k > 1$) |
| cLag | in: | int, highest lag to be used in the ACF |
| fAcf | in: | int, TRUE: draw ACF (optional argument, drawn by default) |
| fPacf | in: | int, TRUE: draw PACF (optional argument, not drawn by default) |

| fErrorBand | in: | int, TRUE: draw error bands (optional argument, not drawn by default) |
| iIndex | in: | int, line index, see Table 10.4, (optional argument, default is 2). |
| fBar | in: | int, TRUE: draw bar plot, else draw index plot (optional argument, using bars by default) |

*No return value.*

*Description*

Draws the autocorrelation function and/or partial autocorrelation function. The autocorrelation at lag zero is always one, and not included in the graph. The $y$-axis is $[0, 1]$ if all autocorrelations are positive, $[-1, 1]$ otherwise. The acf is computed similarly to the acf() library function.

*See also*

acf, DrawCorrelogram for an example.

# DrawAdjust

DrawAdjust(const iType, ...);

| iType | in: | int, type of adjustment |
| d1, ..., d4 | in: | optional extra arguments, int or double (defaults to $-1$ if missing) |

*No return value.*

*Description*

This function adjust the *most recently created* graphics object. For example, immediately after a call to Draw(), you can use DrawAdjust to change the line type.

The iType argument specifies the type of adjustment:

| ADJ_AREA_3D | coordinates of the 3D view point of the specified area, |
| ADJ_AREA_P | pixel coordinates of the specified area, |
| ADJ_AREA_X | $X$ world coordinates of the specified area, |
| ADJ_AREA_Y | $Y$ world coordinates of the specified area, |
| ADJ_AREA_Z | $Z$ world coordinates of the specified area, |
| ADJ_AREAMATRIX | area layout (area matrix), boxing and margin, |
| ADJ_AXISCENTRE | centre the axis labels between the large tick marks, |
| ADJ_AXISGRID | set grid lines for the current axis, |
| ADJ_AXISHIDE | hide the axis, |
| ADJ_AXISLABEL | set the label rotation, font size and tick mark size |
| ADJ_AXISLINE | control the axis line, |
| ADJ_AXISSCALE | set the axis scaling type |

| ADJ_COLOR | change line type and colour, |
|---|---|
| ADJ_COLORMODEL | change display or saved PostScript colour model, |
| ADJ_INDEX | make into index line, |
| ADJ_MINMAX | adjust minimum and maximum $y$ value (also affects area), |
| ADJ_PAPERCOLOR | adjust the colour of the paper (RGB), |
| ADJ_PAPERSCALE | adjust the $Y$ scale of the paper (default is 100%), |
| ADJ_SCALE | adjust scale and shift factor for the vector line, |
| ADJ_SYMBOLUSE | change symbol/line drawing mode, |
| ADJ_SYMBOL | change symbol type and size. |

The expected number of arguments depends on the type of adjustment (use $-1$ to keep the default value):

| constant | d1 | d2 | d3 | d4 | d5 |
|---|---|---|---|---|---|
| ADJ_AREA_3D | area | azimuth | elevation | distance | twist |
| ADJ_AREA_P | area | $x_{min}$ | $y_{min}$ | width | height |
| ADJ_AREA_X | area | $x_{min}$ | $x_{max}$ | grow | |
| ADJ_AREA_Y | area | $y_{min}$ | $y_{max}$ | grow | |
| ADJ_AREA_Z | area | $z_{min}$ | $z_{max}$ | grow | |
| ADJ_AREASCOLOR | *red*:0–255 | *green*:0–255 | *blue*:0–255 | | |
| ADJ_AREAMATRIX | $Y$ areas | $X$ areas | box | margin | |
| ADJ_AXISCENTRE | 0,1 | | | | |
| ADJ_AXISGRID | 0,1 | colour | type | | |
| ADJ_AXISHIDE | 0,1 | | | | |
| ADJ_AXISLABEL | rotation | font size | tick size | | |
| ADJ_AXISLINE | line at $y = 0$ | above | no line | no small | |
| ADJ_AXISSCALE | type | scale | shift | | |
| ADJ_COLOR | colour | type | | | |
| ADJ_COLORMODEL | display:0,1 | print:0-3 | | | |
| ADJ_INDEX | 0,1,2 | base | | | |
| ADJ_LEGEND | area | no columns | font size | resize | box all |
| ADJ_MINMAX | minimum | maximum | | | |
| ADJ_PAPERCOLOR | *red*:0–255 | *green*:0–255 | *blue*:0–255 | | |
| ADJ_PAPERSCALE | percentage | | | | |
| ADJ_SCALE | scale | shift | | | |
| ADJ_SYMBOLUSE | style | | | | |
| ADJ_SYMBOL | type | size | | | |

Some notes and examples:

ADJ_AREA_3D expects the area number as the first argument. The azimuth is the rotation along the $Z$ axis (or, more precisely orthogonal to the line of view). Elevation is the angle with the $X$–$Y$ plane, and twist the rotation along the line of view. Azimuth, elevation and twist are specified in degrees, distance is in area units. The default values of azimuth, elevation, distance and twist for Fig. 10.8 correspond approximately to: $-125, 25, 1800, 0$;

ADJ_AREA_P expects the area number as the first argument.

ADJ_AREA_X, ADJ_AREA_Y, ADJ_AREA_Z all expect the area number as the first argument. Real-world area adjustment does currently not work properly for 3D graphs. All have an optional argument grow; set this to one if the area should only grow if it already has dimensions fixed.

ADJ_AREAMATRIX Adjust the rows and columns of the area matrix from the default For example, when there are two areas, the default layout is $2 \times 1$. To put the graphs next to each other:

```
DrawAdjust(ADJ_AREAMATRIX, 1, 2);
```

Set the third argument to one to box all areas. The margin size can be changed with the fourth argument (the default is 640)

ADJ_AXIS... Unless explicitly created, axes are only made once the graph is displayed. Therefore, adjustments to an axis need to be preceeded by an explicit creation, as for example in:

```
DrawT(1, x, 1960, 1, 4);
DrawAxisAuto(1, 1);              // create a default X axis
DrawAdjust(ADJ_AXISCENTRE, 1);  // and centre the dates
```

ADJ_AXISGRID Use $-1$ for default colour and line type:

```
DrawAxisAuto(0, 1);
DrawAdjust(ADJ_AXISGRID, 1, -1, -1);
```

ADJ_AXISLABEL Rotation changes the label rotation relative to the axis, the value is $0, 1$, or $-1$ to leave the default. The default font size is $300$ and tick size $6$; use $-1$ to leave the default.

ADJ_AXISLINE All arguments are $0, 1$, or $-1$ to leave the default. The second ('above') puts the labels on the opposite side of the axis; ' no line' omits the base line (leaving the tick marks); 'no small' removes the small tick marks.

ADJ_AXISSCALE The type for is one of:

| | |
|---|---|
| AXIS_LINEAR | – standard axis, |
| AXIS_LOG | – log-scale (data is in natural logarithms), |
| AXIS_LOG10 | – log10-scale (data is in base-10 logarithms), |
| AXIS_SCALED | – scaled: set scale and shift as 2nd and 3rd value, |
| AXIS_DATE | – dated: interpret as Julian date/time values, see Fig. 10.6 for an example. |

```
DrawT(0, log(x), 1960, 1, 4);
DrawAxisAuto(0, 0);                      // default Y axis
DrawAdjust(ADJ_AXISSCALE, AXIS_LOG);  // use log scale
```

ADJ_COLOR Colour is $0 \ldots 15$: $0$ = background (white), $1$ = foreground (black), $2 \ldots 15$ are remaining colours. Type is $0 \ldots 15$. By default, the colour and type are equal, with settings given in Table 10.4. Use $-1$ to leave the default.

ADJ_COLORMODEL The display mode can be 0 (colour) or 1 (b&w). The print mode can take the values $0 - 3$: $0$ = black & white, $1$ = black, white & gray, $2$ = gray levels, $3$ = colour. This defines the colour model that is used for saving graphs in PostScript.

ADJ_INDEX  Use d1=1 to change to an index line (in that case d2 defaults to 0), and d1=2 to change to a bar. The base argument is the point to which the index lines or bars are drawn. When omitted, it is assumed to be zero. An index line is a single vertical line, centred on the observation values — multiple index lines will overwrite each other. The bar type is centred on the observation value, and will make space if multiple bars are drawn. If the bars become too thin, they will become a single line drawn in the colour, instead of a black outline filled with the colour.

ADJ_MINMAX  Sets the minimum and maximum of the previous vector or histogram object. This implies that the area will encompass these values, and therefore differs from ADJ_AREA_Y, which enforces a $Y$ range.

ADJ_PAPERCOLOR  Sets the color of the paper (not the areas).

ADJ_PAPERSCALE  This adjust the $Y$ scale as a percentage of the original. To set half size (50%; an example is given under DrawXYZ):

```
DrawAdjust(ADJ_PAPERSCALE, 50);
```

ADJ_SYMBOL  Symbol types are listed in Table 10.1.

ADJ_SYMBOLUSE  Style can be: 0 = draw line, 1 = draw symbols, 2 = draw both.

```
DrawT(0, x, 1960, 1, 4);
DrawAdjust(ADJ_SYMBOL, PL_CIRCLE, 150);
DrawAdjust(ADJ_SYMBOLUSE, 2);
```

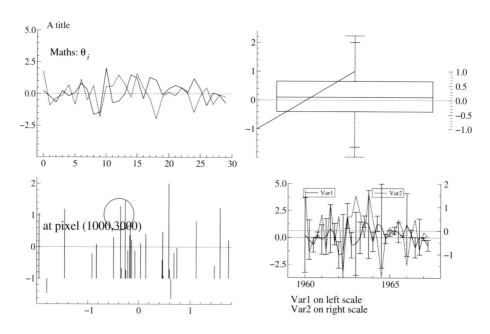

**Figure 10.3**   Illustration of DrawAdjust .

*Example*

A selection of adjustments is used in the following listing, producing Figure 10.3. Another example is given under `DrawCorrelogram()`, and `DrawXYZ()`.

............................................*samples/graphics/draw4.ox*

```
#include <oxstd.h>
#include <oxdraw.h>
main()
{
    decl m = rann(30,2);
    Draw(0, m', 0, 1);                      // draw 2 variables
    DrawAdjust(ADJ_MINMAX, -5, 5);          // adjust y min/max
    DrawTitle(0, "A title");                    // set the title
    DrawText(0, "Maths: $\\theta_i$", 1, 3); // text at (1,3)
                            // add text at pixel coordinates
    DrawPText(0, "at pixel (1000,3000)", 1000, 3000, 0, 400);

    DrawBoxPlot(1, m[][0]', "Var1");        // draw a box plot
    DrawLine(1, 0, -1, 1, 1, 4);      //and a line in the plot
        // draw a circle, is in area 2 but belongs to area 1
    DrawPSymbol(1, 3000, 3000, 4000, 4000, PL_CIRCLE,3);
    DrawAxisAuto(1, FALSE);                 // draw default y axis
                                            // add a second y axis
    DrawAxis(1, FALSE, 2, -1, 1, -1, 0.5, 0.1, 0);
    DrawAdjust(ADJ_AXISLINE, 0, 1, 1, 0);       // adjust axis
                                            // draw a cross plot
    DrawXMatrix(2, m[][0]', "Var1", m[][1]', "Var2");
    DrawAdjust(ADJ_INDEX, 1, -1);       // change to index line
    DrawLegend(2, 0, 0, 1);                 // hide the legend

    DrawTMatrix(3, m[][0]', "Var1", 1960, 1, 4);        // draw
    DrawZ(m[][1]');                     // add 2nd var as error bar
    DrawLegend(3, 100, 50, 0);              // draw the legend
    DrawAdjust(ADJ_AREA_X, 3, 1959, 1968);     //fix x(world)
                        // also fix pixel location of area 3
    DrawAdjust(ADJ_AREA_P, 3, 9000, 1500, 5000, 3000);

    DrawTMatrix(4, m[][1]', "Var2", 1960, 1, 4, 0, 3);
                            // draw area 4 on top of area 3
    DrawAdjust(ADJ_AREA_P, 4, 9000, 1500, 5000, 3000);
    DrawAdjust(ADJ_AREA_X, 4, 1959, 1968);     //same x world
    DrawAxisAuto(4, TRUE, FALSE);           // remove x axis
    DrawAxisAuto(4, FALSE, TRUE, ANCHOR_MAX);   //move axis
    DrawAdjust(ADJ_AXISLINE, TRUE, TRUE);   // labels right
    DrawLegend(4, 550, 50, 0);              // move legend

    DrawPText(4, "Var1 on left scale", 9100, 700);
    DrawPText(4, "Var2 on right scale", 9100, 400);

    DrawAdjust(ADJ_AREAMATRIX, 2, 2);       // 5 areas, use 2x2

    ShowDrawWindow();                       // show this concoction
    SaveDrawWindow("draw4.gwg");
```

```
        SaveDrawWindow("draw4.eps");
    }
```
................................................................................

# DrawAxis, DrawAxisAuto

```
DrawAxis(const iArea, const iIsXaxis, const dAnchor, const dAxmin,
    const dAxmax, const dFirstLarge, const dLargeStep,
    const dSmallStep, const iFreq);
DrawAxis(const iArea, const iIsXaxis, const dAnchor, const dAxmin,
    const dAxmax, const dFirstLarge, const dLargeStep,
    const dSmallStep, const iFreq, const dAnchor2);
DrawAxisAuto(const iArea, const iIsXaxis, ...);
DrawAxisAuto(const iArea, const iIsXaxis, const fShow,
    const iAnchor, const dAnchor, const dAnchor2);
```

| | | |
|---|---|---|
| iArea | in: | area index |
| iIsXAxis | in: | 1: $X$ axis, 0: $Y$ axis, 2: $Z$ axis |
| dAnchor | in: | if iAnchor=ANCHOR_USER: anchor of the axis ($Y$ location of $X$, $X$ location of $Y$ and $Z$ axis) |
| dAnchor2 | in: | if iAnchor=ANCHOR_USER: anchor of the 3D axis ($Z$ location of $X$ and $Y$ axis, $Y$ location of $Z$) |
| dAxmin | in: | axis minimum |
| dAxmax | in: | axis maximum |
| dFirstLarge | in: | location of first large tick |
| dLargeStep | in: | step size between large ticks |
| dSmallStep | in: | step size between small ticks |
| iFreq | in: | frequency (for time series X-axis, set to 0 otherwise) |
| fShow | in: | TRUE: show the axis |
| iAnchor | in: | axis anchor location, ANCHOR_MIN: at minimum, ANCHOR_MAX: at maximum, ANCHOR_USER: at dAnchor |

*No return value.*

*Description*

    DrawAxis draws an axis, fully specified.

    DrawAxisAuto draws an axis with automatic design.

*See also*

    DrawAdjust (for examples)

# DrawBoxPlot

```
DrawBoxPlot(const iArea, const mY, const sY);
DrawBoxPlot(const iArea, const vY, const sY, const iIndex);
```
|        |     |                                                           |
|--------|-----|-----------------------------------------------------------|
| iArea  | in: | int, area index                                           |
| mY     | in: | $k \times T$ matrix, each *row* is a new plot (needs $T > 5$) |
| sY     | in: | string, variable name, or array of strings ($k > 1$)      |
| iIndex | in: | int, line index, see Table 10.4, (optional argument, default is 2). |

*No return value.*

*Description*

Draws a box plot of the data in the specified area.

A box plot shows the distribution of a variable in terms of its quartiles, labelled $Q_1, Q_2, Q_3$ (the 25%, 50% and 75% quartiles). Define the interquartile range as $IQR = 1.5(Q_3 - Q_1)$. The box plot consists of the following elements:

- a box, with horizontal lines at $Q_1, Q_2$ (the median) and $Q_3$;
- a vertical line from $Q_1 - IQR$ to $Q_3 + IQR$ (omitted inside the box);
- individual observations: all observations outside the $(Q_1 - IQR, Q_3 + IQR)$ range, plus the two observations on either end which just fall inside this range.

*See also*

DrawAdjust (for an example)

# DrawCorrelogram

```
DrawCorrelogram(const iArea, const mY, const sY, const cLag);
```
|        |     |                                                      |
|--------|-----|------------------------------------------------------|
| iArea  | in: | int, area index                                      |
| mY     | in: | $k \times T$ matrix, each *row* is a new plot        |
| sY     | in: | string, variable name, or array of strings ($k > 1$) |
| cLag   | in: | int, highest lag to be used in correlogram           |

*No return value.*

*Description*

Draws a correlogram which plots the autocorrelation function. The autocorrelation at lag zero is always one, and not included in the graph. The $y$-axis is $[0, 1]$ if all autocorrelations are positive, $[-1, 1]$ otherwise. The acf is computed differently from that in the acf() library function. The difference is that DrawCorrelogram uses the running mean:

$$\hat{r}_j^* = \frac{\sum_{t=j+1}^{T} (x_t - \bar{x}_0)(x_{t-j} - \bar{x}_j)}{\sqrt{\sum_{t=j+1}^{T} (x_t - \bar{x}_0)^2 \sum_{t=j+1}^{T} (x_{t-j} - \bar{x}_j)^2}}.$$

Here $\bar{x}_0 = \frac{1}{T-j} \sum_{t=j+1}^{T} x_t$ is the sample mean of $x_t$, $t = j+1, \ldots, T$, and

$\bar{x}_j = \frac{1}{T-j} \sum_{t=j+1}^{T} x_{t-j}$ is the sample mean of $x_{t-j}$, so that $\hat{r}_j^*$ corresponds to a proper sample correlation coefficient. The difference with the definition of the sample autocorrelations in (8.1) tends to be small, and vanishes asymptotically.

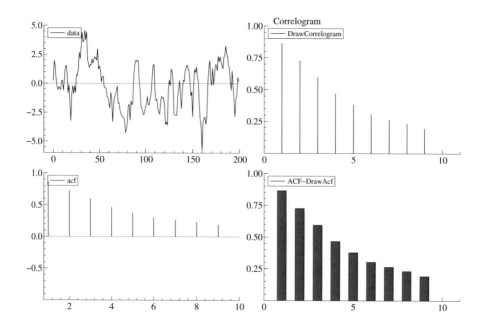

**Figure 10.4**  Autocorrelation functions.

*See also*

    acf, DrawAcf to draw the standard ACF.

*Example*

    The following example compares the two correlograms, with the bottom graph holding the standard ACF, computed using the acf() function.

    ..........................................*samples/graphics/draw5.ox*

```
#include <oxstd.h>
#include <oxdraw.h>
main()
{
    decl lag = 9;
    decl m = cumulate(rann(200,1), 0.9);

    DrawMatrix(0, m', "data", 0, 1);
    DrawCorrelogram(1, m', "DrawCorrelogram", lag);

    decl macf = acf(m, lag);           // compute standard ACF
    DrawMatrix(2, macf[1:][]', "acf", 1, 1);// draw the ACF
```

```
        DrawAdjust(ADJ_INDEX, 1);       // change to index line
        DrawAdjust(ADJ_MINMAX, -1, 1); // set y range to [-1 1]

        DrawAcf(3, m', "DrawAcf", lag);

        ShowDrawWindow();
}
```

# DrawDensity

```
DrawDensity(const iArea, const vY, const sY, ...);
DrawDensity(const iArea, const vY, const sY, const fDens,
    const fHist, const fNormal, BOOL fCdf, BOOL fStand,
    const cBar, const iIndex);
```

| | | |
|---|---|---|
| iArea | in: | int, area index |
| mY | in: | $k \times T$ matrix, each *row* is a new plot |
| sY | in: | string, variable name, or array of strings ($k > 1$) |
| fDens | in: | int, TRUE: draw estimated density (optional, default) |
| fHist | in: | int, TRUE: draw histogram (optional, not drawn by default) |
| fNormal | in: | int, TRUE: add the normal density with same mean and variance for reference (optional, not drawn by default) |
| fCdf | in: | int, TRUE: plot CDF in separate area (optional, not drawn by default); this is drawn as a QQ plot against the normal with same mean and variance (unless fStand=TRUE) |
| fStand | in: | int, TRUE: use standardized data (optional, default uses original data) |
| cBar | in: | int, number of bars (0: use default; optional argument) |
| iIndex | in: | int, line index for density, see Table 10.4, (optional argument, default is 2). |

*No return value.*

*Description*

Draws the histogram and/or density of the data in the specified area. When fNormal is TRUE, a normal density with the same mean and variance as the data will be drawn.

The density estimate is based on a kernel density estimation, with Gaussian kernel, and optimal bandwidth (if the data are indeed from a normal density) of $1.06\hat{\sigma}T^{-0.2}$. The density is estimated at 128 points using the fast Fourier transform due to B.W. Silverman (see Silverman, 1986) and Applied Statistics algorithm AS 176). Also see the *OxMetrics* book.

*See also*

samples/lib/DensEst.ox (which gives examples of the use of density estima-

tion code, in comparison with DrawDensity),
DrawHistogram.

# DrawHistogram

```
DrawHistogram(const iArea, const vBar, ...);
DrawHistogram(const iArea, const vBar, const dMin, const dStep,
    const iIndex, const iColorIn);
```
|  |  |  |
|---|---|---|
| iArea | in: | int, area index |
| vBar | in: | $k \times T$ matrix with bar heights, each *row* is a new plot |
| dMin | in: | double, first $X$-coordinate of histogram (optional argument, default is 1) |
| dStep | in: | double, bar step size (optional argument, default is 1) |
| iIndex | in: | int, line index for outline, see Table 10.4, (optional argument, default is 2). |
| iColorIn | in: | int, colour index for inside of bars, see Table 10.4, (optional argument, default is 0: white). |

*No return value.*

*Description*

Draws a histogram when the data is already in histogram format, i.e. vBar contains the bar heights.

*See also*

DrawDensity

# DrawLegend

```
DrawLegend(const iArea, const iOffsX, const iOffsY,
    const fHidden);
```
|  |  |  |
|---|---|---|
| iArea | in: | area index |
| iOffsetX | in: | $X$ pixel offset from top left of area |
| iOffsetY | in: | $Y$ pixel offset from top left |
| fHidden | in: | TRUE: hide the legend |

*No return value.*

*Description*

DrawLegend determines the location of the legend. By default, a legend is drawn in the top left-hand corner, with a scale that adjusts automatically to the area size. DrawLegend can also be used to hide the legend. The content of the legend is determined by the variable names that are used when drawing vectors.

*See also*

DrawAdjust (for an example)

# DrawLine

```
DrawLine(const iArea, const dX1, const dY1, const dX2, const dY2,
    const iIndex);
DrawLine(const iArea, const dX1, const dY1, const dZ1,
    const dX2, const dY2, const dZ2, const iIndex);
```
  iArea      in:  area index
  dX1,dY1   in:  real-world coordinates of starting point
  dX2,dY2   in:  real-world coordinates of end point
  dZ1,dZ2   in:  real-world $Z$ coordinates for symbol in 3D graph
  iIndex    in:  int, line index for first row, see Table 10.4.

*No return value.*

*Description*
    `DrawLine` draws a line between the specified coordinates.

*See also*
    `DrawAdjust` (for an example)

# DrawMatrix

```
DrawMatrix(const iArea, const mYt, const asY, const dXfirst,
    const dXstep, ...);
DrawMatrix(const iArea, const mYt, const asY, const dXfirst,
    const dXstep, const iSymbol, const iIndex);
```
  iArea    in:  int, area index
  mYt      in:  $m \times T$ matrix with $m$ rows of data
  asY      in:  array of strings (holds variable names), or 0 (no names), or a string (when only one variable to graph)
  dXfirst  in:  double, $X$-value of first observation, $x$
  dXstep   in:  double, gap between $X$-values, $d_x$
  iSymbol  in:  int, 0: draw line, 1: draw symbols, 2: draw both (optional argument, default is 0), see Table 10.3.
  iIndex   in:  int, line index for first row, see Table 10.4, (optional argument, default is 2). Each subsequent row will have the next index.

*No return value.*

*Description*
    This is a more flexible version of the `Draw()` function. `DrawMatrix` draws the $m$ variables in the rows of `mYt`. The $X$ variable consists of evenly spaced observations $x, x + d_x, x + 2d_x, x + 3d_x, \ldots$.
    The following table gives the default settings for each line index. Note that index 0 is the background colour, and 1 the foreground colour.

# DrawPLine, DrawPSymbol, DrawPText

```
DrawPLine(const iArea, const iX1, const iY1, const iX2,
    const iY2, const iIndex);
DrawPSymbol(const iArea, const iX1, const iY1, const iX2,
    const iY2, const iSymType, const iIndex);
DrawPText(const iArea, const sText, const iPx1,
    const iPy1, ...);
DrawPText(const iArea, const sText, const iPx1, const iPy1,
    const iFontNo, const iFontSize, const fTitle);
    iX1,iY1              in:  pixel coordinates
    iX2,iY2              in:  pixel coordinates
```

*No return value.*

*Description*

These are pixel coordinate equivalents of DrawLine, DrawSymbol and DrawText respectively. See under those functions for a description of the remaining arguments.

# DrawQQ

```
DrawQQ(const iArea, const mY, const sY, const iDens,
    const df1, const df2);
    iArea      in:  int, area index
    mY         in:  $k \times T$ matrix, each *row* is a new plot
    sY         in:  string, variable name, or array of strings ($k > 1$)
    iDens      in:  int, one of: QQ_CHI, QQ_F, QQ_N, QQ_T, QQ_U
    df1        in:  double, first parameter for distribution
    df2        in:  double, second parameter for distribution
```

*No return value.*

*Description*

Draws a QQ plot. Each row of mY would normally hold critical values which are hypothesized to come from a certain distribution. This function then draws a cross plot of these observed values (sorted), against the theoretical quantiles. The $45^o$ line is drawn for reference (the closer the cross plot to this line, the better the match).

The following distributions are supported:

| | |
|---|---|
| QQ_CHI | $\chi^2(df1)$, |
| QQ_F | $F(df1, df2)$, |
| QQ_N | $N(0, 1)$, |
| QQ_N_SE | $N(0, 1)$ with pointwise asymptotic $95\%$ standard error bands, as derived in Engler and Nielsen (2009), |
| QQ_T | $t(df1)$, |
| QQ_U | Uniform$(0, 1)$, resulting in a quantile plot. |

# DrawSpectrum

```
DrawSpectrum(const iArea, const mY, const sY, const iOrder);
```
    iArea      in:  int, area index
    mY         in:  $k \times T$ matrix, each *row* is a new plot
    sY         in:  string, variable name, or array of strings ($k > 1$)
    iOrder   in:  int, lag truncation parameter $m$

*No return value.*

*Description*

    Draws the estimated spectral density, which is a smoothed function of the autocorrelations $r_j$. The graph corresponds to the results computed with the periodogram library function using imode = 2, and cpoints = 128. Note that the horizontal axis in the graph is scaled by $\pi$, thus transforming the scale from $[0, \pi]$ to $[0, 1]$.

*See also*

    periodogram

*Example*

    ...................................................*samples/draw6.ox*

```
#include <oxstd.h>
#include <oxfloat.h>
#include <oxdraw.h>
main()
{
    decl m = rann(100,1), cp = 128;

    DrawSpectrum(0, m', "var", 10);
    DrawTitle(0, "Spectral density (SDF) using DrawSpectrum()");

    Draw(1, periodogram(m,10, cp,2)', 0, M_PI / (cp-1));
    DrawTitle(1, "SDF using periodogram(), imode = 2");

    Draw(2, periodogram(m,100,cp,0)', 0, M_PI / (cp-1));
    DrawTitle(2, "Periodogram without truncation");

    Draw(3, periodogram(m,100,cp,1)', 0, M_PI / (cp-1));
    DrawTitle(3, "Smoothed periodogram without truncation");

    ShowDrawWindow();
}
```

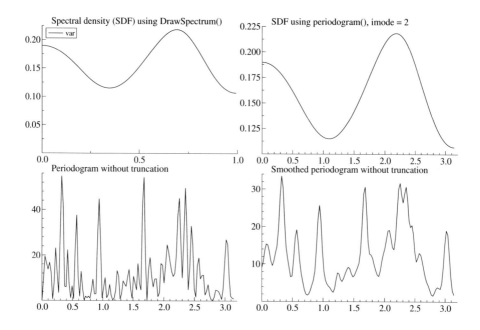

**Figure 10.5**   Periodograms and spectral density estimates.

# DrawSymbol

```
DrawSymbol(const iArea, const dX1, const dY1, const dX2,
    const dY2, const iSymType, const iIndex);
DrawSymbol(const iArea, const dX1, const dY1, const dZ1, const dX2,
    const dY2, const dZ2, const iSymType, const iIndex);
```

| | | |
|---|---|---|
| iArea | in: | area index |
| dX1,dY1 | in: | real-world coordinates, lower-left corner of bounding box |
| dX2,dY2 | in: | real-world coordinates, upper-right corner of bounding box |
| dZ1,dZ2 | in: | real-world $Z$ coordinates for symbol in 3D graph |
| iSymType | in: | symbol type, see Table 10.1 |
| iIndex | in: | int, line index for first row, see Table 10.4, (optional argument, default is 2). |

*No return value.*

*Description*

DrawSymbol draws a symbol in the specified bounding box.

*See also*

DrawAdjust (for an example)

# DrawT

```
DrawT(const iArea, const mYt, const mnYear, const mnPeriod,
    const iFreq);
DrawT(const iArea, const mYt, const vDates, 0, 0);
```
|  |  |  |
|---|---|---|
| iArea | in: | int, area index |
| mYt | in: | $m \times T$ matrix with $m$ $y$ variables |
| mnYear | in: | int, year of first observation |
| mnPeriod | in: | int, period of first observation |
| iFreq | in: | int, frequency of observations |
| vDates | in: | $1 \times T$ matrix with Julian dates (and/or times, see dayofcalendar and timeofday) |

*No return value.*

*Description*

Draws $m$ variables in the specified area against time.  Each variable is drawn by linking up the points.  The first line index is 2.

# DrawText, DrawTitle

```
DrawText(const iArea, const sText, const dX1, const dY1, ...);
DrawText(const iArea, const sText, const dX1, const dY1,
    const iFontNo, const iFontSize, const iTitle, const iRotation,
    const dZ1);
DrawTitle(const iArea, const sText);
```
|  |  |  |
|---|---|---|
| iArea | in: | area index |
| sText | in: | text to draw, this may include LaTeX-style formatting |
| dX1,dY1 | in: | real-world coordinates of text anchor |
| iFontNo | in: | font number (0 for first font; use -1 for the default font) |
| iFontSize | in: | font size (e.g. 330; use -1 for the default size) |
| iTitle | in: | |
|  |  | TEXT_TEXT or 0: normal text, else is graph title (coordinates are ignored): |
|  |  | TEXT_TITLE  – graph title |
|  |  | TEXT_XLABEL – label along $X$-axis |
|  |  | TEXT_YLABEL – label along $Y$-axis |
|  |  | TEXT_ZLABEL – label along $Z$-axis |
| iRotation | in: | rotation (in degrees, default is 0), only effective if the iTitle argument is zero |
| dZ1 | in: | real-world $Z$ coordinate of text anchor (for text in 3D graphs; default is 0) |

*No return value.*

*Description*

DrawText draws text at the specified location. There is optional control of font and font size.

For a summary of the LATEX-style features, see the OxMetrics book. Note that the forward slash for LATEX commands must be doubled, for example:

```
DrawText(0, "$\\leftarrow\\arrowext$", 1962, 1, -1, -1, 0, 45);
```

DrawTitle draws text at the title location. This corresponds to DrawText(iArea, sText, 0, 0, -1, -1, TEXT_TITLE).

Text can also be rotated, by specifying the angle in degrees. This will not work well for multiple line text blocks.

*See also*

DrawAdjust (for an example)

# DrawTMatrix

DrawTMatrix(const iArea, const mYt, const asY, ...);
DrawTMatrix(const iArea, const mYt, const asY, const mnYear,
    const mnPeriod, const iFreq, const iSymbol, const iIndex);
DrawTMatrix(const iArea, const mYt, const asY, const vDates, ...);
DrawTMatrix(const iArea, const mYt, const asY, const vDates,
    0, 0, const iSymbol, const iIndex);

| | | |
|---|---|---|
| iArea | in: | int, area index |
| mYt | in: | $m \times T$ matrix with $m$ $y$ variables |
| asY | in: | array of strings (holds variable names), or 0 (no names), or a string (when only one variable to graph) |
| mnYear | in: | int, year of first observation (optional argument, default is 1) |
| mnPeriod | in: | int, period of first observation (optional argument, default is 1) |
| iFreq | in: | int, frequency of observations (optional argument, default is 1) |
| iSymbol | in: | int, 0: draw line, 1: draw symbols, 2: draw both (optional argument, default is 0), see Table 10.3 |
| iIndex | in: | int, line index for first row, see Table 10.4, (optional argument, default is 2) Each subsequent row will have the next index. |
| vDates | in: | $1 \times T$ matrix with Julian dates (and/or times, see dayofcalendar and timeofday) |

*No return value.*

*Description*

This is a more flexible version of the DrawT() function. Draws $m$ variables in the specified area against time. See under `DrawMatrix` for the default settings for each line index.

See `Modelbase::DbDrawTMatrix` for a version that uses the database sample information for the horizontal axis.

*Example*

The code of `draw10.ox` draws a data against the Julian time values which are representing dates (Fig. 10.6b), and against time (Fig. 10.6c).

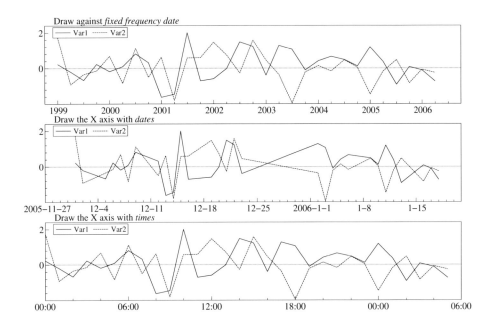

**Figure 10.6**  `DrawTMatrix` example with dates and times.

```
.............................................................samples/draw10.ox
#include <oxstd.h>
#include <oxdraw.h>

main()
{
    decl c = 30, m = rann(30,2);

    decl dates = dayofcalendar(2005, 12, 1) + range(0, 300);
    // drop weekends
    decl drop = dayofweek(dates) .== 1 .|| dayofweek(dates) .== 7;
    // drop period between christmas and newyear
    drop = drop .|| (dates .>= dayofcalendar(2005, 12, 25) .&&
        dates .<= dayofcalendar(2006,  1, 1));
```

```
// drop those dates, and get c dates
dates = deleteifc(dates, drop)[ : c - 1];

println("%C", dates');

DrawTitle(0, "Draw against {\it fixed frequency date}");
DrawTMatrix(0, m', {"Var1", "Var2"}, 1999, 1, 4);

DrawTitle(1, "Draw the X axis with {\it dates}");
DrawTMatrix(1, m', {"Var1", "Var2"}, dates);

DrawTitle(2, "Draw the X axis with {\it times}");
DrawTMatrix(2, m', {"Var1", "Var2"},
    range(0, c - 1) / 24, "", 0);

ShowDrawWindow();
}
```

# DrawX

```
DrawX(const iArea, const mYt, const vX);
   iArea      in:   int, area index
   mYt        in:   m × T matrix with m y variables
   vX         in:   1 × T matrix with x variable
```
*No return value.*

*Description*

Draws $m$ $y$ variables in the specified area against an $x$ variable. Each point is marked, but the points are not linked, resulting in a cross plot. The first line index is 2.

# DrawXMatrix

```
DrawXMatrix(const iArea, const mYt, const asY, const vX, const sX,
   ...);
DrawXMatrix(const iArea, const mYt, const asY, const vX, const sX,
   const iSymbol, const iIndex);
   iArea      in:   int, area index
   vX         in:   1 × T matrix with x variable
   iSymbol    in:   int, 0: draw line, 1: draw symbols, 2: draw both (optional
                    argument, default is 0).
   iIndex     in:   int, line index for first row, see Table 10.4, (optional argu-
                    ment, default is 2), see Table 10.3. Each subsequent row will
                    have the next index.
```

*No return value.*

*Description*

This is a more flexible version of the `DrawX()` function. Draws $m$ variables in the specified area against an $x$ variable See under `DrawMatrix` for the default settings for each line index and a description of the remaining arguments.

*Example*

The code of `draw11.ox` draws a data against the Julian time values which are representing dates (Fig. 10.7b).

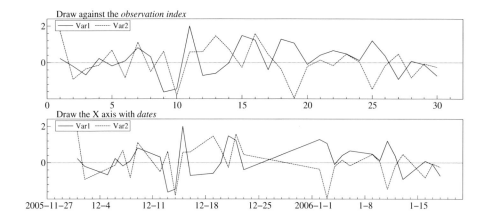

**Figure 10.7**   `DrawXMatrix` example with dates and times.

..................................................*samples/draw11.ox*

```
#include <oxstd.h>
#include <oxdraw.h>

main()
{
    decl c = 30, m = rann(30,2);

    decl dates = dayofcalendar(2005, 12, 1) + range(0, 300);
    // drop weekends
    decl drop = dayofweek(dates) .== 1 .|| dayofweek(dates) .== 7;
    // drop period between christmas and newyear
    drop = drop .|| (dates .>= dayofcalendar(2005, 12, 25) .&&
        dates .<= dayofcalendar(2006,  1, 1));

    // drop those dates, and get c dates
    dates = deleteifc(dates, drop)[ : c - 1];

    println("%C", dates');
```

```
DrawTitle(0, "Draw against the {\it observation index}");
DrawTMatrix(0, m', {"Var1", "Var2"}, 1, 1, 1);

DrawTitle(1, "Draw the X axis with {\it dates}");
DrawAxisAuto(1, 1);
DrawAdjust(ADJ_AXISSCALE, AXIS_DATE);
DrawXMatrix(1, m', {"Var1", "Var2"}, dates, "");

DrawAdjust(ADJ_PAPERSCALE, 70);
DrawAdjust(ADJ_AREAMATRIX, 2, 1);

ShowDrawWindow();
}
```

# DrawXYZ

```
DrawXYZ(const iArea, const vX, const vY, const mZ, ...);
DrawXYZ(const iArea, const vX, const vY, const mZ,
    const iMode, const sX, const sY, const sZ,
    const iPalette, const iIndex);
```

| | | |
|---|---|---|
| iArea | in: | int, area index |
| vX | in: | $1 \times k$ matrix with $X$ variable |
| vY | in: | $1 \times n$ matrix with $Y$ variable |
| mZ | in: | $n \times k$ matrix with $Z$ variable, heights above XY plane |
| | *or* in: | $1 \times n = k$ matrix with $Z$ coordinates for points $(X, Y, Z)$, creates rough approximating surface (scatter format) |
| iMode | in: | int, type of plot (optional argument): |
| | | $-1$: triangulation (only for scatter format) |
| | | 0: surface plot only (default) |
| | | 1: unsupported: surface with contours on ground level |
| | | 2: 2-dimensional contour plot |
| sX | in: | string, name of $X$ variable (optional argument) |
| sY | in: | string, name of $Y$ variable (optional argument) |
| sZ | in: | string, name of $Z$ variable (optional argument) |
| iPalette | in: | int, palette index, see Table 10.5, (optional, default is 2: red). |
| iIndex | in: | int, line index for mesh, see Table 10.4, (optional, default is 1: black). |

*No return value.*

*Description*

　　This function draws a 3-dimensional surface.

*Example*

　　The first example shows a simple 3-dimensional plot of a bivariate independent normal density (without the normalizing constant). In first plot of the second example, the tabular format is different for $x$ and $y$: $x$ is $1 \times 21$, $y$ is $1 \times 14$, $z$ is $14 \times 21$. The second plot of Fig. 10.9 is drawn from a random scatter: the $X, Y, Z$ vectors have the same dimension. It keeps the azimuth, elevation and distance at the approximate default values, but adds a twist of about $25°$.

See `samples/draw8contour.ox` for an example involving contour plots.

..................................................... *samples/draw7.ox*

```
#include <oxstd.h>
#include <oxdraw.h>

main()
{
    decl x, y, z;

    x = y = range(-30,30,3) / 10;
    z = exp(-sqr(x) / 2) .* exp(-sqr(y') / 2);

    DrawXYZ(0, x, y, z);
    DrawAdjust(ADJ_PAPERSCALE, 60);
    ShowDrawWindow();
}
```
......................................................................

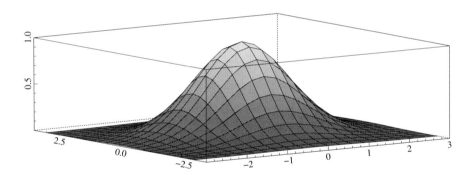

**Figure 10.8**  Three-dimensional plot.

..................................................... *samples/draw8.ox*

```
#include <oxstd.h>
#include <oxdraw.h>

main()
{
    decl x = range(-30,30,3) / 10;
    decl y = quann(range(1,14) / 15) * 2;
    decl z = exp(-sqr(x) / 2) .* exp(-sqr(y') / 2); // table

    DrawXYZ(0, x, y, z);
```

```
x = (ranu(500, 1) - 0.5) * 6;
y = (ranu(500, 1) - 0.5) * 6;
z = exp(-sqr(x) / 2) .* exp(-sqr(y) / 2);  // vector!

DrawXYZ(1, x, y, z);
DrawAdjust(ADJ_AREA_3D, 1, -125, 25, 1000, 25);

DrawAdjust(ADJ_PAPERSCALE, 60);
ShowDrawWindow();
}
```

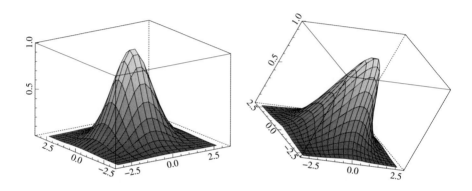

**Figure 10.9**    Three-dimensional plot.

# DrawZ

```
DrawZ(const vZ, ...);
DrawZ(const vZ, const sZ, const iMode, const dFac, const iIndex);
```

| | | |
|---|---|---|
| vZ | in: | $1 \times T$ matrix |
| sZ | in: | $Z$ variable name (optional argument) |
| iMode | in: | type of $Z$ variable (optional argument) |
| dFac | in: | bar/band factor (optional argument, 2.0 is default) |
| iIndex | in: | int, line index for first row, see Table 10.4, (optional argument, default is 2). |

*No return value.*

*Description*

DrawZ adds a $Z$ component to the most recent graphics object. DrawZ should be used immediately after a call to one of the draw functions Draw, DrawMatrix, DrawX, etc.). The iMode argument can have one of the following values:

| ZMODE_SYMBOL | use values as symbol size, |
|---|---|
| ZMODE_VALUE | draw value as text, |
| ZMODE_BAR | draw error bars (the default), |
| ZMODE_BAND | draw error bands, |
| ZMODE_FAN | draw error fans, |
| ZMODE_HILO | draw high-low plot, |
| ZMODE_3D | draw 3-D points. |

To draw a sequence of 3D points, use for example:

```
DrawX(0, y, x);
DrawZ(z, "Z", ZMODE_3D);
```

*See also*
    DrawAdjust (for an example)

# SaveDrawWindow

SaveDrawWindow(const sFilename);
    sFilename            in:   valid file name
*No return value.*

*Description*
    Saves the current graph to the specified file. The file format for saving is derived from the extension. The following formats are supported:

| extension | format |
|---|---|
| .eps | Encapsulated PostScript; |
| .gwg | *OxMetrics* graphics file; |
| .png | Portable Network Graphics, which is a bitmap format; |
| .ps | PostScript. |

See the *OxMetrics* book for a description of these formats. When saving in a format other than .gwg, the .gwg file is automatically saved as well.

# SetDraw

SetDraw(const iOption, ...);
SetDraw(const iOption, const i1, const i2, const i3, const i4,
    const i5);
    iOption            in:   int, option to set
    i1,...,i5        in:   int, optional extra arguments
*No return value.*

*Description*
    This function changes the default settings used in graphics. When run via Ox-Metrics, this will affect the persistent OxMetrics settings. Check first under

`DrawAdjust` if the required customization is available there. The following constants may be used for `iOption`:

| option | changes | option | changes |
|---|---|---|---|
| SET_AXISFORMAT | axis label format | SET_LEGENDHIDE | legend hiding |
| SET_AXISLINE | axis options | SET_LEGENDRESIZE | resize legends |
| SET_AXIS | axis fonts/ticks | SET_LEGEND | legend style |
| SET_BOX | box and grid | SET_LINEBWG | b&w line settings |
| SET_BWG | b&w setting | SET_LINE | line settings |
| SET_COLORMODEL | PostScript model | SET_MARGIN | paper margins |
| SET_COLOR | colour settings | SET_PALETTE_MAX | palette max colour |
| SET_DEFAULT | reset all defaults | SET_PALETTE_MIN | palette min colour |
| SET_FONT | font | SET_PAPERCOLOR | paper colour |
| SET_GRID | grid style | SET_PRINTPAGE | PostScript paper |
| SET_HISTOGRAM | bar colours | SET_SYMBOL | symbol settings |
| SET_LEGENDFONTSIZE | legend font size | SET_XYSTYLE | labels along axes |

The following table lists the integer arguments for each option, with the range of possible values. If no range is given, the argument is a size in pixel coordinates (see §10.1).

| option | i1 | i2 | i3 | i4 | i5 |
|---|---|---|---|---|---|
| SET_AXISFORMAT | *width*:8 | *precision*:6 | *same prec*:0,1 | *lead zero*:0,1 | |
| SET_AXISLINE | *no X-line* | *no Y-line* | *center dates* | *no small Y* | |
| SET_AXIS | *fontsize* | *step* | *tick* | | |
| SET_BOX | *box*:0–1 | *X-grid*:0–1 | *Y-grid*:0–1 | | |
| SET_BWG | *lineno*:0–15 | *red*:0–255 | *green*:0–255 | *blue*:0–255 | |
| SET_COLORMODEL | *model*:0–3 | | | | |
| SET_COLOR | *lineno*:0–15 | *red*:0–255 | *green*:0–255 | *blue*:0–255 | |
| SET_FONT | *fontno*:0–3 | *fontsize* | | | |
| SET_GRID | *color*:0–15 | *type*:0–15 | | | |
| SET_HISTOGRAM | *inside*:0–15 | *outside*:0–15 | | | |
| SET_LEGENDFONTSIZE | *fontsize* | | | | |
| SET_LEGENDHIDE | *hide*:0–1 | | | | |
| SET_LEGENDRESIZE | *resize*:0,1 | | | | |
| SET_LEGEND | *boxed*:0–1 | *columns* | | | |
| SET_LINEBWG | *lineno*:0–15 | *linetype*:0–4 | *width* | *on* | *off* |
| SET_LINE | *lineno*:0–15 | *linetype*:0–4 | *width* | *on* | *off* |
| SET_MARGIN | *left* | *top* | | | |
| SET_PALETTE_MAX | *lineno*:0–7 | *red*:0–255 | *green*:0–255 | *blue*:0–255 | |
| SET_PALETTE_MIN | *lineno*:0–7 | *red*:0–255 | *green*:0–255 | *blue*:0–255 | |
| SET_PAPERCOLOR | *red*:0–255 | *green*:0–255 | *blue*:0–255 | | |
| SET_PRINTPAGE | *papertype*:0–2 | *orientation*:0–1 | *X-size* | *Y-size* | |
| SET_SYMBOL | *lineno*:0–15 | *symtype*:0–4 | *size* | | |
| SET_XYSTYLE | *2D-style*:0,1 | *3D-style*:0,1 | | | |

For *symtype* see Table 10.1 and for *linetype* see Table 10.2. All SET_AXISLINE

arguments are 0 or 1. Paper, orientation and model arguments for SET_PRINTPAGE
and SET_COLORMODEL are:

| *papertype* | *orientation* | *model* | |
|---|---|---|---|
| PAGE_A4 | PAGE_PORTRAIT | 0 | black & white |
| PAGE_LETTER | PAGE_LANDSCAPE | 1 | black, white, gray |
| PAGE_USER | | 2 | gray |
| | | 3 | color |

*Example*

................................................ *samples/draw3.ox*

```
#include <oxstd.h>
#include <oxdraw.h>
main()
{
    decl m = rann(30,2);

    Draw(0, m', 0, 1);
    DrawMatrix(1, m', {"Var1", "Var2"}, 0, 1, 2);
    DrawT(2, m', 1960, 1, 4);
    DrawXMatrix(3, m', {"Var1", "Var2"}, m', "Var1", 1, 3);

    ShowDrawWindow();
    SetDraw(SET_PRINTPAGE, PAGE_LETTER, PAGE_PORTRAIT);
    SaveDrawWindow("draw3.ps");
}
```

# SetDrawWindow

```
SetDrawWindow(const sTitle);
```
    sTitle      in:   string, name of window
*No return value.*

*Description*

This function is only relevant when interacting with *OxMetrics* otherwise it does
nothing. It sets the name of the *OxMetrics* window in which the graphs of the Ox
program appear to sTitle.

# SetTextWindow

```
SetTextWindow(const sTitle);
```
    sTitle      in:   string, name of window
*No return value.*

*Description*

This function is only relevant when interacting with *OxMetrics* otherwise it does nothing. It sets the name of the *OxMetrics* window in which the output (from the print() function) of the Ox program appears to sTitle.

# ShowDrawWindow

ShowDrawWindow();

*No return value.*

*Description*

Shows the drawing. Note that in some implementations the graphs cannot be displayed. Then a message is printed (SaveDrawWindow() will still work in that case!).

A call to ShowDrawWindow also clears the drawing buffer, so does not need to be followed by a call to CloseDrawWindow. Therefore, two subsequent calls to ShowDrawWindow first show, then clear the graph from the active window.

# Chapter 11

# Packages

Packages are extensions and additions to the Ox language. Whereas the core of Ox contains the general purpose functions, packages often solve a specific problem or are ports of existing code to Ox. Sometimes part of the code is available through a Dynamic Link Library (DLL) with accompanying header file. Many packages are third party contributions to Ox, and documented and maintained by their respective authors. The Ox web site maintains an up to date list of available packages. This chapter only describes the packages which are part of the standard release of Ox.

## 11.1 Arma package

The Arma package implements functions which are commonly used in autoregressive-moving average models. The Arma package requires the header file `arma.h`. Note that the Arma package uses the convention of writing the AR and MA coefficients on the right-hand side with a positive sign.

## arma0

```
arma0(const ma, const vp, const cp, const cq);
```
     ma         in:  $T \times n$ matrix $A$

     vp         in:  $1 \times s$ matrix with autoregressive coefficients $\phi_1, \phi_2, \ldots, \phi_p$ followed by the moving average coefficients $\theta_1, \theta_2, \ldots, \theta_q$, $s \geq p + q$

     cp         in:  int, no of autoregressive coefficients (could be 0)

     cq         in:  int, no of moving average coefficients (could be 0)

*Return value*

Returns the residual from applying the ARMA($p, q$) filter to each column of $A$. The result has the same dimensions as `ma`. The first $p$ rows of the return value will be zero.

*Description*

For a column $a = (a_0, \ldots, a_{T-1})'$ of $A$, this function computes (see e.g. Harvey, 1993, §3.3):

$$\epsilon_t = 0 \qquad\qquad\qquad\qquad\qquad\qquad\qquad\qquad t = 0, \ldots, p - 1,$$
$$\epsilon_t = a_t - \phi_1 a_{t-1} \ldots - \phi_p a_{t-p} - \theta_1 \epsilon_{t-1} \ldots - \theta_q \epsilon_{t-q} \quad t = p, \ldots, T - 1,$$

using $\epsilon_t = 0$ for $t < 0$. For example when $p = 1$ and $q = 2$:

$$\epsilon_0 = 0$$
$$\epsilon_1 = a_1 - \phi_1 a_0 - \theta_1 \epsilon_0$$
$$\epsilon_2 = a_2 - \phi_1 a_1 - \theta_1 \epsilon_1 - \theta_2 \epsilon_0$$
$$\epsilon_t = a_t - \phi_1 a_{t-1} - \theta_1 \epsilon_{t-1} - \theta_2 \epsilon_{t-2} \quad t = p, \ldots, T - 1.$$

Comparison with the `cumulate` function shows that in the univariate case `cumulate(y,a0,a1)` corresponds to `arma0(y,-(a0~a1),0,2)`.

*See also*

    `armagen, armaforc, armavar, diff0, diffpow, pacf`

*Example*
```
#include <oxstd.h>
#include <arma.h>
main()
{
    decl mx = <1:5>';
    print(arma0(mx,<0.5, 0.5>, 1, 1) ~ arma0(mx,<0.5>, 0, 1));
}
```

produces

| | |
|---|---|
| 0.00000 | 1.0000 |
| 1.5000 | 1.5000 |
| 1.2500 | 2.2500 |
| 1.8750 | 2.8750 |
| 2.0625 | 3.5625 |

# armaforc

```
armaforc(const mx, const vp, const cp, const cq, ...);
armaforc(const mx, const vp, const cp, const cq,
    const ma, const me);
```
| | | |
|---|---|---|
| mx | in: | $H \times n$ matrix $X$, fixed part of forecasts |
| vp | in: | $1 \times s$ matrix with autoregressive coefficients $\phi_1, \phi_2, \ldots, \phi_p$ followed by the moving average coefficients $\theta_1, \theta_2, \ldots, \theta_q$, $s \geq p + q$ |
| cp | in: | int, no of autoregressive coefficients (could be 0) |
| cq | in: | int, no of moving average coefficients (could be 0) |
| ma | in: | (optional argument) $T \times n$ matrix $A$, pre-forecast data values (default is zero) |
| me | in: | (optional argument) $T \times n$ matrix $E$, pre-forecast residual values (default is zero) |

*Return value*

Returns the forecasts from an ARMA$(p, q)$ model, as an $H \times n$ matrix. The same model is applied to each column of mx.

*Description*

For a column $x = (x_0, \ldots, x_{H-1})'$ of $X$, as the first argument, and assuming the ma and me arguments are omitted, this function computes:

$$\hat{a}_0 = x_0$$
$$\hat{a}_1 = x_1 + \phi_1 \hat{a}_0$$
$$\hat{a}_2 = x_2 + \phi_1 \hat{a}_1 + \phi_2 \hat{a}_0$$
$$\ldots$$
$$\hat{a}_h = x_h + \phi_1 \hat{a}_{h-1} + \ldots + \phi_p \hat{a}_{h-p} \quad h = p, \ldots, H - 1,$$

The ma argument can be used to specify actual values $a = (a_0, \ldots, a_{T-1})'$, which are used in the beginning stages of the forecasting, e.g. when $p = 2$:

$$\hat{a}_0 = x_0 + \phi_1 a_{T-1} + \phi_2 a_{T-2}$$
$$\hat{a}_1 = x_1 + \phi_1 \hat{a}_0 + \phi_2 a_{T-1}$$
$$\hat{a}_2 = x_2 + \phi_1 \hat{a}_1 + \phi_2 \hat{a}_0$$
$$\hat{a}_h = x_h + \phi_1 \hat{a}_{h-1} + \phi_2 \hat{a}_{h-2} \quad h = 2, \ldots, H - 1,$$

Note that the actual values are taken from the end of ma: the first forecast will use the last two values, the second forecast the last value.

When a moving average component is present, it is necessary to specify the actual values for the error term. The me argument is used for this. As for the actual values, the errors are taken from the end of me, and are only used when lagged errors fall in the pre-forecast period. For an ARMA(2,2) model (see e.g. Harvey, 1993, §2.6):

$$\hat{a}_0 = x_0 + \phi_1 a_{T-1} + \phi_2 a_{T-2} + \theta_1 \epsilon_{T-1} + \theta_2 \epsilon_{T-2}$$
$$\hat{a}_1 = x_1 + \phi_1 \hat{a}_0 + \phi_2 a_{T-1} + \theta_2 \epsilon_{T-1}$$
$$\hat{a}_2 = x_1 + \phi_1 \hat{a}_1 + \phi_2 \hat{a}_0$$
$$\hat{a}_h = x_h + \phi_1 \hat{a}_{h-1} + \phi_2 \hat{a}_{h-2} \qquad\qquad h = 2, \ldots, H - 1,$$

*See also*
arma0, armavar, cumulate, modelforc

*Example*
We use an example from Harvey (1993, p.35):

$$y_t = 0.6 y_{t-1} + 0.2 y_{t-2} + \epsilon_t + 0.3 \epsilon_{t-1} - 0.4 \epsilon_{t-2}.$$

Using $y_T = 4$, $y_{T-1} = 5$, $\epsilon_T = 1$ and $\epsilon_{T-1} = 0.5$ four forecasts are computed. The two entries of 100 are ignored, because values are taken from the end:

```
#include <oxstd.h>
#include <arma.h>
main()
{
    print( armaforc(zeros(4,1), <0.6,0.2,0.3,-0.4>, 2, 2,
        <100;100;5.0;4.0>, <0.5;1>) );
}
```

produces

```
    3.5000
    2.5000
    2.2000
    1.8200
```

# armagen

armagen(const mx, const me, const vp, const cp,const cq);

| | | |
|---|---|---|
| mx | in: | $T \times n$ matrix of known component $X$ |
| me | in: | $T \times n$ matrix of errors $E$ |
| vp | in: | $1 \times s$ matrix with autoregressive coefficients $\phi_1, \phi_2, \ldots, \phi_p$ followed by the moving average coefficients $\theta_1, \theta_2, \ldots, \theta_q$, $s \geq p + q$ |
| cp | in: | int, no of autoregressive coefficients (could be 0) |
| cq | in: | int, no of moving average coefficients (could be 0) |

*Return value*

Generates a an ARMA($p, q$) series from an error term (me) and a mean term (mx). The result has the same dimensions as mx. The first $p$ rows of the return value will be identical to those of mx; the recursion will be applied from the $p$th term onward (missing lagged errors are set to zero).

*Description*

For a column $(x_0, \ldots, x_{T-1})'$ of $X$, and a column $(\epsilon_0, \ldots, \epsilon_{T-1})'$ of $E$, this function computes:

$$a_t = x_t \qquad\qquad\qquad\qquad\qquad\qquad\qquad\quad t = 0, \ldots, p-1,$$
$$a_t = x_t + \phi_1 a_{t-1} \ldots \phi_p a_{t-p} + \epsilon_t + \theta_1 \epsilon_{t-1} \ldots \theta_q \epsilon_{t-q} \quad t = p, \ldots, T-1,$$

using $\epsilon_t = 0$ for $t < 0$. For example when $p = 1$ and $q = 2$:

$$a_0 = x_0$$
$$a_1 = x_1 + \phi_1 a_0 + \epsilon_1 + \theta_1 \epsilon_0$$
$$a_2 = x_2 + \phi_1 a_1 + \epsilon_2 + \theta_1 \epsilon_1 + \theta_2 \epsilon_0$$
$$a_t = x_t + \phi_1 a_{t-1} + \epsilon_t + \theta_1 \epsilon_{t-1} + \theta_2 \epsilon_{t-2} \quad t = p, \ldots, T-1.$$

This function could be used to generate an ARMA($p, q$) series from random numbers. In that case it is common to discard intitial observations to remove the effect of starting up the recursion.

*See also*

arma0, armaforc, armavar, cumsum, cumulate

*Example*

```
#include <oxstd.h>
#include <arma.h>
main()
{
    decl mx = ones(5,1), meps = rann(5,1) / 10;
    print( armagen(mx, meps, <0.5, 0.5>, 1, 1)
         ~ armagen(mx, meps, <0.5>, 0, 1) );
}
```

produces

```
        1.0000        1.0225
        1.6852        1.1852
        1.9092        1.0666
        1.8526        0.89803
        1.8130        0.88670
```

# armavar

```
armavar(const vp, const cp, const cq, const dvar,
    const ct);
```

| | | |
|---|---|---|
| vp | in: | $1 \times s$ matrix with autoregressive coefficients $\phi_1, \phi_2, \ldots, \phi_p$ followed by the moving average coefficients $\theta_1, \theta_2, \ldots, \theta_q$, $s \geq p + q$ |
| cp | in: | int, no of autoregressive coefficients (could be 0) |
| cq | in: | int, no of moving average coefficients (could be 0) |
| dvar | in: | double, variance of disturbance, $\sigma_\epsilon^2$. |
| ct | in: | int, number of autocovariance terms required |

*Return value*

Returns a $1 \times$ ct matrix with the autocovariances of the ARMA($p, q$) process. Or 0 if the computations failed (e.g. when all autoregressive coefficients are zero).

*Description*

Computes the theoretical autocovariances c($i$), $i = 0, \ldots, T - 1$ (see equation (8.2) on page 170 for a definition) of the ARMA($p, q$) process specified as

$$a_t = \phi_1 a_{t-1} + \ldots + \phi_p a_{t-p} + \epsilon_t + \theta_1 \epsilon_{t-1} + \ldots + \theta_q \epsilon_{t-q}, \quad \mathrm{E}\epsilon_t = 0, \ \mathrm{E}\epsilon_t^2 = \sigma_\epsilon^2.$$

using $\epsilon_t = 0$ for $t < 0$. Stationary is assumed, but not verified. The computations are based on the algorithm given in McLeod (1975).

*See also*

arma0, pacf

*Example*

In the example below, we set $\sigma_\epsilon^2$ such that we obtain the autocorrelation function:

```
#include <oxstd.h>
#include <arma.h>
main()
{
    print( armavar(<0.5>, 1, 0, (1 - 0.5^2), 5)'
         ~ armavar(<-0.5>, 1, 0, (1 - (-0.5)^2), 5)'
         ~ armavar(<0.5>, 0, 1, 1 / (1 + 0.5^2), 5)' );
}
```

produces

```
        1.0000          1.0000          1.0000
        0.50000        -0.50000         0.40000
        0.25000         0.25000         0.00000
        0.12500        -0.12500         0.00000
        0.062500        0.062500        0.00000
```

# diffpow

```
diffpow(const ma, const d);
diffpow(const ma, const d, const dmisval);
```

| | | |
|---|---|---|
| ma | in: | $T \times n$ matrix $A$ |
| d | in: | double, length of difference $d$, $|d| \leq 10000$ |
| dmisval | in: | (optional argument) double, value to set missing observations to (default is 0) |

*Return value*

Returns a $T \times n$ matrix with $(1 - L)^d A$. The result has the same dimensions as ma.

*Description*

Differences the specified matrix, missing values are replaced by zero (unless a missing value is specified as the third argument). For a column $a = (a_0, \ldots, a_{T-1})'$ of $A$, this function computes $(1 - L)^d a$, defined as:

$$a_t = \sum_{j=0}^{t} \frac{(-d)_j}{j!} a_{t-j}, \quad t = 0, \ldots, T - 1,$$

where the $(\cdot)_j$ symbol is defined as:

$$
\begin{aligned}
(z)_0 &= 1, \\
(z)_j &= z(z+1) \ldots (z+j-1) && \text{for } j > 0 \\
(z)_j &= 1/\left((z-1)(z-2) \ldots (z-j)\right) && \text{for } j < 0
\end{aligned}
$$

and using $a_k = 0$ for $k < 0$.

*See also*

arma0, diff0

*Example*

In this example, `fracdiff` replicates the functionality of the library function `diffpow`.

```
#include <oxstd.h>
#include <arma.h>

fracdiff(const mY, const d)
{
    decl i, mu = mY, fac = -d;

    for (i = 1; i < rows(mY); ++i, fac *= (-d+i-1)/i)
        mu += fac * lag0(mY,i);

    return mu;
}
main()
```

```
{
    decl mx = <1:5>';
    print( diffpow(mx,2) ~ diff0(diff0(mx,1),1) ~
        diffpow(mx,-2) ~ diff0(diff0(mx,-1),-1) );
    print( diffpow(mx,0.2) ~ fracdiff(mx,0.2) ~
        diffpow(mx,-0.2) ~ fracdiff(mx,-0.2) );
}
```

produces

```
        1.0000       0.00000        1.0000       0.00000
        0.00000      1.0000         4.0000       0.00000
        0.00000      0.00000        10.000       0.00000
        0.00000      0.00000        20.000      -1.0000
        0.00000      0.00000        35.000       0.00000

        1.0000       1.0000         1.0000       1.0000
        1.8000       1.8000         2.2000       2.2000
        2.5200       2.5200         3.5200       3.5200
        3.1920       3.1920         4.9280       4.9280
        3.8304       3.8304         6.4064       6.4064
```

# modelforc

```
modelforc(const mU, const mData, const miDep,
    const miSel, const miLag, const mPi, const iTmin);
```

| | | |
|---|---|---|
| mU | in: | 0, or $(T_2 - T_1 + 1) \times n$ matrix $\mathbf{U}$, optional error term |
| mData | in: | $T(= T_2 + 1) \times d$ matrix $\mathbf{D}$, database |
| miDep | in: | $1 \times n$ matrix with indices in $\mathbf{D}$ of dependent variables |
| miSel | in: | $1 \times k$ matrix with indices in $\mathbf{D}$ of explanatory variables |
| miLag | in: | $1 \times k$ matrix with lag lengths of explanatory variables |
| iTmin | in: | $T_1$, observation to start forecasting from (this may be zero) |

*Return value*

Returns the dynamic forecasts from a linear dynamic model as a $(T - T_1 = T_2 - T_1 + 1) \times n$ matrix.

*Description*

This function forecasts from a dynamic model, which may be an estimated (reduced form) model or a DGP:

$$\mathbf{y}_t = \mathbf{\Pi}\mathbf{w}_t + \mathbf{u}_t, \quad t = T_1, \dots, T_2$$

where $\mathbf{w}$ contains $\mathbf{z}$, $r$ lags of $\mathbf{z}$ and $m$ lags of $\mathbf{y}$:

$$\mathbf{w}'_t = \left(\mathbf{y}'_{t-1}, \dots, \mathbf{y}'_{t-m}, \mathbf{z}'_t, \dots, \mathbf{z}'_{t-r}\right).$$

Take $\mathbf{y}_t$ as an $n \times 1$ vector, $\mathbf{z}_t$ as $q \times 1$, and $\mathbf{w}_t$ as $k \times 1$.

Given data on $\mathbf{z}_t$ for $t = 0, \ldots, T_2$, and on $\mathbf{y}_t$ for $t = 0, \ldots, T_1 - 1$, `modelforc` will produce forecasts for $t = T_1 \ldots T_2$. No actual $\mathbf{y}_t$ data is used for $t \geq T_1$, only previously forecasted values. If lagged data is missing ($z_t, y_t$ for $t < 0$), it is assumed to be zero. If the error term is not given (mU argument 0 implies $\mathbf{u}_t = 0$), the output corresponds to model forecasts. Otherwise it could e.g. be the fitted values from a DGP. Note that in that case the first observation in the mU matrix is $\mathbf{u}_{T_1}$.

*See also*
> `armaforc`, `cumulate`, PcFimlDgp class.

# pacf

```
pacf(const macf);
pacf(const macf, const alogdet);
pacf(const macf, const alogdet, const my);
pacf(const macf, const meps);
```
| | | |
|---|---|---|
| macf | in | arithmetic type, $T \times 1$ matrix of autocovariances or autocorrelations |
| alogdet | in: | (optional argument) address of variable |
| | out: | double, the *logarithm* of the the determinant of the filter |
| my | in: | (optional argument) $T \times n$ data matrix $Y$ to apply filter to |
| meps | in: | (optional argument) $T \times n$ data matrix $Y$ to apply inverse filter to |

*Return value*

- `pacf(macf);`
- `pacf(macf, alogdet);`
  Returns a $T \times 1$ matrix with the partial autocorrelation function of the first column of `macf`.
- `pacf(macf, alogdet, my);`
  Returns a $T \times (n + 1)$ matrix with the residuals from the filter based on the specified ACF applied to the columns of `my`. The last column contains the standard devations of the filter.
- `pacf(macf, meps);`
  Returns a $T \times n$ matrix with the fitted values from applying the inverse filter based on the specified ACF applied to the columns of `my`.

Returns 0 if the computations fail (the stochastic process has a root on the unit circle).

*Description*

Given autocovariance (or autocorrelation) functions in the first column of `macf`, this function computes the partial autocorrelations using Durbin's method as described in Golub and Van Loan (1989, §4.7.2). This corresponds to recursively solving the Yule-Walker equations. For example, with autocorrelations, $\rho_0, \rho_1, \rho_2, \ldots$, the first reported partial correlation is 1. The second is the solution $p_1$ from $(\rho_0\rho_1)' = T(\rho_0\rho_1)(p_0p_1)'$, the third is $p_2$ from $(\rho_0\rho_1\rho_2)' = T(\rho_0\rho_1\rho_2)(p_0p_1p_2)'$. This may be verified by repeatedly using the function solvetoeplitz. See under toeplitz for the $T(\cdot)$ notation.

For the theoretical PACF of an ARMA$(p, q)$ process, use the results from armavar as input. For the sample PACF, use the results from acf.

When a data matrix is specified, the filter (corresponding to the specified ACF) is applied to the data, returning the residuals **E**. This corresponds to applying the inverse Choleski factor to the data matrix:

$$T(\rho_0\rho_1 \ldots) = LDL' = PP', \quad \mathbf{E} = D^{-1/2}L^{-1}Y = P^{-1}Y.$$

As in decldl, $L$ is lower diagonal, with ones on the diagonal. $D$ contains the squared diagonal values, which here correspond to the residual variances. The last column of the return value holds the diagonal of $D^{1/2}$. The log-determinant of $T(\cdot)$ corresponds to twice the sum of the log of the last column of the return value.

When logdet is absent, and a data matrix (e.g. white noise) is specified, the inverse filter (corresponding to the specified ACF) is applied to the data, returning the generated data **Y**. This corresponds to applying the Choleski factor to the data matrix:

$$T(\rho_0\rho_1 \ldots) = LDL' = PP', \quad \mathbf{Y} = PE.$$

This allows for generating data according to the specified ACF when the input is standard normal random data. In general, this is slower than applying $P$ directly. However, for large $T$, storage of $P$ may become prohibitive.

*See also*
    acf, arma0, armavar, solvetoeplitz

*Example*
```
#include <oxstd.h>
#include <arma.h>
main()
{
    decl ct = 5;
    decl acf1 = armavar(<0.5>, 1, 0, (1 - 0.5^2), ct)';
    decl acf2 = armavar(<-0.5>, 1, 0, (1 - (-0.5)^2), ct)';
    decl acf3 = armavar(<0.5>, 0, 1, 1 / (1 + 0.5^2), ct)';
    decl y = rann(ct,1), logdet, e;

    print(pacf(acf1) ~ pacf(acf2) ~ pacf(acf3));

    e = pacf(acf3, &logdet, y);
    print(e ~ invert(choleski(toeplitz(acf3))) * y);
    print("logdet = ", logdet, " ",
```

```
        2 * double(sumc(log(e[][1]))) );

    e = pacf(acf1, &logdet, y);
    print(arma0(y, <0.5>, 1, 0) ~ e[][0] .* e[][1]);
    e = pacf(acf3, &logdet, y);
    //differ, but will be the same beyond approx. 10 obs:
    print(arma0(y, <0.5>, 0, 1) ~ e[][0] .* e[][1]);
}
```

produces

```
          1.0000          1.0000          1.0000
          0.50000        -0.50000          0.40000
          0.00000          0.00000        -0.19048
          0.00000          0.00000          0.094118
          0.00000          0.00000        -0.046921

          0.22489          1.0000          0.22489
          1.8004          0.91652          1.8004
         -1.1003          0.89974         -1.1003
         -0.47828          0.89574         -0.47828
         -0.51476          0.89476         -0.51476
logdet = -0.82828 -0.82828
          0.00000          0.22489
          1.6276          1.6276
         -1.0743         -1.0743
         -0.81547         -0.81547
         -0.21537         -0.21537

          0.22489          0.22489
          1.6276          1.6501
         -1.0181         -0.99002
         -0.40857         -0.42842
         -0.46988         -0.46059
```

# 11.2 Maximization package

The maximization package implements maximization of functions of (several) parameters, as well as numerical differentiation. The maximization package requires the
header file `maximize.h`, and linking in of `maximize.oxo`. This is achieved by adding
`#import <maximize>` at the top of your code.

## GetMaxControl, GetMaxControlEps

```
#include <maximize.h>
GetMaxControl();
GetMaxControlEps();
```

*Return value*
> Return an array with three values and two values respectively.
> `GetMaxControl` returns { `mxIter, iPrint, bCompact` }.
> `GetMaxControlEps` returns { `dEps1, dEps2` }.

*See also*
> `MaxControl`, `MaxControlEps`

## MaxBFGS

```
#include <maximize.h>
MaxBFGS(const func, const avP, const adFunc,
    const amInvHess, const fNumDer);
```
| | | |
|---|---|---|
| func | in: | a function computing the function value, option-ally with derivatives |
| avP | in: | address of $p \times 1$ matrix with starting values |
| | out: | $p \times 1$ matrix with final coefficients |
| adFunc | in: | address |
| | out: | double, final function value |
| amInvHess | in: | address of $p \times p$ matrix, initial (inverse negative) quasi-Hessian **K**; a possible starting value is the identity matrix |
| | or: | 0, in which case the identity matrix is used |
| | out: | if not 0 on input: final **K** (not reliable as estimate of actual Hessian) |
| fNumDer | in: | 0: func provides analytical first derivatives |
| | | 1: use numerical first derivatives |

The supplied `func` argument should have the following format:

`func(const vP, const adFunc, const avScore, const amHessian);`

| | | |
|---|---|---|
| vP | in: | $p \times 1$ matrix with coefficients |
| adFunc | in: | address |
| | out: | double, function value at vP |
| avScore | in: | 0, or an address |
| | out: | if !0 on input: $p \times 1$ matrix with first derivatives at vP |
| amHessian | in: | always 0 for MaxBFGS, as it does not need the Hessian |
| returns | | 1: successful, 0: function evaluation failed |

*Return value*

Returns the status of the iterative process:

MAX_CONV *Strong convergence*
Both convergence tests (11.2) and (11.3) were passed, using tolerance $\epsilon = \epsilon_1$.

MAX_WEAK_CONV *Weak convergence (no improvement in line search)*
The step length $s_i$ has become too small. The convergence test (11.2) was passed, using tolerance $\epsilon = \epsilon_2$.

MAX_MAXIT *No convergence (maximum no of iterations reached)*

MAX_LINE_FAIL *No convergence (no improvement in line search)*
The step length $s_i$ has become too small. The convergence test (11.2) was not passed, using tolerance $\epsilon = \epsilon_2$.

MAX_FUNC_FAIL *No convergence (function evaluation failed)*

The chosen default values for the tolerances are:

$$\epsilon_1 = 10^{-4}, \ \epsilon_2 = 5 \times 10^{-3}.$$

*Description*

MaxBFGS maximizes a function, using the quasi-Newton method developed by Broyden, Fletcher, Goldfarb, Shanno (BFGS). The function either uses supplied analytical first derivatives, or numerical first derivatives (in which case only the function values need to be available: this uses the function Num1Derivative).

Using numerical derivatives saves programming (and thinking) time, but analytical dervatives tend to be computable with higher accuracy and over a wider parameter range. The iteration process is unaffected by this choice, other than caused by the slight numerical differences between the two methods (and the lower robustness of numerical derivatives).

A Newton scheme is used to maximize the unconstrained function $f(\boldsymbol{\theta})$:

$$\boldsymbol{\theta}(k+1) = \boldsymbol{\theta}(k) + s(k)\mathbf{Q}(k)^{-1}\mathbf{q}(k), \tag{11.1}$$

with

$\boldsymbol{\theta}(k)$    parameter values at iteration $k$;
$s(k)$    step length, normally 1;
$\mathbf{Q}(k)$    symmetric positive definite matrix (at iteration k);
$\mathbf{q}(k)$    first derivative of the function (the score vector);
$\boldsymbol{\delta}(k)$    $= \boldsymbol{\theta}(k) - \boldsymbol{\theta}(k-1)$, the change in the parameters;
$\boldsymbol{\gamma}(k)$    $= \mathbf{q}(k) - \mathbf{q}(k-1)$, the change in the score.

The BFGS method updates $\mathbf{K} = \mathbf{Q}^{-1}$ directly, avoiding the need for second derivatives. A linear line search is used when necessary.

Owing to numerical problems it is possible (especially close to the maximum) that the calculated $\boldsymbol{\delta}_i$ does not yield a higher likelihood. Then an $s_i \in [0,1]$ yielding a higher function value is determined by a line search. Theoretically, since the direction is upward, such an $s_i$ should exist; however, numerically it might be impossible to find one. When using BFGS with numerical derivatives, it often pays to scale the data so that the initial gradients are of the same order of magnitude.

The *convergence* decision is based on two tests. The first uses likelihood elasticities ($\partial \ell / \partial \log \boldsymbol{\theta}$, switching notation from $f(\boldsymbol{\theta})$ to $\ell(\boldsymbol{\theta})$):

$$
\begin{aligned}
|q_{i,j}\theta_{i,j}| &\leq \epsilon \quad \text{for all } j \text{ when } \theta_{i,j} \neq 0, \\
|q_{i,j}| &\leq \epsilon \quad \text{for all } j \text{ with } \theta_{i,j} = 0.
\end{aligned}
\tag{11.2}
$$

The second is based on the one-step-ahead relative change in the parameter values:

$$
\begin{aligned}
|\delta_{i+1,j}| &\leq 10\epsilon \, |\theta_{i,j}| \quad \text{for all } j \text{ with } \theta_{i,j} \neq 0, \\
|\delta_{i+1,j}| &\leq 10\epsilon \quad \text{for all } j \text{ when } \theta_{i,j} = 0.
\end{aligned}
\tag{11.3}
$$

The final inverse negative quasi-Hessian $\mathbf{K}$ can not reliably used to estimate standard errors. When, for example, iteration starts in the maximum with an identity matrix as initial quasi-Hessian, the final-Hessian will also be the identity matrix. Instead, it is possible to take the inverse of minus the numerical second derivatives.

Note that the code resides in `src/maximize.ox`. To use this function, either include the code, or link the corresponding `maximize.oxo` file using `#import <maximize>`.

*See also*

MaxControl,    MaxConvergenceMsg,    MaxNewton,    Num1Derivative, Num2Derivative

*Example*

The following example minimizes the so-called Rosenbrock function (see Fletcher, 1987):

$$f(\alpha, \beta) = 100 * \left(\beta - \alpha^2\right)^2 + (1 - \alpha)^2 .$$

No data are involved. It is easily seen that the minimum is at $(1, 1)$ with function value $0$. The contours are rather banana-shaped. The program maximizes the function twice, starting from (0,0), once with analytical derivatives, once without:

.......................................... *samples/maximize/maxbfgs.ox*

```
#include <oxstd.h>
#import <maximize>

fRosenbrock(const vP, const adFunc, const avScore, const amHessian)
{
    adFunc[0] = -100 * (vP[1] - vP[0] ^ 2) ^ 2
        - (1 - vP[0]) ^ 2;                  // function value

    if (avScore)                    // if !0: compute score
    {   // this bit is not needed for numerical derivatives
        (avScore[0])[0] = 400 * (vP[1] - vP[0]^2)
            * vP[0] + 2 * (1 - vP[0]);
        (avScore[0])[1] = -200 * (vP[1] - vP[0]^2);
    }
    return 1;                       // 1 indicates success
}

main()
{
    decl vp, dfunc, ir;

    MaxControl(1000, 50);

    vp = zeros(2, 1);                       // starting values
    ir = MaxBFGS(fRosenbrock, &vp, &dfunc, 0, FALSE);

    print("\n", MaxConvergenceMsg(ir),
        " using analytical derivatives",
        "\nFunction value = ", dfunc, "; parameters:",vp);

    vp = zeros(2, 1);                       // starting values
    ir = MaxBFGS(fRosenbrock, &vp, &dfunc, 0, TRUE);

    print("\n", MaxConvergenceMsg(ir),
        " using numerical derivatives",
        "\nFunction value = ", dfunc, "; parameters:",vp);
}
```
..................................................................

This produces:

```
Starting values
parameters
        0.00000         0.00000
gradients
         2.0000         0.00000
Initial function =                      -1


Position after 20 BFGS iterations
Status: Strong convergence
parameters
        1.0000          0.99999
gradients
 -6.7948e-005   3.8365e-005
function value = -2.29573829351e-011


Strong convergence using analytical derivatives
Function value = -2.29574e-011; parameters:
        1.0000
        0.99999


Starting values
parameters
        0.00000         0.00000
gradients
         2.0000         0.00000
Initial function =                      -1


Position after 20 BFGS iterations
Status: Strong convergence
parameters
        1.0000          0.99999
gradients
 -6.7948e-005   3.8365e-005
function value = -2.30014575614e-011


Strong convergence using numerical derivatives
Function value = -2.30015e-011; parameters:
        1.0000
        0.99999
```

# MaxControl, MaxControlEps

```
#include <maximize.h>
MaxControl(const mxIter, const iPrint);
MaxControl(const mxIter, const iPrint, const bCompact);
MaxControlEps(const dEps1, const dEps2);
```

| | | |
|---|---|---|
| mxIter | in: | int, maximum number of iterations; default is 1000, use $-1$ to leave the current value unchanged |
| iPrint | in: | int, print results every iPrint'th iteration; default is 0, use $-1$ to leave the current value unchanged |
| bCompact | in: | int, if TRUE uses compact format for iteration results (optional argument) |
| dEps1 | in: | double, $\epsilon_1$, default is $10^{-4}$, use $\leq 0$ to leave the current value unchanged |
| dEps2 | in: | double, $\epsilon_2$, default is $5 \times 10^{-3}$, use $\leq 0$ to leave the current value unchanged |

*Return value*
> No return value.

*Description*
> The MaxControl and MaxControlEps functions provide control over some iteration parameters. Use a value of –1 for mxIter, iPrint, dEps1 or dEps2 to leave the current value unchanged.

*See also*
> GetMaxControl,    GetMaxControlEps,    MaxBFGS    (for    an    example), MaxSimplex

# MaxConvergenceMsg

```
#include <maximize.h>
MaxConvergenceMsg(const iCode);
```

| | | |
|---|---|---|
| iCode | in: | int, code returned by MaxBFGS or MaxSimplex |

*Return value*
> Returns the text corresponding to the convergence code listed under the return values of MaxBFGS.

*See also*
> MaxBFGS (for an example), MaxNewton, MaxSimplex, MaxSQP, MaxSQPF

# MaxNewton

```
#import <maximize>
MaxNewton(const func, const avP, const adFunc,
    const amInvHess, const fNumDer);
```
|  |  |  |
|---|---|---|
| func | in: | a function computing the function value, optionally with derivatives |
| avP | in: | address of $p \times 1$ matrix with starting values |
|  | out: | $p \times 1$ matrix with final coefficients |
| adFunc | in: | address |
|  | out: | double, final function value |
| amHessian | in: | address, or 0 |
|  | out: | if not 0 on input: final Hessian **H** |
| fNumDer | in: | 0: func provides analytical second derivatives |
|  |  | 1: use numerical second derivatives |

The supplied func argument should have the following format:
```
func(const vP, const adFunc, const avScore, const amHessian);
```
|  |  |  |
|---|---|---|
| vP | in: | $p \times 1$ matrix with coefficients |
| adFunc | in: | address |
|  | out: | double, function value at vP |
| avScore | in: | 0, or an address |
|  | out: | if !0 on input: $p \times 1$ matrix with first derivatives at vP |
| amHessian | in: | 0, or an address |
|  | out: | if !0 on input: $p \times p$ matrix with second derivatives (Hessian matrix) at vP |
| returns |  | 1: successful, 0: function evaluation failed |

*Return value*

Returns the status of the iterative process, see MaxBFGS.

*Description*

MaxNewton maximizes a function, using the Newton method. The function expects analytical first derivatives (scores), and either uses supplied analytical second derivatives (Hessian), or computes the Hessian numerically. The numerical second derivatives are computed using forward differences on the scores.

Using numerical derivatives saves programming (and thinking) time, but analytical dervatives tend to be computable with higher accuracy and over a wider parameter range. The iteration process is unaffected by this choice, other than caused by the small numerical differences between the two methods (and the lower robustness of numerical derivatives).

MaxNewton uses a scheme like (11.1) to maximize $f(\boldsymbol{\theta})$:

$$\boldsymbol{\theta}(k+1) = \boldsymbol{\theta}(k) - s(k)\mathbf{H}(k)^{-1}\mathbf{q}(k),$$

where **H** is the user supplied Hessian matrix. This requires that **H** is negative definite at each step. If this is not the case, a steepest descent step with line search is taken. Otherwise the line search is as discussed in `MaxFBGS`. The *convergence* decision is also the same as for `MaxBFGS`.

Since the Hessian matrix is user supplied, this function can be used to implement various methods, for example:

| **H** | description |
|---|---|
| $\partial^2 f\,(\theta)/\partial\theta\partial\theta'$ | Newton's method |
| $E[\mathbf{H}]$ | method of scoring |
| **I** | steepest descent |
| OPG | outer product of gradients: BHHH method, see Berndt, Hall, Hall and Hausman, 1974 |

Note that the code resides in `src/maximize.ox`. To use this function, either include the code, or link the corresponding `maximize.oxo` file using `#import <maximize>`.

*See also*

> `MaxBFGS`, `MaxControl`, `MaxConvergenceMsg`, `Num1Derivative`, `Num2Derivative`

*Example*

> The following program extends the `MaxBFGS` example by adding second derivatives to the Rosenbrock function. Note that we always should check whether the score and Hessian arguments are of type array. For example, during the line search neither are required, and both will be zero. When numerical second derivatives are used the `amHessian` arguments to `fRosenbrock` will always be zero.

....................................................*samples/maximize/maxnewt.ox*

```
#include <oxstd.h>
#import <maximize>

fRosenbrock(const vP, const adFunc, const avScore, const amHessian)
{
    decl ab2 = vP[1] - vP[0] ^ 2, a1 = 1 - vP[0];

    adFunc[0] = -100 * ab2 ^ 2 - a1 ^ 2;
    if (avScore)                    // if !0: compute score
    {
        (avScore[0])[0] = 400 * ab2 * vP[0] + 2 * a1;
        (avScore[0])[1] = -200 * ab2;
    }
    if (amHessian)                  // if !0: compute Hessian
    {  // this bit is not needed for numerical derivatives
        (amHessian[0])[0][0] =
            400 * vP[1] - 1200 * vP[0]^2 - 2;
        (amHessian[0])[1][1] = -200;
        (amHessian[0])[1][0] =
            (amHessian[0])[0][1] = 400 * vP[0];
    }
```

```
    return 1;                           // 1 indicates success
}

main()
{
    decl vp, dfunc, ir, mhess;

//    MaxControl(100, 1, 1);

    vp = zeros(2, 1);                        // starting values
    ir = MaxNewton(fRosenbrock, &vp, &dfunc,&mhess, TRUE);

    print("\n", MaxConvergenceMsg(ir),
        " using numerical 2nd derivatives",
        "\nFunction value = ", dfunc, "; parameters:", vp,
        "final Hessian:", mhess);

    vp = zeros(2, 1);                        // starting values
    ir = MaxNewton(fRosenbrock, &vp, &dfunc,&mhess,FALSE);

    print("\n", MaxConvergenceMsg(ir),
        " using analytical 2nd derivatives",
        "\nFunction value = ", dfunc, "; parameters:", vp,
        "final Hessian:", mhess);
}
```
..............................................................................

produces

```
Strong convergence using numerical 2nd derivatives
Function value = -2.45742e-009; parameters:
        1.0000
        1.0000
final Hessian:
     -0.49900      -0.99799
     -0.99799      -2.0010

Strong convergence using analytical 2nd derivatives
Function value = -1.22009e-012; parameters:
        1.0000
        1.0000
final Hessian:
     -0.50000      -0.99999
     -0.99999      -2.0050
```

# MaxSimplex

```
#include <maximize.h>
MaxSimplex(const func, const avP, const adFunc, vDelta);
```

| | | |
|---|---|---|
| func | in: | a function computing the function value |
| avP | in: | address of $p \times 1$ matrix with starting values |
| | out: | $p \times 1$ matrix with coefficients at convergence |
| adFunc | in: | address |
| | out: | double, function value at convergence |
| vDelta | in: | 0, or a $p \times 1$ matrix with the initial simplex (if 0 is specified, the score is used for the initial simplex) |

The supplied func argument should have the same format as in MaxBFGS.

*Return value*

Returns the status of the iterative process, as documented under MaxBFGS.

*Description*

Maximizes a function using the simplex method, see for example Applied Statistics algorithm AS 47 (O'Neil, 1971). The simplex method can be rather slow. For reasonably well behaved functions, a preferred derivative free method is MaxBFGS using numerical derivatives.

Note that the code resides in src/maximize.ox. To use this function, either include the code, or link the corresponding maximize.oxo file using #import <maximize>.

*See also*

MaxBFGS

*Example*

. . . . . . . . . . . . . . . . . . . . . . . . . . . . . . . . . . . . . . . . . . . . *samples/maximize/maxboth.ox*

```
#include <oxstd.h>
#include <oxfloat.h>
#import <maximize>


fRosenbrock(const vP, const adFunc, const avScore, const amHessian)
{
    adFunc[0] =
        -100 * (vP[1][0] - vP[0][0] ^ 2) ^ 2 - (1 - vP[0][0]) ^ 2;

return 1;
}
fPowell(const vP, const adFunc, const avScore, const amHessian)
{
    adFunc[0] =
    -((vP[0][0] + 10*vP[1][0]) ^ 2 + 5 * (vP[2][0] - vP[3][0]) ^ 2
    +(vP[1][0] - 2*vP[2][0]) ^ 4 + 10 * (vP[0][0] + vP[3][0]) ^ 4);
```

```
    return 1;
    }
fQuad(const vP, const adFunc, const avScore, const amHessian)
{
    adFunc[0] = -double(sumc(vP .^ 4));

    return 1;
    }

main()
{
    decl vp, vf, mh;

    format(66);                 // shorter lines than normal
    MaxControl(-1,1000);

    vp = <-1.2;1>;  mh = unit(2);
    MaxBFGS(fRosenbrock, &vp, &vf, &mh, TRUE);
    vp = <-1.2;1>;  mh = unit(2);
    MaxSimplex(fRosenbrock, &vp, &vf, 0 /*<1;1>*/);

    vp = <3;-1;0;1>;  mh = unit(4);
    MaxBFGS(fPowell, &vp, &vf, &mh, TRUE);
    vp = <3;-1;0;1>;  mh = unit(4);
    MaxSimplex(fPowell, &vp, &vf, 0 /*<1;1;1;1>*/);

    vp = ones(10,1); mh = unit(10);
    MaxBFGS(fQuad, &vp, &vf, &mh, TRUE);
    vp = ones(10,1); mh = unit(10);
    MaxSimplex(fQuad, &vp, &vf, 0 /*vp*/);
}
```
.............................................................................

produces after some editing of the output:

```
Starting values
parameters
      -1.2000        1.0000
gradients
      215.60        88.000
Initial function =                 -24.2

Position after 33 BFGS iterations
Status: Strong convergence
parameters
       1.0000        1.0000
gradients
 -6.6755e-008  4.8263e-008
function value =  -4.0124066543e-016

Starting values
parameters
      -1.2000        1.0000
Initial function =                 -24.2
```

```
Position after 132 Simplex iterations
Status: Strong convergence
parameters
        1.0000          1.0000
gradients
  3.1028e-005 -1.5521e-005
function value = -6.02226722279e-013


Starting values
parameters
        3.0000         -1.0000         0.00000          1.0000
gradients
       -2546.0          144.00          2.0000         -2570.0
Initial function =                      -2615

Position after 50 BFGS iterations
Status: Strong convergence
parameters
  -4.2609e-005   4.2609e-006  -0.00017248  -0.00017248
gradients
   6.0617e-010   1.9090e-009 -2.5012e-010   9.8933e-010
function value = -3.62744789919e-014


Starting values
parameters
        3.0000         -1.0000         0.00000          1.0000
Initial function =                      -2615

Position after 239 Simplex iterations
Status: Strong convergence
parameters
  -0.00081637   8.1527e-005   0.00029861   0.00029848
gradients
   2.2137e-006   2.2082e-005  -1.3407e-006   1.3451e-006
function value = -2.09880254028e-012


Starting values
parameters
        1.0000          1.0000          1.0000          1.0000          1.0000
        1.0000          1.0000          1.0000          1.0000          1.0000
gradients
       -4.0000         -4.0000         -4.0000         -4.0000         -4.0000
       -4.0000         -4.0000         -4.0000         -4.0000         -4.0000
Initial function =                      -10

Position after 1 BFGS iterations
Status: Strong convergence
parameters
        0.00000         0.00000         0.00000         0.00000         0.00000
        0.00000         0.00000         0.00000         0.00000         0.00000
gradients
        0.00000         0.00000         0.00000         0.00000         0.00000
```

```
        0.00000      0.00000      0.00000      0.00000      0.00000
function value =                  0   steplen = 0.25

Starting values
parameters
        1.0000       1.0000       1.0000       1.0000       1.0000
        1.0000       1.0000       1.0000       1.0000       1.0000
Initial function =                  -10

Position after 454 Simplex iterations
Status: Strong convergence
parameters
    0.00012390  -0.00040964    0.00099913   7.2798e-005  -0.00027496
    0.00085512  -0.00076729   -0.00081975   0.00052821   -0.00060839
gradients
 -7.6214e-012  2.7501e-010  -3.9896e-009  -1.5505e-012   8.3175e-011
 -2.5012e-009  1.8070e-009   2.2036e-009  -5.8956e-010   9.0080e-010
function value =   -2.5783761224e-012
```

# MaxSQP, MaxSQPF

```
#import <maxsqp>
MaxSQP(const func, const avP, const adFunc, const amHessian,
    const fNumDer, const cfunc_gt0, const cfunc_eq0, vLo, vHi);
MaxSQP(const func, const avP, const adFunc, const amHessian,
    const fNumDer, const cfunc_gt0, const cfunc_eq0, vLo, vHi,
    const cfunc_gt0_jac, const cfunc_eq0_jac, ...);
MaxSQPF(const func, const avP, const adFunc, const amHessian,
    const fNumDer, const cfunc_gt0, const cfunc_eq0, vLo, vHi);
MaxSQPF(const func, const avP, const adFunc, const amHessian,
    const fNumDer, const cfunc_gt0, const cfunc_eq0, vLo, vHi,
    const cfunc_gt0_jac, const cfunc_eq0_jac, ...);
```

| | | |
|---|---|---|
| func | in: | a function computing the function value, optionally with derivatives |
| avP | in: | address of $p \times 1$ matrix with starting values |
| | out: | $p \times 1$ matrix with final coefficients |
| adFunc | in: | address |
| | out: | double, final function value |
| amHessian | in: | address, or 0 |
| | out: | if not 0 on input: final Hessian (BFGS-style) approximation $\mathbf{B}$ |
| fNumDer | in: | 0: func provides analytical first derivatives |
| | | 1: use numerical first derivatives |
| vLo | in: | $p \times 1$ matrix with lower bounds, or <> |
| vHi | in: | $p \times 1$ matrix with upper bounds, or <> |

The supplied func argument should have the same format as in MaxBFGS.

The cfunc_gt0 argument can be zero, or a function evaluating the nonlinear constraints (which will be constrained to be positive) with the following format:

```
cfunc_gt0(const avF, const vP);
```

| | | |
|---|---|---|
| avF | in: | address |
| | out: | $m \times 1$ matrix with inequality constraints at vP |
| vP | in: | $p \times 1$ matrix with coefficients |
| returns | | 1: successful, 0: constraint evaluation failed |

The cfunc_eq0 argument can be zero, or a function evaluating the nonlinear constraints (which will be constrained to zero) with the following format:

```
cfunc_eq0(const avF, const vP);
```

| | | |
|---|---|---|
| avF | in: | address |
| | out: | $m_e \times 1$ matrix with equality constraints at vP |
| vP | in: | $p \times 1$ matrix with coefficients |
| returns | | 1: successful, 0: constraint evaluation failed |

The `cfunc_gt0_jac` and `cfunc_eq0_jac` are optional functions that return the analytical Jacobian matrix of the constraints. They have the same format, returning in `avF` an $m \times 1$ and an $m_e \times p$ matrix respectively.

*Return value*

Returns the status of the iterative process, see `MaxBFGS`.

*Description*

`MaxSQP` implements a sequential quadratic programming technique to maximize a non-linear function subject to non-linear constraints, similar to Algorithm 18.7 in Nocedal and Wright (1999).

`MaxSQPF` enforces all iterates to be feasible, using the Algorithm by Lawrence and Tits (2001). The current version does not support equality constraints. If a starting point is infeasible, `MaxSQPF` will try to minimize the squared constraint violations to find a feasible point.

Note that the code resides in `src/maxsqp.ox`. To use these functions add the line #import <maxsqp> at the top of the file.

*See also*

`MaxBFGS`,     `MaxControl`,     `MaxConvergenceMsg`,     `Num1Derivative`, `Num2Derivative`

*Example*

See ox\samples\maximize.

# Num1Derivative, Num2Derivative

```
#include <maximize.h>
Num1Derivative(const func, vP, const avScore);
Num2Derivative(const func, vP, const amHessian);
```

| func | in: | a function computing the function value, option-ally with derivatives |
|---|---|---|
| vP | in: | $p \times 1$ matrix with parameter values |
| mHessian | in: | $p \times p$ matrix, initial Hessian |
| avScore | in: | an address |
| | out: | $p \times 1$ matrix with 1st derivatives at vP |
| amHessian | in: | an address |
| | out: | $p \times p$ matrix with 2nd derivatives at vP |

The supplied func argument should have the format as documented under
MaxBFGS.

*Return value*

Returns 1 if successful, 0 otherwise.

*Description*

These functions take numerical first and second differences of a function based
on a central finite difference approximation. The numerical derivatives are calculated using:

$$\frac{f\left(\theta + \epsilon \imath\right) - f\left(\theta - \epsilon \imath\right)}{\mu} \simeq \frac{\partial f\left(\theta\right)}{\partial\left(\imath'\theta\right)}$$

where $\imath$ is a unit vector (for example, $(1\ 0 \dots 0)'$ for the first element of $\theta$), $\epsilon$ is
a suitably chosen step length. Thus, $\epsilon$ represents a compromise between round-
off error (cancellation of leading digits when subtracting nearly equal numbers)
and truncation error (ignoring terms of higher order than $\epsilon$ in the approximation).
Although the Ox code chooses $\epsilon$ carefully, there may be situations where the
numerical derivative performs poorly.

If in Num1Derivative one-side fails, the procedure will use a one-sided difference.

The numerical values of second derivatives can be computed in a corresponding
way using:

$$\frac{f(\theta + \epsilon_1\imath + \epsilon_2\jmath) + f(\theta - \epsilon_1\imath - \epsilon_2\jmath) - f(\theta - \epsilon_1\imath + \epsilon_2\jmath) - f(\theta + \epsilon_1\imath - \epsilon_2\jmath)}{4\epsilon_1\epsilon_2}$$

where $\imath$ or $\jmath$ is zero except for unity in the $i^{th}$ or $j^{th}$ position.

Note that the code resides in src/maximize.ox. Add #import <maximize>
to use this function.

*See also*

MaxBFGS

*Example*

The following example is based on the Rosenbrock function (see MaxBFGS):

.............................................. *samples/maximize/numder.ox*

```
#include <oxstd.h>
#import <maximize>

fRosenbrock(const vP, const adFunc, const avScore, const amHessian)
{
    adFunc[0] = -100 * (vP[1][0] - vP[0][0] ^ 2) ^ 2
        - (1 - vP[0][0]) ^ 2;                    // function value

    if (avScore)                      // if !0: compute score
    { // this bit is not needed for numerical derivatives
        (avScore[0])[0][0]= 400 * (vP[1][0] - vP[0][0]^2)
            * vP[0][0] + 2 * (1 - vP[0][0]);
        (avScore[0])[1][0]=-200 * (vP[1][0] - vP[0][0]^2);
    }
    return 1;
}

main()
{
    decl vp, dfunc, vscore, mhess;

    vscore = vp = zeros(2, 1);              // starting values

    fRosenbrock(vp, &dfunc, &vscore, 0);
    print("analytical first derivative at <0;0>", vscore);

    if (Num1Derivative(fRosenbrock, vp, &vscore))
        print("numerical 1st derivative at <0;0>", vscore);

    if (Num2Derivative(fRosenbrock, vp, &mhess))
        print("numerical 2nd derivative at <0;0>", mhess);
}
```
..................................................................................

produces

```
analytical first derivative at <0;0>
       2.0000
       0.00000
numerical 1st derivative at <0;0>
       2.0000
       0.00000
numerical 2nd derivative at <0;0>
      -2.0000        0.00000
       0.00000       -200.00
```

# NumJacobian

```
#include <maximize.h>
NumJacobian(const func, vU, const amJacobian);
    func                in:  function mapping from restricted to unrestricted
                             parameters
    vU                  in:  of u × 1 matrix with parameters
    amJacobian          in:  address
                        out: r × u Jacobian matrix corresponding to mapping
```

The supplied `func` argument should have the following format:
```
func(const avR, const vU);
```

```
    avR        in:  address
               out: r × 1 matrix with restricted coefficients
    vU         in:  u × 1 matrix with unrestricted coefficients
    returns         1: successful, 0: function evaluation failed
```

*Return value*
> Returns 1 if successful, 0 otherwise.

*Description*
> Computes the Jacobian matrix of the restrictions imposed of the form $\theta = f(\phi)$:
> $J = \partial f(\phi)/\partial \theta'$; $f(\cdot)$ is an $r$-vector, $\phi$ is an $u$-vector.
> Note that the code resides in `src/maximize.ox`. Add `#import <maximize>`
> to use this function.

*See also*
> Num1Derivative

*Example*
> . . . . . . . . . . . . . . . . . . . . . . . . . . . . . . . . . . . . . . . . . . . . . . . . . . *samples/maximize/jacobian.ox*
```
#include <oxstd.h>
#import <maximize>

fMap(const avR, const vU)
{
    decl cu = rows(vU);

    avR[0] = vU[ : cu-2][] .^ 2; // drop last row, square

    return 1;
}

main()
{
    decl vp, mjacob;

    if (NumJacobian(fMap, ones(4, 1), &mjacob))
        print("numerical Jacobian at <1;1;1;1>", mjacob);
```

```
        if (NumJacobian(fMap, zeros(4, 1), &mjacob))
            print("numerical Jacobian at <0;0;0;0>", mjacob);
}
```

produces

```
numerical Jacobian at <1;1;1;1>
        2.0000        0.00000        0.00000        0.00000
        0.00000        2.0000        0.00000        0.00000
        0.00000        0.00000        2.0000        0.00000
numerical Jacobian at <0;0;0;0>
        0.00000        0.00000        0.00000        0.00000
        0.00000        0.00000        0.00000        0.00000
        0.00000        0.00000        0.00000        0.00000
```

# SolveNLE

```
#import <solvenle>
SolveNLE(const func, const avX);
SolveNLE(const func, const avX, iMode, funcJac, dEps1, dEps2,
    mxIter, iPrint, mxItInner);
```

|          |      |                                                                 |
|----------|------|-----------------------------------------------------------------|
| func     | in:  | Ox function evaluating the nonlinear equations (see below)       |
| avX      | in:  | address of $n \times 1$ matrix with starting values             |
|          | out: | $n \times 1$ matrix with final coefficients                     |
| iMode    | in:  | int, mode of operation:                                         |

$-1$ (default): mode 1 if $n < 80$, else mode 3
0: Newton's method using analytical Jacobian
1: Newton's method using numerical Jacobian
2: using Broyden's approximation to Jacobian
3: large scale problem (tensor-gmres method, avoiding $n \times n$ Jacobian matrix)

| funcJac   | in: | a function computing the function value, optionally with derivatives |
| dEps1     | in: | double, $\epsilon_1$, default is $10^{-4}$, use $\leq 0$ to leave the current value unchanged (can also be set with MaxControlEps) |
| dEps2     | in: | double, $\epsilon_2$, default is $5 \times 10^{-3}$, use $\leq 0$ to leave the current value unchanged (can also be set with MaxControlEps) |
| mxIter    | in: | int, maximum number of iterations; default is 1000, use $-1$ to leave the current value unchanged (can also be set with MaxControl) |
| iPrint    | in: | int, print results every iPrint'th iteration; default is 0, use $-1$ to leave the current value unchanged (can also be set with MaxControl) |
| mxItInner | in: | int, int, number of inner iterations for large scale problems, default is $\max(50, 10 * \log_{10}(n))$ |

- The supplied `func` argument should have the following format:

`func(const avF, const vX)`

| | | |
|---|---|---|
| avF | in: | address |
| | out: | $n \times 1$ matrix with with nonlinear system $f(x)$ evaluated at $x$ |
| vX | in: | $n \times 1$ matrix with coefficients $x$ |
| returns | | 1: successful, 0: function evaluation failed |

*Return value*
Returns 1 if successful, 0 otherwise.

- When the analytical Jacobian is used, the `funcJac` argument should have the following format:

`funcJac(const amJac, const vX)`

| | | |
|---|---|---|
| amJac | in: | address |
| | out: | $n \times n$ Jacobian matrix evaluated at $x$ |
| vX | in: | $n \times 1$ matrix with coefficients $x$ |
| returns | | 1: successful, 0: function evaluation failed |

*Return value*
Returns 1 if successful, 0 otherwise.

*Return value*
Returns the status of the iterative process:

MAX_CONV *Strong convergence*
norm($f(x)$) $< 0.001\epsilon_1$.
MAX_WEAK_CONV *Weak convergence (no improvement in line search)*
The step length has become too small, but norm($f(x)$) $< \epsilon_2$.
MAX_MAXIT *No convergence (maximum no of iterations reached)*
MAX_LINE_FAIL *No convergence (no improvement in line search)*
The step length has become too small and weak convergence was not achieved.
MAX_FUNC_FAIL *No convergence (function evaluation failed)*
MAX_NOCONV *No convergence*
Probably not yet attempted to solve the system.

The chosen default values for the tolerances are:

$$\epsilon_1 = 10^{-4}, \ \epsilon_2 = 5 \times 10^{-3}.$$

*Description*
Solves a system $f(x)$ of $n$ nonlinear equations in $n$ unknowns. The principle method implemented is the tensor–Newton method, using either a numerical or analytical Jacobian matrix. The tensor–Newton method is similar (but not identical) to that discussed in Schnabel and Frank (1985). There is an option to use the

Broyden approximation to the Jacobian instead, but that often works less well in practice. Finally, a large scale option avoids the $n \times n$ Jacobian matrix and uses the gmres method to approximately solve the linear system, and nonlinear gmres to solve the tensor system (so is different from Feng and Pulliam, 1997).

For a general overview see, e.g., Dennis Jr. and Schnabel (1983) and Nocedal and Wright (1999).

Note that the code resides in `src/solvenle.ox`. Add `#import <solvenle>` to use this function.

*See also*

    MaxControl, MaxControlEps

*Example*

    . . . . . . . . . . . . . . . . . . . . . . . . . . . . . . . . *samples/maximize/solvenle1.ox (part of)*

```
#include <oxstd.h>
#import <maximize>
#import <solvenle>

test813(const avF, const vX)
{
    avF[0] = vX[0] + vX[1] - 3 | sqr(vX[0]) + sqr(vX[1]) - 9;
    return 1;
}
test813_jac(const amJac, const vX)
{
    amJac[0] = (1 ~ 1) | (2 * vX[0] ~ 2 * vX[1]);
    return 1;
}

main()
{
    decl x;
    MaxControl(-1, 1, 1);

    x = <1;5>;
    println("==== Using numerical Jacobian:");
    SolveNLE(test813, &x);
    println("x=", x);

    x = <1;5>;
    println("\n==== Using analytical Jacobian:");
    SolveNLE(test813, &x, 0, test813_jac);
    println("x=", x);
}
```

    . . . . . . . . . . . . . . . . . . . . . . . . . . . . . . . . . . . . . . . . . . . . . . . . . . . . . . . . . . . . . . . . . . . . . . . .

produces

```
==== Using numerical Jacobian:
it0     f'f/2=    149.0000 ||f||=    17.000
it1     f'f/2=    10.26612 ||f||=     4.5313 slope=      -298.00
it2     f'f/2=   0.1598528 ||f||=    0.56543 slope=      -20.550
```

```
it3      f'f/2= 0.0001087224 ||f||=   0.014746 slope=    -0.32032
it4      f'f/2=3.744902e-022 ||f||=2.2677e-011 slope= -0.00021762
SolveNLE(1): Strong convergence
x=
   1.1541e-011
       3.0000


==== Using analytical Jacobian:
it0      f'f/2=     149.0000 ||f||=     17.000
it1      f'f/2=     10.26611 ||f||=     4.5312 slope=    -298.00
it2      f'f/2=    0.1598527 ||f||=    0.56543 slope=    -20.550
it3      f'f/2= 0.0001087224 ||f||=   0.014746 slope=    -0.32032
it4      f'f/2=3.243347e-023 ||f||=8.0540e-012 slope= -0.00021762
SolveNLE(0): Strong convergence
x=
  -1.3427e-012
       3.0000
```

# SolveQP

```
#import <solveqp>
SolveQP(const mG, const vG, const mA, const vB, const mC,
    const vD, const vLo, const vHi);
SolveQPE(const mG, const vG, const mC, const vD);
SolveQPS(const sFile, const iVerbose)
SolveQPS(const sFile, const iVerbose, const fnSolveQP)
```

| | | |
|---|---|---|
| mG | in: | $n \times n$ matrix $G$ with quadratic weights, or $n \times 1$ vector with diagonal of $G$ |
| vG | in: | $n \times 1$ vector $g$ with linear weights |
| mA | in: | $m \times n$ matrix $A$ with linear inequality constraints $Ax \geq b$ (may be empty) |
| vB | in: | $m \times 1$ vector $b$ with right-hand side for linear inequality constraints (empty if $A$ is empty) |
| mC | in: | $m_e \times n$ matrix $C$ with linear equality constraints (may be empty) |
| vD | in: | $m_e \times 1$ vector $d$ with right-hand side for linear equality constraints (empty if $C$ is empty) |
| vLo | in: | $n \times 1$ vector with lower bounds (may be empty) |
| vHi | in: | $n \times 1$ vector with upper bounds (may be empty) |
| sFile | in: | string with .qps file name |
| iVerbose | in: | int, 0 for no output, 1 for one line summary output, 2 to print all matrices and results |
| fnSolveQP | in: | (optional argument) QP solver with call syntax as SolveQP. If absent SolveQP is used. |

*Return value*

SolveQP returns an array with three elements:

[0] integer return value:

> 0  success
> 1  initial point not feasible (should only be possible when `SolveQPIF` is called directly)
> 2  maximum number of iterations reached

[1] $n \times 1$ vector with solution $x$

[2] $m^* \times 1$ vector with Lagrange multipliers $\lambda$, $m^* = m_e + m + 2n$
in order: equality constraints, inequality constraints, lower bounds, upper bounds.

`SolveQPE` returns an array with three elements:

[0] $n \times 1$ vector with solution $x$

[1] $m_e \times 1$ vector with Lagrange multipliers $\lambda$

[2] $p \times 1$ vector with index of redundant constraint ($p = 0$ if all constraints were used)

`SolveQPS` returns an array with four elements: the first three as *SolveQP*, the fourth is the value of the objective function $f(x)$.

*Description*

`SolveQP` solves the quadratic program

$$\min f(x) = x'Gx/2 + x'g, \text{ subject to:}$$
$$Ax \geq b,$$
$$Cx = d,$$
$$x_{lo} \leq x \leq x_{hi}.$$

using an active set method based on a QR decomposition of $G^{-1}A'$. This is updated using `decqrupdate` to achieve reasonable speed. If $G$ is not positive definite, a small number is added to its diagonal. Sparseness is not taken into account, so `SolveQP` is not appropriate for large problems (say more than 1000 variables or constraints). `SolveQP` implements a pre-processing step, where bounds which are part of $A$ are moved to the explicit bound variables, and the remaining restrictions are checked for the tightest bounds. See, for example, Nocedal and Wright (1999) or Fletcher (1987) for an overview.

Note that the code resides in `src/solveqp.ox`. Add `#import <solveqp>` to use this function.

*See also*

`MaxFSQP`

*Example*

. . . . . . . . . . . . . . . . . . . . . . . . . . . . . . . . . . . . . . . . . . . . . . . *samples/maximize/solveqp1.ox*

```
#include <oxstd.h>
#import  <solveqp>

main()
```

```
{
    decl mg, vg, ma, vb, x, iret;
    mg = <4,2,2;2,4,0;2,0,2>;
    vg = <-8;-6;-4>;
    ma = <-1,-1,-2>;
    vb = <-3>;

    [iret,x] = SolveQP(mg, vg, ma, vb, <>, <>, <>, <>);
    println("HS35    result from SolveQP: ", iret, " (0=OK)",
        " x'= ", x', "f=", (x'mg*x) / 2 + vg'x + 9);

    [iret,x] = SolveQP(mg, vg, ma, vb, <>, <>,
        <-.Inf;0.5;-.Inf>, <.Inf;0.5;.Inf>);
    println("HS35MOD result from SolveQP: ", iret, " (0=OK)",
        " x'= ", x', "f=", (x'mg*x) / 2 + vg'x + 9);

    [iret,x] = SolveQP(mg, vg, ma, vb, <0,1,0>, <0.5>, <>, <>);
    println("HS35MOD result from SolveQP: ", iret, " (0=OK)",
        " x'= ", x', "f=", (x'mg*x) / 2 + vg'x + 9);

    mg = <0.02;2>;
    vg = <0;0>;
    ma = <10,-1;1,0;-1,0;0,1;0,-1>;
    vb = <10;2;-50;-50;-50>;
    [iret,x] = SolveQP(mg, vg, ma, vb, <>, <>, <>, <>);
    println("HS21    result from SolveQP: ", iret, " (0=OK)",
        " x'= ", x', "f=", (x'(mg.*x)) / 2 + vg'x - 10);
}
```
·······································································

produces

```
HS35    result from SolveQP: 0 (0=OK) x'=
      1.3333        0.77778       0.44444
f=
      0.11111
HS35MOD result from SolveQP: 0 (0=OK) x'=
      1.5000        0.50000       0.50000
f=
      0.25000
HS35MOD result from SolveQP: 0 (0=OK) x'=
      1.5000        0.50000       0.50000
f=
      0.25000
HS21    result from SolveQP: 0 (0=OK) x'=
      2.0000        0.00000
f=
     -9.9600
```

# 11.3 Probability package

The probability package contains various probability distributions (the standard library only defines the standard sampling distributions). It also contains random number generators for many distributions. This package requires #include <oxprob.h>.

## dens...

```
densbeta(const ma, const a, const b);
densbinomial(const ma, const n, const p);
denscauchy(const ma);
densexp(const ma, const lambda);
densextremevalue(const ma, const alpha, const beta);
densgamma(const ma, const dr, const da);
densgeometric(const ma, const p);
densgh(const ma, const nu, const delta, const gamma, const beta);
densgig(const ma, const nu, const delta, const gamma);
denshypergeometric(const ma, const n, const k, const m);
densinvgaussian(const ma, const mu, const lambda);
denskernel(const ma, const itype);
denslogarithmic(const ma, const alpha);
denslogistic(const ma, const alpha, const beta);
denslogn(const ma);
densmises(const ma, const mu, const kappa);
densnegbin(const ma, const k, const p);
denspareto(const ma, const k, const a);
denspoisson(const ma, const mu);
densweibull(const ma, const a, const b);
```

| | | |
|---|---|---|
| ma | in: | arithmetic type |
| a,b | in: | arithmetic type, arguments for Beta distribution |
| alpha,beta | in: | arithmetic type, location and scale parameter |
| lambda | in: | arithmetic type, parameter of exponential distribution |
| mu | in: | arithmetic type, von Mises: mean direction (use M_PI for symmetric between 0 and $\pi$); Poisson: mean |
| kappa | in: | arithmetic type, dispersion |

*Return value*
Returns the requested density at ma (the returned densities are positive):

| *function* | | |
|---|---|---|
| *density (for discrete distributions: $Pr\{X = x\}$)* | | |
| densbeta | | |
| Beta $(a, b)$, | $\frac{1}{B(a,b)} x^{a-1}(1-x)^{b-1}$ | $0 < x < 1; a > 0, b > 0$ |
| densbinomial | | |
| Binomial(n,p) | $\binom{n}{x} p^x q^{n-x}$ | $x = 0, 1, \ldots, n;\ 0 \le p \le 1$ |
| denscauchy | | |
| Cauchy, | $\left(\pi\left(1+x^2\right)\right)^{-1}$ | |
| densexp | | |
| Exponential, | $\lambda e^{-\lambda x}$ | $x > 0; \lambda > 0$ |
| densextremevalue | | |
| Extreme Value, | $\frac{e^{-(x-\alpha)/\beta}}{\beta} F(x)$ where | $\beta > 0$ |
| (Type I or Gumbel) | $F(x) = \exp\left[-e^{-(x-\alpha)/\beta}\right]$ | |
| densgamma | | |
| Gamma | $\frac{a^r}{\Gamma(r)} x^{r-1} e^{-ax}$ | $x > 0; r > 0, a > 0$ |
| densgeometric | | |
| Geometric | $pq^x$ | $x = 0, 1, \ldots;\ \mu > 0$ |
| densgh | | |
| Generalized hyperbolic, see (11.5) | | |
| densgig | | |
| Generalized inverse Gaussian, see (11.4) | | |
| denshypergeometric | | |
| Hypergeometric | $\binom{K}{x}\binom{M-K}{n-x} / \binom{M}{n}$ | $x = 0, 1, \ldots, n$ |
| Pr[$x$ white balls $\mid$ sample $n$ without replacement from $K$ white balls and $M$ in total] | | |
| densinvgaussian | | |
| Inverse Gaussian, | $\left(\frac{\lambda}{2\pi x^3}\right)^{1/2} \exp\left[-\frac{\lambda(x-\mu)^2}{2\mu^2 x}\right]$ | $x > 0; \lambda > 0, \mu > 0$ |
| denskernel | | |
| kernel, | see below | |
| denslogarithmic | | |
| Logarithmic | $\frac{-\alpha^x}{x \log(1-\alpha)}$ | $x = 1, 2 \ldots;\ 0 < \alpha < 1$ |
| denslogistic | | |
| Logistic, | $\frac{F(x)(1-F(x))}{\beta}$ | $F(x) = \left[1 + e^{-(x-\alpha)/\beta}\right]^{-1}, \beta > 0,$ |
| denslogn | | |
| Lognormal, | $\frac{1}{x(2\pi)^{1/2}} \exp\left[-(\log x)^2/2\right]$ | $x > 0$ |
| densmises | | |
| von Mises, | see (11.7) below | |
| densnegbin | | |
| Negative Binomial | $\binom{k+x-1}{x} p^k q^x$ | $x = 0, 1, \ldots;\ 0 < p \le 1,\ k > 0$ |
| denspareto | | |
| Pareto$(k, a)$ | $ak^a x^{-(a+1)}$ | $x \ge k > 0;\ a > 0$ |
| denspoisson | | |
| Poisson | $\frac{e^{-\mu}\mu^x}{x!}$ | $x = 0, 1, \ldots;\ \mu > 0$ |
| densweibull | | |
| Weibull | $abx^{b-1} \exp\left(-ax^b\right)$ | $x > 0;\ a > 0, b > 0$ |

`denskernel` arguments:

| itype | kernel name | form | |
|-------|-------------|------|---|
| 'e' | Epanechnikov | $0.75(1 - x^2)$ | $|x| < 1$ |
| 'b' | Biweight (Quartic) | $(15/16)(1 - x^2)^2$ | $|x| < 1$ |
| 't' | Triangular | $1 - |x|$ | $|x| < 1$ |
| 'g' | Gaussian (Normal) | $(2\pi)^{-1/2} \exp\left[-x^2/2\right]$ | |
| 'r' | Rectangular (Uniform) | $0.5$ | $|x| < 1$ |

The return type is derived as follows:

| returns | ma | degrees of freedom arguments |
|---------|-----|------------------------------|
| $m \times n$ matrix | $m \times n$ matrix | scalar |
| $m \times n$ matrix | scalar | $m \times n$ matrix |
| $m \times n$ matrix | $m \times n$ matrix | $m \times n$ matrix |
| double | scalar | scalar |

## Description

The information regarding the generalized inverse Gaussian and generalized hyperbolic distributions is based on Barndorff-Nielsen and Shephard (2001). The generalized inverse Gaussian distribution is a rather general model for positive random variables.

If $X \sim GIG(\nu, \delta, \gamma)$ then it has a generalized inverse Gaussian density:

$$\frac{(\gamma/\delta)^\nu}{2K_\nu(\delta\gamma)} x^{\nu-1} \exp\left\{-\frac{1}{2}(\delta^2 x^{-1} + \gamma^2 x)\right\}, \quad \gamma, \delta \geq 0, \quad \nu \in \mathbb{R}, \quad x > 0, \tag{11.4}$$

where $K_\nu$ is a modified Bessel function of the third kind.

The generalized hyperbolic distribution with $\mu = 0$, $GH(\nu, \delta, \gamma, \beta)$ has support on the real line. The density is :

$$\frac{(\gamma/\delta)^\nu}{\sqrt{2\pi}\alpha^{\nu-\frac{1}{2}} K_\nu(\delta\gamma)} \left\{\delta^2 + x^2\right\}^{\frac{1}{2}\left(\nu-\frac{1}{2}\right)} K_{\nu-\frac{1}{2}}\left(\alpha\left[\delta^2 + x^2\right]^{1/2}\right) e^{\beta x}, \tag{11.5}$$

where $\alpha = \sqrt{\beta^2 + \gamma^2}$. For $\mu \neq 0$ replace $x$ by $x - \mu$.

Some special cases of the GIG distribution are:

| | | | |
|---|---|---|---|
| Gamma: | $\Gamma(\nu, \gamma^2/2)$ | $=$ | $GIG(\nu > 0, 0, \gamma),$ |
| Reciprocal Gamma: | $R\Gamma(\nu, \delta^2/2)$ | $=$ | $GIG(-\nu, \delta, 0),$ |
| Inverse Gaussian: | $IG(\delta, \gamma)$ | $=$ | $GIG(-\frac{1}{2}, \delta, \gamma),$ |
| Reciprocal inverse Gaussian: | $RIG(\delta, \gamma)$ | $=$ | $GIG(\frac{1}{2}, \delta, \gamma),$ |
| Positive hyperbolic: | $PH(\delta, \gamma)$ | $=$ | $GIG(1, \delta, \gamma).$ |
| Reciprocal positive Hyperbolic: | $PH(\delta, \gamma)$ | $=$ | $GIG(-1, \delta, \gamma).$ |

Some special cases of the GH distribution are:

| | | | |
|---|---|---|---|
| Normal | $N(0, \sigma^2)$ | $=$ | $\lim_{\gamma \to \infty} GH(\nu, \gamma, 0, \sigma^2 \gamma),$ |
| Normal inverse Gaussian | $NIG(\alpha, \beta, \delta)$ | $=$ | $GH\left(-\frac{1}{2}, \alpha, \beta, \delta\right),$ |
| Reciprocal NIG | $NRIG(\alpha, \beta, \delta)$ | $=$ | $GH\left(\frac{1}{2}, \alpha, \beta, \delta\right),$ |
| Hyperbolic | $H(\alpha, \beta, \delta)$ | $=$ | $GH(1, \alpha, \beta, \delta),$ |
| Skewed Student's t | $T(\nu, \delta, \beta)$ | $=$ | $GH(-\nu, \beta, \beta, \delta),$ |
| Student's t | | $=$ | $\lim_{\alpha \to \infty} GH(-\nu, \beta, \beta, \delta),$ |
| Laplace | $La(\alpha, \beta)$ | $=$ | $GH(1, \alpha, \beta, 0)$ |
| Normal Gamma | $N\Gamma(\nu, \delta, \beta)$ | $=$ | $GH(\nu, \beta, \beta, \delta),$ |
| Reciprocal hyperbolic | $RH(\alpha, \beta, \delta)$ | $=$ | $GH(-1, \alpha, \beta, \delta).$ |

*See also*

    `prob...,quan...,tail...`

# prob...

```
probbeta(const ma, const a, const b);
probbinomial(const ma, const n, const p);
probbvn(const da, const db, const drho);
probcauchy(const ma);
probexp(const ma, const lambda);
probextremevalue(const ma, const alpha, const beta);
probgamma(const ma, const dr, const da);
probgeometric(const ma, const p);
probhypergeometric(const ma, const n, const k, const m);
probinvgaussian(const ma, const mu, const lambda);
problogarithmic(const ma, const alpha);
problogistic(const ma, const alpha, const beta);
problogn(const ma);
probmises(const ma, const mu, const kappa);
probmvn(const mx, const msigma);
probnegbin(const ma, const k, const p);
probpareto(const ma, const k, const a);
probpoisson(const ma, const mu);
probweibull(const ma, const a, const b);
```

| | | |
|---|---|---|
| ma | in: | arithmetic type |
| a,b | in: | arithmetic type, arguments for Beta distribution |
| dr | in: | arithmetic type |
| da | in: | arithmetic type |
| mu | in: | arithmetic type, von Mises: mean direction (use M_PI for symmetric between 0 and $\pi$); Poisson: mean |
| alpha,beta | in: | arithmetic type, location and scale parameter |
| lambda | in: | arithmetic type, parameter of exponential distribution |
| kappa | in: | arithmetic type, dispersion |
| nc | in: | arithmetic type, non-centrality parameter |
| da,db | in: | arithmetic type, upper limits of integration |
| drho | in: | arithmetic type, correlation coefficient |
| mx | in: | $m \times n$ matrix for $n$-variate normal |
| msigma | in: | $n \times n$ variance matrix $\Sigma$ |

*Return value*

Returns the requested cumulative distribution functions at ma ($P[X \leq x]$; the returned probabilities are between zero and one):

| | |
|---|---|
| `probbvn` | bivariate normal distribution, |
| `probbinomial` | Bin$(n, p)$ distribution, |
| `probbeta` | Beta$(a, b)$ distribution, |
| `probcauchy` | Cauchy distribution, |
| `probexp` | exp$(\lambda)$ distribution with mean $1/\lambda$, |
| `probextremevalue` | Extreme Value (type I or Gumbel) distribution, |
| `probgamma` | $\Gamma$ distribution, |
| `probgeometric` | Geometric distribution, |
| `probhypergeometric` | Hypergeometric distribution, |
| `probinvgaussian` | Inverse Gaussian distribution, |
| `problogarithmic` | Logarithmic distribution, |
| `problogistic` | Logistic distribution, |
| `problogn` | Lognormal distribution, |
| `probmises` | VM$(\mu, \kappa)$ distribution, |
| `probmvn` | normal distribution N$_n(0, \Sigma), n \leq 3$, |
| `probnegbin` | Negative Binomial distribution, |
| `probpareto` | Pareto distribution, |
| `probpoisson` | Poisson $\mu$ distribution, |
| `probweibull` | Weibull distribution. |

The functional forms are listed under the density functions.

The probabilities are accurate to about 10 digits, except for `probbvn` and `probmvn` which are accurate to $10^{-15}$.

The return type for `probbvn` is a double if all arguments are scalar, or an $m \times n$ matrix if one or more arguments are an $m \times n$ matrix.

The return type for `probbeta`, `probgamma`, `probmises`, `probpoisson` is derived as follows:

| returns | ma | degrees of freedom arguments |
|---|---|---|
| $m \times n$ matrix | $m \times n$ matrix | scalar |
| $m \times n$ matrix | scalar | $m \times n$ matrix |
| $m \times n$ matrix | $m \times n$ matrix | $m \times n$ matrix |
| double | scalar | scalar |

The return type for `probmvn` is a double if $m = 1$, or an $m \times 1$ vector if $m > 1$, where $m$ is the number of rows of the first argument. *Note that* `probmvn` *currently only computes up to a trivariate normal distribution.*

### Description

The bivariate normal distribution with mean zero and correlation $\rho$ is defined as:

$$\left(2\pi\sqrt{1 - \rho^2}\right)^{-1} \int_{-\infty}^{a} \int_{-\infty}^{b} \exp\left(-\frac{1}{2}\frac{x^2 - 2\rho xy + y^2}{1 - \rho^2}\right) \mathrm{d}x\mathrm{d}y.$$

The Beta distribution is defined as $I_x(a, b)$ under `betafunc`.

The Gamma distribution, $\Gamma(z; r, a)$, is defined as:

$$\Gamma(z; r, a) = \int_0^z \frac{a^r}{\Gamma(r)} x^{r-1} e^{-ax} \mathrm{d}x, \quad z > 0, r > 0, a > 0. \tag{11.6}$$

so that $\Gamma(z; r, 1)$ corresponds to the incomplete gamma function. Note that $\chi(df)$ can be computed as $\Gamma(\cdot; 0.5df, 0.5)$.

The von Mises distribution $\mathrm{VM}(\mu, \kappa)$ is defined as:

$$F(z) = \int_0^z \frac{[2\pi I_0(\kappa)]^{-1}}{e^{\kappa \cos(x-\mu)}} \mathrm{d}x, \quad 0 \le z < 2\pi, \kappa \ge 0, \tag{11.7}$$

where $I_0(\kappa)$ is the modified Bessel function. Note that the density is defined from 0 to $2\pi$, which means that the mean direction is $\pi$ and not zero. Usually, $\mathrm{VM}(0, \kappa)$ is written for the symmetric von Mises distribution. In the current notation, that corresponds to $\mathrm{VM}(\pi, \kappa)$. For applications of the von Mises distribution, see e.g. Fisher (1993).

The multivariate normal distribution with mean zero and $n \times n$ variance matrix $\Sigma$ is defined as:

$$[(2\pi)^n |\Sigma|]^{-1/2} \int_{-\infty}^a \int_{-\infty}^b \int_{-\infty}^c \exp\left(-\frac{1}{2} \mathbf{x}' \Sigma^{-1} \mathbf{x}\right) \mathrm{d}x,$$

where $\mathbf{x}' = (x_1, x_2, \ldots, x_n)$.

Sources: `probmises` uses AS 86 (Mardia and Zemroch, 1975). The bivariate and trivariate normal distributions are derived from Genz (2000).

*See also*

> `bessel`, `betafunc`, `gammafunc`, `dens...`, `quan...`, `tail...`

*Example*

```
#include <oxstd.h>
#include <oxprob.h>
main()
{
    decl m = <0,4.61,5.99>;

    print("%r", {"chi:  "}, probchi(m, 2));
    print("%r", {"gamma:"}, probgamma(m, 1, 0.5));

    println("Bivariate normal probabilities (rho=0 and 1):");
    println("BVN=", probbvn(<0,0>, <1.645,1.645>, <0,1>));

    println("Multivariate normal probabilities (unit variance):");
    println("TVN=", probmvn(<0,0,0;1.645,1.645,1.645>, unit(3))');
    println("BVN=", probmvn(<0,0;1.645,1.645>, unit(2))');
    println("N=", probmvn(<0;1.645>, unit(1))');
}
```

produces

```
chi:                  0.00000     0.90024     0.94996
gamma:                0.00000     0.90024     0.94996
Bivariate normal probabilities (rho=0 and 1):
BVN=
      0.47501     0.50000
Multivariate normal probabilities (unit variance):
TVN=
      0.12500     0.85742
BVN=
      0.25000     0.90253
N=
      0.50000     0.95002
```

# quan...

```
quanbeta(const ma, const a, const b);
quanbinomial(const ma, const n, const p);
quancauchy(const ma);
quanexp(const ma, const lambda);
quanextremevalue(const ma, const alpha, const beta);
quangamma(const ma, const dr, const da);
quangeometric(const ma, const p);
quanhypergeometric(const ma, const n, const k, const m);
quaninvgaussian(const ma, const mu, const lambda);
quanlogarithmic(const ma, const alpha);
quanlogistic(const ma, const alpha, const beta);
quanlogn(const mx);
quanmises(const mp, const mu, const kappa);
quannegbin(const ma, const k, const p);
quanpareto(const ma, const k, const a);
quanpoisson(const ma, const mu);
quanweibull(const ma, const a, const b);
```

| | | |
|---|---|---|
| ma | in: | arithmetic type, probabilities: all values must be between 0 and 1 |
| a,b | in: | arithmetic type, arguments for Beta distribution |
| dr | in: | arithmetic type |
| da | in: | arithmetic type |
| alpha,beta | in: | arithmetic type, location and scale parameter |
| lambda | in: | arithmetic type, parameter of exponential distribution |
| mu | in: | arithmetic type, mean direction (use M_PI for symmetric between 0 and $\pi$) |
| kappa | in: | arithmetic type, dispersion |

*Return value*

Returns the requested quantiles (inverse probability function; percentage points) at ma:

| | |
|---|---|
| quanbeta | quantiles from Beta $(a, b)$ distribution |
| quanbinomial | quantiles from Bin$(n, p)$ distribution, |
| quancauchy | quantiles from the Cauchy distribution, |
| quanexp | quantiles from the exp$(\lambda)$ distribution with mean $1/\lambda$, |
| quanextremevalue | quantiles from the Extreme Value (type I or Gumbel), |
| quangamma | quantiles from $\Gamma(r, a)$ distribution |
| quangeometric | quantiles from the Geometric distribution, |
| quanhypergeometric | quantiles from the Hypergeometric distribution, |
| quaninvgaussian | quantiles from the Inverse Gaussian distribution, |

| `quanlogarithmic` | quantiles from the Logarithmic distribution, |
| `quanlogistic` | quantiles from the Logistic distribution, |
| `quanlogn` | quantiles from the Lognormal distribution, |
| `quanmises` | quantiles from $\mathrm{VM}(\mu, \kappa)$ distribution |
| `quannegbin` | quantiles from the Negative Binomial distribution, |
| `quanpareto` | quantiles from the Pareto distribution, |
| `quanpoisson` | quantiles from the Poisson $\mu$ distribution, |
| `quanweibull` | quantiles from the Weibull distribution. |

The functional forms are listed under the density functions.
The quantiles are accurate to about 10 digits.
The return type is derived as follows:

| returns | `ma` | degrees of freedom arguments |
| --- | --- | --- |
| $m \times n$ matrix | $m \times n$ matrix | scalar |
| $m \times n$ matrix | scalar | $m \times n$ matrix |
| $m \times n$ matrix | $m \times n$ matrix | $m \times n$ matrix |
| double | scalar | scalar |

*See also*
> `dens...`, `prob...`, `tail...` `lib/Quantile.ox` (to compute quantiles of other distributions)

# ran...

```
ranbeta(const r, const c, const a, const b);
ranbinomial(const r, const c, const n, const p);
ranbrownianmotion(const r, const times);
ranchi(const r, const c, const df);
rancauchy(const r, const c);
randirichlet(const r, const valpha);
ranexp(const r, const c, const lambda);
ranextremevalue(const r, const c, const alpha, const beta);
ranf(const r, const c, const df1, const df2);
rangamma(const r, const c, const dr, const da);
rangeometric(const r, const c, const p);
rangh(const r, const c, const nu, const delta, const gamma,
    const beta);
rangig(const r, const c, const nu, const delta, const gamma);
ranhypergeometric(const r, const c, const n, const k, const m);
raninvgaussian(const r, const c, const mu, const lambda);
ranlogarithmic(const r, const c, const alpha);
ranlogistic(const r, const c);
ranlogn(const r, const c);
ranmises(const ma, const kappa);
ranmultinomial(const n, const vp);
rannegbin(const r, const c, const k, const p);
ranpareto(const r, const c, const k, const a);
ranpoisson(const r, const c, const mu);
ranpoissonprocess(const r, const times, const mu);
ranshuffle(const c, const x);
ranstable(const r, const c, const alpha, const beta);
ransubsample(const c, const n);
rant(const r, const c, const df);
ranuorder(const c);
ranweibull(const r, const c, const a, const b);
ranwishart(const n, const p);
```

| | | |
|---|---|---|
| r | in: | int, number of rows |
| c | in: | int, number of columns |
| a,b | in: | double or $r \times c$ matrix, arguments for Beta distribution |
| n | in: | int, number of trials |
| p | in: | double, probability of success |
| | | (rangeometric also allows $r \times c$ matrix) |
| vp | in: | column or row vector with $c$ probabilities of success (must sum to one) |

| | | |
|---|---|---|
| `lambda` | in: | double or $r \times c$ matrix |
| `df` | in: | double or $r \times c$ matrix, degrees of freedom |
| `df1` | in: | double or $r \times c$ matrix, degrees of freedom in the numerator |
| `df2` | in: | double or $r \times c$ matrix, degrees of freedom in the denominator |
| `dr` | in: | double or $r \times c$ matrix |
| `da` | in: | double or $r \times c$ matrix |
| `mu` | in: | or $r \times c$ matrixdouble, mean |
| `kappa` | in: | double or $r \times c$ matrix, dispersion (mean direction is $\pi$) |
| `alpha` | in: | double or $r \times c$ matrix |
| `beta` | in: | double or $r \times c$ matrix |
| `nu` | in: | double, parameter for GH and GIG distributions |
| `valpha` | in: | vector with $c + 1$ shape parameters for Dirichlet distribution |
| `times` | in: | column or row vector with $c$ time points (must be non-decreasing) |
| `x` | in: | column or row vector to sample from |

*Return value*

The following return a $r \times c$ matrix of random numbers which is filled by row. Note that, if both r and c are 1, the return value is a scalar of type double!

| function | Generates random numbers from |
|---|---|
| `ranbeta` | Beta$(a, b)$ distribution, |
| `ranbinomial` | Binomial$(n, p)$ distribution, |
| `ranbrownianmotion` | $r$ realizations of the Brownian motion, |
| *rancauchy* | equals `rant(r, c, 1)`, |
| `ranchi` | $\chi^2(df)$ distribution, |
| `randirichlet` | Dirichlet$(\alpha_1, \ldots, \alpha_{c+1})$ distribution (each row is a realization of the $c$-variate random variable), |
| `ranexp` | $\exp(\lambda)$ distribution with mean $1/\lambda$, |
| `ranextremevalue` | Extreme Value (type I or Gumbel) distribution, |
| `ranf` | $F(df1, df2)$ distribution, |
| `rangamma` | Gamma$(r, a)$ distribution, see (11.6), p. 310, |
| `rangeometric` | Geometric distribution, |
| `rangh` | $GH(\nu, \delta, \gamma, \beta)$ distribution (see `densgh`) |
| `rangig` | $GIG(\nu, \delta, \gamma)$ distribution (see `densgig`) |
| `ranhypergeometric` | Hypergeometric distribution, |
| `raninvgaussian` | Inverse Gaussian$(\mu, \lambda)$ distribution, |
| `ranlogarithmic` | logarithmic distribution, |
| `ranlogistic` | logistic distribution, |
| `ranlogn` | log normal distribution, |
| `ranmises` | VM$(\pi, \kappa)$ distribution, see (11.7), p. 310, |
| `rannegbin` | Negative binomial$(k, p)$ distribution, |

| function | Generates random numbers from |
|----------|-------------------------------|
| ranpareto | Pareto$(k, a)$ distribution, |
| ranpoisson | Poisson$(\mu)$ distribution, |
| ranpoissonprocess | $r$ realizations of the Poisson process, |
| ranstable | Stable distribution, $S(\alpha, \beta)$, $0 < \alpha \leq 2$, $-1 \leq \beta \leq 1$ with location 0, and scale 1, $S(2, 0) \sim N(0, 2)$, |
| rant | Student $t(df)$, df need not be integer. |
| ranweibull | Weibull distribution. |
| ranwishart | Wishart$(n, \mathbf{I}_p)$ distribution, returns a $p \times p$ matrix. Let $V = \sum_{i=1}^{n} x_i x_i'$ where $x_i \sim N_p(0, \mathbf{I}_p)$, then $V \sim \text{Wishart}(n, \mathbf{I}_p)$. |

The functional forms are listed under the density functions.

The following return a $1 \times$ c matrix of random numbers:

| function | Generates random numbers from |
|----------|-------------------------------|
| ranmultinomial | Multinomial$(n, p_1, p_2, \ldots, p_c)$ distribution, vp must hold the $m$ probabilities which sum to one, |
| ranshuffle | draws c elements from x without replacement, |
| ransubsample | draws c numbers from the integers $0, \ldots, n-1$ without replacement, |
| ranuorder | generates c uniform order statistics. |

*Description*

All these functions use uniform random numbers generated as described under ranu.

The rangamma function uses algorithms 3.19 and 3.20 from Ripley (1987), rangamma is used for ranchi: rangamma$(n_1/2, 1/2)$, and ranf: ranchi$(n_1)$ $n_2$ / $(n_1$ ranchi$(n_2))$, ranbinomial is based on a simple execution of the Bernoulli trials, rannegbin sums $k$ independent geometric random numbers, ranmultinomial generates $n$ order statistics and counts the bin contents, ranpoisson uses algorithms 3.3 and 3.15 from Ripley (1987). Drawings from the Beta and Dirichlet distributions are generated as a ratio of Gamma's.

The ranmises function generates random numbers between 0 and $2\pi$ from the von Mises distribution with mean direction $\pi$. For a different mean use:

```
fmod(ranmises(r, c, kappa) + mu, M_2PI)
```

(M_2PI requires oxfloat.h). The algorithm is given in Best and Fisher (1979). The inverse Gaussian distribution is generated according to Michael, Schucany and Haas (1976). The logistic distribution uses algorithm LBM from Kemp (1981). The stable distribution with location zero and scale 1 has characteristic function:

$$\phi(t) = \exp\left[|t|^\alpha \left\{1 + i\beta \frac{t}{|t|} w(|t|, \alpha)\right\}\right]$$

where

$$w(|t|, \alpha) = \begin{cases} \tan(\frac{1}{2}\pi\alpha), & \alpha \neq 1, \\ \frac{2}{\pi}\log|t|, & \alpha = 1. \end{cases}$$

The skewness parameter is $\beta$ ($-1 \leq \beta \leq 1$), and the characteristic component $\alpha$ ($0 < \alpha \leq 2$). Stable random number generation is implemented according to Chambers, Mallows and Sturk (1976) (but without the corrections for $\alpha$ close to but not equal to one).

The uniform random order statistics are generated using the method of exponential spacing (see, e.g., Ripley, 1987, p.97). This may be combined with a quantile function to generate random order statistics of other distributions, e.g. for 100 standard normal order statistics use quann(ranuorder(100)).

The Wishart($n, \mathbf{I}_p$) random numbers are generated as in Applied Statistics algorithm AS 53 (Smith and Hocking, 1972). To generate from a Wishart($n, \mathbf{\Sigma}_p$) use **PWP'** where **PP'** $= \mathbf{\Sigma}_p$ and **W** is generated as Wishart($n, \mathbf{I}_p$).

Several generators use rejection methods (notably rann, rangamma, and hence rannt and ranchi). Such generators may suffer from a lattice structure in the uniform rng (i.e. correlation between successive values). This may be noticeable in the higher moments (skewnewss and kurtosis) of the generated data. If this is a problem, use quantiles of the uniform rng, such as quanchi(ranu(), ...)). (Also see Ripley, 1987, p.55–59.)

ransubsample draws without replacement. To draw $c$ numbers with replacement from $0, \ldots, n-1$, simply use int(ranu(1,c) * n). Note that the return value from ransubsample is ordered (so ransubsample(n,n) just returns $0, \ldots, n-1$). Use ranshuffle(c, range(0,n-1))) if a random ordering is required.

A simple generic method to draw random numbers from the GIG distribution (11.4) has been derived by Dagnapur (1988, pp. 133-5), and adjusted by Lehner (1989). This technique is used in rangig. If $\sigma^2 \sim GIG(\nu, \delta, \gamma)$ and is independent of $\varepsilon \sim N(0, 1)$, then $\beta\sigma^2 + \sigma\varepsilon$ has the generalized hyperbolic distribution (11.5). This is used in rangh.

For ranbrownianmotion, the increment has an $N[0, \Delta\tau]$ distribution. Defining $\tau$ as the $T$-vector of time steps:

$$\begin{aligned} y_0 &= \varepsilon_0 * \tau_0^{1/2}, \\ y_t &= y_{t-1} + \varepsilon_t * (\tau_t - \tau_{t-1})^{1/2}, \quad t = 1, \ldots, T-1, \end{aligned}$$

where $\varepsilon_t$ is $\text{IN}[0, 1]$. In the case of ranpoissonprocess, the increment has a Poisson($\mu\Delta\tau$) distribution:

$$\begin{aligned} y_0 &= z_0 & z_0 \sim \text{Poisson}(\mu\tau_0), \\ y_t &= y_{t-1} + z_t, & z_t \sim \text{Poisson}(\mu[\tau_t - \tau_{t-1}]), \quad t = 1, \ldots, T-1. \end{aligned}$$

The function argument times represents the vector $\tau$. If the r argument is set to one, one column of length vec(times) is generated. If r is greater than one, *r* independent columns are generated, and the return value is a matrix with *r* columns.

*See also*

rann, ranseed, ranu

*Example*

```
#include <oxstd.h>
#include <oxprob.h>
main()
{
    print( double(sumc( ranchi(1000,1,5) )) / 1000, " " );
    print( double(sumc( ranexp(1000,1,5) )) / 1000, " " );
    print( double(sumc( rann(1000,1) )) / 1000 );

    ranseed(-1);
    print(rann(1,5));
    ranseed(-1);
    print(rann(1,3) ~ rann(1,2));

    ranseed(-1);
    println("%4.0f", ransubsample(5, 9));
    println("%4.0f", ranshuffle(5, range(0,9)));
}
```

produces

```
4.97999 0.206975 0.0173497
        0.22489          1.7400       -0.20426      -0.91760      -0.67417

        0.22489          1.7400       -0.20426      -0.91760      -0.67417

     2   3   4   5   7

     4   7   6   5   8
```

# 11.4 QuadPack

QuadPack (documented in Piessens, de Donker-Kapenga, Überhuber and Kahaner, 1983) is a Fortran library for univariate numerical integration ('quadrature') using adaptive rules. The main driver functions are exported to Ox from quadpack.dll, using the header file quadpack.h. At the end of this section is a sample program using several of these functions. Full documentation is in Piessens, de Donker-Kapenga, Überhuber and Kahaner, 1983.

## QNG, QAG, QAGS, QAGP, QAGI

```
QNG (const func, const a, const b, const aresult,
    const aabserr);
QAG (const func, const a, const b, const key,
    const aresult, const aabserr);
QAGS(const func, const a, const b, const aresult,
    const aabserr);
QAGP(const func, const a, const b, const vpoints,
    const aresult, const aabserr);
QAGI(const func, const bound, const inf, const aresult,
    const aabserr);
```

| | | |
|---|---|---|
| func | in: | function to integrate; func must be a function of one argument (a double), returning a double |
| a | in: | double, lower limit of integration |
| b | in: | double, upper limit of integration |
| key | in: | int, key for choice of local integration rule, which determines the number of points in the Gauss-Kronrod pair: $\leq 1$ (7–15 points), 2 (10–21 points), 3 (15–31 points), 4 (20–41 points), 5 (25–51 points), $\geq 6$ (30–61 points). |
| vpoints | in: | row vector with singularities of integrand |
| bound | in: | double, lower bound (inf == 1) or upper bound (inf == −1) |
| inf | in: | int, $1 : \int_b^\infty, -1 : \int_{-\infty}^b, 2 : \int_{-\infty}^\infty$ |
| aresult | in: | address of variable |
| | out: | double, approximation to the integral |
| aabserr | in: | address of variable |
| | out: | double, estimate of the modulus of the absolute error |

*Return value*

Result of the QuadPack routine:

   0   normal and reliable termination of routine;

   1   maximum number of steps has been executed;

   2   roundoff error prevents reaching the desired tolerance;

   3   extremely bad integrand behaviour prevents reaching tolerance;

4       algorithm does not converge;
5       integral is probably convergent or slowly divergent;
6       invalid input;
10      not enough memory;
An error message greater than 0 is reported unless switched off with QPWARN.

*Description*

QNG: simple non-adaptive automatic integrator for a smooth integrand.

QAG: simple globally adaptive Gauss-Kronrod-based integrator, with choice of formulae.

QAGS: globally adaptive integrator with extrapolation, which can handle integrand singularities of several types.

QAGP: as QAGS, but allows the user to specify singularities, discontinuities and other difficulties of the integrand.

QAGI: as QAGS, but handles integration over infinite integrals.

# QAWO, QAWF, QAWS, QAWC

```
#include <quadpack.h>
QAWO(const func, const a, const b, const omega, const fcos,
    const maxp1, const aresult, const aabserr);
QAWF(const func, const a, const omega, const fcos, const limlst,
    const maxp1, const aresult, const aabserr);
QAWS(const func, const a, const b, const alpha, const beta,
    const type, const aresult, const aabserr);
QAWC(const func, const a, const b, const c, const aresult,
    const aabserr);
```

| | | |
|---|---|---|
| func | in: | function to integrate; func must be a function of one argument (a double), returning a double |
| a | in: | double, lower limit of integration |
| b | in: | double, upper limit of integration |
| omega | in: | double, factor in cosine or sine function |
| fcos | in: | int, 1: function to integrate is $\cos(\omega x)f(x)$, else it is $\sin(\omega x)f(x)$ |
| maxp1 | in: | in: int, upper bound on the number of Chebyshev moments which can be stored. |
| limlst | in: | int, upper bound on the number of cycles (must be 3). |
| alpha,beta | in: | double, powers in $w(x)$, both $> -1$. |
| itype | in: | int, 1: $v(x) = 1$; 2: $v(x) = \log(x-a)$; 3: $v(x) = \log(b-x)$; 4: $v(x) = \log(x-a) * \log(b-x)$. |
| c | in: | double, term for Cauchy principal value ($!= a$ and $!= b$). |
| aresult | in: | address of variable |
| | out: | double, approximation to the integral |
| aabserr | in: | address of variable |
| | out: | double, estimate of the modulus of the absolute error |

*Return value*

Result of the QuadPack routine:

0     normal and reliable termination of routine;

1     maximum number of steps has been executed;

2     roundoff error prevents reaching the desired tolerance;

3     extremely bad integrand behaviour prevents reaching tolerance;

4     algorithm does not converge;

5     integral is probably convergent or slowly divergent;

6     invalid input;

10    not enough memory;

An error message greater than 0 is reported unless switched off with `QPWARN`.

*Description*

`QAWO`: integrates $\cos(\omega x) f(x)$ or $\sin(\omega x) f(x)$ over a finite interval $(a, b)$.

`QAWF`: Fourier cosine or Fourier sine transform of $f(x)$, from a to infinity. (`QAWF` returns error 6 if epsabs is zero, use `QPEPS` to change the value of epsabs.)

`QAWS`: integrates $w(x) * f(x)$ over a finite interval $(a, b)$, where $w(x) = [(x - a)^{\alpha}][(b - x)^{\beta}]v(x)$, and $v(x)$ depends on the `itype` argument.

`QAWC`: Cauchy principal value of $f(x)/(x - c)$ over a finite interval $(a, b)$ and for user-determined $c$.

## QPEPS, QPWARN

```
QPEPS(const epsabs, const epsrel);
QPWARN(const ion);
```

    epsabs     in:   double, absolute accuracy requested (the default value is $\epsilon_a = 0$)

    epsrel     in:   double, relative accuracy requested (the default value is $\epsilon_r = 10^{-10}$)

    ion       in:   1: print warning and error messages (the default), or 0: don't print

*No return value.*

*Description*

QPEPS Sets the accuracy which the integration routines should try to achieve. Let $\hat{I}$ be the approximation from the QuadPack routines to the integral:

$$I = \int_a^b f(x)\mathrm{d}x,$$

then the result will hopefully satisfy:

$$\left|I - \hat{I}\right| \leq \texttt{abserr} \leq \max\left\{\epsilon_a, \epsilon_r \left|I\right|\right\}.$$

QPWARN controls whether warning/error messages are printed or not.

*Example*

```
#include <oxstd.h>
#include <quadpack.h>

output(const sFunc, const result, const abserr)
{
    print(sFunc, result, " abserr=", abserr, "\n");
}
mydensn(const x)
{
    return densn(x);
}
main()
{
    decl result, abserr, pn = probn(1) - probn(0);

    QNG(densn, 0.0, 1.0, &result, &abserr);
    output("QNG: ", result, abserr);

    QAG(densn, 0.0, 1.0, 5, &result, &abserr);
    output("QAG: ", result, abserr);

    QAG(densn, 0.0, 1.0, 15, &result, &abserr);
    output("QAG: ", result, abserr);

    QAGS(densn, 0.0, 1.0, &result, &abserr);
    output("QAGS:", result, abserr);

    QAGP(densn, 0.0, 1.0, <0.1,0.9>, &result, &abserr);
    output("QAGP:", result, abserr);

    QAGI(mydensn, 0, 1, &result, &abserr);
    output("QAGI:", result, abserr);

    print("using probn(): ", probn(1) - probn(0),
          " and ", probn(0), "\n");
}
```

produces

```
QNG: 0.341345 abserr=3.78969e-015
Quadpack warning 1
QAG: 0.330835 abserr=0.0101865
QAG: 0.341345 abserr=3.78969e-015
QAGS:0.341345 abserr=3.78969e-015
QAGP:0.341345 abserr=3.78969e-015
QAGI:0.5 abserr=1.24255e-011
using probn(): 0.341345 and 0.5
```

# Chapter 12

# Class reference

This chapter documents the preprogrammed classes which are provided with the Ox system. All classes in this chapter are located as follows in the Ox installation:

| | |
|---|---|
| ox/include | header file (.h) |
| ox/include | compiled code (.oxo file) |
| ox/src | source code (.ox file) |

To use these classes, it is necessary to include the header file, and import the .ox or .oxo file. This is most easily achieved using the #import <...> statement (see 13.9.3). For example:

```
#import <database>
```

which automatically inserts database.h at that point, and links database.oxo when the program is executed (or database.ox if the .oxo file does not exist).

# 12.1 Database and Sample class

### 12.1.1 Introduction

The Sample class stores a time interval, and the frequency, e.g. 1980 (1) – 1990 (1), with frequency 4 (i.e. quarterly observations). Although we talk about year and period to denote a point in time, the year denotes the major time period, and the period the minor, so that, for example, 20 (3) could be day 3 in week 20, when the frequency is 7 (daily data). The member functions of Sample return information about the sample. Use frequency 1 for cross-section data.

The Sample class forms the basis for the Database class and has no constructor function of its own. Because it will be mostly used as part of the Database class, the documentation of the two is presented together.

The Database class stores a matrix of data, together with the sample period (the class derives from the Sample class), and the names of the variables. Functions to create a database from disk files (ASCII, *OxMetrics*, *PcGive*, and Excel spreadsheet formats) are provided. The Database class supports the use of daily and weekly data.

In addition, the Database class has built-in support to select variables (for modelling) from the database. Variables are selected by name, optionally with a lag length, and allocated to a group (e.g. to distinguish between dependent and independent variables). A sample period for the selection can be set. This selection can then be extracted from the database. The selected sample is always adjusted so as not to include missing values. Some examples follow. Remember to import the database code when using this class. This is achieved using the #import <database> statement, which also automatically inserts database.h.

*Example*

........................................... *samples/database/dbclass.ox*

```
#include <oxstd.h>
#import <database>        // required to use Database class

main()
{   decl dbase, y, dy, names;

    dbase = new Database();          // create new object
    dbase.Load("data/data.in7");        // load data

    dbase.Info();                 // print database info
                                  // select variables
    dbase.Select(0, { "CONS", 0, 0, "INC", 0, 0 } );
    dbase.Select(1, { "CONS", 1, 1, "INC", 1, 1 } );
    dbase.SetSelSample(1953, 1, 1992, 3);    // and sample

    y = dbase.GetGroup(0);            // extract group 0
    dy  = y - dbase.GetGroup(1);

    names = {"CONS", "INC", "DCONS", "DINC"};
    print("\nsample variance over ",
```

```
                dbase.GetSelSample(),
                "%r", names, "%c", names, variance(y ~ dy) );

        println("\nnumber of observations:  ", dbase.GetSize());
        println("period of observation 9: ", dbase.ObsYear(9),
            " (", dbase.ObsPeriod(9), ")");
        println("database index 1985(4):  ", dbase.GetIndex(1985,4));

        delete dbase;               // done with object, delete it
    }
```

The program produces:

```
---- Database information ----
Sample:    1953 (1) - 1992 (3) (159 observations)
Frequency: 4
Variables: 4

Variable #obs #miss   type      min     mean      max   std.dev
CONS      159     0 double     853.5   875.94   896.83   13.497
INC       159     0 double    870.22   891.69   911.38   10.725
INFLAT    159     0 double   -0.6298   1.7997   6.4976   1.2862
OUTPUT    159     0 double    1165.9   1191.1   1213.3   10.974

sample variance over 1953 (2) - 1992 (3)
                CONS         INC       DCONS         DINC
CONS          181.97      135.71      2.9314       3.7989
INC           135.71      114.01      1.9820       5.4127
DCONS         2.9314      1.9820      4.8536       5.5060
DINC          3.7989      5.4127      5.5060       11.183

number of observations:  159
period of observation 9: 1955 (2)
database index 1985(4):  131
```

The following code uses the Dow Jones data to give an example involving weekly data. This is different from the previous database, because some years have 52 and others 53 weeks. Therefore, the method of using a fixed frequency, as implemented in the Sample class from which the Database class derives, does not work. Instead, a database can now be dated:

- the first column must be of type DB_DATE,
- the first column holds date indices as created by dayofcalendar,
- the optional fractional part of this indicates time,
- the first and last observation must be valid, i.e. cannot be missing.

These criteria are satisfied in dowjones.xls, and the Excel dates are translated in Ox dates when reading the file[1]

---

[1]Excel inherits a mistake that was made by the Lotus developers, assuming wrongly that 1900 was a leap year. Instead, the rule for centuries is that they are only a leap year when divisible by 400. Ox takes this into account when loading and saving Excel files.

Note that the underlying fixed frequency information is set to a frequency of one (equivalent to undated data), so that `GetSize` and other `Sample` functions still work.

As the example illustrates, there are several functions to facilitate the handling of dated data.

*Example*

............................................. *samples/database/dbdates.ox*

```
#include <oxstd.h>
#import <database>          // required to use Database class

main()
{   decl dbase, y, dy, names;

    dbase = new Database();              // create new object
    dbase.Load("data/dowjones.xls");            // load data

    dbase.Info();                      // print database info

    if (!dbase.IsDated())
    {
        println("Expecting a dated database");
        return;
    }
    decl dum = dbase.GetVar("d408");

    println("\nSome dates: ", "%r", {"start","dummy","end"},
        "%C", dbase.GetDateByIndex(
            0 ~ vecindex(dum) ~ dbase.GetSize() - 1));

    dbase.Select(0, { "DLDOWJONES", 0, 1 } );// select vars
    dbase.SetSelDates(1987, 1, 1, 1987, 12, 31);// & sample
    println("\nSelecting dates: 1987-01-01 - 1987-12-31");
    println("Selected sample: ", dbase.GetSelSample(),
        " (database is weekly)");

    delete dbase;            // done with object, delete it
}
```
..................................................................

The program produces:

```
---- Database information ----
Sample:    1980-01-02 - 1994-09-28 (770 observations)
Frequency: 1
Variables: 5

Variable  #obs #miss   type     min      mean     max   std.dev
Date       770     0   date  1980-01-02    1994-09-28
DOWJONES   770     0 double   762.12      2055   3975.5   961.68
LDOWJONES  770     0 double   6.6361    7.5076   8.2879  0.50376
DLDOWJONES 769     1 double -0.17377 0.0020133 0.07242 0.021404
d408       770     0 double        0 0.0012987        1 0.036014
```

```
Some dates:
start     1980-01-02
dummy     1987-10-21
end       1994-09-28

Selecting dates: 1987-01-01 - 1987-12-31
Selected sample: 1987-01-07 - 1987-12-30 (database is weekly)
```

## 12.1.2 Database and Sample overview

### Creation/Information

| | |
|---|---|
| Database | Constructor function. |
| Create | create a database (not needed when using Load...) |
| Empty | empties the database and sample |
| GetDbName | get the database name |
| Info | prints summary of database contents |
| SetDbName | set the database name |

### Data input/output

| | |
|---|---|
| Load | load data set |
| LoadDht | load Gauss data file |
| LoadDta | load Stata data file |
| LoadFmtVar | load ASCII formated by variable |
| LoadIn7 | load PcGive 7 data set |
| LoadObs | load ASCII file by observation |
| LoadVar | load ASCII file by variable |
| LoadWks | load Lotus spreadsheet file |
| LoadXls | load Excel spreadsheet file |
| Save | save the database |
| SaveFmtVar | save as ASCII formated by variable |
| SaveIn7 | save as PcGive 7 data set |
| SaveObs | save as ASCII file by observation |
| SaveVar | save as ASCII file by variable |
| SaveWks | save as Excel spreadsheet file |
| SaveXls | save as Lotus spreadsheet file |

### Adding/removing variables/observations

| | |
|---|---|
| Append | append variable(s) to the database |
| Deterministic | create Constant, Trend and Seasonals |
| Grow | grows the sample size |
| Remove | remove a variable from the database |
| RemoveObsIf | remove observations from the database |
| Rename | rename a variable |
| Renew | renew the observations of a variable |
| RenewBlock | renews a block of variables |
| SetVar | sets variable(s) by name |

### Extraction

| | |
|---|---|
| GetAll | returns the whole database data matrix |
| GetAllNames | returns all the variable names |
| GetSample | returns text with database sample |
| GetSampleByIndex | virtual funcrion returning sample text |

| GetVar | gets variable(s) by name |
|---|---|
| GetVarByIndex | gets variable(s) by database index |
| GetVarIndex | gets the database index of a named variable |
| GetVarNameByIndex | gets variable name(s) by database index |

**Database sample information**: Sample class

| GetFrequency | data frequency |
|---|---|
| GetIndex | index of time point |
| GetPeriod1 | period of first observation |
| GetPeriod2 | period of last observation |
| GetSize | number of observations in sample |
| GetYear1 | year of first observation |
| GetYear2 | year of last observation |
| ObsPeriod | finds period of observation index |
| ObsYear | finds year of observation index |

**Dated data and variable types**

| GetDateByIndex | get the date of a database index |
|---|---|
| GetDates | returns date variable or <> if undated |
| GetIndexByDate | get the index for a date (must be dated) |
| GetIndexByDates | get the indices for a date range (must be dated) |
| GetVarTypeByIndex | gets the variable type |
| IsDated | returns TRUE if the database is dated |
| SetDates | sets the date variable |
| SetVarTypeByIndex | sets the variable type |

**Variable selection**

| DeSelect | remove the current variable and sample selection |
|---|---|
| DeSelectByIndex | remove a variable (by database index) from selection |
| DeSelectByName | remove a named variable from selection |
| FindSelection | find a variable name with lag in the selection |
| GetGroup | get a group selection matrix |
| GetGroupLag | get group with specific lag range |
| GetGroupLagNames | get the names of group with specific lag range |
| GetGroupNames | get the names of variables in a group |
| GetMaxGroupLag | gets maximum lag length in group |
| GetMaxSelLag | get maximum lag length |
| GetSelInfo | get array with selection info |
| Select | select variables into a group |
| SelectByIndex | select variables by their database index |
| SetSelInfo | set array with selection info |

**Variable and sample selection**

| ForceSelSample | forces a selection sample |
|---|---|

| `GetSelEnd` | index of last selection observation |
|---|---|
| `GetSelSample` | get text with selected sample |
| `GetSelSampleMode` | returns the current selection sample mode |
| `GetSelStart` | index of first selection observation |
| `SetSelDates` | select a sample by year, month, day |
| `SetSelSample` | select a sample (fixed frequency) |
| `SetSelSampleByDates` | select a sample by date value |
| `SetSelSampleByIndex` | select a sample by datebase indices |
| `SetSelSampleMode` | set the selection sample mode |

**Database data members (all protected)**

| `m_mData` | data matrix ($T \times k$) |
|---|---|
| `m_sDbName` | database name (string) |
| `m_asNames` | variable names (array with $k$ strings) |
| `m_iSampleSelMode` | sample selection mode (argument to `findsample` in `SetSelSample`) |
| `m_vVarType` | variable types ($1 \times k$) |
| | Remainder is for sample selection: |
| `m_mLagsel` | lag length of each entry in `m_mVarsel` ($1 \times s$ matrix) |
| `m_mSelgroup` | group number of each entry in `m_mVarsel` ($1 \times s$ matrix) |
| `m_iT1sel` | row index in `m_mData` of first selected observation (int) |
| `m_iT2sel` | row index in `m_mData` of last selected observation (int) |
| `m_mVarsel` | variable selection ($1 \times s$ matrix with selection) the selection consists of indices in `m_mData` and `m_asNames` |

**Sample data members**

| `m_iFreq` | data frequency (int) |
|---|---|
| `m_iYear1` | year of first observation (int) |
| `m_iPeriod1` | period of first observation (int) |
| `m_iYear2` | year of last observation (int) |
| `m_iPeriod2` | period of last observation (int) |

## 12.1.3 Database and Sample function members

# Database::Append

```
Database::Append(const mNew, const asNew);
Database::Append(const mNew, const asNew, const iT1);
```
| `mNew` | in: | $T \times k$ matrix with the new variables |
|---|---|---|
| `asNew` | in: | array with $k$ variable names of the new variables, may be a single string if $k = 1$ |
| `iT1` | in: | starting observation index in database (0 if missing) |

*No return value.*

*Description*

Appends the $k$ new variables to the database, storing the observations and variable names. The first observation has database index iT1 (omit the third argument, or use 0 if the variables start at the same sample point as the database), the last is the end of the database sample, or the end of mNew, whichever comes first.

The following error and warning messages can occur:

Append(): one data column expected
Append(): need same number of names as variables
Append(): asNew has wrong type
Append(): variable(s) already exist(s), use Renew()
Append() warning: cannot grow sample, use Grow()

*Example*

The following example shows how you could load a matrix file into a database, assuming that that matrix file contains a $T \times 2$ matrix:

```
decl dbase, mx;

dbase = new Database();
mx = loadmat("./mydata.mat");
dbase.Create(1,1,1,rows(mx),1);
dbase.Append(mx, {"Y1", "Y2"}, 0);
```

Here the database is created with frequency 1 (annual data), and first observation year 1, period 1. We give the two variables the names "Y1" and "Y2", and match the first observation of mx to the first in the database (which has index 0).

## Database::Create

```
Create(const iFreq, const iYear1, const iPeriod1, const iYear2,
    const iPeriod2);
```
| | | |
|---|---|---|
| iFreq | in: | int, frequency |
| iYear1 | in: | int, start year |
| iPeriod1 | in: | int, start period |
| iYear2 | in: | int, end year |
| iPeriod2 | in: | int, end period |

*No return value.*

*Description*

Creates a database. Use this when the database is not to be loaded from disk. The Append member function allows adding data to the database.

## Database::Database

```
Database::Database();
```

*No return value.*

*Description*
> Constructor. Calls `Empty` and sets the sample selection mode to `SAM_ALLVALID`.

## Database::DeSelect

```
Database::DeSelect();
```
*No return value.*

*Description*
> Clears the current variable and sample selection completely.

## Database::DeSelectByIndex, Database::DeSelectByName

```
Database::DeSelectByIndex(const iSel);
Database::DeSelectByName(const sVar, const iGroup, const iLag);
```
| | | |
|---|---|---|
| iSel | in: | int or matrix: selection indices of variables to delete |
| sVar | in: | string: database name of variable to delete |
| iGroup | in: | int: group identifier of variable to delete |
| iLag | in: | int: lag length of variable to delete |

*No return value.*

*Description*
> Delete specific variable(s) from the current selection. The selection sample is not changed.

## Database::Deterministic

```
Database::Deterministic(const iCseason);
```
| | | |
|---|---|---|
| iCseason | in: | 0: create $n$ normal seasonals |
| | | 1: create $n$ centred seasonals |
| | | 2: create 1 normal seasonal |
| | | 3: create 1 centred seasonal |
| | | < 0: do not create any seasonals |

*No return value.*

*Description*
> Appends constant, trend and seasonals to the database. These variables are named `Constant`, `Trend` and `Season Season_1`, ..., `Season_x`, where $x$ is the frequency.
>
> `Season` has a 1 in quarter 1 (for quarterly data), and zeros elsewhere, `Season_1` has a 1 in quarter 2, etc.
>
> If `iCseason` is 1, the seasonals are centred (with quarterly observations, for quarter 1: $0.75, -0.25, -0.25, -0.25, \ldots$), in which case the names are `CSeason`, `CSeason_1`, ..., `CSeason_x`.

When a single variable is created, the name is `Seasonal` and `CSeasonal` respectively.

# Database::Empty

```
Database::Empty();
```
*No return value.*

*Description*

Empties the database.

# Database::FindSelection

```
Database::FindSelection(const sVar, const iLag);
```
     sVar       in:   string, variable name
     iLag       in:   int, lag length

*Return value*

Returns the selection index of the specified variable with the specified lag, or $-1$ if it is not selected.

# Database::ForceSelSample

```
Database::ForceSelSample(const iYear1, const iPeriod1,
    const iYear2, const iPeriod2);
```
     iYear1             in:   int, start year of selection, use $-1$ for earliest year and period
     iPeriod1       in:   int, start period of selection
     iYear2             in:   int, end year of selection, use $-1$ for latest year and period
     iPeriod2       in:   int, end period of selection

*Return value*

Returns the number of observations in the sample.

*Description*

Sets a selection a sample for the variables previously selected with the `Select` function. This function does not check for missing values. Use `SetSelSample()` to set a sample with checking for missing values.

# Database::GetAll, Database::GetAllNames

```
Database::GetAll();
Database::GetAllNames();
```
*Return value*

`GetAll` returns the whole database matrix. `GetAllNames` returns an array of strings with all the variable names.

## Database::GetDateByIndex

```
Database::GetDateByIndex(const iT1)
     iT1          in:  int, observation index in database
```
*Return value*

Returns the date at the specified index (the same as `GetDates()`

$$iT1$$

). This can be printed with the "%C" format, or translated using `dayofcalendar`. The database must be dated.

## Database::GetDates

```
Database::GetDates();
```
*Return value*

Returns a column vector with the date variable or <> if the database is undated.

## Database::GetDbName

```
Database::GetDbName();
```
*Return value*

Returns the current database name.

## Sample::GetFrequency

```
Sample::GetFrequency();
```
*Return value*

The data frequency.

## Database::GetGroup, Database::GetGroupLag

```
Database::GetGroup(const iGroup);
Database::GetGroupLag(const iGroup, const iLag1, const iLag2);
     iGroup       in:  int, group number
     iLag1        in:  int, first lag
     iLag2        in:  int, last lag
```
*Return value*

`GetGroup` returns a $T \times n$ matrix with all selected variables of group `iGroup`. `GetGroupLag` returns only those with the specified lag length. If no database sample has been selected yet, the return value is a 0.

*Description*

`GetGroup` extracts all selected variables of group `iGroup`.

`GetGroupLag` extracts all selected variables of group `iGroup` which have a lag in `iLag1 ... iLag2`. The selection sample period must have been set.

## Database::GetGroupLagNames, Database::GetGroupNames

```
Database::GetGroupLagNames(const iGroup, const iLag1, const iLag2,
  aasNames);
Database::GetGroupNames(const iGroup, const aasNames);
```
| | | |
|---|---|---|
| iGroup | in: | int, group number |
| iLag1 | in: | int, first lag |
| iLag2 | in: | int, last lag |
| aasNames | in: | array |
| | out: | will hold an array of strings with the names of the variables with specified group and lag |

*No return value.*

*Description*

GetGroupLagNames gets the names of all selected variables of group iGroup which have a lag in iLag1 ... iLag2. The selection sample period must have been set. GetGroupNames gets all the variables of the specified group.

The following code section gets all names of X_VAR variables and prints them.

```
decl as, i;
db.GetGroupNames(X_VAR, &as);
for (i = 0; i < columns(as); ++i)
    println(as[i]);
```

## Sample::GetIndex

```
Sample::GetIndex(const iYear, const iPeriod);
```
| | | |
|---|---|---|
| iYear | in: | int, year |
| iPeriod | in: | int, period |

*Return value*

The index of the specified time point.

## Database::GetIndexByDate, Database::GetIndexByDates

```
Database::GetIndexByDate(const dDate1)
Database::GetIndexByDates(const dDate1, const dDate2)
```
| | | |
|---|---|---|
| dDate1 | in: | double, date value |
| dDate2 | in: | double, date value |

*Return value*

GetIndexByDate returns the index closest to the specified date.

GetIndexByDates returns the start and end indices of the specified period as an array of two integers. This can be used, e.g., as [t1,t2]= GetIndexByDates( dayofcalendar(1990, 1, 1), dayofcalendar(1990, 12, 31)).

## Database::GetMaxGroupLag, Database::GetMaxSelLag

```
Database::GetMaxSelLag();
Database::GetMaxGroupLag(iGroup);
    iGroup      in: int, group number
```

*Return value*

GetMaxSelLag returns the highest lag in all selected variables.

GetMaxGroupLag returns the highest lag in selected variables of the specified group.

*Description*

Gets lag information on the selection.

## Sample::GetPeriod1, Sample::GetPeriod2

```
Sample::GetPeriod1();
Sample::GetPeriod2();
```

*Return value*

GetPeriod1 returns the period of the first observation.

GetPeriod2 returns the period of the last observation.

## Database::GetSample

```
Database::GetSample();
virtual Database::GetSampleByIndex(const iT1, const iT2)
    iT1         in: int, first observation index in database
    iT2         in: int, last observation index in database
```

*Return value*

GetSample returns a string with the full database sample, e.g. "1980(1) - 1990(2)". GetSampleByIndex is called to create the text.

GetSampleByIndex writes the sample text for the sample with database indices iT1, iT2.

If iT1< 0 the output is "no sample"; if iT2< 0 the end-period is omitted, so only a sample date is returned.

## Database::GetSelEnd, Database::GetSelStart

```
Database::GetSelStart();
Database::GetSelEnd();
```

*Return value*

GetSelStart returns the database index of the first observation of the selected sample.

GetSelEnd returns the database index of the last observation of the selected sample.

## Database::GetSelInfo

```
Database::GetSelInfo();
```

*Return value*

Returns a $1 \times 5$ array with the selection information as follows ($c$ is the number of selected variables):

0    $1 \times c$ matrix with database indices of selected variables
1    $1 \times c$ matrix with group index of selected variables
2    $1 \times c$ matrix with lag lengths of selected variables
3    integer, first selection observation
4    integer, last selection observation

## Database::GetSelSample

```
Database::GetSelSample();
```

*Return value*

GetSelSample returns a string with the text of the selected database sample, e.g. `"1980(1) - 1984(2)"`. GetSampleByIndex is called to create the text.

## Database::GetSelSampleMode

```
Database::GetSelSampleMode();
```

*Return value*

GetSelSampleMode returns the current sample selection mode (also see findsample), one of: SAM_ALLVALID , SAM_ENDSVALID, SAM_ANYVALID .

## Sample::GetSize

```
Sample::GetSize();
```

*Return value*

The number of observations in the sample.

## Database::GetVar, Database::GetVarByIndex

```
Database::GetVar(const sName);
Database::GetVarByIndex(const iVar);
```

     sName      in:    string or array of strings with variable names
     iVar       in:    int or matrix of database indices of variables

*Return value*

Returns a matrix with the specified variable(s), or <> if the variable(s) cannot be found.

## Database::GetVarIndex

```
Database::GetVarIndex(const asName);
```
        asName       in:  string, or array of strings: variable names

*Return value*
    Returns the database indices of the specified variable(s), or the empty matrix if none are found.

## Database::GetVarNameByIndex, Database::GetVarTypeByIndex

```
Database::GetVarNameByIndex(const iVar);
Database::GetVarTypeByIndex(const iVar);
```
        iVar         in:  int or matrix of database indices of variables

*Return value*
    GetVarNameByIndex returns an array with the names of the specified variable(s). If iVar is a scalar, a single string is returned.
    GetVarTypeByIndex returns the variable type, one of: DB_DOUBLE, DB_DATE .

## Sample::GetYear1, Sample::GetYear2

```
Sample::GetYear1();
Sample::GetYear2();
```

*Return value*
    GetYear1 returns the year of the first observation.
    GetYear2 returns the year of the last observation.

## Database::Grow

```
Database::Grow(const cTadd);
```
        cTadd        in:  int, number of observations to grow database sample by (> 0: cTadd observations are added at the end; <0: -cTadd observations are added at the beginning)
*No return value.*

## Database::Info

```
Database::Info();
```
*No return value.*

*Description*
    Prints information on the contents of the database.

## Database::IsDated

```
Database::IsDated();
```

*Return value*
   TRUE if the database is dated, FALSE otherwise.


## Database::Load

```
Database::Load(const sFilename);
     sFilename             in:   string, filename
```

*Return value*
   FALSE if the loading failed, TRUE otherwise.

*Description*
   Load creates the database and loads the specified data file from disk. The file type
   is derived from the extension. Supported are: .csv, .dat (see LoadFmtVar),
   .dht, .dta, .in7, .xls.

*See also*
   loadmat


## Database::LoadDht, Database::LoadDta

```
Database::LoadDht(const sFilename, const iYear1, const iPeriod1,
     const iFreq);
Database::LoadDta(const sFilename, const iYear1, const iPeriod1,
     const iFreq);
     sFilename             in:   string, filename
     iYear1                in:   int, start year
     iPeriod1              in:   int, start period
     iFreq                 in:   int, frequency
```

*Return value*
   FALSE if the loading failed, TRUE otherwise.

*Description*
   LoadDht creates the database and loads the specified *Gauss* (small and extended
   v86) data file from disk. Such files come in pairs: the .dht is a binary file which
   specifies the number of columns, the corresponding .dat file (with the same base
   name) is a binary file with the data.
   LoadDta creates the database and loads the specified *Stata* (version 4–6) data file
   from disk.

## Database::LoadFmtVar, Database::LoadIn7

```
Database::LoadFmtVar(const sFilename);
Database::LoadIn7(const sFilename);
    sFilename            in:  string, filename
```

*Return value*

    FALSE if the loading failed, TRUE otherwise.

*Description*

    LoadIn7 creates the database and loads the specified *OxMetrics* file (which is the same as a PcGive 7 data file) from disk.

    LoadFmtVar creates the database and loads the ASCII file with formatting information from disk. In *OxMetrics* this is called 'Data with load info'. Such a file is human-readable, with the data ordered by variable, and each variable preceded by a line of the type:

    > *name year1 period1 year2 period2 frequency.*

    For example:

```
>CONS 1953 1 1955 4 4
      890     886     886     884
      885     884     884     884
      887     889     890     894
```

*See also*

    loadmat

## Database::LoadObs, Database::LoadVar

```
Database::LoadObs(const sFilename, const cVar,const cObs,
    const iYear1, const iPeriod1, const iFreq, const fOffendMis);
Database::LoadVar(const sFilename, const cVar,const cObs,
    const iYear1, const iPeriod1, const iFreq, const fOffendMis);
    sFilename            in:  string, filename
    cVar                 in:  int, number of variables
    cObs                 in:  int, number of observations
    iYear1               in:  int, start year
    iPeriod1             in:  int, start period
    iFreq                in:  int, frequency
    fOffendMis           in:  int, TRUE:offending text treated as missing
                              value; FALSE: offending text skipped
```

*Return value*

    FALSE if the loading failed, TRUE otherwise.

*Description*

    Creates the database and loads the specified human-readable data file from disk.

The data is ordered by observation (LoadObs), or by variable. Since there is no information on the sample or the variable names in these files, the sample must be provided as function arguments. The variable names are set to Var1, Var2, etc., use Rename to rename the variables.

As the name suggests, a human-readable (or ASCII) data file is a file that can be read using a file viewer or editor. (A binary file cannot be read in this way.) The default extension is .DAT.

Each variable must have the same number of observations. So variables that have too short a sample have to be padded by missing values (M_NAN). Text following ; or // up to the end of the line is considered to be comment, and skipped. Data files can be ordered by observation (first observation on all variables, second observation on all variables, etc.) or by variable (all observations of first variable, all observations of second variable, etc.). Examples are:

| // by variable | //by observation |
|---|---|
| // cons | 891 2.8 //1953 (1) |
| 883 884 885 | 883 2.7 //1953 (2) |
| 889 891 900 | 884 3.5 // etc. |
| // inflat | 891 2.8 |
| 2.7 3.5 3.9 | 885 3.9 |
| 2.6 2.8 3.4 | 889 2.6 |
| | 891 2.8 |

The fOffendMis argument gives additional flexibility in reading human- readable files, by giving the option to treat offending words as missing values, or to skip them. The former can be used to read files with a . or a word for missing values, the latter for comma-separated files. Treating offending words or symbols as missing values (fOffendMis is TRUE) can be visualized as:

| 10 M 30 |
|---|
| 20 . 40 |

read as →

| 10 . 30 |
|---|
| 20 . 40 |

When read by observation (LoadObs), the second variable will be removed (consisting of missing values only), and the database variables will be labelled Var1 and Var3.

And for a comma separated example using the skip option (fOffendMis is FALSE):

| 10,5,30, |
|---|
| 20,6,40, |

read as →

| 10 5 30 |
|---|
| 20 6 40 |

## Database::LoadWks, Database::LoadXls

```
Database::LoadWks(const sFilename);
Database::LoadXls(const sFilename);
```

sFilename                    in:   string, filename

*Return value*
   FALSE if the loading failed, TRUE otherwise.

*Description*
   Creates the database and loads the specified spreadsheet file from disk. A `.wks`
   or `.wk1` file is a Lotus file, an `.xls` file is an Excel worksheet.

   The Database class can read and write the following spreadsheet files:

   • Excel: `.xls` files;
   • Lotus: `.wks`, `.wk1` files;

   provided the following convention is adopted:

   • Ordered by observation (that is, variables are in columns).
   • Columns with variables are labelled.
   • There is an *unlabelled column* with the dates (as a string), in the form year–
     period (the – can actually be any single character), for example, 1980–1 (or:
     1980Q1 1980P1 1980:1 etc.). This doesn't have to be the first column.
   • The data form a contiguous sample (non-numeric fields are converted to
     missing values, so you can leave gaps for missing observations).

   Database class can read the following types of Excel file:

   • Excel 2.1, 3.0, 4.0 worksheets;
   • Excel 5.0, 95, 97, XP, 2003, 2007 workbooks.

   When saving an Excel file, it is written as an Excel 2.1 worksheet. Workbooks
   are compound files, and only the first sheet in the file is read. If OxMetrics cannot
   read a workbook file, it is recommended to retry with a worksheet file.

   For example, the format for writing is (this is also the optimal format for reading):

   |   |        | A    | B    | C    | D   |
   |---|--------|------|------|------|-----|
   | 1 |        | CONS | INFL | DUM  |     |
   | 2 | 1980-1 | 883  | 2.7  | 3    |     |
   | 3 | 1980-2 | 884  | 3.5  | 5    |     |
   | 4 | 1980-3 | 885  | 3.9  | 1    |     |
   | 5 | 1980-4 | 889  | 2.6  | 9    |     |
   | 6 | 1981-1 | 900  | 3.4  | 2    |     |

   If these conventions are not adopted the file can still be read, but you will have to
   check the final result.

*See also*
   loadmat

## Sample::ObsPeriod

```
Sample::ObsPeriod(iObs);
   iObs        in:  int, observation index
```

*Return value*
>    The period of the observation index.

## Sample::ObsYear

```
Sample::ObsYear(iObs);
   iObs        in:  int, observation index
```

*Return value*
>    The year of the observation index.

## Database::Remove, Database::RemoveObsIf

```
Database::Remove(const sName);
Database::RemoveObsIf(const vRemove)
     sName      in:  string or array of strings, variable name(s)
     vRemove    in:  matrix T × 1 or 1 × T matrix, non-zero at position of obser-
                     vations to remove, 0 for observations to keep
```

*No return value.*

*Description*
>    Removes the named variable or specified observations from the database.

## Database::Rename

```
Database::Rename(const sNewName, const sOldName);
     sNewName         in:  string or array of strings, new name(s)
     sOldName         in:  string or array of strings, old name(s) of database
                           variable(s)
```

*No return value.*

*Description*
>    Renames a database variable. To rename more than one variable at once, both
>    most be arrays of the same size, and all old names must exist in the database.

## Database::Renew

```
Database::Renew(const mNew, const asName);
Database::Renew(const mNew, const asName, const iT1);
```

| mNew   | in: | $T \times k$ matrix |
|--------|-----|---------------------|
| asName | in: | array with $k$ variable names, may be a single string if $k = 1$ |
| iT1    | in: | first observation (0 if argument is missing) |

*No return value.*

*Description*

Renews the observations on the named variable. The first new observation has database index iT1, the last is the end of the database sample, or the end of mNew, whichever comes first.

If a non-existent variable is renewed, the variable is created first using Append. The database sample can be changed by Grow, not by Renew or Append. If that fails, the following error message will appear:

Renew(): could not append variable(s)

## Database::RenewBlock

RenewBlock(const mNew, const iVarIndex);

| mNew      | in: | $T \times k$ matrix |
|-----------|-----|---------------------|
| iVarIndex | in: | int, database index of first variable to renew |

*No return value.*

*Description*

Renews the observations on the $k$ variables starting from the first, without any checking for existence.

## Database::Save, Database::SaveFmtVar, Database::SaveIn7

Database::Save(const sFilename);
Database::SaveIn7(const sFilename);
Database::SaveFmtVar(const sFilename);

| sFilename | in: | string, filename |
|-----------|-----|------------------|

*No return value.*

*Description*

Save derives the file type from the file extension (using .in7/.bn7 if no extension is given). Supported are: .csv, .dat (see SaveFmtVar), .dht, .in7, .xls. SaveIn7 saves the database as a *OxMetrics* file.

SaveFmtVar saves the database as a formatted ASCII file. Also see under LoadFmtVar.

*See also*

savemat

## Database::SaveObs, Database::SaveVar

```
Database::SaveObs(const sFilename);
Database::SaveVar(const sFilename);
      sFilename            in:   string, filename
```
*No return value.*

*Description*

Saves the database as a human-readable data file, ordered by observation, or by variable. Also see under `LoadObs`, `LoadVar`.

## Database::SaveWks, Database::SaveXls

```
Database::SaveWks(const sFilename);
Database::SaveXls(const sFilename);
      sFilename            in:   string, filename
```
*No return value.*

*Description*

Saves the database as a Lotus or Excel spreadsheet file.

*See also*

Database::LoadWks, Database::LoadXls, savemat

## Database::Select, Database::SelectByIndex

```
Database::Select(const iGroup, const aSel);
Database::SelectByIndex(const iGroup, const iVar, const iLag0,
    const iLag1);
```

| | | |
|---|---|---|
| iGroup | in: | int, group number |
| aSel | in: | $3k$ array, specifying name, start lag, end lag |
| iVar | in: | int: database index of variable to select |
| | | matrix: database index of $k$ variables to select |
| iLag0 | in: | int: initial lag length of variables to select |
| | | matrix: $k$ initial lag lengths of variables to select |
| iLag1 | in: | int: final lag length of variables to select |
| | | matrix: $k$ final lag lengths of variables to select |

*No return value.*

*Description*

Selects variables by name and with specified lags, and assigns the `iGroup` number to the selection. The `aSel` argument of `Select` is an array consisting of sequences of three values: name, start lag, end lag. For example:

```
Select(0, {"CONS", 0, 0});    // select CONS as group 0
                              //  from lag 0 to 0
Select(0, {"INC", 0, 0}); // also select INC as group 0
Select(1, {"CONS", 1, 1, "INC", 1, 1});
                    // the first lag of CONS and INC as group 1
```

After a sample period is set, the selection can be extracted from the database.
If CONS and INC are variables 0 and 1 in the database, the same selection could
be written as:

```
            // select CONS,INC as group 0 from lag 0 to 0
SelectByIndex(0, <0,1>, 0, 0);
                    // the first lag of CONS and INC as group 1
SelectByIndex(1, <0,1>, 1, 1);
```

## Database::SetDbName

```
Database::SetDbName(const sName);
```
*No return value.*

*Description*
> Sets the current database name.

## Database::SetDates

```
Database::SetDates(const vDates);
```
*No return value.*

*Description*
> If the database is not yet dated, vDates is set as the date column (the first col-
> umn). Otherwise vDates replaces the current date column.

## Database::SetSelInfo

```
Database::SetSelInfo(const asInfo);
    asInfo      in:  1 × 5 array with selection info
```
*Description*
> Sets the selection based on the specified input array. No checking is done on the
> input values.
>
> The selection information should be organized as follows ($c$ is the number of
> selected variables):
>
> 0   $1 \times c$ matrix with database indices of selected variables
> 1   $1 \times c$ matrix with group index of selected variables
> 2   $1 \times c$ matrix with lag lengths of selected variables
> 3   integer, first selection observation
> 4   integer, last selection observation
>
> The last two arguments may be omitted, in which case a call to SetSelSample
> may be required.

## Database::SetSelDates

```
Database::SetSelDates(const iYear1, const iMonth1, const iDay1,
    const iYear2, const iMonth2, const iDay2)
```

| | | |
|---|---|---|
| iYear1  | in: | int, start year of selection |
| iMonth1 | in: | int, start month of selection |
| iDay1   | in: | int, start day of selection |
| iYear2  | in: | int, end year of selection |
| iMonth2 | in: | int, end month of selection |
| iDay2   | in: | int, end day of selection |

*Return value*

Returns the number of observations in the sample.

*Description*

This is the equivalent of SetSelSample that can be used when the database is dated.

Selects a sample for the variables previously selected with the Select function. The actually selected sample will be the largest starting from the specified starting date (but not exceeding the specified end date) without any missing values when using the default selection mode. Use SetSelSampleMode to change the selection mode. Use DeSelect to deselect the current sample and variables.

```
Database::SetSelSample(const iYear1, const iPeriod1,
    const iYear2, const iPeriod2);
```

| | | |
|---|---|---|
| iYear1  | in: | int, start year of selection, use –1 for earliest year and period |
| iPeriod1 | in: | int, start period of selection |
| iYear2  | in: | int, end year of selection, use –1 for latest year and period |
| iPeriod2 | in: | int, end period of selection |

*Return value*

Returns the number of observations in the sample.

*Description*

Selects a sample for the variables previously selected with the Select function. The actually selected sample will be the largest starting from the specified starting date (but not exceeding the specified end date) without any missing values when using the default selection mode. Use SetSelSampleMode to change the selection mode. Use DeSelect to deselect the current sample and variables.

## Database::SetSelSampleByDates, Database::SetSelSampleByIndex

```
Database::SetSelSampleByDates(const dDate1, const dDate2);
Database::SetSelSampleByIndex(const iT1, const iT2);
```

|          |     |                                   |
|----------|-----|-----------------------------------|
| `dDate1` | in: | double, date value                |
| `dDate2` | in: | double, date value                |
| `iT1`    | in: | int, first observation index in database |
| `iT2`    | in: | int, last observation index in database  |

*Return value*
Returns the number of observations in the sample.

## Database::SetSelSampleMode

```
Database::SetSelSampleMode(const iMode);
```
    `iMode`               in:   int, the new sample selection mode, see `findsample`

*No return value.*

## Database::SetVar

```
Database::SetVar(const mNew, const asName);
```
    `mNew`     in:  $T \times k$ matrix
    `asName`   in:  array with $k$ variable names, may be a single string if $k = 1$

*No return value.*

*Description*
If any of the named variables exist in the database, the content is changed, otherwise the new variables are appended. If $T$ is larger than the sample size of the database, the database is extended (unlike `Renew`); if it is shorter, the new (or changed) variable will have missing values for the remainder. If the database has not been created yet, it is created with frequency of unity (annual/undated).

## Database::SetVarTypeByIndex

```
Database::SetVarTypeByIndex(const iVar, const iType);
```
    `iVar`    in:  int or matrix of database indices of variables
    `iType`   in:  int, type DB_DOUBLE (the default) or DB_DATE

*No return value.*

*Description*
Sets the variable type.

# 12.2 Modelbase class

### 12.2.1 Introduction

The Modelbase class derives from the Database class to implement model estimation features. Modelbase is not intended to be used directly, but as a base for a more specialized class. A range of virtual member functions allows for customization of the class. Modelbase facilitates interactive use with OxMetrics through the **OxPack** program. Dialogs and a test menu are easily created by overriding just a few virtual functions. More information is on using Modelbase with OxPack is in the separate Ox Appendices.

In most cases, model estimation involves the following steps (key virtual functions are given in parentheses):

- Call constructor (Modelbase), specify package name and version (GetPackage, GetVersion).
- Initialize data: extract estimation data from underlying database (InitData).
- Initialize parameters (InitPar): specify the number of parameters; set fixed parameters (if any); determine starting values (if necessary).
- Estimate model (Estimate or DoEstimation).
- Produce model output and evaluation (GetParNames, Covar, Output, etc.).

Modelbase has a few essential properties to track this procedure:

| | |
|---|---|
| Model status | GetModelStatus, SetModelStatus |
| Maximization method | GetMethod, SetMethod |
| Estimation result | GetResult, SetResult |
| Parameters | GetPar, SetPar, GetParCount, SetParCount |
| Fixed/Free parameters | GetFreeParCount, GetFreePar, SetFreePar, FixPar, FreePar |
| Covariance | Covar |

The following example shows a minimal Modelbase implementation.

*Example*

.............................................*samples/database/mbclass.ox*

```
#include <oxstd.h>
#import   <modelbase>

class Ols : Modelbase
{
    decl m_mRes;
    decl m_dSigmaSqr;

    Ols();
    GetPackageName();
    GetPackageVersion();
    DoEstimation(vP);
};

Ols::Ols()
```

```
{
    Modelbase();
}
Ols::GetPackageName()
{
    return "Ols";
}
Ols::GetPackageVersion()
{
    return "1.0";
}
Ols::DoEstimation(vP)
{
    decl cp = columns(m_mX);
    SetParCount(cp);

    olsc(m_mY, m_mX, &vP, &m_mCovar);
    m_mRes = m_mY - m_mX * vP;
    m_dSigmaSqr = m_mRes'm_mRes / (rows(m_mY) - cp);
    m_mCovar *= m_dSigmaSqr;

    SetResult(MAX_CONV);

    return vP;
}

main()
{
    decl ols = new Ols();

    ols.Load("data/data.in7");
    ols.Deterministic(FALSE);

    ols.Select(Y_VAR, {"CONS", 0, 2});
    ols.Select(X_VAR, {"Constant", 0, 0, "INC" , 0, 2});

    ols.Estimate();
}
```
......................................................................

The program produces:

```
Ols package version 1.0, object created on  8-12-2005

---- Ols ----
The estimation sample is:  1953(3) -  1992(3)
The dependent variable is: CONS  (data/data.in7)
                  Coefficient  Std.Error  t-value  t-prob
CONS_1               1.31039    0.07564     17.3   0.000
CONS_2              -0.352108   0.07915    -4.45   0.000
Constant            -2.17250   11.19       -0.194  0.846
INC                  0.508481   0.03606     14.1   0.000
INC_1               -0.577251   0.05816    -9.92   0.000
INC_2                0.112122   0.05325      2.11  0.037
```

```
log-likelihood           .NaN
no. of observations        157  no. of parameters        6
AIC.T                     .NaN  AIC                    .NaN
mean(CONS)              875.78  var(CONS)           182.397
```

At first sight it may be somewhat surprising how much this program achives with so little coding. But, with an understanding of virtual functions, the documentation below, and the actual source code of `Modelbase` (in `ox\src`), it should be possible to implement a `Modelbase` derived package. Other examples of the use of `Modelbase` are the Arfima and DPD packages.

### 12.2.2 Modelbase overview

Functions which are used in a minimal implementation are marked as follows:

    *   virtual function to override,
  **   need to be called as part of the estimation procedure.

**general**

| | |
|---|---|
| `Modelbase` | constructor |
| `ClearEstimation` | removes results fom previous estimation |
| `ClearModel` | sets model status to MS_NONE |
| `GetMethod` | get the estimation method |
| `GetMethodLabel` | get the label for the current estimation method |
| `GetModelLabel` | get the label for the model |
| `GetModelStatus` | get the model status (MS_....) |
| `GetPackageName`* | returns name of the package |
| `GetPackageVersion`* | returns version of the package |
| `GetResult` | get the estimation result |
| `Grow` | extend database and update the deterministic terms |
| `Init` | resets all variables to default |
| `IsUnivariate` | returns TRUE if only one Y_VAR allowed |
| `SetForecasts` | set the number of forecasts |
| `SetMethod` | set the estimation method |
| `SetModelStatus`** | set the model status (MS_....) |
| `SetPrint` | switch printing on or off |
| `SetResult`** | set the estimation result |
| `SetRecursive` | set the number of recursive steps |

**parameter related**

| | |
|---|---|
| `FixPar` | fixes parameters |
| `FreePar` | frees parameters |
| `GetFreePar` | get the vector of free parameters, $p \times 1$ |
| `GetFreeParCount` | get number of free parameters $p$ |
| `GetFreeParNames` | get the names of free parameters, array of length $p$ |

| | |
|---|---|
| `GetPar` | get the vector of all parameters, $q \times 1$ |
| `GetParCount` | get number of parameters $q$ (including fixed) |
| `GetParNames`* | get the names of all parameters, array of length $q$ |
| `GetParStatus` | returns full parameter info |
| `GetParTypes` | returns array of type letters for each model variable |
| `MapParToFree` | return the free parameters from the argument |
| `ResetFixedPar` | reset the values of the fixed parameters |
| `SetFreePar` | set the free parameters |
| `SetPar`** | set the full parameter vector |
| `SetParCount`** | set the number of parameters $q$ (including fixed) |

**move up in model status**

| | |
|---|---|
| `DoEstimation` | low level estimate |
| `Estimate` | high level estimate |
| `InitData` | get the data: $Y, X$ |
| `InitPar` | initializes the parameter values |
| `SetStartPar` | set the starting values |

**covariance evaluation**

| | |
|---|---|
| `Covar`* | sets `m_mCovar` |

**get model results**

| | |
|---|---|
| `GetCovar` | returns $p \times p$ covariance matrix |
| `GetCovarRobust` | returns `<>` or $p \times p$ robust covariance matrix |
| `GetLogLik` | return the log-likelihood, `m_dLogLik` |
| `GetResVar` | returns residual variance, $n \times n$ |
| `GetResiduals` | returns residual matrix, $T \times n$ |
| `GetStdErr` | returns the std.errors (0 for fixed) $q \times 1$ |
| `GetStdErrRobust` | returns `<>` or robust standard errors |
| `GetcDfLoss` | returns degrees of freedom lost (for tailt, AIC) |
| `GetcT` | returns actual no of variables to use in output, `m_cT` |

**post estimation**

| | |
|---|---|
| `DbDrawTMatrix` | draws using the database sample information |
| `GetForecastData` | returns avilable data over a forecast period |
| `Output` | prints output |
| `OutputHeader` | prints output header, returns TRUE to print rest |
| `OutputPar` | prints parameter estimates |
| `OutputLogLik` | prints log-likelihood, AIC, etc. |
| `OutputMax` | prints maximization result and starting values |
| `PrintTestVal` | prints a test statistic |
| `TestRestrictions` | tests restrictions on the parameters |

**OxPack related**, see the separate Ox Appendices for documentation

| | |
|---|---|
| `GetLongRunInfo` | returns 0 or info on long-run |
| `GetLongRunNames` | returns 0 or names of long-run parameters |
| `ReceiveData` | receive the data for estimation |
| `ReceiveDialog` | receive output from a dialog |
| `ReceiveModel` | receive the model specification |
| `SendDialog` | send a dialog |
| `SendFunctions` | send specification of special functions |
| `SendMenu` | send a menu list |
| `SendMethods` | send the estimation methods |
| `SendResults` | send an output variable |
| `SendSpecials` | send the names of special variables |
| `SendVarStatus` | send the types of variables |

### 12.2.3 Modelbase function members

## Modelbase::ClearEstimation, Modelbase::ClearModel

```
virtual ClearEstimation()
virtual ClearModel();
```
*No return value.*

*Description*

> `ClearEstimation()` clears the model estimation settings. `ClearModel()` sets the model status to `MS_NONE`, and calls `ClearEstimation()`.

## Modelbase::Covar

```
virtual Covar();
```
*No return value.*

*Description*

> In some models, the evaluation of the variance-covariance matrix of the estimated parameters is costly, therefore, this matrix is only computed on demand: when the covariance matrix does not yet exist, `Covar()` is called to compute it.
>
> By default, the `m_mCovar` member variable of `Modelbase` is $-1$ when estimation commences (through a call to `ClearEstimation()`). `Covar()` should set `m_mCovar` to the variance-covariance matrix (but `Estimate()` or `DoEstimation()` may also do this, as in the example above). `Covar()` can optionally set `m_mCovarRobust` as well. If the covariance matrix does not exist, `Covar()` is automatically called when using `GetCovar()`, `GetCovarRobust()`, `GetStdErr()`, or `GetStdErrRobust()`.
>
> This procedure ensures that the covariance is only computed once when required, and not at all when not required (in some Monte Carlo experiments, for example).

## Modelbase::DbDrawTMatrix

```
DbDrawTMatrix(const iArea, const mYt, const asY, const iT1);
DbDrawTMatrix(const iArea, const mYt, const asY, const iT1,
        const iSymbol, const iIndex);
```

| | | |
|---|---|---|
| iArea | in: | int, area index |
| mYt | in: | $m \times T$ matrix with $m$ $y$ variables |
| asY | in: | array of strings (holds variable names), or 0 (no names), or a string (when only one variable to graph) |
| iT1 | in: | int, database index of first observation |
| iSymbol | in: | int, 0: draw line, 1: draw symbols, 2: draw both (optional argument, default is 0). |
| iIndex | in: | int, line index for first row, see Table 10.4, (optional argument, default is 2). Each subsequent row will have the next index. |

*No return value.*

*Description*

This is equivalent to DrawTMatrix, but using sample information from the underlying database. The function will automatically draw a proper date axis if the database is dated.

## Modelbase::DoEstimation, Modelbase::Estimate

```
virtual DoEstimation(vPar);
virtual Estimate();
```

| | | |
|---|---|---|
| vPar | in: | matrix, vector of starting values (free parameters), $p \times 1$ |

*Return value*

DoEstimation() returns:

- Direct estimation: $p \times 1$ matrix with the estimated parameters.
- Iterative estimation: array of length 3, with respectively:
    - $p \times 1$ matrix with the estimated parameters,
    - string, name of the iterative procedure ("BFGS" for example),
    - TRUE if numerical derivatives were used, FALSE otherwise.

Estimate() returns TRUE if estimation was successful, FALSE otherwise.

*Description*

There are two ways to implement estimation:

- Override DoEstimation(), which is called from Modelbase::Estimate. In this case, the derived DoEstimation() returns the estimated parameters, and sets m_iResult, see SetResult(). Prior to calling DoEstimation(), Modelbase::Estimate() will call InitData(),

InitPar() and ClearEstimation(). Afterwards, it will update the model status, and, if estimation was successful, Output(), and, if iterative estimation was used: OutputMax().

- Override Estimate(), in which case DoEstimation() is not automatically called. This provides complete control, but requires more code. For example, a slightly simplified version of Modelbase::Estimate() is given below, showing the essential properties which must be set:

    - estimated free parameters: SetFreePar(),
    - m_iResult, see SetResult()
    - m_iModelStatus, see SetModelStatus().

```
Modelbase::Estimate()
{   decl  vpstart, vpfree, estout;

    if (!InitPar())             // calls InitData() if necessary
        return FALSE;

    vpstart = GetFreePar();  // map pars to estimation format
    estout = DoEstimation(vpstart); // do the estimation
    vpfree = isarray(estout) ? estout[0] : estout;

    SetFreePar(vpfree);// map estimated pars to normal format

    if (m_iResult >= MAX_CONV && m_iResult < MAX_MAXIT)
        m_iModelStatus = MS_ESTIMATED;
    else
        m_iModelStatus = MS_EST_FAILED;

    if (m_fPrint)
    {   Output();
        if (isarray(estout))
            OutputMax(estout[1],m_iResult,vpstart,estout[2]);
    }
    return m_iModelStatus == MS_ESTIMATED;
}
```

## Modelbase::FixPar

```
FixPar(const iP, const dFix);
```
| | | |
|---|---|---|
| iP | in: | int, index of parameter to fix |
| dFix | in: | double, value to fix parameter at |

*No return value.*

*Description*

FixPar() is used to fix a parameter at the specified value. Subsequently, this parameter is omitted from the vector returned by GetFreePar().

## Modelbase::FreePar

```
FreePar(const iP)
```
　　　　iP　　　　　　in:　int, index of parameter to free, use −1 to free all

*No return value.*

*Description*
　　　　Frees a parameter which was previously fixed by `FixPar()`.

## Modelbase::GetcDfLoss

```
virtual GetcDfLoss();
```

*Return value*
　　　　The loss in degrees of freedom in the estimated model. The default is the number of estimated parameters.

*Description*
　　　　Only override this function if the number to be used in the output is different from that number of free parameters in the estimation.

## Modelbase::GetcT

```
virtual GetcT();
```

*Return value*
　　　　Returns an integer with the actual number of observations to be used in the output.

*Description*
　　　　Only override this function if the number reported in the output is different from that used in the estimation (`m_cT`).

## Modelbase::GetCovar, Modelbase::GetCovarRobust

```
GetCovar();
GetCovarRobust();
```

*Return value*
　　　　Returns the $p \times p$ variance-covariance matrix of the free parameters.

*Description*
　　　　See `Covar` for an explanation of the implementation.

## Modelbase::GetForecastData

```
GetForecastData(const iGroup, const mnLag, const mxLag,
    const cTforc);
GetForecastData(const iGroup, const mnLag, const mxLag,
    const cTforc, const iT1forc);
```
|  |  |  |
|---|---|---|
| iGroup | in: | int, group number |
| mnLag | in: | int, start lag |
| mxLag | in: | int, end lag |
| cTforc | in: | int, number of forecasts |
| iT1forc | in: | int, first forecasts observation (default is m_iT2est+1) |

*Return value*

Returns a matrix with the available forecasts data (or an empty matrix if no there is no data).

## Modelbase::GetFreePar, Modelbase::GetFreeParCount, Modelbase::GetFreeParNames

```
GetFreePar();
GetFreeParCount();
GetFreeParNames();
```

*Return value*

GetFreePar returns the $p \times 1$ vector with free parameters.

GetFreeParCount returns the free parameter count $p$.

GetFreeParNames returns an array of length $p$ with the names of the free parameters.

*Description*

GetFreePar returns the current values of the free parameters. Parameters are fixed with FixPar(). The value of free parameters is set with SetFreePar().

## Modelbase::GetLogLik

```
GetLogLik();
```

*Return value*

Returns the log-likelihood, which is the value of the m_dLogLik member variable.

## Modelbase::GetMethod, Modelbase::GetMethodLabel

```
GetMethod();
virtual GetMethodLabel();
```

*Return value*

GetMethod returns the integer representing the estimation method, which is the value of the m_iMethod member variable.

GetMethodLabel returns the text label for the current estimation method m_iMethod.

## Modelbase::GetModelLabel, Modelbase::GetModelStatus

```
virtual GetModelLabel();
GetModelStatus();
```

*Return value*

GetModelLabel returns the text label for the current model.

GetModelStatus returns the model estimation status:

| value | description |
|---|---|
| MS_NONE | no model preparatory action has been taken, |
| MS_DATA | estimation data has been extracted from the database, |
| MS_PARAMS | the starting values for estimation have been set, |
| MS_ESTIMATED | the model has been estimated, |
| MS_EST_FAILED | model estimation has failed. |

This value is stored in the m_iModelStatus member variable.

## Modelbase::GetPackageName

```
virtual GetPackageName();
```

*Return value*

Name of the modelling package.

*Description*

This virtual function should be overridden by the derived class.

## Modelbase::GetPackageVersion

```
virtual GetPackageVersion();
```

*Return value*

Version number of the modelling package.

*Description*

This virtual function should be overridden by the derived class.

# Modelbase::GetPar,   Modelbase::GetParCount,   Modelbase::Get-ParNames

```
GetPar();
GetParCount();
virtual GetParNames();
```

*Return value*

GetPar returns the $q \times 1$ vector with the current parameter values (both fixed and free).

GetParCount returns the total parameter count $q$ (both fixed and free parameters).

GetParNames returns an array of length $q$ with the names of the parameters.

*Description*

GetParNames should be overridden to use proper labels in the output.

# Modelbase::GetParStatus

```
GetParStatus();
```

*Return value*

Returns array with:

    0  total number of parameters $q$,

    1  $q \times 1$ matrix with 1 in position of free parameters, and 0 for fixed,

    2  $q \times 1$ matrix with fixed value in position of fixed parameters (free positions are unused),

*Description*

This function is infrequently used.

# Modelbase::GetParTypes

```
virtual GetParTypes();
```

*Return value*

Override the default to return an array of strings indicating the type of each model variable, e.g. `"Y","X","X","U"`. The default returns 0, so that no types are indicated in the output.

# Modelbase::GetResiduals

```
virtual GetResiduals();
```

*Return value*

Returns the $T \times n$ matrix with residuals ($n$ equals 1 for univariate models).

*Description*

Must be overridden by the derived class to return residuals.

# Modelbase::GetResult

```
GetResult();
```

*Return value*
> The estimation result (normally a value from `MaxBFGS`), which is the value of the
> `m_iResult` member variable.

# Modelbase::GetResVar

```
virtual GetResVar();
```

*Return value*
> Returns the $n \times n$ matrix with the residual variance ($n$ equals 1 for univariate
> models).

*Description*
> Must be overridden by the derived class.

# Modelbase::GetStdErr, Modelbase::GetStdErrRobust

```
GetStdErr();
GetStdErrRobust();
```

*Return value*
> Returns the $q \times 1$ vector with standard errors (0 at position of fixed parameters).

*Description*
> See `Covar` for an explanation of the implementation.

# Modelbase::Grow

```
Modelbase::Grow(const cTadd);
```
>     cTadd     in:  int, number of observations to grow database sample by ($>$
>                     0: `cTadd` observations are added at the end; $<0$: `-cTadd`
>                     observations are added at the beginning)

*No return value.*

*Description*
> Calls `Database::Grow` and updates the deterministic variables ("Constant",
> "Trend", "Seasonal", "CSeasonal").

# Modelbase::InitData

```
virtual InitData();
```

*Return value*
> TRUE if successful.

*Description*
> Extracts the data for estimation from the underlying database.  Sets the model status to MS_DATA if successful.

# Modelbase::InitPar

```
virtual InitPar();
```

*Return value*
> TRUE if successful.

*Description*
> Gets starting values for the estimation procedure.  Sets the model status to MS_PARAMS if successful.

# Modelbase::IsUnivariate

```
virtual IsUnivariate();
```

*Return value*
> TRUE if only one dependent variable (Y_VAR) is allowed.

*Description*
> This virtual function should be overridden by the derived class if multivariate models are implemented.

# Modelbase::MapParToFree

```
MapParToFree(const vPar);
```
> vPar       in:   int, $q$ vector with parameter values (both fixed and free)

*Return value*
> Returns a $p \times 1$ vector with free parameter values.

*Description*
> Extracts and returns the free parameter values from a full parameter vector.

# Modelbase::Modelbase

```
Modelbase();
```

*No return value.*

*Description*
> Constructor function.

## Modelbase::Output

```
virtual Output();
```
*No return value.*

*Description*
> Prints the estimation output.

## Modelbase::OutputHeader

```
OutputHeader(const sTitle);
    sTitle      in:   string, title
```
*No return value.*

*Description*
> Called by Output to print the header section.

## Modelbase::OutputLogLik

```
OutputLogLik();
```
*No return value.*

*Description*
> Called by Output to print the loglikelihood and other summary statistics.

## Modelbase::OutputMax

```
OutputMax(const sMethod, const iResult, const vPstart,
    const bNumerical);
    sMethod              in:   maximization method
    iResult              in:   int, maximization result
    vPstart              in:   vector with starting values
    bNumerical           in:   int, TRUE if using numerical derivatives
```
*No return value.*

*Description*
> Called by Estimate to print the starting values and method used for iterative estimation.

## Modelbase::OutputPar

```
OutputPar();
```
*No return value.*

*Description*
> Called by Output to print the parameter estimates.

## Modelbase::PrintTestVal

```
static PrintTestVal(const dTest, const cR, const cTdf,
    const sLabel);
```
|          |     |                          |
|----------|-----|--------------------------|
| dTest    | in: | test statistic           |
| cR       | in: | first degrees of freedom |
| cTdf     | in: | second degrees of freedom |
| sLabel   | in: | name of test             |

*No return value.*

*Description*

Prints a test statistic and its significance. If cTdf is zero, the test is assumed to have $\chi^2(\text{cR})$ distribution, otherwise an $F(\text{cR,cTdf})$ distribution.

## Modelbase::ResetFixedPar

```
ResetFixedPar();
```
*No return value.*

*Description*

Resets the fixed parameters to their prespecified values.

## Modelbase::SetForecasts

```
virtual SetForecasts(const cForc, const bIsLessForecasts);
```
|                  |     |                                                  |
|------------------|-----|--------------------------------------------------|
| cForc            | in: | int, number of forecasts,                        |
| bIsLessForecasts | in: | int, TRUE: the forecasts are subtracted from the selection sample. |

*No return value.*

*Description*

The Modelbase version sets m_cTforc.

## Modelbase::SetFreePar

```
SetFreePar(const vParFree);
```
|          |     |                                |
|----------|-----|--------------------------------|
| vParFree | in: | $p$ vector with free parameter values |

*No return value.*

## Modelbase::SetMethod

```
SetMethod(const iMethod);
```
|         |     |                                                          |
|---------|-----|----------------------------------------------------------|
| iMethod | in: | int, estimation method (no values are predefined in Modelbase) |

*No return value.*

*Description*

Sets m_iMethod.

## Modelbase::SetModelStatus

```
SetModelStatus(const iModelStatus);
```
    iModelStatus      in:  int, model status to set, one of: MS_NONE, MS_DATA, MS_PARAMS, MS_ESTIMATED, MS_EST_FAILED

*No return value.*

*Description*

Sets m_iModelStatus.

## Modelbase::SetPar, Modelbase::SetParCount

```
SetPar(const vPar);
SetParCount(const cPar);
SetParCount(const cPar, const bAdd);
```
    vPar      in:  $q \times 1$ vector with new parameter values (both fixed and free)

    cPar      in:  int, total number of parameters (fixed and free)

    bAdd      in:  (optional) int, TRUE: add parameters to current count; else set the count.

*No return value.*

*Description*

SetParCount() be called for the other parameter functions to work.

## Modelbase::SetPrint

```
SetPrint(fPrint);
```
    fPrint    in:  int, TRUE to switch printing on, FALSE to switch off.

*No return value.*

*Description*

For Monte Carlo experiments, it can be useful to switch off printing.

## Modelbase::SetRecursive

```
virtual SetRecursive(const bSet, const cInit);
```
    bSet    in:  int, TRUE to switch recursive estimation on

    cInit    in:  int, number of initialization steps

*No return value.*

*Description*

The Modelbase version sets m_bRecursive and m_cTinit.

## Modelbase::SetResult

```
SetResult(const iResult);
```

*No return value.*

*Description*

Sets the estimation result (normally a value from `MaxBFGS`), which is the value of the `m_iResult` member variable.

## Modelbase::SetStartPar

```
virtual SetStartPar(const vParFree);
```
    vParFree                in:  $p$ vector with the starting values for the free parameters

*No return value.*

*Description*

This is an alternative to `InitPar`, allowing for direct setting of the starting parameters prior to estimation.

## Modelbase::TestRestrictions

```
virtual TestRestrictions(vSel);
virtual TestRestrictions(mR, const vR);
```
    vSel                    in:  $p$ vector, with a 1 for the coefficients which tested to be zero, 0 otherwise
    mR                    in:  $s \times p$ matrix $R$
    vR                    in:  $s$ vector $r$

*No return value.*

*Description*

The one-argument version tests whether one or more coefficients are zero. The second form tests restrictions of the type $R\theta = r$. Both are implemented as a Wald test with a $\chi^2(s)$ distribution.

This function requires that `Covar()` and `GetParNames()` are implemented, and `SetPar()` or `SetParFree()` are used to set the estimated parameters.

## 12.3 PcFiml class

The PcFiml class provides part of the advanced computations available in the menu driven computer program *PcGive*, see Doornik and Hendry (2009). The class is derived from the Database class, and provides model formulation using variable names.

The class allows for estimating a Vector Autoregression (VAR), cointegration analysis ('Johansen procedure'), and multivariate regression model (such as an unrestricted reduced form, URF), as well as a simultaneous equations model (2SLS, 3SLS, FIML). Identities equations are currently not supported. Mis-specification tests include: vector autoregression, vector normality, vector heteroscedasticity, vector portmanteau, as well as a Chow test.

The documentation here is rather cursory, the actual source code (pcfiml.ox) gives more documentation. The required header file is pcfiml.h, which is imported here (togther with the actual code) using #import <pcfiml>.

*Example*

.................................................*samples/pcfiml/pcf1.ox*

```
#include <oxstd.h>
#import <pcfiml>

main()
{
    decl system;

    system = new PcFiml();

    system.LoadIn7("data/data.in7");
    system.Deterministic(FALSE);
                                // formulate the system
    system.Select(Y_VAR, { "CONS", 0, 2, "INC", 0, 2 } );
    system.Select(X_VAR, { "INFLAT", 0, 0 } );
    system.Select(U_VAR, { "Constant", 0, 0 } );

    system.SetSelSample(1953, 1, 1992, 3);
    system.Estimate();          // estimate the system (VAR)
    system.Cointegration();     // cointegration analysis

    system.Chow(1980, 1);                   // some tests
    system.Portmanteau(12);
    system.NormalityTest();
    system.ArTest(1, 5);
    system.HeteroTest(FALSE, FALSE);
    system.HeteroTest(FALSE, TRUE);

    delete system;
}
```

.................................................................

The output of this program is (omitting the $\chi^2$ form of some tests):

```
---- System estimation by OLS ----
```

```
The estimation sample is 1953(3) - 1992(3)
CONS        lag 0 status Y
CONS        lag 1 status Y
CONS        lag 2 status Y
INC         lag 0 status Y
INC         lag 1 status Y
INC         lag 2 status Y
INFLAT      lag 0
Constant    lag 0 status U
```

coefficients

|          | CONS      | INC       |
|----------|-----------|-----------|
| CONS_1   | 0.90553   | 0.083906  |
| CONS_2   | 0.039957  | 0.17361   |
| INC_1    | 0.060179  | 0.73816   |
| INC_2    | -0.033528 | -0.089942 |
| INFLAT   | -0.95629  | 0.0023221 |
| Constant | 25.505    | 87.920    |

coefficient standard errors

|          | CONS     | INC      |
|----------|----------|----------|
| CONS_1   | 0.13261  | 0.21549  |
| CONS_2   | 0.12260  | 0.19923  |
| INC_1    | 0.086063 | 0.13986  |
| INC_2    | 0.075989 | 0.12349  |
| INFLAT   | 0.17341  | 0.28179  |
| Constant | 15.216   | 24.727   |

equation standard errors

| CONS   | INC    |
|--------|--------|
| 1.9275 | 3.1323 |

residual covariance

|      | CONS   | INC    |
|------|--------|--------|
| CONS | 3.7152 | 4.9906 |
| INC  | 4.9906 | 9.8111 |

log-likelihood=-185.911118 det-omega=10.6792 T=157

Cointegration analysis

| eigenvalues | trace  | [pval] | max-eval | [pval] |
|-------------|--------|--------|----------|--------|
| 0.40306     | 101.97 | 0.0000 | 81.002   | 0.0000 |
| 0.12502     | 20.967 | 0.0000 | 20.967   | 0.0000 |

beta

|        |          |          |
|--------|----------|----------|
| CONS   | 0.22102  | 0.17651  |
| INC    | -0.24747 | -0.25253 |
| INFLAT | 1.0903   | -0.22638 |

alpha

|      |          |         |
|------|----------|---------|
| CONS | -0.74698 | 0.62647 |
| INC  | 0.24209  | 1.1558  |

standardized beta

```
CONS                1.0000      -0.69898
INC                -1.1197       1.0000
INFLAT              4.9332       0.89643


standardized alpha
CONS       -0.16510      -0.15820
INC         0.053507     -0.29187


long run matrix
                  CONS           INC        INFLAT
CONS       -0.054518      0.026651      -0.95629
INC         0.25752      -0.35178       0.0023221
Unrestricted constant
```

```
Chow test for break after 1980(1) in sample up to 1992(3):
Scalar Chow tests:  F(50,101)=
            1.2555        1.0587
Vector Chow test:   F(100,200)=1.18615 [0.1558]
Vector portmanteau:   Chi(38)=45.8927 [0.1776]
Vector normality:     Chi(4)=3.49129 [0.4792]
Vector AR 1-5 test:  F(20,280)=1.74601 [0.0265]
Vector hetero test:  F(30,405)=0.977499 [0.5030]
Vector hetero-X test: F(60,382)=1.07614 [0.3357]
```

The next example involves simultaneous equations estimation.

. . . . . . . . . . . . . . . . . . . . . . . . . . . . . . . . . . . . . . . . . . . . . . . . . . . . *samples/pcfiml/pcf3.ox*

```
#include <oxstd.h>
#import <pcfiml>
main()
{
    decl system = new PcFiml();

    system.LoadIn7("data/data.in7");
    system.Deterministic(FALSE);
                                // formulate the system
    system.Select(Y_VAR, { "CONS", 0, 2, "INC", 0, 2 } );
    system.Select(X_VAR, { "INFLAT", 0, 0 } );
    system.Select(U_VAR, { "Constant", 0, 0 } );

    system.SetSelSample(1953, 1, 1992, 3);
    system.SetPrint(FALSE);     // don't print URF results
    system.Estimate();                  // estimate URF

    system.SetPrintUrf(FALSE);
    system.SetPrint(TRUE);          // but print model output
                                    // formulate a model
    system.SetEquation("CONS", {"CONS",1,2, "INC",0,0 });
    system.SetEquation("INC",  {"INC", 1,2 } );

    system.Fiml();              // estimate the model by FIML
    system.Portmanteau(12);             // do some tests
    system.EgeArTest(1, 1);
```

```
        system.EgeArTest(1, 5);
        system.NormalityTest();
        system.HeteroTest(FALSE, FALSE);
        system.HeteroTest(FALSE, TRUE);

        delete system;                    // done with the system
}
```
..................................................................................

```
---- Model estimation by FIML ----
The estimation sample is 1953 (3) 1992 (3)

coefficients
                         CONS              INC
CONS              -1.0000          0.00000
INC               -0.0024770      -1.0000
CONS_1             1.2238          0.00000
CONS_2            -0.24947         0.00000
INC_1              0.00000         0.99701
INC_2              0.00000        -0.044041
INFLAT             0.00000         0.00000
Constant          24.527          41.792

coefficient standard errors
                         CONS              INC
CONS              0.00000          0.00000
INC               0.035193         0.00000
CONS_1            0.063435         0.00000
CONS_2            0.062315         0.00000
INC_1             0.00000          0.065539
INC_2             0.00000          0.063625
INFLAT            0.00000          0.00000
Constant          16.305           22.300

equation standard errors
            CONS         INC
        2.1822       3.3125
residual covariance
                 CONS             INC
CONS         4.7620         5.5795
INC          5.5795         10.972

log-likelihood=-236.414419 det-omega=20.3209 T=157
FIML estimation: Strong convergence
```

```
Vector portmanteau:    Chi(43)=77.2487 [0.0010]
Vector EGE-AR 1-1 test: F(4,302)=1.53528 [0.1918]
Vector EGE-AR 1-5 test: F(20,286)=2.23427 [0.0022]
Vector normality:      Chi(4)=4.07116 [0.3965]
Vector hetero test:    F(30,405)=2.10415 [0.0008]
Vector hetero-X test:  F(60,382)=2.67075 [0.0000]
```

## PcFiml function members

ArTest(const iAr1, const iAr2);
  System vector AR test for lags iAr1...iAr2.
Chow(const iYear, const iPeriod);
  Forecast Chow tests for break on or after iYear (iPeriod).
Cointegration();
  Estimate cointegrating space.
CointegrationI2();
  I(2) cointegration analysis.
EgeArTest(const iAr1, const iAr2);
  Model vector AR test for lags iAr1...iAr2.
Estimate();
  Estimate the system (NB: use .SetSelSample() first).
Fiml();
  Do FIML estimation.
GetOmega();
  Returns $n \times n$ matrix of URF/RRF residual variance $\mathbf{V}'\mathbf{V}/(T-k)$.
GetPi();
  Returns $n \times k$ matrix of URF/RRF coefficients.
GetResiduals();
  Returns $T \times n$ matrix $\mathbf{V}$ of URF/RRF residuals.
GetResult();
  Returns results from FIML estimation (return code from MaxBFGS).
GetStatus(const aiConst, const aiTrend);
  Returns status of Constant & Trend (0: no constant; 1: restricted constant;
  2: unrestricted constant; 4: unrestricted trend; 3: restricted trend)
GetVarNames(const aasY, const aasW);
  Returns n  n1  k (n1 is no of lagged $Y$s); puts list of varnames in arguments.
GetVarPi();
  Returns $n \times k$ matrix with variances of RRF/URF coefficients.
GetVarRf();
  System: returns full $nk \times nk$ variance-covariance matrix of URF coefficients;
  Model: returns full $nk \times nk$ variance-covariance matrix of RRF coefficients.
GetVarTheta();
  System: returns full $nk \times nk$ variance-covariance matrix of URF coefficients;
  Model: returns full $np \times np$ variance-covariance matrix of model coefficients.
HeteroTest(const fStand, const fCross);
  Vector heteroscedasticity test.
NormalityTest();
  Vector normality test.

Output(const fSys, const fCoint);
  Print System and/or Cointegration results.

```
PcFiml();
```
   Constructor.
```
Portmanteau(const iLag);
```
   Vector portmanteau test up to lag iLag.
```
SetEquation(const sEquation, const aModel);
```
   Delete or add variable from model.
```
SetPrint(fPrint);
```
   Toggles print switch.
```
SetPrintUrf(fPrintUrf);
```
   Toggles URF print switch.
```
ThreeSLS();
```
   Do 3SLS estimation.
```
TwoSLS();
```
   Do 2SLS estimation.

# 12.4 PcFimlDgp class

The `PcFimlDgp` class is a data generation process (DGP), designed for use in dynamic econometric Monte Carlo experiments. Unlike the `PcNaiveDgp` class, it derives from `Database` to formulate the DGP and store the generated data. This makes the DGP more general, but somewhat more complex. The class is used through the header file `pcfimldgp.h`.

The form of the DGP in mathematical formulation is a reduced form model:

$$
\begin{aligned}
\mathbf{y}_t &= \mathbf{\Pi}\mathbf{w}_t + \mathbf{u}_t, \quad t = T_1, \ldots, T_2, \\
\mathbf{z}_t &= \mathbf{C}_0\mathbf{z}_{t-1} + \mathbf{v}_t, \quad t = T_1, \ldots, T_2.
\end{aligned}
$$

where $\mathbf{w}$ contains $\mathbf{z}$, $r$ lags of $\mathbf{z}$ and $m$ lags of $\mathbf{y}$:

$$
\mathbf{w}'_t = \left( \mathbf{y}'_{t-1}, \ldots, \mathbf{y}'_{t-m}, \mathbf{z}'_t, \ldots, \mathbf{z}'_{t-r} \right).
$$

Take $\mathbf{y}_t$ as an $n \times 1$ vector, $\mathbf{z}_t$ as $q \times 1$, and $\mathbf{w}_t$ as $k \times 1$.

The database is constructed as follows:

| | |
|---|---|
| $0 \ldots s - 1$ | initial values for lagged observations, $s \geq \max(1, m, r)$ |
| $T_1 = s \ldots s + d - 1$ | space to allow for discarded observations, |
| $T_1 + d \ldots T_2^*$ | remainder of generated data. |

$T_2^*$, the sample size of the database, is determined by the call to `Create()`. $T_2$, the endpoint for data generation, is determined by the call to `GenerateTo()`; $T_2 \leq T_2^*$.

*Example*

.......................................................... *samples/simula/pcfdgp.ox*

```
#include <oxstd.h>
#import <pcfimldgp>

main()
{
    decl dgp = new PcFimlDgp(2,1);

    dgp.Create(1, 1980, 1, 0, 1, 100);

    dgp.Select(Y_VAR, {"Ya", 0, 1});
    dgp.Select(Y_VAR, {"Yb", 0, 1});
    dgp.Select(Z_VAR, {"Za", 0, 0});
    dgp.Select(Z_VAR, {"Constant", 0, 0});

    dgp.SetYParameter((<0.9,0;0.1,0.8> ~ <0.2;0.2> ~ <1;0>)');
    dgp.SetZParameter(<0.5>);
    dgp.SetDistribution(U_DGP, MVNORMAL, zeros(2,1),
        ones(2,2)/10 + unit(2)/5);

    dgp.Prepare();
    dgp.Print();

    print("%c", {"Ya", "Yb", "Ua", "Ub"}, dgp.GenerateTo(6));
```

```
    delete dgp;
}
```
..............................................................................

produces (all non specified parameters are zero by default):

```
---- PcFiml (2.00) DGP ----
y is (2 x 1), z is (1 x 1) and fixed.

DGP: y[t] = e[t] + Pi w
Ya              Y_VAR: dependent variable
Yb              Y_VAR: dependent variable
Ya_1            Y_VAR: lagged dependent variable
Yb_1            Y_VAR: lagged dependent variable
Za              X_VAR: regressor
Constant        X_VAR: regressor
Database sample: 1979 - 2079

Coefficients, Pi'=
                        Ya              Yb
Ya_1              0.90000         0.10000
Yb_1              0.00000         0.80000
Za                0.20000         0.20000
Constant          1.0000          0.00000
e ~ MVN(0,sigma)
sigma=
        0.30000         0.10000
        0.10000         0.30000

z[t] = v[t] + C0 z[t-1]
C0 =
        0.50000
v ~ N(0,1)


             Ya             Yb             Ua             Ub
          1.1673       0.012740        0.12233      -0.032237
          2.3206        0.81527       -0.10044        0.31785
          3.2826        0.61491       0.049601       -0.41377
          4.2886         1.4344        0.44557        0.72554
          4.8417         1.1850        0.17252       -0.20085
          4.3026         1.2911       -0.89102       0.022867
```

## PcFimlDgp::Asymp

```
Asymp();
```
*No return value.*

*Description*
    Prints an asymptotic analysis of the current DGP.

## PcFimlDgp::Create

```
Create(const iFreq, const iYear1, const iPeriod1, const cTdiscard,
    const mxDgpLag, const mxT);
```
| | | |
|---|---|---|
| iFreq | in: | int, database frequency |
| iYear1 | in: | int, start year of observation $T_1 + d$ |
| iPeriod1 | in: | int, start period of observation $T_1 + d$ |
| cTdiscard | in: | int, number of discards, $d$ |
| mxDgpLag | in: | int, maximum lag $s$ to be used in DGP |
| mxT | in: | int, maximum sample size to be used, $= T_2^* - T_1 - d + 1$ (this excludes lags and discards) |

*No return value.*

*Description*
    Creates the database. After this, Select may be used to formulate the DGP, with group identifier Y_VAR or Z_VAR. The database name of the variables are "Ya", "Yb", ..., and "Za", "Zb", .... The Constant, Trend and normal Seasonals are automatically created.

## PcFimlDgp::DiscardZ

```
DiscardZ();
```
*No return value.*

*Description*
    Discards the current $\mathbf{z}_t$; the next call to Generate() will generate new observations on $\mathbf{z}_t$.

## PcFimlDgp::GenerateTo

```
GenerateTo(const cT);
```
| | | |
|---|---|---|
| cT | in: | int, sample size $T$ |

*Return value*
    GenerateTo returns generated $\mathbf{Y} : \mathbf{U}$, as a $T \times 2n$ matrix.

*Description*
    Generates cT observation of the current DGP.

## PcFimlDgp::GenerateU, GenerateV, GenerateY, GenerateZ

```
virtual GenerateU(const cT);
virtual GenerateV(const cT);
virtual GenerateZ(const cT, const mC0t, const mV);
virtual GenerateY(const cT, const mPit, const mU);
```

| | | |
|---|---|---|
| cT | in: | int, sample size $T$ |
| mPit | in: | $k \times n$ matrix $\mathbf{\Pi}'$ |
| mC0t | in: | $q \times q$ matrix $\mathbf{C}'_0$ |
| mV | in: | $T \times q$ matrix $\mathbf{V}$ |
| mU | in: | $T \times n$ matrix $\mathbf{U}$ |

*Return value*

GenerateU returns generated $\mathbf{U} = (\mathbf{u}_{T-1} \ldots \mathbf{u}_{T_2})'$.
GenerateV returns generated $\mathbf{V} = (\mathbf{v}_{T-1} \ldots \mathbf{u}_{T_2})'$.
GenerateY returns generated $\mathbf{Y} = (\mathbf{y}_{T-1} \ldots \mathbf{y}_{T_2})'$.
GenerateZ returns generated $\mathbf{Z} = (\mathbf{z}_{T-1} \ldots \mathbf{z}_{T_2})'$.

*Description*

These virtual functions are called by GenerateTo to generate the data using matrix expressions (the default).

## PcFimlDgp::GenerateU_t, GenerateV_t, GenerateY_t, GenerateZ_t

```
virtual GenerateU_t(const iT);
virtual GenerateV_t(const iT);
virtual GenerateZ_t(const iT, const mC0t);
virtual GenerateY_t(const iT, const mPit);
```

| | | |
|---|---|---|
| iT | in: | int, observation $t$ |
| mPit | in: | $k \times n$ matrix $\mathbf{\Pi}'$ |
| mC0t | in: | $q \times q$ matrix $\mathbf{C}'_0$ |

*Return value*

GenerateU_t returns generated $\mathbf{u}'_t$.
GenerateV_t returns generated $\mathbf{v}'_t$.
GenerateY_t returns generated $\mathbf{y}'_t$.
GenerateZ_t returns generated $\mathbf{z}'_t$.

*Description*

These virtual functions are called by GenerateTo to generate the data when using a for loop. This is the case after a call to UseObsLoop(TRUE).

## PcFimlDgp::GetU, GetV, GetY, GetZ

```
GetU();
GetV();
GetY();
GetZ();
```

*Return value*

GetU returns current $\mathbf{U} = (\mathbf{u}_{T_1} \ldots \mathbf{u}_{T_2})'$, as a $T \times n$ matrix.
GetV returns current $\mathbf{V} = (\mathbf{v}_{T_1} \ldots \mathbf{u}_{T_2})'$, as a $T \times q$ matrix.
GetY returns current $\mathbf{Y} = (\mathbf{y}_{T_1} \ldots \mathbf{y}_{T_2})'$, as a $T \times n$ matrix.
GetZ returns current $\mathbf{Z} = (\mathbf{z}_{T_1} \ldots \mathbf{z}_{T_2})'$, as a $T \times q$ matrix.

## PcFimlDgp::PcFimlDgp

```
PcFimlDgp(const cY, const cZ);
```
|  |  |  |
|------|-----|-----|
| cY | in: | int, $n$, dimension of $\mathbf{y}_t$ |
| cZ | in: | int, $q$, dimension of $\mathbf{z}_t$ |

*No return value.*

*Description*

Constructor.

## PcFimlDgp::Prepare

```
virtual Prepare();
```
*No return value.*

*Description*

Virtual function which must be called prior to data generation.

## PcFimlDgp::Print

```
Print();
```
*No return value.*

*Description*

Prints the setup of the current DGP.

## PcFimlDgp::SetDistribution

```
SetDistribution(const iEqn, const iDist, mM, mS);
```

*Description*

See PcNaiveDgp::SetDistribution().

# PcFimlDgp::SetFixedZ

```
SetFixedZ(const fSetting);
```

*Description*
> See `PcNaiveDgp::SetFixedZ()`.

# PcFimlDgp::SetInit

```
SetInit(const iDgp, const mInit);
    iEqn       in:   one of: Y_DGP, Z_DGP
    mInit      in:   0, or
                     Y_DGP: $s \times n$ matrix
                     Z_DGP: $s \times q$ matrix
```
*No return value.*

*Description*
> This function is used to specify initial values for the data generation. By default the initial values are 0.
>
> The first row of `mInit` will be stored at observation $0 = T_1 - d - s$ in the database.

# PcFimlDgp::SetU, SetV, SetY, SetZ

```
SetU(const m);
SetY(const m);
    m                in:   $T \times n$ matrix
SetV(const m);
SetZ(const m);
    m                in:   $T \times q$ matrix
```
*No return value.*

*Description*
> SetU sets $\mathbf{U} = \mathbf{u}_{T_1} \ldots \mathbf{u}_{T_1 + T - 1}$.
> SetV sets $\mathbf{V} = \mathbf{v}_{T_1} \ldots \mathbf{v}_{T_1 + T - 1}$.
> SetY sets $\mathbf{Y} = \mathbf{y}_{T_1} \ldots \mathbf{y}_{T_1 + T - 1}$.
> SetZ sets $\mathbf{Z} = \mathbf{z}_{T_1} \ldots \mathbf{z}_{T_1 + T - 1}$.

# PcFimlDgp::SetYParameter

```
SetYParameter(const mPit);
    mPit       in:   $k \times n$ matrix $\mathbf{\Pi}'$
```
*No return value.*

*Description*
> Sets the parameters for the $\mathbf{y}_t$ equation.

## PcFimlDgp::SetZParameter

```
SetZParameter(const mC0);
```
      mC0         in:   $q \times q$ matrix $\mathbf{C}_0$

*No return value.*

*Description*
    Sets the parameters for the $\mathbf{z}_t$ equation.

## PcFimlDgp::UseObsLoop

```
UseObsLoop(const bUseObsLoop);
```
      bUseObsLoop         in:   TRUE: generate data by looping over observa-
                                            tions

*No return value.*

*Description*
    By default, the data are generated using matrix expressions. Use this to generate the data in a `for`-loop. This is considerably slower, but gives more flexibility.

## 12.5 PcNaiveDgp class

The `PcNaiveDgp` class is a data generation process (DGP), designed for use in dynamic econometric Monte Carlo experiments. The class is used through the header file `pcnaive.h`. The design is an $n$-variate version of the DGP used in Hendry, Neale and Ericsson (1991). The form of the DGP in mathematical formulation is:

$$\begin{aligned}
\mathbf{y}_t &= \mathbf{A}_0\mathbf{y}_t + \mathbf{A}_1\mathbf{y}_{t-1} + \mathbf{A}_2\mathbf{z}_t + \mathbf{a}_3 + \mathbf{A}_5\mathbf{y}_{t-2} + \mathbf{u}_t, \\
\mathbf{u}_t &= \mathbf{B}_0\mathbf{u}_{t-1} + \mathbf{e}_t + \mathbf{B}_1\mathbf{e}_{t-1}, \\
\mathbf{z}_t &= \mathbf{C}_0\mathbf{z}_{t-1} + \mathbf{c}_1 + \mathbf{c}_2 t + \mathbf{v}_t.
\end{aligned} \tag{12.1}$$

The vectors $\mathbf{y}_t, \mathbf{u}_t, \mathbf{e}_t$ are $n \times 1$, so that the coefficient matrices $\mathbf{A}_0, \mathbf{A}_1, \mathbf{B}_0, \mathbf{B}_1$ are $n \times n$, and $\mathbf{a}_3$ is $n \times 1$. The $\mathbf{z}_t$ vector is $q \times 1$, making $\mathbf{a}_2$ $n \times q$, $\mathbf{C}_0$ $q \times q$, and $\mathbf{c}_1, \mathbf{c}_2$ $q \times 1$. The $z$s can be kept fixed between experiments, or regenerated for the experiment. A distribution for $\mathbf{e}_t$ and $\mathbf{v}_t$ can be specified.

The DGP can also be formulated in equilibrium correction form:

$$\Delta\mathbf{y}_t = \boldsymbol{\alpha}\boldsymbol{\beta}'\mathbf{y}_{t-1} + \mathbf{A}_2\mathbf{z}_t + \mathbf{a}_3 + \mathbf{A}_5^*\Delta\mathbf{y}_{t-1} + \mathbf{u}_t. \tag{12.2}$$

*Example*

............................................*samples/simula/pcndgp.ox*

```
#include <oxstd.h>
#import <pcnaive>

main()
{
    decl dgp = new PcNaiveDgp(2,1);

    dgp.SetYParameter(zeros(2,2), <0.9,0;0.1,0.8>,
        <0.2;0.2>, <1;0>);
    dgp.SetZParameter(<0.5>, <0>, <0>);
    dgp.SetDistribution(U_DGP, MVNORMAL, zeros(2,1),
        ones(2,2)/10 + unit(2)/5);

    dgp.Print();
    print("%c", {"Ya", "Yb", "Ua", "Ub"}, dgp.GenerateTo(6));

    delete dgp;
}
```

............................................................................

produces (all non specified parameters are zero by default):

```
---- PcNaive (2.00) DGP ----
y is (2 x 1), z is (1 x 1) and fixed.

y[t] = e[t] + A1 y[t-1] + A2 z[t] + a3
A1 =
        0.90000        0.00000
        0.10000        0.80000
A2 =
```

```
        0.20000
        0.20000
a3 =
        1.0000
        0.00000

e ~ MVN(0,sigma)
sigma=
        0.30000        0.10000
        0.10000        0.30000

z[t] = v[t] + C0 z[t-1]
C0 =
        0.50000

v ~ N(0,1)
```

|       Ya |        Yb |        Ua |         Ub |
|---------:|----------:|----------:|-----------:|
|   1.1673 |  0.012740 |   0.12233 |  -0.032237 |
|   2.3206 |   0.81527 |  -0.10044 |    0.31785 |
|   3.2826 |   0.61491 |  0.049601 |  -0.41377 |
|   4.2886 |    1.4344 |   0.44557 |    0.72554 |
|   4.8417 |    1.1850 |   0.17252 |  -0.20085 |
|   4.3026 |    1.2911 |  -0.89102 |   0.022867 |

# PcNaiveDgp::Asymp

`PcNaiveDgp::Asymp();`

*No return value.*

*Description*

Prints an asymptotic analysis of the current DGP: companion matrix with eigenvalues, together with cointegrating space and level of integration of DGP: I(0), I(1) or I(2).

# PcNaiveDgp::DiscardZ

`PcNaiveDgp::DiscardZ();`

*No return value.*

*Description*

Discards the current $\mathbf{z}_t$; the next call to `Generate()` will generate new observations on $\mathbf{z}_t$.

# PcNaiveDgp::Generate, PcNaiveDgp::GenerateTo

`PcNaiveDgp::Generate(const cT);`
`PcNaiveDgp::GenerateTo(const cT);`
    cT         in:   int, sample size $T$

*Return value*

Generate returns generated $\mathbf{Y} = (\mathbf{y}_0 \dots \mathbf{y}_T)'$, as a $T \times n$ matrix.
GenerateTo returns generated $\mathbf{Y} : \mathbf{U}$, as a $T \times 2n$ matrix.

*Description*

Generates cT observation of the current DGP.

# PcNaiveDgp::GenerateBreakTo

`PcNaiveDgp::GenerateBreakTo(const cT,const iTbreak,const iTreset,`
    `const mA0, const mA1, const mA2, const mA3, const mA5);`
    cT         in:   int, sample size $T$
    iTbreak   in:   int, $T_1$, first observation with break
    iTreset   in:   int, $T_2$, first observation after the break
    mA0       in:   $n \times n$ matrix $\mathbf{A}_0^*$ *must have zeros on the diagonal*
    mA1       in:   $n \times n$ matrix $\mathbf{A}_1^*$
    mA2       in:   $n \times q$ matrix $\mathbf{A}_2^*$
    mA3       in:   $n \times 1$ matrix $\mathbf{a}_3^*$
    mA5       in:   $n \times n$ matrix $\mathbf{A}_5^*$

*Return value*

Returns generated generated $\mathbf{Y} : \mathbf{U}$, as a $T \times 2n$ matrix.

*Description*

Generates cT observation of the current DGP. For observations $[0, T_1 - 1]$ and $[T_2, T - 1]$ the original DGP is used. For observations $[T_1, T_2 - 1]$ the DGP as specified in the arguments is used. Note that only the $Y$ equation can have a break.

## PcNaiveDgp::GetU, GetY, GetZ

```
PcNaiveDgp::GetU();
PcNaiveDgp::GetY();
PcNaiveDgp::GetZ();
```

*Return value*

GetU returns current $\mathbf{U} = (\mathbf{u}_0 \ldots \mathbf{u}_{T-1})'$, as a $T \times n$ matrix.

GetY returns current $\mathbf{Y} = (\mathbf{y}_0 \ldots \mathbf{y}_{T-1})'$, as a $T \times n$ matrix (as does `Generate`).

GetZ returns current $\mathbf{Z} = (\mathbf{z}_0 \ldots \mathbf{z}_{T-1})'$, as a $T \times q$ matrix.

## PcNaiveDgp::PcNaiveDgp

```
PcNaiveDgp::PcNaiveDgp(const cY, const cZ);
```
|       |     |                                |
|-------|-----|--------------------------------|
| cY    | in: | int, $n$, dimension of $\mathbf{y}_t$ |
| cZ    | in: | int, $q$, dimension of $\mathbf{z}_t$ |

*No return value.*

*Description*

Constructor.

## PcNaiveDgp::Print

```
PcNaiveDgp::Print();
```
*No return value.*

*Description*

Prints the setup of the current DGP.

## PcNaiveDgp::SetDistribution

```
PcNaiveDgp::SetDistribution(const iEqn, const iDist, mM, mS);
```

| iEqn | in: | one of: U_DGP, Z_DGP |
|------|-----|----------------------|
| iDist | in: | one of: NO_DIST, NORMAL, MVNORMAL, MVNORMAL_CORR, LOGNORMAL, T_DIST, F_DIST, EXPONENTIAL, MVNARCH, MVNHETERO |
| mM | in: | first parameter of distribution, $\alpha$ MVNARCH, MVNHETERO: $n \times n$ for $\mathbf{y}_t, \mathbf{u}_t$; $q \times q$ for $\mathbf{z}_t$ others: $n \times 1$ for $\mathbf{y}_t, \mathbf{u}_t$; $q \times 1$ for $\mathbf{z}_t$ |
| mS | in: | second parameter of distribution, $\beta$ MVNORMAL, MVNARCH, MVNHETERO: $n \times n$ for $\mathbf{y}_t, \mathbf{u}_t$; $q \times q$ for $\mathbf{z}_t$ others: $n \times 1$ for $\mathbf{y}_t, \mathbf{u}_t$; $q \times 1$ for $\mathbf{z}_t$ |

*No return value.*

*Description*

Specifies the distribution for the $\mathbf{u}$, or $\mathbf{z}$ equation in (12.1). The first argument indicates the equation, the second the distribution. The last two arguments parametrize the distribution.

Write $\epsilon_t$ for either $\mathbf{e}_t$ or $\mathbf{v}_t$, then:

| argument | distribution |
|----------|-------------|
| NO_DIST | 0 (no distribution) |
| NORMAL | $\epsilon_{it} \sim \mathsf{N}(\alpha_i, \beta_i) = \mathsf{N}(0, 1) \times \sqrt{\beta_i} + \alpha_i$ |
| MVNORMAL | $\epsilon_t \sim \mathsf{N}_n(\boldsymbol{\alpha}, \boldsymbol{\beta})$ |
| MVNORMAL_CORR | $\epsilon_t \sim \mathsf{N}_n(\boldsymbol{\alpha}, \boldsymbol{\beta})$ specified with standard deviations on diagonal, correlations on lower diagonal |
| LOGNORMAL | $\epsilon_{it} \sim \Lambda(\alpha_i, \beta_i) = \exp\{N(0, 1)\} \times \sqrt{\alpha_i} + \beta_i$ |
| T_DIST | $\epsilon_{it} \sim \mathsf{t}(\alpha_i)$ |
| F_DIST | $\epsilon_{it} \sim \mathsf{F}(\alpha_i, \beta_i)$ |
| EXPONENTIAL | $\epsilon_{it} \sim \exp(\alpha_i)$ |
| MVNARCH | $\epsilon_t \sim \mathsf{N}_n(\mathbf{0}, \boldsymbol{\alpha} + \boldsymbol{\beta}\epsilon_{t-1}\epsilon'_{t-1}\boldsymbol{\beta}')$ |
| MVNHETERO | $\mathbf{e}_t \sim \mathsf{N}_n(\mathbf{0}, \boldsymbol{\alpha} + \boldsymbol{\beta}\mathbf{y}_{t-1}\mathbf{y}'_{t-i}\boldsymbol{\beta}')$ |

# PcNaiveDgp::SetFixedZ

```
PcNaiveDgp::SetFixedZ(const fSetting);
```
　　　fSetting　　　　　　　in:　0: $\mathbf{z}_t$ is fixed, 1: $\mathbf{z}_t$ not fixed

*No return value.*

*Description*

Specifies whether $\mathbf{z}_t$ is fixed or not. Fixed $\mathbf{z}_t$ is only generated once, until a call to DiscardZ or SetFixedZ is made. By default $\mathbf{z}_t$ is fixed.

# PcNaiveDgp::SetInit

```
PcNaiveDgp::SetInit(const iDgp, const mInit);
```

| iEqn  | in: | one of: Y_DGP, Z_DGP |
|-------|-----|----------------------|
| mInit | in: | 0, or |
|       |     | Y_DGP: $1 times n$ or $2 times n$ matrix |
|       |     | Z_DGP: $1 times q$ matrix |

*No return value.*

*Description*

    This function is used to specify initial values for the data generation. By default the initial values are 0.

    The $Z$ equation has only one lag, and mInit specifies $z_{-1}$.

    The $Y$ equation can have up to two lags. If mInit has two rows, the first row specifies $y_{-2}$, and the second $y_{-1}$. If mInit has one row, that row is used for both $y_{-2}$ and $y_{-1}$.

# PcNaiveDgp::SetUParameter

```
PcNaiveDgp::SetUParameter(const mB0, const mB1);
```
| mB0 | in: | $n \times n$ matrix $\mathbf{B}_0$ |
|-----|-----|-----------------------------------|
| mB1 | in: | $n \times n$ matrix $\mathbf{B}_1$ |

*No return value.*

*Description*

    Sets the parameters for the $\mathbf{e}_t$ equation.

# PcNaiveDgp::SetYParameter

```
PcNaiveDgp::SetYParameter(const mA0, const mA1, const mA2,
    const mA3);
PcNaiveDgp::SetYParameter(const mA0, const mA1, const mA2,
    const mA3, const mA5);
```
| mA0 | in: | $n \times n$ matrix $\mathbf{A}_0$ *must have zeros on the diagonal* |
|-----|-----|-----------------------------------|
| mA1 | in: | $n \times n$ matrix $\mathbf{A}_1$ |
| mA2 | in: | $n \times q$ matrix $\mathbf{A}_2$ |
| mA3 | in: | $n \times 1$ matrix $\mathbf{a}_3$ |
| mA5 | in: | (optional argument) $n \times n$ matrix $\mathbf{A}_5$ |

*No return value.*

*Description*

    Sets the parameters for the $\mathbf{y}_t$ equation.

# PcNaiveDgp::SetYParameterEcm

```
PcNaiveDgp::SetYParameterEcm(const mAlpha, const mBeta, const mA2,
    const mA3);
PcNaiveDgp::SetYParameterEcm(const mAlpha, const mBeta, const mA2,
    const mA3, const mA5);
```

| mAlpha | in: | $n \times p$ matrix $\boldsymbol{\alpha}$ |
|--------|-----|-------------------------------------------|
| mBeta  | in: | $n \times p$ matrix $\boldsymbol{\beta}$ |
| mA2    | in: | $n \times q$ matrix $\mathbf{A}_2$ |
| mA3    | in: | $n \times 1$ matrix $\mathbf{a}_3$ |
| mA5    | in: | (optional argument) $n \times n$ matrix $\mathbf{A}_5^*$ |

*No return value.*

*Description*

Sets the parameters for the $\mathbf{y}_t$ equation in equilibrium correction form. The rank of the cointegration space is $p$.

## PcNaiveDgp::SetZParameter

PcNaiveDgp::SetZParameter(const mC0, const mC1, const mC2);

| mC0 | in: | $q \times q$ matrix $\mathbf{C}_0$ |
|-----|-----|------------------------------------|
| mC1 | in: | $q \times 1$ matrix $\mathbf{c}_1$ |
| mC2 | in: | $q \times 1$ matrix $\mathbf{c}_2$ |

*No return value.*

*Description*

Sets the parameters for the $\mathbf{z}_t$ equation.

## PcNaiveDgp::SetZCustom

PcNaiveDgp::SetZCustom(mCZ);

| mCZ | in: | $T \times q$ matrix with custom $Z$ |
|-----|-----|-------------------------------------|

*No return value.*

*Description*

Installs a custom $Z$. This is added to $\mathbf{Z}$ after generation of $\mathbf{Z}$, but before $Z$ is used in the $Y$ equation.

# 12.6 RanMC class

The RanMC class provides random number generation of specific distribution for use by the PcNaiveDgp and PcFimlDgp classes. All member functions are static, and can be used without constructing an object, for example as:

```
x = RanMC::Choleski(x);
```

## RanMC::Choleski

```
static Choleski(const mSig);
```
  mSig      in:   square symmetric matrix

*Return value*
> The Choleski decomposition of mSig. mSig may have zeros on the diagonal; the corresponding rows and columns are ignored in the decomposition, and will be zero in the return value.

## RanMC::CheckDist

```
static CheckDist(const sFunc, iDist, mPar1, mPar2);
```
  iDist      in:   int, see PcNaiveDgp::SetDistribution()
  mPar1     in:   matrix, see PcNaiveDgp::SetDistribution()
  mPar2     in:   matrix, see PcNaiveDgp::SetDistribution()

*Return value*
> Returns an array of three values:
>   iDist   int, distribution
>   mPar1  matrix, adjusted input value
>   mPar2  matrix, adjusted input value

*Description*
> The following adjustments are made:
> - column vectors are made into row vectors;
> - MVNORMAL_CORR: matrix with standard deviations/correlations is translated to covariance matrix; distribution is set to MVNORMAL;
> - MVNORMAL: second argument returned as transposed Choleski factor;
> - NORMAL: second argument returned as square root of input value.

## RanMC::RanDist

```
RanDist(const iDist, const cT, const cY, const mDf1, const mDf2);
```
  iDist      in:   int, distribution, may not be MVNHETERO
  cT        in:   int, desired sample size $T$
  cY        in:   int, number of variables $n$
  mDf1     in:   matrix, first parameter
  mDf2     in:   matrix, second parameter

*Return value*

Returns a $T \times n$ matrix of random numbers from the specified distribution. The distribution parameters must be as returned from CheckDist().

*Example*

The following program generates the same bivariate normal random numbers twice (also see page 5):

```
#include <oxstd.h>
#import <ranmc>

main()
{
    decl x, par1, par2, idist, mu = <9,3>, sigma = <4,1;1,2>;
    [idist, par1, par2] =
        RanMC::CheckDist("text", MVNORMAL, mu, sigma);
    // use RanMC class, note: calling CheckDist first
    ranseed(-1);
    x = RanMC::RanDist(MVNORMAL, 5, 2, par1, par2);
    // or use as described in How to chapter
    ranseed(-1);
    x ~= rann(5, 2) * choleski(sigma)' + mu;
    print(x);
}
```

# RanMC::RanDist1

```
static RanDist1(const iDist, const cY, const mDf1, const mDf2,
    const mUlag, const mYlag);
```

| | | |
|---|---|---|
| iDist | in: | int, distribution |
| cY | in: | int, number of variables $n$ |
| mDf1 | in: | matrix, first parameter |
| mDf2 | in: | matrix, second parameter |
| mUlag | in: | matrix, last period error term, used for MVNARCH |
| mYlag | in: | matrix, last period generated numbers, used for MVNHETERO |

*Return value*

Returns a $1 \times n$ matrix of random numbers from the specified distribution. The distribution parameters must be as returned from CheckDist().

# RanMC::WriteDist

```
static WriteDist(const sPar, const iDist, const mDf1, const mDf2);
```

| | | |
|---|---|---|
| sPar | in: | string, name of generated variable (e.g. "Y") |

*No return value.*

*Description*

Writes the used distribution. The distribution parameters must be as returned from CheckDist().

## 12.7 Simulation class

The `Simulation` class can be used to set up Monte Carlo experiments. Derive your own simulation experimentation class from this, overriding the virtual functions. `Simulation` will handle the replications and storage, and print the final results. The type of data it can handle are coefficients, test statistics and p-values of test statistics. The class is used through the header file `simula.h`.

   An extensive example, using the `PcFiml` class for estimation, is given in the file `samples/simula/artest.ox`. An example more in line with the one here is `samples/simula/simnor.ox`. This program compares the small sample size of two tests for normality. When run in *OxRun*, it will plot the distribution of the test statistics as the Monte Carlo experiment proceeds. A more elaborate example can be found in the *Introduction to Ox*.

   The example discussed here generates data from a standard normal distribution, and estimates the mean and variance. It also tests whether the mean is different from zero. The properties of the estimated coefficients and test statistic are studied by repeating the experiment $M$ times, and averaging the outcome of the $M$ experiments. So the data generation process is:

$$y_t = \mu + \epsilon_t \text{ with } \epsilon_t \sim N(0, \sigma^2),$$

together with $\mu = 0$ and $\sigma^2 = 1$. We estimate the parameters from a sample of size $T$ by:

$$\hat{\mu} = T^{-1} \sum_{t=0}^{T-1} y_t, \quad \hat{\sigma}^2 = (T)^{-1} \sum_{t=0}^{T-1} (y_t - \hat{\mu})^2,$$

and

$$\hat{s} = \left\{ (T-1)^{-1} \sum_{t=0}^{T-1} (y_t - \hat{\mu})^2 \right\}^{\frac{1}{2}} = \left\{ \frac{T}{T-1} \hat{\sigma}^2 \right\}^{\frac{1}{2}}.$$

The $t$-test which tests the hypothesis $H_0$: $\hat{\mu} = 0$ is:

$$T^{\frac{1}{2}} \frac{\hat{\mu}}{\hat{s}}.$$

The code for this Monte Carlo experiment is in `simtest.ox` (remember that the simula code needs to be imported in):

*Example*
.................................................. *samples/simula/simtest.ox*

```
#include <oxstd.h>
#import <simula>

/*---------------- SimNormal : Simulation ----------------*/
class SimNormal : Simulation          // inherit from simulation
{
    decl m_mCoef;                              // coefficient
    decl m_mTest;                              // test statistic
```

```
    decl m_mPval;                           // p-value of t-test

    SimNormal();                                    // constructor
    Generate(const iRep, const cT, const mxT);
                                        // generate replication
    GetCoefficients();              // return coefficient values
    GetPvalues();                      // return p-values of tests
    GetTestStatistics();                  // return test statistics
    IsTwoSided();
};
SimNormal::SimNormal()
{
    Simulation(<50>, 100, 1000, TRUE, -1,
        <0.2,0.1,0.05,0.01>,        // p-values to investigate
        <0,1>);                     // true coefs: mean=0, sd=1
    SetTestNames({"t-value"});
    SetCoefNames({"constant", "std.dev"});
}
SimNormal::IsTwoSided()
{
    return <1>;
}
SimNormal::Generate(const iRep, const cT, const mxT)
{
    decl my, sdevy, meany;

    my = rann(cT, 1);                           // generate data

    meany = meanc(my);                          // mean of y
    sdevy = sqrt(cT * varc(my) / (cT-1));     // std.dev of y

    m_mCoef = meany | sdevy;                    // mean,sdev of y
    m_mTest = meany / (sdevy / sqrt(cT));     //t-value on mean
    m_mPval = tailt(m_mTest, cT-1);     // t(T-1) distributed

return 1;
}
SimNormal::GetCoefficients()
{
    return m_mCoef;
}
SimNormal::GetPvalues()
{
    return m_mPval;
}
SimNormal::GetTestStatistics()
{
    return m_mTest;
}
/*-------------- END SimNormal : Simulation ----------------*/

main()
{
```

```
        decl experiment = new SimNormal();        // create object
        experiment.Simulate();                     // do simulations
        delete experiment;                         // remove object
}
```
. . . . . . . . . . . . . . . . . . . . . . . . . . . . . . . . . . . . . . . . . . . . . . . . . . . . . . . . . . . . . . . .

produces

```
T=50, M=1000, RNG=MWC_52, common seed=-1

moments of test statistics
                        mean         std.dev      skewness  ex.kurtosis
t-value              0.019533        0.98938      -0.013264    0.037059

critical values (two sided: left tail quantiles)
                        10%            5%           2.5%         0.5%
t-value              -1.2420        -1.6862        -2.0192     -2.4008

critical values (two sided: right tail quantiles)
                        10%            5%           2.5%         0.5%
t-value               1.2384         1.5872         1.8257      2.8318

rejection frequencies
                        20%            10%            5%           1%
t-value              0.21100        0.089000       0.039000   0.0080000
[ASE]                0.012649       0.0094868      0.0068920  0.0031464

moments of estimates
                        mean          MCSD
constant             0.0024543       0.13648
std.dev              0.99797         0.10294

biases of estimates
                     mean bias        MCSE          RMSE       true value
constant             0.0024543       0.0043160      0.13651     0.00000
std.dev             -0.0020337       0.0032554      0.10296     1.0000
```

The sample size is $T = 50$, with $M = 1000$ experiments. Setting the seed enables us to use common random numbers (i.e. the same random numbers in different experiments). Note that Ox always starts with a fixed seed, so exactly the same results will be obtained when rerunning the program. The first table gives the empirical critical values for the test statistic, at the $p$-values we provided. These should correspond to the theoretical distribution, namely t(49). The value 1.276 is the 900th number in the 1000 t-values after sorting the t values (computed using `quantiler`). The empirical rejection frequencies give the percentage of experiments which were rejected at the specified probability points, based on the $p$-values returned by `GetPvalues`. The final table gives the results for the coefficients. If $\hat{\mu}_m$ is the estimated mean for experiment

$m$, and $\mu$ the true parameter then:

mean $\qquad \bar{\hat{\mu}} = M^{-1} \sum_{m=0}^{M-1} \hat{\mu}_m,$

std.dev $\qquad \hat{\sigma}_{\hat{\mu}} = \left\{ M^{-1} \sum_{m=0}^{M-1} (\hat{\mu}_m - \bar{\hat{\mu}})^2 \right\}^{\frac{1}{2}},$

mean bias $\qquad \bar{\hat{\mu}} - \mu,$

se mean bias $\qquad \hat{\sigma}_{\bar{\hat{\mu}}} = M^{-\frac{1}{2}} \hat{\sigma}_{\hat{\mu}},$

rmse $\qquad \left\{ M^{-1} \sum_{m=0}^{M-1} (\hat{\mu}_m - \mu)^2 \right\}^{\frac{1}{2}} = \left\{ (\text{std.dev})^2 + (\text{mean bias})^2 \right\}^{\frac{1}{2}},$

where RMSE is the root of the mean squared error. The standard deviation of the simulated coefficient is also called MCSD (Monte Carlo Standard Deviation). When simulating coefficients, it is also possible to compute the mean of the estimated coefficient standard error, this is called the MCSE.

## Simulation::Generate

```
virtual Simulation::Generate(const iRep, const cT, const mxT);
```
    iRep      in:  int, index of current replication (0 is first)
    cT        in:  int, sample size to be used for replication
    mxT      in:  int, maximum sample size to be used for replication (this is only relevant when using common random numbers)

*Return value*

The functions should return 1 if successful, 0 if the replications failed.

If the call to the Generate function fails, it is retried until a successful return (*so always returning 0, or not returning a value could result in an infinite loop*). The number of rejected replications is reported in the output.

*Description*

Virtual function which the derived class must override. It is called for every replication, and must perform the actual replication. The results from this replication are obtained by the simula class by calling GetCoefficients, GetPvalues and GetTestStatistics.

## Simulation::GetCoefficients, GetPvalues, GetTestStatistics

```
virtual Simulation::GetCoefficients();
virtual Simulation::GetPvalues();
virtual Simulation::GetTestStatistics();
```

*Return value*

The functions return 0 if the information is not generated, otherwise:

    GetCoefficients     $s_c \times 1$ matrix with the observed coefficients
    GetPvalues          $s_p \times 1$ matrix with observed $p$-values of the tests
    GetTestStatistics   $s_t \times 1$ matrix with the observed test statistics

*Description*

Virtual functions which the derived class must override.

# Simulation::IsTwoSided

```
virtual Simulation::IsTwoSided();
```

*Return value*

Returns a vector of 0–1 values, with a 1 for each test statistics which is two-sided. If this function is not provided, all tests are one-sided.

# Simulation::Plot

```
virtual Simulation::Plot(const iRep, const iT)
    iRep        in:  int, index of current replication (0 is first)
    iT          in:  int, sample size of current replication
```
*No return value.*

*Description*

Virtual plot function. The default version does nothing.

# Simulation::SaveIn7, Simulation::SaveRecIn7

```
Simulation::SaveIn7(const sFilename);
Simulation::SaveRecIn7(const sFilename);
    sFilename               in:  destination file name
```

*Return value*

Returns TRUE if results were saved.

*Description*

Saves simulation results to the named file.

SaveIn7   stores the test and coefficient values.

SaveRecIn7 stores: coefficients, MCSE, Bias, RMSE, test critical values (right tail), rejection frequencies and moments.

# Simulation::SetCoefNames, Simulation::SetTestNames

```
Simulation::SetCoefNames(const asNames);
Simulation::SetTestNames(const asNames);
    asNames     in:  SetCoefNames: array with s_c names
                     SetTestNames: array with s_t names
```
*No return value.*

*Description*

Installs the names of tests statistics and coefficients, to make the report more readable.

## Simulation::SetPlotRep, SetRecursive, SetStore

```
Simulation::SetPlotRep(const iPlotRep);
Simulation::SetRecursive(const bRecursive);
Simulation::SetStore(const bStore);
```

| | | |
|---|---|---|
| iPlotRep | in: | call `Plot()` every `iPlotRep` replications (default is 0) |
| bRecursive | in: | int, TRUE: do recursive Monte Carlo (default is FALSE) |
| bStore | in: | int, store results of all replications for later access (default is FALSE) |

*No return value.*

## Simulation::Simulate

```
Simulation::Simulate()
```

*No return value.*

*Description*

This is the core function.  It runs the Monte Carlo experiment, and prints the results.

## Simulation::Simulation

```
Simulation::Simulation(const mT, const mxT, const cRep,
    const fCommon, const dSeed, const mPvalue, const mTrueParam);
```

| | | |
|---|---|---|
| mT | in: | $1 \times r$ matrix of sample sizes |
| mxT | in: | int, maximum sample size |
| cRep | in: | int, number of replications |
| fCommon | in: | 1: reset seed for each experiment; else 0 |
| dSeed | in: | double, resets seed to `dSeed` if `fCommon` == TRUE |
| mPvalue | in: | $1 \times s_p$ matrix with $p$-values to test at, only used if `GetPvalues` returns $p$-values |
| mTrueParam | in: | $1 \times s_c$ matrix with true parameters, only used if `GetCoefficients` returns coefficients |

*No return value.*

*Description*

Constructor function. The `mT`, `mPvalue`, and `mTrueParam` arguments are automatically changed to a row vector when they are a column vector on input.

# Chapter 13

# Language reference

## 13.1 Introduction

The Ox syntax is formalized in a fashion similar to Kernighan and Ritchie (1988) and Stroustrup (1997). These two books describe the C and C++ languages on which the Ox language is modelled (although the object-oriented features in Ox are closer to those of Java than C++).

As an example, consider the syntax of `enum` declaration statements:

> `enum {` *enumerator-list* `} ;`
>
> *enumerator-list:*
>> *enumerator*
>> *enumerator-list* `,` *enumerator*
>
> *enumerator:*
>> *identifier*
>> *identifier* = *int-constant-expression*

Symbols which have to be typed literally are given in `typewriter` font; these are called terminal symbols. *Italic* symbols are non-terminal, and require further definition. Ultimately, the whole syntax can be reduced to terminal statements. The subscript $_{opt}$ denotes an optional element. In this example, *identifier* and *int-constant-expression* remain as yet undefined. An *enumerator-list* is defined recursively: consisting of one or more enumerators, separated by columns. This can be visualized as follows:

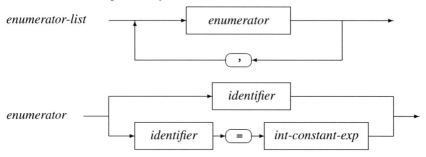

394

# 13.2 Lexical conventions

### 13.2.1 Tokens

The first action of a compiler is to divide the source code into units it can understand, so-called tokens. There are four kinds of tokens: identifiers, keywords, constants (also called literals) and operators. White space (newlines, formfeeds, tabs, comments) is ignored, but can serve to separate tokens.

### 13.2.2 Comment

Anything between /* and */ is considered comment. This comment *can* be nested (unlike C and C++). Everything following // up to the end of the line is also comment, but is ignored inside /* ... */ type comment. So nested comment is possible:

```
one = cons + 1;        // comment
/* two = cons + 1;     // comment
*/
```
This is also legal:

```
two = cons + 1;    /* comment /* nested comment */ */
```
Note that code can also be removed using preprocessor statements, see §13.9.4.

# 13.3 Identifiers

Identifiers are made up of letters and digits. The first character must be a letter. Underscores (_) count as a letter. Valid names are CONS, cons, cons_1, _a_1_b, etc. Invalid are #CONS, 1_CONS, log(X), etc. Ox is case sensitive, so CONS and cons are different identifiers. It is better not to use identifiers with a leading underscore, as several compilers use these for internal names. The maximum length of an identifier is 60 characters; additional characters are ignored.

### 13.3.1 Keywords

The following keywords are reserved:

*keyword:* one of

| | | | | |
|---|---|---|---|---|
| array | default | goto | private | switch |
| break | delete | if | protected | switch_single |
| case | do | inline | public | this |
| char | double | int | return | virtual |
| class | else | matrix | short | while |
| const | enum | namespace | static | |
| continue | extern | new | string | |
| decl | for | operator | struct | |

### 13.3.2 Constants

Arithmetic types, string type and array type (see §13.4.1) have corresponding constants.

> *constant:*
> > *scalar-constant:*
> > > *int-constant*
> > > *double-constant*
> > *vector-constant:*
> > > *matrix-constant*
> > *string-constant*
> > *array-constant*

#### 13.3.2.1 Integer constants

A sequence of digits is an integer constant. A hexadecimal constant is a sequence of digits and the letters A to F or a to f, prefixed by 0x or 0X. Examples are:

```
1236
0x1a        (26 decimal)
0xFF        (255 decimal)
0xffffffff  (–1 decimal using 32 bit integers)
```

#### 13.3.2.2 Character constants

Character constants are interpreted as an integer constant. A character constant is an integer constant consisting of a single character enclosed in single quotes (e.g. 'a' and '0') or an escape sequence enclosed in single quotes.

*escape-sequence:* one of

| | | | |
|---|---|---|---|
| \" | double quote (") | \' | single quote (') |
| \0 | null character | \\ | backslash (\) |
| \a | alert (bel) | \b | backspace |
| \f | formfeed | \n | newline |
| \r | carriage return | \t | horizontal tab |
| \v | vertical tab | \x*hh* | hexadecimal number (*hh*) |

So '\n' is the integer constant corresponding to the newline character. On most systems the newline character has decimal value 10, and in that case could also be written as '\x0A' or '\x0a', but not '\X0a'.

#### 13.3.2.3 Double constants

A double constant consists of an integer part, a decimal point, a fraction part, an e, E, d or D and an optionally signed integer exponent. Either the integer or the fraction part may be missing (not both); either the decimal point or the full exponent may be missing (not both). A hexadecimal double constant is written as 0x.*hhhhhhhhhhhhhhhh*. The format used is an 8 byte IEEE real. The hexadecimal string is written with the most significant byte first (the sign and exponent are on the left). If any hexadecimal digits are missing, the string is left padded with 0's. Examples of correct double constants:

| | | | |
|---|---|---|---|
| `0.` | | `1.2` | |
| `.5` | | `-.5e-10` | |
| `2.1E-112` | | `1D-1` | (0.1) |
| `1E1` | (10.0) | `0x.7FF0000000000000` | (infinity) |
| `0x.3ff0000000000000` | (1) | `0x.3fb999999999999a` | (−0.1) |

The last example shows that most numbers which can be expressed exactly in decimal notation, cannot be represented exactly on the computer.

Double constants in an external declaration (see §13.5.3) may use a dot to represent a missing values. This sets the variable to `.NaN` (Not a Number).

### 13.3.2.4 Matrix constants

A matrix constant lists within < and > the elements of the matrix, row by row. Each row is delimited by a semicolon, successive elements in a row are separated by a comma. For example:

```
< 00, 01, 02; 10, 11, 12 >
< 0.0, 0.1, 0.2 >
< 1100 >
```

which are respectively a $2 \times 3$ matrix, a $1 \times 3$ matrix and a $1 \times 1$ matrix:

$$\begin{pmatrix} 00 & 01 & 02 \\ 10 & 11 & 12 \end{pmatrix} \quad \begin{pmatrix} 0.0 & 0.1 & 0.2 \end{pmatrix} \quad \begin{pmatrix} 1100 \end{pmatrix}$$

Elements in a matrix constant can be specified as:

> *matrix element:*
> > *constant-expression*
> > *constant-expression* : *constant-expression*
> > *constant-expression* : [ *constant-expression* ]
> > > *constant-expression*
> > [ *constant-expression* ] [ *constant-expression* ] =
> > > *constant-expression*
> > [ *constant-expression* ] *
> > > *constant-expression*

The constant expressions must evaluate to an integer or a double. The index of each row is one higher than the previous row. Within each row, the column index of an element is one higher than that created with the previous element in the same row.

We have seen examples of the first element type. The second specifies an integer range, e.g. `2:5` corresponds to `2,3,4,5`. The range may decrease, so that `5.3:2.8` corresponds to `5.3,4.3,3.3`. It is also possible to specify a step size as in `2:[2]8`, which gives `2,4,6,8`. The third form sets a specific element in the matrix (which overrides the location implicit in the position of the element in the matrix constant).

Note that the top left element is [0][0], the second element in the first row [0][1], etc. Consider for example:

$$\begin{pmatrix} 1 & 2 & 3 \\ 4 & 5 & 6 \\ 7 & 8 & 9 \end{pmatrix} \quad \text{indexed as} \quad \begin{matrix} [0][0] & [0][1] & [0][2] \\ [1][0] & [1][1] & [1][2] \\ [2][0] & [2][1] & [2][2] \end{matrix}$$

Finally, it is possible to specify a number of identical elements, e.g. [3]*0 corresponds to 0,0,0. Unspecified elements are set to zero.

As an example involving all types, consider:

```
< [4]*1,2; 10,11,14-2; 1:4; [3][4]=99,2;8:[-2-1]2 >
```

The 2 in the first row will be in column 4, as columns 3 was the last created previously. The 2 in the penultimate row gets column 5. The last specified row is equivalent to 8:[-3]2. The result is:

$$\begin{pmatrix} 1 & 1 & 1 & 1 & 2 & 0 \\ 10 & 11 & 12 & 0 & 0 & 0 \\ 1 & 2 & 3 & 4 & 0 & 0 \\ 0 & 0 & 0 & 0 & 99 & 2 \\ 8 & 5 & 2 & 0 & 0 & 0 \end{pmatrix}$$

Further examples are given in §13.5.3.

Missing values in a matrix constant could be represented with a dot, or .NaN which represents NaN (Not a Number), e.g.: < .,2,3; 4,.,6 > Similarly, .Inf represents infinity.

An empty matrix can be written as: <>

### 13.3.2.5 String constants

A string constant is a text enclosed in double quotes. Adjacent string constants are concatenated. A null character is always appended to indicate the end of a string. The maximum length of a string constant is 1024 characters. Escape sequences can be used to represent special characters, as in §13.3.2.2. At least one and at most two hexadecimal digits must be given for the hexadecimal escape sequence. A single quote need not be escaped. Some examples of string constants:

```
"a simple string"
"two strings" " joined together"
"with double quote \" and a newline character:\n"
"three ways to include a tab: \t, \x9 and \x09"
"use \\ to include a backslash,e.g. c:\\ox\\include"
```

### 13.3.2.6 Array constants

An array constant is a list of constants in braces, separated by a comma. This is a recursive definition, because the constant can itself be an array constant. The terminating level consists of non-array constants. Each level of array constants creates an array of references. An empty array is written as {}. For example:

```
{ "tinker", "tailor", "soldier" }
{{ "tinker", "tailor"}, {"soldier"} }
```

The first creates an array of three references to strings, the second an array of two references, the first references an array of two references to strings, the second to an array of one reference to the word soldier:

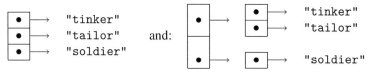

Remember that { "tinker" "tailor" "soldier" } is identical to an array consisting of one string: { "tinkertailorsoldier" }.

# 13.4 Objects

### 13.4.1 Types

Variables in Ox are implicitly typed, and can change type during their lifetime. The life of a variable corresponds to the level of its declaration. Its scope is the section of the program in which it can be seen. Scope and life do not have to coincide.

There are three basic types and four derived types. The integer type int is a signed integer. The double precision floating point type is called double. A matrix is a two-dimensional array of doubles which can be manipulated as a whole. A string-type holds a string, while an array-type is an array of references.

| | |
|---:|:---|
| *arithmetic-type:* | int, double, matrix |
| *string-type:* | string |
| *scalar-type:* | int, double |
| *vector-type:* | string, matrix |
| *derived-type:* | array, function, class, reference to class object |

#### 13.4.1.1 Type conversion

When a double is converted to an int, the fractional part is discarded; if the resulting value cannot be represented, the behaviour is undefined. When an int is converted to a double, the nearest representation will be used. For example, conversion to int of 1.3 and 1.7 will be 1 on both occasions. Explicit type conversion is discussed in §13.8.2.3.

A single element of a string (a character) is of type int. An int or double can be assigned to a string element, which first results in conversion to int, and then to a single byte character.

### 13.4.2 Lvalue

An lvalue is an object to which an assignment can be made.

### 13.4.3 Scope

Variables declared at the start of a statement block have scope and life restricted to the block. These variables are called automatic: they are created and initialized whenever the block is entered, and removed as soon as the block is exited. Variables declared outside any statement block have global scope and life; these are called static. Note that Ox assignment of arithmetic types and string type implies copying over the contents from the right-hand side to the left-hand side. Automatic variables of any type can be assigned to variables with broader scope.

# 13.5 External declarations

> *external-declaration:*
>> enum { *enumerator-list* } ; $_{opt}$
>> *specifier*$_{opt}$ const$_{opt}$ decl *ext-variable-decl-list* ;
>> *specifier*$_{opt}$ *function-declaration* ;
>> *specifier*$_{opt}$ *function-definition*
>> inline$_{opt}$ *function-definition*
>> inline$_{opt}$ *member-function-definition*
>> *class-specifier* ; $_{opt}$

An Ox program consists of a sequence of external declarations. These either reserve storage for an object, or serve to inform of the existence of objects created elsewhere. Each program must define one function called main, where execution of the program will start.

### 13.5.1 Enumerations

> enum { *enumerator-list* } ; $_{opt}$
> *enumerator-list:*
>> *enumerator*
>> *enumerator-list* , *enumerator*
> *enumerator:*
>> *identifier*
>> *identifier* = *int-constant-expression*

An enumeration defines a list of integer constants. They provide a convenient way of centralizing parameters which have a constant value. Members of an enumeration cannot be assigned to, but can occur in a constant expression. By default, the first member will have value 0, and each successive member will have a value of one plus that of the previous member. The value of a member can be set by assigning it a constant integer value. The names of enumerators cannot coincide with names of other objects in the same scope (but a previously defined scalar constant may be redefined, as long as it is set to the same value). Enumerator names only exist in the file in which they occur. Enumerations should be placed in header files if they need to be shared between several source files.

Here are some examples with corresponding values:

```
enum { C_FIRST, C_SECOND, C_THIRD };                 // 0,1,2
enum { T_INT, T_DBL=2, T_STR, T_MAT=C_THIRD };       // 0,2,3,2
enum { FLAG0,FLAG1, FLAG2=FLAG1*2, FLAG3=FLAG2*2};   //0,1,2,4
enum { T_ERR = 1.0 } ;                               // error
```

### 13.5.2 Specifiers

*specifier:* one of
static
extern

The static specifier restricts the scope of the declared object to the remainder of the file. Although it will exist throughout the program's life, it cannot be seen from other files. In classes (§13.5.6), the static keyword is used with a different meaning. The extern specifier informs the remainder of the file that the object can be accessed, although defined (created) in another file. The extern and static specifiers are mutually exclusive. External declarations are most conveniently placed in header files.

### 13.5.3 External variable declarations

*specifier*$_{opt}$ const$_{opt}$ decl *ext-variable-decl-list* ;

*ext-variable-decl-list:*
    *ext-init-declarator*
    *ext-variable-decl-list , ext-init-declarator*

*ext-init-declarator:*
    *identifier*
    *identifier = constant-expression*
    *mat-identifier*
    *mat-identifier = int-constant-expression*

*mat-identifier:*
    *identifier* [ *int-constant-expression* ] [ *int-constant-expression* ]

The static or extern specifier and the const qualifier preceding an external variable declaration list applies to all variables in the list. Each identifier creates space for an object with global lifetime, unless declared extern or const.

A const object must be initialized (unless declared extern) but its value may not be changed thereafter. Unless declared extern, a const object cannot be accessed from other files. If of scalar type (see §13.4.1), a const can appear in a constant-expression.

At the external level of declarations, as treated here, it is possible to specify a matrix size, and initialize that matrix to zero. If an external variable is created without explicit value and without dimensions, it will default to an int with value 0. Here are some examples:

```
decl a, b;                          // default to type int, value 0
enum { AAP, NOOT, MIES, WIM };
const decl ia = NOOT, ib = NOOT + WIM;            // type: int
const decl ma = < NOOT, AAP; 0, 1 >;         // type: matrix
const decl aa = {"tinker", "tailor"};         // type: array
decl id = ia * (WIM - 1) * MIES + ib;         // type: int
decl da = ia + 0.;                           // type: double
decl mb = <0:3; 4:7; 8:11>;                  // type: matrix
decl ab = { ma, ma};                          // type: array
extern decl elsewhere;              // defined in other file

decl mc[3][3] = 1.5;         // 3 x 3 matrix with values 1.5
decl md[2][1];               // 2 x 1 matrix of zeros

enum { ZUS = id };           // error: id is not const
decl ih = id;                // error: id is not const
decl ia;                     // error: already defined
```

### 13.5.4 Function declarations

> *specifier$_{opt}$ function-declaration ;*
> extern *string-constant function-declaration ;*
> *function-declaration:*
>> *identifier ( argument-type-list$_{opt}$ )*
> *argument-type-list:*
>> *argument-list ,  . . .*
> *argument-list:*
>> *argument*
>> *argument-list , argument*
> *argument:*
>> const$_{opt}$ *identifier*

A function declaration communicates the number of arguments and their types to a file, so that the function can be called correctly from that file. The actual creation of the function is done through a function definition (which at the same time declares the function). A function can be declared many times, but type and number of arguments must always be identical:

```
test0();                     // function takes no arguments
test1(const a1);                   // one const argument
test2(const a2, a3);         // two arguments, first is const
static test3(a1);            // cannot be used outside this file
extern test4(a1);            // function defined outside this file
print(a1, ...);              // variable number of arguments
test1(a1);         // error: previous declaration was different
```

The second form, which uses `extern` *string-constant*, provides dynamic linking of extension functions (which could be written in C, FORTRAN, etc.; creation of dynamic link libraries is platform dependent). In the following example, `test5` corresponds to the external function `MyCFunc()`, located in the dynamic library `mydll`.[1] When the Ox program is linked, `mydll` will be automatically loaded, and the function imported.

```
extern "mydll,MyCFunc" test5(a1);
```

### 13.5.5 Function definitions

>*specifier*<sub>opt</sub> *function-definition*
>`inline`<sub>opt</sub> *function-definition*
>*function-definition:*
>        *identifier* ( *argument-type-list*<sub>opt</sub> ) *compound-statement*

A function definition specifies the function header and body, and declares the function so that it can be used in the remainder of the file. A function can be declared many times, but defined only once.

The use of `const` is recommended: arguments declared `const` can be referenced, but cannot be changed inside the function. If the argument is a `const` reference, the reference cannot be changed, but what it references can. The `decl` keyword is optional in front of an argument. An empty argument list indicates that the function takes no arguments at all. The ... indicates a variable number of arguments; it must have the last position in the header, but cannot be the first.

```
test1(const a1);                    // declaration of test1
print(a1, ...);             // variable number of arguments
test2(const a1, a2)                  // definition of test2
{
    test1(a2);                        // call function test1
    print(a1, 1, 2, "\n");          // at least one argument
    test1(a2, 1);       // error: wrong number of arguments
    a2 = 1;                            // a2 may be changed
    a1 = 1;                          // error: a1 is const
    /* ... */
}
```

All function arguments are passed by value. This means that a copy of the actual object is made. For int, double, matrix and string types the whole object is copied. Any

---

[1]The 64-bit version will try to load `mydll_64` first, then try `mydll`; the appropriate extension is appended automatically. The following table lists the defaults that are searched first (thus allowing the folder structure to be shared between platforms):

| | |
|---|---|
| `mydll.dll` | Windows 32-bit |
| `mydll_64.dll` | Windows 64-bit |
| `mydll.so` | Linux 32-bit |
| `mydll_64.so` | Linux 64-bit |
| `mydll_osx.so` | OS X 32-bit |
| `mydll_sparc.so` | Solaris on Sparc, 32-bit |
| `mydll_sunx86.so` | Solaris on x86, 32-bit |

changes to the copy are lost as soon as the function returns. Derived types (see §13.4.1) are accessed through a reference, and that reference is passed by value. However, what is referenced may be changed, and that change will remain in effect after function return. So passing references allows a function to make a permanent change to a variable, for examples see §13.8.2.2. It is good practice to label an argument const if a function doesn't change the variable. This increases program clarity and enables the compiler to generate more efficient code (i.e. it avoids the need for the internal code to make a copy).

### 13.5.5.1 Returning a value

All functions may have a return value, but this return value need not be used by the caller. *If a function does not return a value, its actual return value is undefined.*

The return statement returns a value from the function, *and also exits the function*. So, when the program flow reaches a return statement, control returns to the caller, without executing the remainder of the function. The syntax of the return statement is:

        return *return_value* ;

Or, to exit from a function which does not have a return value:

        return;

The following example illustrates the use of return:

```
threes(const r, const c)                // definition of threes
{
    return constant(3, r, c);
}
otherfunc()
{
    println(threes(2, 2));
}
```

Multiple returns can be implemented through the multiple assignment statement, see §13.8.1.1:

```
func(const r, const c)                  // definition of threes
{
    return {zeros(r,c), ones(r,c)};     // array with 2 elements
}
otherfunc()
{
    decl x1, x2;
    [x1, x2] = func(3, 3);//get element [0] in x1 and [1] in x2
}
```

### 13.5.5.2 Variable length argument list

A special library function va_arglist() is used to access arguments in the variable argument list. It returns the arguments supplied for the ellipse as an array. An example illustrates:

```
test(const a, ...)
{
    decl i, args = va_arglist();

    for (i = 0; i < sizeof(args); i++)
        print (" vararg ", i, ": ", args[i]);
}
main()
{
    test("tinker", "tailor", "soldier");
}
```

which prints `vararg 0:   tailor vararg 1:   soldier`.

### 13.5.5.3 Inline function definitions

A function can be defined as `inline`. This instructs the compiler to expand the function body wherever it is called, and tends to be used for very small functions. The compiler may ignore the `inline` instruction. Inline functions can only be defined, not declared. If an inline function is to be shared accross several files, the whole definition must be put in a header file.

### 13.5.6 Classes

A class is a collection of data objects combined with functions operating on those objects. Access to data members from outside the class is through member functions: only member functions can access data directly (at least, that is the default, see §13.5.7.2 below). So by default, all data members are protected, and all function members public, using C++ parlance.

*class-specifier* ; *opt*

*class-specifier:*
        class *identifier base-class*$_{opt}$ { *member-list* }
        struct *identifier base-class*$_{opt}$ { *member-list* }

*base-class:*
        : *identifier*

*member-list:*
        *member*
        *member-list member*
        public:
            *member-list member*
        protected:
            *member-list member*

*member:*
        static$_{opt}$ decl *member-variable-decl-list* ;
        const$_{opt}$ decl *member-variable-decl-list* ;
        static const decl *ext-variable-decl-list* ;
        static$_{opt}$ *function-declaration* ;
        virtual$_{opt}$ *function-declaration* ;
        enum { *enumerator-list* } ; *opt*

*member-variable-decl-list:*
        *identifier*
        *member-variable-decl-list , identifier*

Consider a simple line class, which supports drawing lines from the current cursor position to the next, and moving the cursor:

```
class Line                           // Line is the class name
{
    decl m_x, m_y;                       // two data members
    const decl m_origin;              // const data member
    static decl sm_cLines;          // static data member
    Line(const orig);                      // constructor
    moveto(const x, const y);              // move cursor
    lineto(const x, const y);    // draw line and move cursor
    static getcLines();                // static function
    static setcLines(c);               // static function
public:
    static const decl M_CONST = 1;    // value must be set here
    enum { M_AA, M_BB = -1};
};                            // ; is optional in Ox (unlike C++)
```

All member names within a class must be unique. A class declaration introduces a type, and can be shared between source files through inclusion in header files. Ox accesses an object through a reference to the object which is created using the new operator.

Data members that are static const must be initialized in the class declaration. Data members that are not static but are const can only be initialized in the constructor function, see §13.5.7.1. Otherwise data members can be initialized in the constructor function, or anywhere else they are accessible.

Enumerations of constants can be defined within the class through the enum keyword (§13.5.3). Constants defined through enum behave the same as static const decl member variables. In the example above, the public keyword means that M_CONST, M_AA and M_BB can be accessed from outside the class as Line::M_CONST, etc.

### 13.5.7 Member function definitions

inline*opt* *member-function-definition*

*member-function-definition:*
>        *identifier* :: *identifier* (*argument-type-list*<sub>opt</sub>) *compound-statement*

A member function provides access to data members of an object. It is defined as its class name, followed by :: and the function name. The function name must have been declared in the class. Member functions cannot be declared outside a class; the class declaration contains the member function declaration. Only a member function can use data members of its own class directly.

Here are the definitions of the member functions of class Line:

```
Line::Line(const orig)
{
    m_x = m_y = orig;               // set cursor at the origin
    m_origin = orig;                // only allowed in constructor
    sm_cLines++;                    // count number of Line objects
}
Line::moveto(const x, const y)
{
    m_x = x;   m_y = y;
    println("moved to ", x, " ", y);
    return this;
}
Line::lineto(const x, const y)
{
                        // draw the line from (x,y) to (ax,ay) ...
    m_x = x;   m_y = y;
    println("line to ", x, " ", y);
    return this;
}
```

The new operator creates an object of the specified class, calls the constructor function, and returns a reference to it. A member function is called through a member reference, which is a class object name followed by -> or a dot. For example:

```
decl lineobj;
lineobj = new Line(0);                        // create object and
                                              // set cursor to (0,0)
lineobj.lineto(10, 10);             // draw line to (10, 10)
lineobj->Line::lineto(10, 10);             // same call
lineobj::lineto(10, 10);            // error, needs -> or .
```

```
    delete lineobj;          // delete object from memory when done
```
Since `lineobj` is of class `Line`, both calls to `lineto` are to the same function. The only difference is one of efficiency. Ox has implicit typing, so can only know the class of `lineobj` at run time. In the second case the class is specified, and the function address can be resolved at compile time.

### 13.5.7.1 Constructor and destructor functions

The member function with the same name as the class is called the constructor, and is automatically invoked when creating an object of the class. If the constructor function is absent, a default constructor function will be assumed which takes no arguments. A constructor may not be static. A constructor always returns a reference to the object for which it was called and may not specify a return value. Only the constructor function may set `const` data members. In the `Line` class, the origin is only set during construction, and not thereafter. However, each `Line` object has its own origin (unless origin is made `static`).

A destructor is called after a request to delete an object, and before the object is actually removed. It may be used to clear up any allocated objects inside the object to be deleted. A destructor function has the same name as the class, is prefixed by ~, and may neither take arguments, nor return a value. It does however receive the `this` reference.

```
    class Line
    {   /* ... */
        Line(const orig);                        // constructor
        ~Line();                                 // destructor
        /* ... */
    };
    test()
    {
        decl lineobj;

        lineobj = new Line(0);     //create object, call constructor
        delete lineobj;            // call destructor, delete object
    }
```

### 13.5.7.2 public and protected members, structs

All function members are public and data members are protected by default in a class. This means that function members can be called from anywhere by accessing an object, while data members can only be accessed from inside a class or derived class:

```
    class Line
    {   /* ... */
        decl m_x;
        Func();
    };
    Line::Func()
```

```
{
    m_x = 0;                  // can access data member from inside
}
test()
{
    decl lineobj = new Line(0);
    lineobj.Func();           // can access function member
    lineobj.m_x = 1;          // error: cannot access data member
}
```

A struct differs from a class only in that *all members are public*. So, if in the above example we would have used struct Line, then the last line (lineobj.m_x = 1) would have been allowed.

More fine-grained control is available using the public and protected specifiers: some variables can be made accessible, and others not. The following code illustrates:

```
class Line
{   /* ... */
public:
    decl m_x;
    decl m_y;
protected:
    decl m_z;
    Func();
};
test()
{
    decl lineobj = new Line(0);
    lineobj.Func();               // can access function member
    lineobj.m_y = 1;              // OK: m_y is public
    lineobj.m_z = 1;              // error: m_z is protected
}
```

Note, however, that in Ox, the addition of public and protected only applies to variables. Functions remain public.

### 13.5.7.3 The this reference and member scope

All non-static member functions receive a hidden argument called this, which points to the object for which the function is called. So the constructor function Line obtains in this a reference to the newly created object. The assignment to m_x and m_y refer to the members of the this object. When accessing a variable in a member function, it is determined first whether the function is a local variable or an argument. Next it is considered as a member of this. If all these fail, it is considered as a global variable. So local variables and arguments hide members, together these hide global variables. The following example shows how the scope resolution operator :: may be used to resolve conflicts:

```
decl x, y;                            // global variables
extern moveto(x, y);                  // external function

Line::moveto(const x, const y)
```

```
    {
        ::x = x;            // assign arguments to global variables
        ::y = y;
        this.m_x = x;           // assign arguments to data members
        this.m_y = y;       // this. needed if these were als x and y

        ::moveto(x, y);              // call non-member function
        moveto(x, y);            // error: call to itself will
    }                                 // cause infinite loop
```

### 13.5.7.4 Static members

There is only one copy of a static member, shared by all objects of a class. A static member may not have the same name as the class it is in. A static member function can only make direct access to static data members.

```
Line::getcLines()
{   return sm_cLines;
}
Line::setcLines(c)
{   sm_cLines = c;
    m_x = 0;                 // error: must be static member
    lineto(1, 1);            // error: must be static member
}
```

A static member function can be called directly, and indirectly:

```
Line::setcLines(0);                       // no Line objects yet
lineobj = new Line(0);                        // create object
lineobj2 = new Line(3);               // create another object
i = Line::getcLines();                             // i = 2
i = lineobj.getcLines();                           // i = 2
i = lineobj2.getcLines();                          // i = 2
Line::moveto(0, 0);            // error: function is not static
Line.getcLines();                      // error, needs ::
```

Since there is only one instance of the static function, in all cases the same `getcLines` function is called (assuming both `lineobj` and `lineobj2` are an object of class Line).

### 13.5.7.5 Derived classes

A class may derive from a previously declared class. A derived class will inherit all members from its base class, and can access these inherited members as its own members. However, if the derived class has members with the same name as members of the base class, the former take precedence. In this way, a class can redefine functionality of its base class. If a function is redefined, the base class name followed by : : may be used to refer to the base class function.

Deriving from the Line class:

```
class Angle : Line               // Line is the base class
{
    Angle();                               // constructor
    lineto(const x, const y);     // draw dash, move cursor
```

```
};
Angle::Angle()
{
    Line(0);                                    // starts at zero
}
Angle::lineto(const x, const y)
{
    Line::lineto(x, m_y);                       // horizontal line
    Line::lineto(x, y);                         // vertical line
    print("is angle to ", x, " ", y, "\n");
    moveto(x, y);
}
```

Angle's constructor just calls the base class constructor, as the body may be read as this.Line(0);. Note that the base class constructor and destructor functions are *not* called automatically (unlike in C++). In the new lineto object, Line::lineto is used to make sure that we call the correct function (otherwise it would make a recursive call). For the moveto that is no problem, moveto calls the base function, as it was not redefined in the Angle class. Non-static member functions may be declared as virtual (that is, they can be redefined by a derived class), this is discussed in the next section.

New classes may be derived from a class which is itself derived, but Ox only supports single inheritance: a class can only derive from one other class at a time.

### 13.5.7.6 Virtual functions

Virtual functions allow a derived class to supply a new version of the virtual function in the derived class, replacing the version of the base class. When the base class calls the virtual function, it will actually use the function of the derived class. For a virtual function, the call can only be resolved at run time. Then, the object type is known, and the called function is the one first found in the object, when moving from the highest class towards the base class. The effect of using virtual functions is most easily explained by the following example.

```
#include <oxstd.h>
class Base
{
    basefunc();
    virtual vfunc();
};
Base::basefunc()
{
    vfunc();                                    // call the virtual function
}
Base::vfunc()
{   print("Base vfunc()\n");
}

class Derived : Base
{
    derfunc();
```

```
        vfunc();
    };
    Derived::derfunc()
    {
        this.Base::basefunc();
        Base::basefunc();
        basefunc();                         // three equivalent calls
    }
    Derived::vfunc()
    {   print("Derived vfunc()\n");
    }

    main()
    {
        decl obj = new Derived();
        obj.basefunc();
        obj.derfunc();
    }
```

The output is:

```
Derived vfunc()
Derived vfunc()
Derived vfunc()
Derived vfunc()
```

Even though Base has its own vfunc(), the derived class provides a new version of this function. This is used whenever Basefunc() is called for an object of class Derived. Were we to remove the virtual keyword, the output would be four times Base vfunc(). If we replace vfunc() with Base::vfunc() inside Base::basefunc, the result would also be four times vfunc() from Base.

# 13.6 Namespace

> namespace *identifier*
> {
>        *external-declaration*
> }

A namespace surrounds a section of external declarations, separating it from functions and variables in other namespaces, or from those outside the namespace. If the namespace is called ns, then identifiers inside the namespace are first resolved within that namespace, and then in the unnamed space. From another namespace, access is by prefix ns::.

Namespaces in Ox cannot be nested, and unnamed namespaces are unsupported.

```
foo()
{
    println("foo");
}
bar()
```

```
{
    println("bar");
}
namespace test
{
bar()
{
    println("test::bar");
}
foo()
{
    println("in test::foo");
    bar();      // calls test::bar
    ::bar();    // calls bar
}
}   // end of namespace
main()
{
    println("calling ::foo");
    foo();
    println("calling test::foo");
    test::foo();
}
```

which prints:

```
calling ::foo
in foo
calling test::foo
in test::foo
in test::bar
in bar
```

## 13.7 Statements

> *statement-list:*
>> *statement*
>> *statement-list statement*
>
> *statement:*
>> *labelled-statement*
>> *expression-statement*
>> *compound-statement*
>> *selection-statement*
>> *switch-statement*
>> *iteration-statement*
>> *jump-statement*
>> *declaration-statement*
>
> *expression-statement:*
>> *expression*$_{opt}$ ;
>
> *compound-statement:*
>> { *statement-list*$_{opt}$ }
>
> *labelled-statement:*
>> : *label statement*

The executable part of a program consists of a sequence of statements. Expression statements are expressions or function calls. It can be a do-nothing expression, as in:

```
for (i = 0; i < 10; i++)
    ;
```

A compound statement groups statements together in a block, e.g.:

```
for (i = 0; i < 10; i++)
{
    a = test(b);
    b = b + 10;
}
```

A statement can be prefixed by a label as in:

```
:L001
    for (i = 0; i < 10; i++)
        ;
```

Labels are the targets of `goto` statements (see §13.7.4); labels are local to a function and have separate name spaces (which means that variables and labels may have the same name). Note that labels are defined in a non-standard way: the colon is prefixed, rather than suffixed as in C or C++.

### 13.7.1 Selection statements

> *selection-statement:*
> > `if` ( *expression* ) *statement*
> > `if` ( *expression* ) *statement* `else` *statement*

The conditional expression in an `if` statement is evaluated, and if it evaluates to true (*for a matrix: no element evaluates to false*), the statement is executed. Zero (0), the empty matrix (`<>`) and a missing value (`.NaN`) all evaluate to false. The conditional expression may not be a declaration statement. Some examples for the `if` statement:

```
if (i == 0)
    i++;                              // do only if i equals 0

if (i >= 0)
    i = 1;                            // do only if i >= 0
else
    i = 0;                            // set negative i to 0

if (i == 0)
    if (k > 0)
        j = 1;                    // do only if i != 0 and k > 0
    else                      // this else matches the inner if
        j = -1;               // do only if i != 0 and k <= 0

if (i == 0)
{   if (k > 0)
        j = 1;                    // do only if i != 0 and k > 0
}
else                      // this else matches the outer if
    j = -1;                       // do only if i != 0
```

Each `else` part matches the closest previous `if`, but this can be changed by using braces. When coding nested `if`s, it is advisable to use braces to make the program more readable and avoid potential mistakes.

Further examples involving matrices are given in §13.8.9.

### 13.7.2 Switch statements

> *switch-statement:*
> > `switch` ( *expression* ) { *case-list default$_{opt}$* }
> > `switch_single` ( *expression* ) { *case-list default$_{opt}$* }
>
> *case-list:*
> > *case*
> > *case-list case*
>
> *case:*
> > `case` *expression* : *statement-list*
>
> *default:*
> > `default` : *statement-list*

A `switch` statement is a compact way of writing a sequence of `if` statements involving the same variable for comparison:

```
decl i = 1;
switch (i)
{
    case 0:
        println("zero");
        break;
    case 1:
        println("one");
        break;
    default:
        println("not zero, not one");
        break;
}
```

which prints: "one". There is a sequence of `case` blocks, and an optional `default` block, which must be the last. The `break` statement jumps out of the `switch` statement.

Here, the value of `i` is compared to each value in turn, until a comparison is true. Then all the statements for that case *and all subsequent cases* are executed (including the default) until a `break` is encountered. If no case is true, the default statements are executed. So, once inside a case, we automatically fall through to the next case. The advantage is that several cases can be grouped together:

```
switch (i)
{
    case 0:
        println("zero");
        break;
    case 1:
    case 2:
        println("one,two");
        break;
    default:
        println("default");
        break;
}
```

printing one,two when i is 1 or 2.

The drawback is that is easy to forget the `break` statements, and get unexpected results. The following code

```
switch (i)
{
    case 0:
        println("zero");
    case 1:
    case 2:
        println("one or two");
    default:
        println("default");
}
```

will print when i equals zero:

```
zero
one or two
default
```

To emphasize that distinction, and allow for more readable code, Ox also has the switch_single statement. Then, one and only one case (or default) is executed:

```
switch_single (i)
{
    case 0:
        println("zero");
    case 1:
        println("one");
    case 2:
        println("two");
    default:
        println("default");
}
```

### 13.7.3 Iteration statements

*iteration-statement:*
>   while ( *expression* ) *statement*
>   do *statement* while ( *expression* ) ;
>   for ( *expression*$_{opt}$ ; *expression*$_{opt}$ ; *expression*$_{opt}$) *statement*
>   for ( *declaration-statement*$_{opt}$; *expression*$_{opt}$ ; *expression*$_{opt}$) *statement*

The while statement excutes the substatement as long as the test expression is nonzero (for a matrix: all elements are nonzero). The test is performed before the substatement is executed.

The do statement excutes the substatement, then repeats this as long as the test expression is nonzero (for a matrix: all elements are nonzero). The test is performed after the substatement is executed. So for the do statement the substatement is executed one or more times, whereas for the while statement this is zero or more times.

The while and do statements can be envisaged respectively as:

```
:startwhile                      :startdo
    if (expression)                  statement
    {                                if (expression)
        statement                        goto startdo;
        goto startwhile;
    }
```

The for expression:

>   for (*init_expr*; *test_expr* ; *increment_expr*) *statement*

corresponds to:

```
{
    init_expr;
    while (test_expr )
    {
        statement
        increment_expr;
    }
}
```

Note that, when the *init_expr* is a declaration statement, the declaration is local to the for statement.

### 13.7.4 Jump statements

> *jump-statement:*
> break ;
> continue ;
> goto *label*;

A continue statement may only appear within an iteration statement and causes control to pass to the loop-continuation portion of the smallest enclosing iteration statement.

The use of goto should be kept to a minimum, but could be useful to jump out of a nested loop, jump to the end of a routine or when converting Fortran code. It is always possible to rewrite the code such that no gotos are required.

A break statement may only appear within an iteration statement and terminates the smallest enclosing iteration statement.

Two examples:

```
for (i = 0; i < 10; i++)
{
    if (test1(i))
        continue;
    test2();                     // only done if test1(i) returns 0
}
for (i = 0; i < 10; i++)
{
    if (test1(i) == 0)
        break;         // jump out of loop if test1(i) returns 0
    test2();
}
```

### 13.7.5 Declaration statements

*declaration-statement:*
    `decl` *declaration-list* ;

*declaration-list:*
    *init-declaration*
    *declaration-list* , *init-declaration*

*declaration-list:*
    *identifier*
    *identifier* = *expression*

Declarations at the external level were discussed in §13.5. Here we treat declaration within a block. Declaration statements create a variable for further manipulation as long as it stays within scope. The created object is removed as soon as the block in which it was created is exited. Variables can be intitialized in a declaration statement. Variables in Ox are implicitly typed, and their type can change during program execution. Non-externally declared variables must be initialized before they can be used in an expression. It is not possible to specify matrix dimension as can be done at the external level, so instead of `decl ma[3][3] = 1.5` write `decl ma = constant(1.5,3,3)`. Unlike C, declaration statements do not have to occur at the start of a block. Consider for example:

```
test1(arg0)
{
    decl k, a = arg0;
    decl ident = <1, 0; 0, 1>;
    decl identsq = ident * ident;

    print("test\n");

    decl i, j;
    for (i = 0; i < 10; i++)
    {
        test2(i);
        test3(j);                       // error: j has no value
    }
```

Variables declared in an inner block hide variables in the outer block:

```
decl i = 3;                             // external declaration

test2(a)
{
    print(i, "\n");                                             // 3

    {   decl i = 0;
        print(i, "\n");                                        // 0
        if (i == 0)                                       // is true
        {
            decl i = 1;
            print(i, "\n");                                   // 1
```

```
        print(::i, "\n");                              // 3
    }
    decl a;                    // error: conflict with argument
  }
}
```

# 13.8 Expressions

**Table 13.1**   Ox operator precedence.

| Category | operators | associativity |
|---|---|---|
| primary | () :: [] {} | left to right |
| postfix | -> . () [] ++ -- ' | left to right |
| power | ^ .^ | left to right |
| unary | ++ -- + - ! & new delete | right to left |
| multiplicative | ** * .* / ./ | left to right |
| additive | + - | left to right |
| horizontal concatenation | ~ | left to right |
| vertical concatenation | \| | left to right |
| relational | < > <= >= .< .> .<= .>= | left to right |
| equality | == != .== .!= | left to right |
| logical dot-and | .&& | left to right |
| logical-and | && | left to right |
| logical dot-or | .\|\| | left to right |
| logical-or | \|\| | left to right |
| conditional | ? : .? .: | right to left |
| assignment | = *= /= += -= ~= \|= .*= ./= | right to left |
| comma | , | left to right |

Table 13.1 gives a summary if the operators available in Ox, together with their precedence (in order of decreasing precedence) and associativity. The precedence is in decreasing order. Operators on the same line have the same precedence, in which case the associativity gives the order of the operators. Note that the order of evaluation of expressions is not fully specified. In:

    i = a() + b();

it is unknown whether a or b is called first.

Subsections below give a more comprehensive discussion. Several operators require an *lvalue*, which is a region of memory to which an assignment can be made. Note that an object which was declared const is not an lvalue. Many operators require operands of arithmetic type, that is int, double or matrix.

The most common operators are *dot-operators* (operating element-by-element) and relational operators (element by element, but returning a single boolean value). The resulting value is given Tables 13.2 and 13.3 respectively. In addition, there are special matrix operations, such as matrix multiplication and division; the result from these operators is explained below. A scalar consists of: int, double or $1 \times 1$ matrix.

**Table 13.2**  Result from dot operators.

| left $a$ | operator | right $b$ | result | computes |
|---|---|---|---|---|
| int | *op* | int | int | $a \; op \; b$ |
| int/double | *op* | double | double | $a \; op \; b$ |
| double | *op* | int/double | double | $a \; op \; b$ |
| scalar | *op* | matrix $m \times n$ | matrix $m \times n$ | $a \; op \; b_{ij}$ |
| matrix $m \times n$ | *op* | scalar | matrix $m \times n$ | $a_{ij} \; op \; b$ |
| matrix $m \times n$ | *op* | matrix $m \times n$ | matrix $m \times n$ | $a_{ij} \; op \; b_{ij}$ |
| matrix $m \times n$ | *op* | matrix $m \times 1$ | matrix $m \times n$ | $a_{ij} \; op \; b_{i0}$ |
| matrix $m \times n$ | *op* | matrix $1 \times n$ | matrix $m \times n$ | $a_{ij} \; op \; b_{0j}$ |
| matrix $m \times 1$ | *op* | matrix $m \times n$ | matrix $m \times n$ | $a_{i0} \; op \; b_{ij}$ |
| matrix $1 \times n$ | *op* | matrix $m \times n$ | matrix $m \times n$ | $a_{0j} \; op \; b_{ij}$ |
| matrix $m \times 1$ | *op* | matrix $1 \times n$ | matrix $m \times n$ | $a_{i0} \; op \; b_{0j}$ |
| matrix $1 \times n$ | *op* | matrix $m \times 1$ | matrix $m \times n$ | $a_{0j} \; op \; b_{i0}$ |

### 13.8.1 Primary expressions

> *primary-expression:*
> > ( *expression* )
> > [ *assignment-expression-list* ]
> > { *expression-list* }
> > *constant*
> > *identifier*
> > : : *identifier*
> > *class-name* : : *identifier*
> > `this`

An expression in parenthesis is a primary expression. Its main use is to change the order of evaluation, or clarify the expression.

An expression in curly braces creates an array of the comma-separated expressions. All types of constants discussed in §13.3.2 form a primary expression.

The operator : : followed by an identifier references a variable declared externally (see §13.5). Section 13.5.7.3 gives examples. A class name followed by : : and a function member of that class references a static function member, or any function member if preceded by an object reference, see sections 13.5.7.4 and 13.5.7.

The `this` reference is only available inside non-static class member functions, and points to the object for which the function was called.

**Table 13.3**   Result from relational operators.

| left $a$ | operator | right $b$ | result | computes |
|---|---|---|---|---|
| int | $op$ | int | int | $a$ $op$ $b$ |
| int/double | $op$ | double | int | $a$ $op$ $b$ |
| double | $op$ | int/double | int | $a$ $op$ $b$ |
| scalar | $op$ | matrix $m \times n$ | int | $a$ $op$ $b_{ij}$ |
| matrix $m \times n$ | $op$ | scalar | int | $a_{ij}$ $op$ $b$ |
| matrix $m \times n$ | $op$ | matrix $m \times n$ | int | $a_{ij}$ $op$ $b_{ij}$ |
| matrix $m \times n$ | $op$ | matrix $m \times 1$ | int | $a_{ij}$ $op$ $b_{i0}$ |
| matrix $m \times n$ | $op$ | matrix $1 \times n$ | int | $a_{ij}$ $op$ $b_{0j}$ |
| matrix $m \times 1$ | $op$ | matrix $m \times n$ | int | $a_{i0}$ $op$ $b_{ij}$ |
| matrix $1 \times n$ | $op$ | matrix $m \times n$ | int | $a_{0j}$ $op$ $b_{ij}$ |
| string | $op$ | string | int | $a$ $op$ $b$ |

**Table 13.4**   Result from operators involving an empty matrix as argument.

| operator | either argument empty | both arguments empty |
|---|---|---|
| == | FALSE | TRUE |
| != | TRUE | FALSE |
| >= | FALSE | TRUE |
| > | FALSE | FALSE |
| <= | FALSE | TRUE |
| < | FALSE | FALSE |
| other | <> | <> |

### 13.8.1.1 Multiple assignment

A comma-separated list of lvalues in square brackets can be used for multiple assignments. When the right-hand side is an array, each array value in turn is assigned to the next value of the left-hand side. The return value of a multiple assignment expression is zero (the examples below illustrate). When there is one lvalue in the square brackets, the right-hand side need not be an array. Fewer array elements on the right than lvalues on the left leads to a runtime error. The converse is no problem. A multiple assignment expression can be used to implement multiple returns from a function.

The following examples illustrate multiple assignments:

```
decl x1, x2, x3, x4, as;
as = {"a", <10,11>, "b"};
[x1, x2, x3] = as;
println("x1=", x1, " x2=", x2, "x3=", x3);
```

**Table 13.5**  Result from relational operators involving missing values.

| $a$ op $b$ | one of $a, b$ missing | both $a, b$ missing |
|:---:|:---:|:---:|
| == | 0 | 1 |
| <= | 0 | 1 |
| >= | 0 | 1 |
| < | 0 | 0 |
| > | 0 | 0 |
| != | 1 | 0 |

```
[x1] = 10;
[x2, x3] = {11,12,13};
    //[x2, x3, x4] = {11,12};            // error
println("x1=", x1, " x2=", x2, " x3=", x3);

x3 = 10 + ([x1, x2] = as[<0,2>]);
println("x1=", x1, " x2=", x2, " x3=", x3);

x1=<1,2,3,4>;
[x1[0], x1[3]] = {-1, -3};
println("x1=", x1);
```

Which prints:

```
x1=a x2=
      10.000        11.000
x3=b
x1=10 x2=11 x3=12
x1=a x2=b x3=10
x1=
      -1.0000       2.0000       3.0000      -3.0000
```

### 13.8.2 Postfix expressions

> *postfix-expression:*
>> *primary-expression*
>> *postfix-expression* ->
>> *postfix-expression* .
>> *postfix-expression* ( *expression-list$_{opt}$* )
>> *postfix-expression* [ *index-expression$_{opt}$* ]
>> *postfix-expression* ++
>> *postfix-expression* --
>> *postfix-expression* '

    *expression-list:*
       *assignment-expression*
       *expression-list , assignment-expression*

### 13.8.2.1 Member reference

The -> operator selects a member from an object reference (. may also be used). The left-hand expression must evaluate to a reference to an object, the right-hand expression must result in a member of that object. See section 13.5.6.

### 13.8.2.2 Function calls

A function call is a postfix expression consisting of the function name, followed in parenthesis by a possibly empty, comma-separated list of assignment expressions. All argument passing is by value, but when an array is passed, its contents may be changed by the function (unless they are const). The order of evaluation of the arguments is unspecified; all arguments are evaluated before the function is entered. Recursive function calls are allowed. A function must be declared before it can be called, and the number of arguments in the call must coincide with the number in the declaration, unless the declaration has ... as the last argument, see §13.5.4.

    Some examples:

```
func1(a0, a1, a2, a3)
{   print("func1(", a0, ",", a1, ",", a2, ",", a3, ")\n");
}
func2()
{   return 0;
}
func3(a0)
{   a0[0] = 1;
}
test1()
{   decl a, b;

    a = 1;
    func1(a, b = 10, func2(), a != 0);      // func1(1,10,0,1)
    a = func2();                            // a = 0
    func3(&a);                              // a = 1
    func3(a);                               // error
}
```

In the latter example a will have been changed by func3. Function arguments are passed by giving the name of the function:

```
func4(a0, a1)
{   a1(a0);                                 // make function call
}
func5(a0)
{   print("func5(", a0, ")\n");
}
```

```
test2()
{   decl a = func5;

    func4(1, func5);                        // prints "func5(1)"
    func4(1, a);                            // prints "func5(1)"
    func4(1, func5(a));             // error: requires function
    func4(1, func2);            // error: func2 takes incorrect
}                               //         number of arguments
```

Note that the parentheses in func5() indicate that it is a function call, whereas lack of brackets just passes the function itself.


### 13.8.2.3 Explicit type conversion

Explicit type conversion has the same syntax as a function call, using types int, double, matrix and string:

|            | int    | double  | matrix    | string        |
|------------|--------|---------|-----------|---------------|
|            | v=0;   | v=0.6;  | v=<0.6,1>; | v="tinker";  |
| matrix(v)  | < 0 >  | < 0.6 > | $v$       | < 116 >       |
| double(v)  | 0.0    | $v$     | 0.6       | see below     |
| int(v)     | $v$    | 0       | 0         | 116           |

The double to string conversion function and its reverse are for packing string values in a double and subsequently extracting it. This is usually better avoided, as it restricts the string length to eight characters (more flexibility is offered by using arrays of strings). Use the sprint library function to express double (or any other) value as a string.

For example, double("tinker") packs the string in a double value. Since a double is 8 bytes, the string is truncated at 8 characters (or padded by null characters). Conversely, string(dbl) extracts the string from a double value, automatically appending a null character.


### 13.8.2.4 Indexing vector and array types

Vector types (that is, string or matrix) and array types are indexed by postfixing square brackets. A matrix can have one or two indices, a string only one. For an array type it depends on the level of indirection. *Note that indexing always starts at zero.*[2] So a 2 × 3 matrix has elements:

[0][0]   [0][1]   [0][2]
[1][0]   [1][1]   [1][2]

Three ways of indexing are distinguished:

---
[2]But see §13.9.5 for the option to change that.

| indexing type | matrix, string | array | example |
|---|:---:|:---:|---|
| scalar | √ | √ | m[0][0] |
| matrix | √ | √ | m[0][<0,1,2>] |
| range | √ | √ | m[][1:] |

In the first indexing case (allowed for all non-scalar types), the expression inside square brackets must have scalar type, whereby double is converted to integer.

Vector types may also be indexed by a matrix or have a range expression inside the brackets. In a matrix index to a string the first *column* of the matrix specifies the selected elements of the string.

It is possible to use only one index to a matrix. If a matrix x is a column or row vector, x[i] it will pick the *i*th element from the vector. If x is a matrix, it will treat the matrix as a vector (row by row, which corresponds to the vecr).

If a matrix is used as an index to a matrix, then each element (row by row, i.e. the vecr of the argument) is used as an index. As a consequence, indexing by a column vector or its transpose (a row vector) has the same effect. A matrix in the first index selects rows, a matrix in the second index selects columns. The resulting matrix is the intersection of those rows and columns.

A range index has the form *start-index : end-index*. Either the start-index or the end-index may be missing, which results in the lower-bound or upper-bound being used respectively. An empty index selects all elements. The resulting type from a range or empty index is always a vector type.

Indexing beyond the end will result in a fatal run-time error. An exception is indexing a string for reference: this can be done one position beyond the end, which returns 0. For example, i=s[sizeof(s)] sets i to 0.

Some examples:

```
decl mat = < 0:3; 10:13 >, d, m;
decl str = "tinkertailor", s;
decl arr = { "tinker", "tailor", "soldier" };
                              // mat = <0,1,2,3; 10,11,12,13>
d = mat[0][0];                                         // d = 0
d = mat[1][2];                                         // d = 12
m = mat[1][];                           // m = <10,11,12,13>
i = 1;
m = mat[1][i:];                            // m = <11,12,13>

d = m[1];                                          // d = <11>
d = m'[1];                          // the same: d = <11>
d = mat[5];                                        // d = <11>

m = mat[][2];                                  // m = <2; 12>
m = mat[][];                          // same as: m = mat;
m = mat[0][<1:3>];        // matrix indexes columns: m = <1,2,3>
m = mat[<1,0,1>][<1,3>];          // m = < 11,13; 1,3; 11,13 >
mat[0][1:3] = 9;                       // range indexes columns:
                              // mat = <0,9,9,9; 10,11,12,13>
s = str[6:11];                                 // s = "tailor"
str[6:11] = 'a';                       // str = "tinkeraaaaaa"
```

```
s = arr[1];                                    // s = "tailor"
arr[1][0] = 'a';                               // arr[1] = "aailor"
```

### 13.8.2.5 Postfix incrementation

A postfix expression followed by ++ or -- leads to the value of the expression being evaluated and then incremented or decremented by 1. The operand must be an lvalue and must have arithmetic type. For a matrix the operator is applied to each element separately. The result of the expression is the value prior to the increment/decrement operation.

```
decl mat = < 0:3; 10:13 >, m, i, j;
decl str = "tinkertailor", s;
j = 0;
i = j++;                                       // i = 0, j = 1
m = mat++;                        // mat = <1,2,3,4; 11,12,13,14>
                                 // m   = <0,1,2,3; 10,11,12,13>
str[0]++;                              // str = "uinkertailor"
str++;                                                // error
```

### 13.8.2.6 Transpose

The postfix operator ' takes the transpose of a matrix. It has no effect on other arithmetic types of operands. The following translations are made when parsing Ox code:

> ' *identifier*   into   ' * *identifier*
> ' (             into   ' * (
> ' this          into   ' * this

A single quote is also used in a character constant; the context avoids ambiguity:

```
mat = m' * a';
mat = m'a';                            // interpreted as m' * a'
mat = m'';                                 // two '' cancel out
mat = m + 'a';                    // 'a' is a character constant
```

### 13.8.3 Power expressions

> *power-expression:*
>    *unary-expression*
>    *power-expression ^ unary-expression*
>    *power-expression .^ unary-expression*

The operands of the power operator must have arithmetic type, and the result is given in the table. If the first operand is not a matrix .^ and ^ are the same. A scalar consists of: int, double or $1 \times 1$ matrix.

| left $a$ | operator | right $b$ | result | computes |
|----------|----------|-----------|--------|----------|
| int | ^    .^ | int or double | int | $a^b$ |
| int/double | ^    .^ | double | double | $a^b$ |
| double | ^    .^ | scalar | double | $a^b$ |
| scalar | ^    .^ | matrix $m \times n$ | matrix $m \times n$ | $a^{b_{ij}}$ |
| matrix $m \times n$ | .^ | scalar | matrix $m \times n$ | $a_{ij}^{b}$ |
| matrix $m \times n$ | .^ | matrix $m \times n$ | matrix $m \times n$ | $a_{ij}^{b_{ij}}$ |
| matrix $m \times m$ | ^ | scalar | matrix $m \times m$ | $a^{\mathrm{int}(b)}$ |

When $a$ and $b$ are integers, then a ^ b is an integer if $b \geq 0$ and if the result can be represented as a 32 bit signed integer. If $b < 0$ and $a \neq 0$ or the integer result would lead to overflow, the return type is double, giving the outcome of the floating point power operation.

The first line in the example shows that power has higher precedence than unary minus:

```
i = - 2 ^ 2;                                        // i = -4
decl r, m1 = <1,2; 2,1>, m2 = <2,3; 3,2>;
r = m1 .^ 3;                            // <1,8; 8,1>
r = m1 .^ 3.7;                 // <1,12.996; 12.996,1>
r =  3 .^ m1;                          // <3,9; 9,3>
r =  3 ^  m1;                          // <3,9; 9,3>
r = m1 .^ m2;                          // <1,8; 8,1>
r = m1 ^  3;                       // <13,14; 14,13>
r = m1 ^  3.7;                     // <13,14; 14,13>
r = m1 ^  -3;         // equivalent to: r = (1 / m1) ^ 3;
r = m1 ^  m2;                               // error
```

The following code prints 14 zero matrices of dimension $2 \times 2$:

```
decl i, ma, m1 = <1,2; 2,1>;

for (i = 0, ma = <1,0; 0,1>; i <= 13; i++, ma *= m1)
     print("i = ", i, ma - m1^i);
```

### 13.8.4 Unary expressions

> *unary-expression:*
> > *postfix-expression*
> > ++ *unary-expression*
> > -- *unary-expression*
> > + *unary-expression*
> > - *unary-expression*
> > ! *unary-expression*
> > & *unary-expression*
> > new *class-name* ( *expression-list* )
> > new matrix [ *expression-list* ]
> > new matrix [ *expression-list* ] [ *expression-list* ]
> > new string [ *expression-list* ]
> > new array [ *expression-list* ]
> > new array [ *expression-list* ] [ *expression-list* ]
> > delete *unary-expression*

#### 13.8.4.1 Prefix incrementation

A prefix expression preceded by ++ or -- leads to the lvalue being incremented or decremented by 1. This new value is the result of the operation. The operand must be an lvalue and must have arithmetic type. For a matrix the operator is applied to each element separately.

```
j = 0;
i = ++j;                                    // i = 1, j = 1
```

#### 13.8.4.2 Unary minus and plus

The operand of the unary minus operator must have arithmetic type, and the result is the negative of the operand. For a matrix each element is set to its negative. Unary plus is ignored.

#### 13.8.4.3 Logical negation

The operand of the logical negation operator must have arithmetic type, and the result is 1 if the operand is equal to 0 and 0 otherwise. For a matrix, logical negation is applied to each element. Negating a missing value returns 0, and negating an empty matrix returns an empty matrix.

```
j = 0;  k = 10;
i = !j;                                      // i = 1
i = !k;                                      // i = 0
```

### 13.8.4.4 Address operator

The operand of the address operator & must be an lvalue. In addition, it must be an object: it is possible to take the address of a class object, a function, or an array element, but not of a matrix element. The result is a reference to the operand as an array of one element, pointing to the region of space occupied by the lvalue. Referencing works through arrays; unlike C and C++ (but like the Java programming language), Ox does not have pointers.

```
test5(const arrstring)
{
    arrstring[0][0] = 'x';
}
test6(astring)
{
    astring[0] = 'a';
}
test4()
{
    decl a, str = "spy";

    a = &str;
    a[0][0]--;                              // str="rpy"
    test5(&str);                            // str="xpy"
    test6(str);                          // str unchanged
}
```

### 13.8.4.5 New and delete

The new operator can be used to create an object of a class, or to create a matrix, string or array. The delete operator removes an object created by new. Note that matrices, strings and arrays are automatically removed when they go out of scope. Only one or two array levels at a time can be created by new; however, delete removes all sublevels. A string created by new consists of null characters, a matrix will have all elements zero. Matrix, string and array objects with dimension zero are allowed (this can be useful to start concatenation in an iterative loop; remember that an empty matrix constant is <>, and an empty array {}). Matrices and arrays can be created with either one or two dimensions.

```
decl i, m1, a1;

m1 = new matrix[2][2];                   // m1 = <0,0; 0,0>
m1[0][0] = 1;

delete m1;
a1 = m1[0][0];               // error: contents of m1 deleted

a1 = new array[3];

for (i = 0; i < sizeof(a1); i++)
{
```

```
    a1[i] = new string[3];
    a1[i][0] = 'a' + i;
    a1[i][1] = '0' + i;
}
```

The a1 variable has the following structure:

Examples involving objects of classes are given in §13.5.6.

### 13.8.5 Multiplicative expressions

> *multiplicative-expression:*
>     *power-expression*
>     *multiplicative-expression* ** *power-expression*
>     *multiplicative-expression* * *power-expression*
>     *multiplicative-expression* .* *power-expression*
>     *multiplicative-expression* / *power-expression*
>     *multiplicative-expression* ./ *power-expression*

The operators **, *, .*, /, and ./ group left-to-right and require operands of arithmetic type. A scalar consists of: int, double or $1 \times 1$ matrix. These operators conform to Table 13.2, except for:

| left $a$ | operator | right $b$ | result | computes |
|---|---|---|---|---|
| matrix $m \times n$ | * | matrix $n \times p$ | matrix $m \times p$ | $a_{i.}b_{.k}$ |
| matrix $m \times n$ | ** | matrix $p \times q$ | matrix $mp \times nq$ | $a_{ij}b$ |
| scalar | * | matrix $n \times p$ | matrix $n \times p$ | $ab_{ij}$ |
| matrix $m \times n$ | * | scalar | matrix $m \times n$ | $a_{ij}b$ |
| matrix $m \times n$ | / | matrix $p \times n$ | matrix $p \times m$ | $a_{i.}b_{.k}^{+}$ |
| scalar | / | matrix $m \times n$ | matrix $n \times m$ | $ab_{ij}^{+}$ |
| matrix $m \times n$ | / | scalar | matrix $m \times n$ | $a_{ij}/b$ |
| scalar | / ./ | scalar | double | $a/b$ |

This implies that * ** are the same as .* when one or both arguments are scalar, and similarly for / and verb./ when the right-hand operand is not a matrix.

Kronecker product is denoted by **. If neither operand is a matrix, this is identical to normal multiplication.

The binary * operator denotes multiplication. If both operands are a matrix and neither is scalar, this is matrix multiplication and the number of columns of the first operand has to be identical to the number of rows of the second operand.

The .* operator defines element by element multiplication. It is only different from * if both operands are a matrix (these must have identical dimensions, however, if one or both of the arguments is a $1 \times 1$ matrix, * is equal to .*).

The product of two integers remains an integer. This means that overflow could occur (when it would not occur in operations where one of the argument is a double). For example 5000 ∗ 50000 fits in an integer and yields 250 000 000, but 50000 ∗ 50000 overflows, yielding −1.794 967 296. When using double arithmetic: 50000.0 ∗ 50000 = 2500 000 000.0.

The binary / operator denotes division. If the second operand is a non-scalar matrix, this is identical to post-multiplication by the inverse (if the matrix is square the matrix is inverted using the `invert()` library function; if that fails, or the matrix is non-square, the generalized inverse is used, see §13.8.5.1). If the second operand is a scalar, each element of the first is divided by it. If the first operand is a scalar, it is multiplied by the inverse of the second argument.

The ./ operator defines element by element division. If either argument is not a matrix, this is identical to normal division. It is only different from / if both operands are a matrix (these must have identical dimensions).

Note that / does not support integer division (such as e.g. 3 / 2 resulting in 1). In Ox, the result of dividing two integers is a double (3 / 2 gives 1.5). Integer division can be performed using the `idiv` library function. The remainder operator (% in C and C++) is supported through the library function `imod`. Multiplication of two integers returns an integer.

Some examples of multiplication and division involving matrices:

```
decl m1 = <1,2; 2,1>, m2 = <2,3; 3,2>, r;

r = m1 * 2.;                                     // <2,4; 4,2>
r = 2. * m2;                                     // <4,6; 6,4>
r = m1 * m2;                                     // <8,7; 7,8>
r = m1 .* m2;                                    // <2,6; 6,2>
r = m1 .* <2,3>;                                 // <2,6; 4,3>
r = m1 ** m2;        // <2,3,4,6; 3,2,6,4; 4,6,2,3; 6,4,3,2>
r = 2 / 3;                                      // 0.666667
r = 2 / 3.;                                     // 0.666667
r = m1 / 2.;                                 // <0.5,1; 1,0.5>
r = m1 ./ <2;3>;                    // <0.5,1; 0.66667,0.33333>
r = 2./ m2;                          // <-0.8,1.2; 1.2,-0.8>
r = 2 ./ m2;                        // <1,0.66667; 0.66667,1>
r = m2 / m2;                                   // <1,0; 0,1>

r = 1/<1;2>;                                   // <0.2,0.4>
r = 1/<1,2>;                                   // <0.2; 0.4>
r = 1/<0,0;0,0>;                               // <0,0; 0,0>
```

Notice the difference between 2./ m2 and 2 ./ m2. In the first case, the dot is interpreted as part of the real number 2., whereas in the second case it is part of the ./ dot-division operator. The white space is used here to change the syntax (as in the example in §13.8.2.6); it would be more clear to write the second case as 2.0 ./ m2. The same difference applies for dot-multiplication, but note that 2.0∗m2 and 2.0.∗m2 give the same result.

### 13.8.5.1 Generalized inverse

The $n \times m$ generalized inverse $A^+$ of an $m \times n$ matrix $A$ is determined using the singular value decomposition:

$$A = UWV',$$

with:

$U$ is $m \times n$ and $U'U = I_n$,
$W$ is $r \times n$ and diagonal, with non-negative diagonal elements $w_i$,
$V$ is $n \times n$ and $V'V = I_n$.

The generalized inverse $A^+$ is computed as:

$$A^+ = VW^+U',$$

where the diagonal elements of $W^+$ are given by:

$$w_i^{-1} = \begin{cases} 1/w_i & \text{if } w_i > 10\epsilon_{inv}||A||_\infty, \\ 0 & \text{otherwise.} \end{cases}$$

The rank of $A$ is the number of non-zero $w_i$. The inversion epsilon, $\epsilon_{inv}$, is set by the `inverteps` function. By default $\epsilon_{inv} = 1000\epsilon_m$, where $\epsilon_m$ is the machine precision for doubles ($\approx 2 \times 10^{-16}$) and

$$||A||_\infty = \max_{0 \le i < m} \sum_{j=0}^{n-1} |a_{ij}|.$$

When $n > m$ the singular value decomposition is applied to $A'$ to avoid a large $V$ matrix:

$$A^+ = UW^+V',$$

where $U$ and $V$ derive from $A' = UWV'$.

Note that the generalized inverse of a square non-singular matrix corresponds to the normal inverse. The generalized inverse of a matrix consisting of zeros only is a matrix of zeros. This follows from the four Moore–Penrose conditions for $A^+$:

$$AA^+A = A, \ A^+AA^+ = A^+, \ \left(AA^+\right)' = AA^+, \ \left(A^+A\right)' = A^+A.$$

### 13.8.6 Additive expressions

*additive-expression:*
*multiplicative-expression*
*additive-expression* + *multiplicative-expression*
*additive-expression* − *multiplicative-expression*

The additive operators + and − are dot-operators, conforming to Table 13.2. Both operators group left-to-right. They respectively return the sum and the difference of the operands, which must both have arithmetic type. Matrices must be conformant in both dimensions, and the operator is applied element by element. For example:

```
decl m1 = <1,2; 2,1>, m2 = <2,3; 3,2>;

r = 2 - m2;                              // <0,-1; -1,0>
r = m1 - m2;                             // <-1,-1; -1,-1>
```

### 13.8.7 Concatenation expressions

> *horizontal-concatenation-expression:*
>> *additive-expression*
>> *horizontal-concatenation-expression* ~ *additive-expression*

> *vertical-concat-expression:*
>> *horizontal-concatenation-expression*
>> *vertical-concat-expression* | *horizontal-concatenation-expression*

| left | operator | right | result |
|---|---|---|---|
| int/double | ~ | int/double | matrix $1 \times 2$ |
| int/double | ~ | matrix $m \times n$ | matrix $m \times (1+n)$ |
| matrix $m \times n$ | ~ | int/double | matrix $m \times (n+1)$ |
| matrix $m \times n$ | ~ | matrix $p \times q$ | matrix $\max(m,p) \times (n+q)$ |
| int/double | | | int/double | matrix $2 \times 1$ |
| int/double | | | matrix $m \times n$ | matrix $(1+m) \times n$ |
| matrix $m \times n$ | | | int/double | matrix $(m+1) \times n$ |
| matrix $m \times n$ | | | matrix $p \times q$ | matrix $(m+p) \times \max(n,q)$ |
| int | ~ | | | string | string |
| string | ~ | | | int | string |
| string | ~ | | | string | string |
| array | ~ | | | array | array |
| array | ~ | | | any basic type | array |

If both operands have arithmetic type, the concatenation operators are used to create a larger matrix out of the operands. If both operands are scalar the result is a row vector (for ~) or a column vector (for |). If one operand is scalar, and the other a matrix, an extra column (~) or row (|) is pre/appended. If both operands are a matrix, the matrices are joined. Note that the dimensions need not match: missing elements are set to zero (however, a warning is printed of non-matching matrices are concatenated). Horizontal concatenation has higher precedence than vertical concatenation.

Two strings or an integer and a string can be concatenated, resulting in a longer string. Both horizontal and vertical concatenation yield the same result.

The result is most easily demonstrated by examples:

```
print(1 ~ 2 ~ 3 | 4 ~ 5 ~ 6);              // <1,2,3; 4,5,6>
print("tinker" ~ '&' ~ "tailor" );        // "tinker&tailor"
print(<1,0; 0,1> ~ 2);                     // <1,0,2; 0,1,2>
print(2 | <1,0; 0,1>);                     // <2,2; 1,0; 0,1>
print(<2> ~ <1,0; 0,1>);                   // <2,1,0; 0,0,1>
```

The first two lines could have been written as:

```
print(<1,2,3; 4,5,6>);
print("tinker" "&" "tailor" );
```

In the latter case, the matrix and string are created at compile time, whereas in the former case this is done at run time. Clearly, the compile time evaluation is more efficient. However, only the concatenation expressions can involve non-constant variables:

```
decl  i1 = 1, i2 = 2, s1 = "tinke";

print(i1 ~ i2);                            // <1,2>
print(s1 ~ 'r');                           // "tinker"
```

Array concatenation results in an array with combined size, with assignment of each member of both arrays to the new array.

```
decl  i, a1 = {"tinker", "tailor"}, a2 = {"soldier"};

a1 ~= a2;
print(a1);
```

prints:

```
[0] = tinker
[1] = tailor
[2] = soldier
```

Often, concatenation is required in a loop. In that case, it is convenient to start from a matrix of dimension zero, for example:

```
decl m, i;

for (i = 0, m = <>; i < 4; ++i)
    m ~= i;
print(m);                                  // m = <0, 1, 2, 3>
```

### 13.8.8 Relational expressions

> *relational-expression:*
>> *vertical-concat-expression*
>> *relational-expression* < *vertical-concat-expression*
>> *relational-expression* > *vertical-concat-expression*
>> *relational-expression* <= *vertical-concat-expression*
>> *relational-expression* >= *vertical-concat-expression*
>> *relational-expression* .< *vertical-concat-expression*
>> *relational-expression* .> *vertical-concat-expression*
>> *relational-expression* .<= *vertical-concat-expression*
>> *relational-expression* .>= *vertical-concat-expression*

The relational operators are <, <=, >, >=, standing for 'less', 'less or equal', 'greater', 'greater or equal'. They all yield 0 if the specified relation is false, and 1 if it is true. The type of the result is always an integer, see Table 13.3. If both operands are a matrix, the return value is true if the relation holds for each element. If one of the operands is of scalar-type, and the other of matrix-type, each element in the matrix is compared to the scalar, and the result is true if each comparison is true.

The dot relational operators are .<, .<=, .>, .>=, standing for 'dot less', 'dot less or equal', 'dot greater', 'dot greater or equal'. They conform to Table 13.2, except when both arguments are a string, in which case the result is as for the non-dotted versions.

If both arguments are scalar, the result type inherits the higher type, so 1 >= 1.5 yields a double with value 0.0. If both operands are a matrix the return value is a matrix with a 1 in each position where the relation is true and zero where it is false. If one of the operands is of scalar-type, and the other of matrix-type, each element in the matrix is compared to the scalar returning a matrix with 1 at each position where the relation holds.

String-type operands can be compared in a similar way. If both operands are a string, the results is int with value 1 or 0, depending on the case sensitive string comparison.

Examples are given in the next section.

### 13.8.9 Equality expressions

> *equality-expression:*
> > *relational-expression*
> > *equality-expression* == *relational-expression*
> > *equality-expression* != *relational-expression*
> > *equality-expression* .== *relational-expression*
> > *equality-expression* .!= *relational-expression*

The == (is equal to), != (is not equal to), .== (is dot equal to) and .!= (is not dot equal to) are analogous to the relational operators, but have lower precedence.

The non-dotted versions conform to Table 13.3. The dotted versions conform to Table 13.2, except when both arguments are a string, in which case the result is as for the non-dotted versions. String comparison is case sensitive (also see isfeq).

For example:

```
decl m1 = <1,2; 2,1>, m2 = <2,3; 3,2>, s1 = "tinke";

print(m1 == 1);                               // 0
print(m1 != 1);                               // 0
print(!(m1 == 1));                            // 1
print(m1 > m2);                               // 0
print(m1 < m2);                               // 1
print(s1 <= "tinker");                        // 1
print(s1 <= "tink" );                         // 0
print(s1 == "tinker");                        // 0
print(s1 >= "tinker");                        // 0
```

```
print(s1 == "Tinke");                                    // 0

print(m1 .== 1);                                         // <1,0; 0,1>
print(m1 .!= 1);                                         // <0,1; 1,0>
print(m1 .> m2);                                         // <0,0; 0,0>
print(m1 .< m2);                                         // <1,1; 1,1>
```

The non-dotted versions only return true if the relation holds for each element. In the first two examples neither m1 == 1 nor m1 != 1 is true for each element, hence the return value 0. The third example shows how to test if a matrix is not equal to a value. The parenthesis are necessary, because ! has higher precedence than ==, and !m1 == 1 results in <0,0; 0,0> == 1 which is false.

The last four examples use dot-relational expressions, resulting in a matrix of zeros and ones. In if statements, it is possible to use such matrices. Remember that a matrix is true if all elements are true (i.e. no element is zero). In the example below, both if (m1 .== 1) and if (m1 .!= 1) result in the else part being executed:

|  | evaluates to | leads to |
|---|---|---|
| if (m1 .== 1) | if (<1,0;0,1>) | else part |
| if (m1 .!= 1) | if (<0,1;1,0>) | else part |
| if (m1 == 1) | if (0) | else part |
| if (m1 != 1) | if (0) | else part |

and both have at least one zero, so that both test statements are false.

The any library function evaluates to TRUE if any element is TRUE, e.g.

|  | evaluates to | leads to |
|---|---|---|
| if (any(m1 .== 1)) | if (any(<1,0;0,1>)) | if part |
| if (any(m1 .!= 1)) | if (any(<0,1;1,0>)) | if part |
| if (m1 == 1) | if (0) | else part |
| if (m1 != 1) | if (0) | else part |

Consider a few more examples, using the matrix m2 = <2 2;2 2>:

|  | evaluates to | leads to |
|---|---|---|
| if (m2 .== 2) | if (<1,1;1,1>) | if part |
| if (m2 .!= 2) | if (<0,0;0,0>) | else part |
| if (m1 .== <1,2; 2,1>) | if (<1,1;1,1>) | if part |
| if (m1 - 1) | if (<0,1;1,0>) | else part |
| if (m1 .>= 1) | if (<1,1;1,1>) | if part |
| if (m1 .> 1) | if (<0,1;1,0>) | else part |
| if (m2 == 2) | if (1) | if part |
| if (m2 != 2) | if (0) | else part |
| if (m1 >= 1) | if (1) | if part |
| if (m1 > 1) | if (0) | else part |

### 13.8.10 Logical dot-AND expressions

> *logical-dot-and-expression:*
>    *equality-expression*
>    *logical-dot-and-expression* `.&&` *equality-expression*

The `.&&` operator groups left-to-right. It returns 1 if both of its operands compare unequal to 0, 0 otherwise. Both operands must have arithmetic type. Handling of matrix-type is as for dot-relational operators: if one or both operands is a matrix, the result is a matrix of zeros and ones. Unlike the non-dotted version, both operands will always be executed. For example, in the expression `func1() .&& func2()` the second function is called, regardless of the return value of `func1()`.

### 13.8.11 Logical-AND expressions

> *logical-and-expression:*
>    *logical-dot-and-expression*
>    *logical-and-expression* `&&` *logical-dot-and-expression*

The `&&` operator groups left-to-right.

It returns the integer 1 if both of its operands compare unequal to 0, and the integer 0 otherwise. Both operands must have arithmetic type. First the left operand is evaluated, if it is false (for a matrix: there is at least one zero element), the result is false, and the right operand will not be evaluated. So in the expression `func1() && func2()` the second function will *not* be called if the first function returned false.

### 13.8.12 Logical dot-OR expressions

> *logical-dot-or-expression:*
>    *logical-and-expression*
>    *logical-dot-or-expression* `.||` *logical-and-expression*

The `.||` operator groups left-to-right. It returns 1 if either of its operands compares unequal to 0, 0 otherwise. Both operands must have arithmetic type. Handling of matrix-type is as for dot-relational operators: if one or both operands is a matrix, the result is a matrix of zeros and ones. Unlike the non-dotted version, both operands will always be executed. For example, in the expression `func1() .|| func2()` the second function is called, regardless of the return value of `func1()`.

### 13.8.13 Logical-OR expressions

> *logical-or-expression:*
>    *logical-dot-or-expression*
>    *logical-or-expression* `||` *logical-dot-or-expression*

The `||` operator groups left-to-right. It returns the integer 1 if either of its operands compares unequal to 0, integer value 0 otherwise. Both operands must have arithmetic type. First the left operand is evaluated, if it is true (for a matrix: no element is zero), the result is true, and the right operand will not be evaluated. So in the expression `func1() .|| func2()` the second function will *not* be called if the first function returned true.

### 13.8.14 Conditional expression

> *conditional-expression:*
> > *logical-or-expression*
> > *logical-or-expression* ? *expression* : *conditional-expression*
> > *logical-or-expression* .? *expression* .: *conditional-expression*

Both the conditional and the dot-conditional expression are ternary expressions. For the conditional expression, the first expression (before the ?) is evaluated. If it is unequal to 0, the result is the second expression, otherwise the third expression.

The dot-conditional expression only differs from the conditional expression if the first expression evaluates to a matrix, here called the test matrix. In that case the result is a matrix of the same size as the test matrix, and the test matrix can be seen as a filter: non zero elements get a value corresponding to the second expression, zero elements corresponding to the third expression. If the second or third expression is scalar, each matrix element will get the appropriate scalar value. If it is a matrix, the corresponding matrix element will be used, unless the matrix is too small, in which case the value 0. will be used. *Note that in the dot-conditional expression both parts are executed, whereas in the conditional expression only one of the two parts is executed.*

```
decl r, m2;

r = <1,0; 0,1> ? 4 : 5;    // 5, matrix is true if no element is 0
r = <1,0; 0,1> .? 4 .: 5;                      // <4,5; 5,4>
m2 = <1>;
r = r .== 4 .? m2 .: 0;                        // <1,0; 0,0>
```

### 13.8.15 Assignment expressions

> *assignment-expression:*
> > *conditional-expression*
> > *unary-expression assignment-operator assignment-expression*
>
> *assignment-operator:* one of
> > =   *=   /=   +=   -=   ~=   |=   .*=   ./=

The assignment operators are the =   *=   /=   +=   -=   ~=   |=   .*=   ./= symbols. An lvalue is required as the left operand. The type of an assignment is that of its left operand. The combined assignment *l op= r* is equivalent to *l = l op (r)*.

If the left-hand side is a comma-separated list in square brackets, the statement is a multiple assignment expression, see §13.8.1.1.

The following code:

```
decl i, k;
for (i = 0, k = 1; i < 5; i += 2)
    k *= 2, print("i = ", i, " k = ", k, "\n");
```

writes:

```
i = 0 k = 2
i = 2 k = 4
i = 4 k = 8
```

Assignment of an array to part of an array (i.e. using selection on the left-hand side) uses the array contents of right-hand side. So, when both as1 and as2 are arrays (of strings e.g.)

```
as1[0:1] = as2
```

is executed as:

```
as1[0] = as2[0], as1[1] = as2[1];
```

thus preserving the array level in as1.

### 13.8.16 Comma expression

> *expression:*
>> *assignment-expression*
>> *expression , assignment-expression*

A pair of expressions separated by a comma is evaluated left to right, and the value of the left expression is discarded. The result will have type and value corresponding to the right operand. The example in the previous section has two instances of the comma operator. The second could be omitted as follows:

```
for (i = 0, k = 1; i < 5; i += 2)
{   k *= 2;
    print("i = ", i, " k = ", k, "\n");
}
```

or as:

```
for (i = 0, k = 1; i < 5; i += 2)
    print("i = ", i, " k = ", k *= 2, "\n");
```

### 13.8.17 Constant expressions

An expression that evaluates to a constant is required in initializers and certain preprocessor expressions. A constant expression can have the operators * / + -, but only if the operands have scalar type. Some examples were given in sections 13.5.1 and 13.5.3.

## 13.9 Preprocessing

Preprocessing in Ox is primarily used for inclusion of files and conditional compilation of code. As such it is more restricted than the options available in C or C++. Escape sequences in strings literals are interpreted when used in preprocessor statements.

### 13.9.1 File inclusion

A line of the form
> #include "*filename*"

will insert the contents of the specified file at that position. The file is searched for as follows:

(1) in the directory containing the source file (if just a filename, or a filename with a relative path is specified), or in the specified directory (if the filename has an absolute path);
(2) the directories specified on the compiler command line (if any);
(3) the directories specified in the OX6PATH environment string (if any).
(4) in the current directory.

A line of the form
> #include <*filename*>

will skip the first step, and search as follows:

(1) the directories specified on the compiler command line (if any);
(2) the directories specified in the OX6PATH environment string (if any);
(3) in the current directory.

The quoted form is primarily for inclusion of user created header or code files, whereas the second form will be mainly for system and library files.

For example if OX6PATH is defined as (which corresponds to the Windows default if it is not set, and the executable is in c:\ox\bin):
> set OX6PATH=c:\ox\include;c:\ox;

Then include <maximize.h> will look for:
> c:/ox/include/maximize.h
> c:/ox/maximize.h
> maximize.h

In this case the first try finds the file. The method in angular brackets is used for Ox header files, whereas the other method is appropriate for your own header files. If the source file is specified to Ox as d:\mycode\test.ox, and run from c:\user, the search for include "test.h" is:
> d:/mycode/test.h
> c:/user/test.h
> c:/ox/include/test.h
> c:/ox/test.h
> test.h

### 13.9.2 Using file names in Ox

Note that escape sequences *are* interpreted in the include string, but not in the version which uses <...> (so in #include "dir\nheader.h", the \n is replaced by a newline character). Both forward and backslashes are allowed (use #include "dir/nheader.h", to avoid the newline character).

### 13.9.3 Import of modules

The `#import` preprocessor statement makes it easier to import compiled code modules. The statement can only happen at the external level, and has the form:

> `#import <`*modulename*`>`

For example
> `#import <pcnaive>`

has the following effect:

(1)      `#include <pcnaive.h>`
   The header file is inserted at that location.
(2)  link the `pcnaive.oxo` file when the program is run, or if this is not found:
(3)  compile and link the `pcnaive.ox` file when the program is run.

Similarly:
> `#import "pcnaive"`

has the following effect:

(1)      `#include "pcnaive.h"`
   The header file is inserted at that location.
(2)  link `pcnaive.oxo` (or `pcnaive.ox` if the `.oxo` file is not found) when the program is run.

The import statement marks the file for linking, but that linking only happens when the file is executed. Even when a module is imported multiple times, it will only be linked in once. Similarly, the header file will not be included more than once in the same source code file.

When a relative path is included, that path will be searched when trying to find a DLL or loading a data file into Ox. If the import name ends in a backward/forward slash, no header file is included, but the path will be searched. For example, when OX6PATH is set to `c:/ox/include;c:/ox;`, and the source file has:

> `#import <packages/arfima/arfima>`
> `#import <packages/arfima/data/>`

Then include `arfima.h` is searched for:

> `c:/ox/include/packages/arfima/arfima.h`
> `c:/ox/packages/arfima/arfima.h`
> `arfima.h`

when a DLL or data file is needed in the code (say ukm1.in7 from source file `d:\mycode\test.ox`), it will be searched as:

> `ukm1.in7`
> `d:/mycode/ukm1.in7`
> `c:/ox/include/ukm1.in7`
> `c:/ox/ukm1.in7`
> `c:/ox/include/packages/arfima/ukm1.in7`
> `c:/ox/packages/arfima/ukm1.in7`

```
c:/ox/include/packages/arfima/data/ukm1.in7
c:/ox/packages/arfima/data/ukm1.in7
```

### 13.9.4 Conditional compilation

The first step in conditional compilation is to define (or undefine) identifiers:

```
#define identifier
#undef identifier
```

Identifiers so defined only exist during the scanning process of the input file, and can subsequently be used by #ifdef and #ifndef preprocessor statements:

```
#ifdef identifier
#ifndef identifier
#else
#endif
```

As an example, consider the following header file:

```
#ifndef OXSTD_INCLUDED
#define OXSTD_INCLUDED

    // header statements

#endif
```

Now multiple inclusion of the header file into a source code file will only once include the actual header statements; on second inclusion, OXSTD_INCLUDED will be defined, and the code skipped.

Another example uses some predefined constants (see Ch. 9):

```
#include <oxstd.h>

main()
{
#ifdef OX_BIG_ENDIAN
    print("This is a big endian machine.\n");
#else
    print("This is a little endian machine.\n");
#endif

#ifdef OX_Windows
    print("This program is running under Windows.\n");
#endif
}
```

### 13.9.5 Pragmas

Pragmas influence the parsing process of the Ox compiler. Pragmas may only occur at the level of external declarations. Defined is:

```
#pragma array_base(integer)
```

As discussed at various points, indices in matrices, arrays and strings always start
at 0. This is the C and C++ convention. Ox, however, allows circumventing this
convention by using the `array_base` pragma. Library functions which return a set
of indices, are aware of the `array_base` settings, and will return appropriate values.
*It is recommended to adopt the zero-based convention, and not use the* `array_base`
*pragma.* The following example shows the difference:

```
#include <oxstd.h>

base0(const m)
{   decl i;
    i = m[0][0];              // first row, first element: i = 0
    i = m[][1:2];                               // i = <1,2>
}
#pragma array_base(1)
base1(const m)
{   decl i;
    i = m[1][1];              // first row, first element: i = 0
    i = m[][1:2];                               // i = <0,1>
    i = m[0][0];                              // error
}
#pragma array_base(0)                    // reset to base 0

main()
{   decl m = <0,1,2,3>;

    base0(m);
    base1(m);
}
```

## 13.10 Difference with ANSI C and C++

This section lists some of the differences between Ox and C/C++ which might cause
confusion:

- */* */* type comments can be nested in Ox.
- `sizeof` is a function in Ox, not an operator (and not a reserved word).
- Labels (targets of `goto` statements) have the colon prefixed, rather than suffixed.
- By default, all data members of a class are private, all function members public.
- The base class constructor and destructor functions are *not* called automatically.
- Integer division is not used, so 1 / 2 yields 0.5, instead of 0. Use `idiv(1, 2)`
  for integer division of 1 by 2.
- The preprocessor does not allow: #define XXX value, for integer constants,
  enums could be used, but more convenient is: const decl XXX = value;.

# References

Abramowitz, M. and Stegun, I. A. (1984). *Pocketbook of Mathematical Functions*. Frankfurt/Main: Verlag Harri Deutsch.

Anderson, T. W. (1984). *An Introduction to Multivariate Statistical Analysis,* 2nd edition. New York: John Wiley & Sons.

Barndorff-Nielsen, O. E. and Shephard, N. (2001). *Lévy Based Dynamic Models for Financial Economics*. Oxford: Draft book, Nuffield College.

Barnett, S. (1990). *Matrices – Methods and Applications*. Oxford: Clarendon Press.

Berndt, E. K., Hall, B. H., Hall, R. E. and Hausman, J. A. (1974). Estimation and inference in nonlinear structural models, *Annals of Economic and Social Measurement*, **3**, 653–665.

Berry, K. J., Mielke Jr, P. W. and Cran, G. W. (1977). Remark AS R83: A remark on algorithm AS 109: Inverse of the incomplete beta function ratio, *Applied Statistics*, **39**, 309–310.

Best, D. J. and Fisher, N. I. (1979). Efficient simulation of the von Mises distribution, *Applied Statistics*, **28**, 152–157.

Best, D. J. and Roberts, D. E. (1975). Algorithm AS 91: The percentage points of the $\chi^2$ distribution, *Applied Statistics*, **24**, 385–389.

Brockwell, P. J. and Davis, R. A. (1991). *Time Series: Theory and Methods*. New York: Springer-Verlag.

Chambers, J. M., Mallows, C. L. and Sturk, B. W. (1976). A method for simulating stable random variables, *Journal of the American Statistical Association*, **71**, 340–344.

Cooper, B. E. (1968). Algorithm AS 3: The integral of student's $t$-distribution, *Applied Statistics*, **17**, 189–190.

Cran, G. W., Martin, K. J. and Thomas, G. E. (1977). Remark AS R19 and algorithm AS 109: A remark on algorithms AS 63: The incomplete beta integral; AS 64: Inverse of the incomplete beta function ratio, *Applied Statistics*, **26**, 111–114.

Dagnapur, J. (1988). *Principles of Random Variate Generation*. Oxford: Clarendon Press.

Dennis Jr., J. E. and Schnabel, R. B. (1983). *Numerical Methods for Nonlinear Equations and Unconstrained Optimization,*. Englewood Cliffs, NJ: Prentice Hall.

Devroye, L. (1986). *Non-Uniform Random Variate Generation*. New York: Springer-Verlag.

Dhrymes, P. J. (1984). *Mathematics for Econometrics,* 2nd edition. New York: Springer-Verlag.

Ding, C. G. (1992). Algorithm AS 275: Computing the non-central $\chi^2$ distribution function, *Applied Statistics*, **41**, 478–483.

Doornik, J. A. (2005). An improved ziggurat method to generate normal random samples, Mimeo, Nuffield College.

Doornik, J. A. (2006). The role of simulation in econometrics, In Mills, T. and Patterson, K. (eds.), *Palgrave Handbook of Econometrics*, pp. 787–811. Basingstoke: Palgrave MacMillan.

Doornik, J. A. (2007). Conversion of high-period random numbers to floating point, *ACM Transactions on Modeling and Computer Simulation*, **17**.

Doornik, J. A. and Hendry, D. F. (2009). *Modelling Dynamic Systems using PcGive: Volume II*

4th edition. London: Timberlake Consultants Press.

Doornik, J. A. and Ooms, M. (2006). *Introduction to Ox* 2nd edition. London: Timberlake Consultants Press.

Dubrulle, A. (1970). A short note on the implicit *ql* algorithm for symmetric tridiagonal matrices, *Numerische Mathematik*, **15**, 450.

Engler, E. and Nielsen, B. (2009). The empirical process of autoregressive residuals, *Econometrics Journal*, forthcoming.

Feng, R. B. and Pulliam, P. D. (1997). Tensor-gmres method for large systems of nonlinear equations, *SIAM Journal of Optimization*, **7**, 757–779.

Fisher, N. I. (1993). *Statistical Analysis of Circular Data*. New York: Cambridge University Press.

Fletcher, R. (1987). *Practical Methods of Optimization,* 2nd edition. New York: John Wiley & Sons.

Genz, A. (2000). Numerical computation of bivariate and trivariate normal probabilities, Mimeo, Washington State University, Pullman, WA.

Golub, G. H. and Van Loan, C. F. (1989). *Matrix Computations*. Baltimore: The Johns Hopkins University Press.

Granger, C. W. J. and Newbold, P. (1986). *Forecasting Economic Time Series,* 2nd edition. New York: Academic Press.

Green, P. J. and Silverman, B. W. (1994). *Nonparametric Regression and Generalized Linear Models. A Roughness Penalty Approach*. London: Chapman and Hall.

Harvey, A. C. (1993). *Time Series Models,* 2nd edition. Hemel Hempstead: Harvester Wheatsheaf.

Hastie, T. J. and Tibshirani, R. J. (1994). *Generalized Additive Models*. London: Chapman and Hall.

Hendry, D. F., Neale, A. J. and Ericsson, N. R. (1991). *PC-NAIVE, An Interactive Program for Monte Carlo Experimentation in Econometrics. Version 6.0.* Oxford: Institute of Economics and Statistics, University of Oxford.

Hill, G. W. (1981). Remark on Algorithm 396: Student's t-quantiles [s14], *ACM Transactions on Mathematical Software*, **7**, 250–251.

Hill, I. D. (1973). Algorithm AS 66: The normal integral, *Applied Statistics*, **22**, 424–427.

Kemp, A. W. (1981). Efficient generation of logarithmically distributed pseudo-random variables, *Applied Statistics*, **30**, 249–253.

Kernighan, B. W. and Ritchie, D. M. (1988). *The C Programming Language* 2nd edition. Englewood Cliffs, NJ: Prentice Hall.

Kiefer, N. M. (1989). The ET interview: Arthur S. Goldberger, *Econometric Theory*, **5**, 133–160.

Lacey, S. and Box, R. (1991). A fast, easy sort, *Byte*, **April**.

LAPACK (1999). *LAPACK Users' Guide* 3rd edition. Philadelphia: SIAM. By Anderson, E. and Bai, Z. and Bischof, C. and Blackford, S. and Demmel, J. and Dongarra, J. and Du Croz, J. and Greenbaum, A. and Hammarling, S. and McKenney, A. and Sorensen, D.

Lawrence, C. T. and Tits, A. L. (2001). A computationally efficient feasible sequential quadratic programming algorithm, *SIAM Journal of Optimization*, **11**, 1092–1118.

L'Ecuyer, P. (1999). Tables of maximally-equidistributed combined LFSR generators, *Mathematics of Computation*, **68**, 261–269.

Lehner, K. (1989). Erzeugung von zufallszahlen für zwei exotische verteilungen, Diplomarbeit, Techn. Universität Graz.

Lenth, R. V. (1987). Algorithm AS 226: Computing noncentral Beta probabilities, *Applied Statistics*, **36**, 241–244.

Lenth, R. V. (1989). Algorithm AS 243: Cumulative distribution function of the non-central $t$ distribution, *Applied Statistics*, **38**, 185–189.

Longley, G. M. (1967). An appraisal of least-squares for the electronic computer from the point of view of the user, *Journal of the American Statistical Association*, **62**, 819–841.

Magnus, J. R. and Neudecker, H. (1988). *Matrix Differential Calculus with Applications in Statistics and Econometrics*. New York: John Wiley & Sons.

Majunder, K. L. and Bhattacharjee, G. P. (1973). Algorithm AS 64. Inverse of the incomplete beta function ratio, *Applied Statistics*, **22**, 411–414.

Mardia, K. V. and Zemroch, P. J. (1975). Algorithm AS 86: The von Mises distribution function, *Applied Statistics*, **24**, 268–272.

Marsaglia, G. (1997). A random number generator for C, Posting, Usenet newsgroup sci.stat.math. 29-Sep-1997.

Marsaglia, G. (2003). Re: good C random number generator, Posting, Usenet newsgroup sci.lang.c. 13-May-2003.

Martin, R. S., Reinsch, C. and Wilkinson, J. H. (1968). Householder's tridiagonalization of a symmetric matrix, *Numerische Mathematik*, **11**, 181–195.

Martin, R. S. and Wilkinson, J. H. (1968a). The implicit $ql$ algorithm, *Numerische Mathematik*, **12**, 377–383.

Martin, R. S. and Wilkinson, J. H. (1968b). Similarity reduction of a general matrix to Hessenberg form, *Numerische Mathematik*, **12**, 349–368.

McLeod, I. (1975). Derivation of the theoretical autocovariance function of autoregressive-moving average time series, *Applied Statistics*, **24**, 255–256. Correction in *Applied Statistics*, **26**, 194.

Michael, J. R., Schucany, W. R. and Haas, R. W. (1976). Generating random variates using transformations with multiple roots, *American Statistician*, **30**, 88–90.

Nocedal, J. and Wright, S. J. (1999). *Numerical Optimization*. New York: Springer-Verlag.

O'Neil, R. (1971). Algorithm AS 47: Function minimization using a simplex procedure, *Applied Statistics*, **20**, 338–345. Improved version in Griffiths, P. and Hill, I. D. (eds) (1985), *Applied Statistics Algorithms*. Chichester: Horwood.

Ooura, T. (1998). Special functions – gamma/error functions, mimeo, Kyoto University. www.kurims.kyoto-u.ac.jp/ ooura.

Park, S. K. and Miller, K. W. (1988). Random number generators: Good ones are hard to find, *Communications of the ACM*, **31**, 1192–1201.

Parlett, B. N. and Reinsch, C. (1969). Balancing a matrix for calculation of eigenvalues and eigenvectors, *Numerische Mathematik*, **13**, 293–304.

Peters and Wilkinson, J. H. (1970). Eigenvectors of real and complex matrices by $lr$ and $qr$ triangulazations, *Numerische Mathematik*, **16**, 181–204.

Petzold, C. (1992). *Programming Windows 3.1*. Redmond: Microsoft Press.

Piessens, R., de Donker-Kapenga, E., Überhuber, C. W. and Kahaner, D. K. (1983). *QUADPACK, A Subroutine Package for Automatic Integration*. Heidelberg: Springer-Verlag.

Press, W. H., Flannery, B. P., Teukolsky, S. A. and Vetterling, W. T. (1988). *Numerical Recipes in C*. New York: Cambridge University Press.

Priestley, M. B. (1981). *Spectral Analysis and Time Series*. London: Academic Press.

Rao, C. R. (1973). *Linear Statistical Inference and its Applications,* 2nd edition. New York: John Wiley & Sons.

Ripley, B. D. (1987). *Stochastic Simulation*. New York: John Wiley & Sons.

Schnabel, R. B. and Frank, P. D. (1985). Tensor methods for nonlinear equations, *SIAM Journal of Numerical Analysis*, **21**, 815–843.

Shea, B. L. (1988). Algorithm AS 239: Chi-squared and incomplete gamma integral, *Applied Statistics*, **37**, 466–473.

Shea, B. L. (1991). Algorithm AS R85: A remark on algorithm AS 91: The percentage points of the $\chi^2$ distribution, *Applied Statistics*, **40**, 233–235.

Silverman, B. W. (1986). *Density Estimation for Statistics and Data Analysis*. London: Chapman and Hall.

Smith, W. B. and Hocking, R. R. (1972). Algorithm AS 53: Wishart variate generator, *Applied Statistics*, **21**, 341–345.

Stroustrup, B. (1997). *The C++ Programming Language* 3rd edition. Reading, MA: Addison Wesley.

Wichura, M. J. (1988). Algorithm AS 241: The percentage points of the normal distribution, *Applied Statistics*, **37**, 477–484.

Wilkinson, J. H. (1965). *The Algebraic Eigenvalue Problem*. Oxford: Oxford University Press.

Wirth, N. (1987). *Compilerbouw*. Schoonhoven, The Netherlands: Academic Service. Dutch version. Original German version published in 1986 by B.G. Teubner Verlag, Stuttgart.

# Subject Index